The pre-colonial kingdom of Buganda, nucleus of the present state of Uganda, has long attracted scholarly interest. Since written records are lacking entirely until 1862, historians have had to rely on oral traditions that were recorded from the end of the nineteenth century. These sources provide rich materials on Buganda in the late eighteenth and nineteenth centuries, but Christopher Wrigley, a senior and highly respected scholar, endeavours to show that the stories that appear to relate to earlier periods are largely mythology. He argues that this does not reduce their value, since they are of interest in their own mythical right, revealing ancient traces of sacred kingship, and also throwing oblique light on the development of the recent state. The author has written an elegant, wide-ranging and original study of one of Africa's most famous kingdoms.

Kingship and state

African Studies Series 88

A list of books in this series will be found at the end of this volume

Kingship and state

The Buganda dynasty

Christopher Wrigley

University of Sussex

CAMBRIDGE
UNIVERSITY PRESS

PUBLISHED BY THE PRESS SYNDICATE OF THE UNIVERSITY OF CAMBRIDGE
The Pitt Building, Trumpington Street, Cambridge, United Kingdom

CAMBRIDGE UNIVERSITY PRESS
The Edinburgh Building, Cambridge CB2 2RU, UK
40 West 20th Street, New York NY 10011–4211, USA
477 Williamstown Road, Port Melbourne, VIC 3207, Australia
Ruiz de Alarcón 13, 28014 Madrid, Spain
Dock House, The Waterfront, Cape Town 8001, South Africa

http://www.cambridge.org

First published 1996
First paperback edition 2002

A catalogue record for this book is available from the British Library

Library of Congress Cataloguing in Publication data
Wrigley, Christopher.
Myth and history in Buganda: a study of an African tradition /
Christopher Wrigley.
          p.   cm. – (African studies series: 88)
Includes bibliographical references.
ISBN 0 521 47370 5
1. Uganda – History – To 1890.   2. Mythology, Ganda.
3. Oral tradition – Uganda.   4. Ganda (African people) – Kings
and rulers.
I. Title.   II. Series.
DT433.265.W75   1996
967.6′01–dc20   95-4678   CIP

ISBN 0 521 47370 5   hardback
ISBN 0 521 89435 2   paperback

To the Republic of Uganda

Contents

List of illustrations   *page* x
Preface   xi
Notes on language   xiii
List of abbreviations   xv

1   Preamble   1

2   The story and its making   20

3   Introduction to myth   43

4   Introduction to Buganda   57

5   The remoter past   69

6   Genesis   79

7   The cycle of the kings   122

8   Fragments of history   169

9   Foreign affairs   192

10   The making of the state   207

11   Reflections   230

Notes   253
Bibliography   275
Index   288

Illustrations

Maps
1 The Lakeland   *page* 2
2 Buganda in 1880   58
3 Busiro, land of tombs   80

Figures
1 The dynasty   *page* 21
2 The principal king-lists   31
3 The beginnings   140
4 The frog's nephew   148
5 The father of the rivers   156
6 The death of the hero   160
7 The middle kingdom   170
8 The eighteenth-century crisis   183
9 The new state   216

Preface

This book is about three decades overdue; and my first acknowledgements must be to my several paymasters, who have seen so little for their money: the Colonial Social Science Research Council, the Leverhulme Trust, the University of Ibadan and the University of Sussex. My other greatest debts are to the dead: to my parents, to Sir Keith Hancock, who encouraged and enabled me to do history, and to Audrey Richards, who inducted me into Africa. Under Audrey's wise and friendly direction the East African Institute of Social Research in the 1950s was a most agreeable and stimulating place, and I owe a great deal to my fellow-workers of that time: the late Lloyd ('Tom') Fallers, the late Wilfred Whiteley, Aidan Southall, Walter Elkan, Anthony Low, Cyril Ehrlich, Jean La Fontaine, Martin Southwold among others, as well as to those who guided my steps into Buganda: Eridadi Muliira, Paulo Tamukedde, Yowana Kasagala, Hezekiah Matovu.

I cannot offer the usual list of people who have read and commented on my manuscript, because I was too insecure to show it to anyone. But Benjamin Ray did belatedly see some fragments and I am grateful for his comments, also for the constructive criticisms of the publisher's two anonymous readers. Over the years I have had fruitful (to me) discussions on Buganda's history with Martin Southwold, Michael Kenny and Michael Twaddle, and I have a particular debt to David Henige, who made scepticism respectable.

I must thank the archivist of the White Fathers in Rome for a copy of an important document, John Rowe for a copy of a crucial text, David Schoenbrun for a copy of his monumental thesis, and Grace Natoolo and Mrs L. Bosa who, at a time when I felt unable to visit Uganda, furnished me with translated extracts from documents available only in the Makerere University Library. It is difficult to express adequate gratitude to the many people in Buganda who, long ago and recently, gave me friendship, hospitality and forbearance.

Finally I would like to thank John Lonsdale, series editor, for his encouragement and for allowing the book to be published, and all those at the Press, especially Jessica Kuper, Marigold Acland, Mary Starkey and Jayne Matthews, who turned my over-long and slapdash manuscript into a publishable book.

Notes on language

Since a good deal of use is made of the etymology of words and names, the non-Ganda reader needs to have some idea of how the Ganda language works. As in other members of the great Bantu family, nouns and adjectives normally consist of a stem, which conveys a general idea, and a prefix, which indicates the precise meaning. Thus *ba-ntu* are 'people', while *mu-ntu* is 'a person' and *bu-ntu* is the quality of being human; there is no such word as *ntu*. Likewise the *ba-ganda* people, one of whom is a *mu-ganda*, live in *Bu-ganda*, speak *Lu-ganda* and behave in a *ki-ganda* way. In the English text, according to standard convention, prefixes are omitted, except in the name of the country: thus the Ganda live in Buganda and speak the Ganda language. In the writing of Ganda terms hyphens between prefix and stem are not part of the normal orthography but will be used here when they are needed to display the structure of the word.

Early European visitors were introduced to Buganda through the medium of the related Swahili language, in which the prefix *bu-* has been reduced to *u-*, and thus called the country 'Uganda'. Later, this term (pronounced English fashion as though with an initial *Y-*) was applied to the wider colonial unit of which the 'Buganda' kingdom became a constituent province.

In some grammatical contexts nouns and adjectives have an initial vowel as well as a prefix: *o-mu-ganda*, 'the Ganda person'; *a-ba-ganda*, 'the Ganda people'. This will usually be ignored but will appear in a few quotations.

The prefix sometimes causes an alteration of the stem. Thus the addition of the prefix *n-* to a stem beginning in *w-* results in the combination *mp-*.

Consonants are pronounced more or less as in English, except that *c* has the sound of *ch-* in 'church'. *L* and *r* constitute a single phoneme – that is, the people hear no difference between these sounds and may utter either of them. More often than not, *r* appears before *e* or *i*, but *l* after other vowels, and this has become the spelling convention. Though *d* is a distinct phoneme it is easily interchangeable with *l*, so that *n + l* produces *nd*.

There is a distinction between *ng*, as in the word 'English', and *ng*' (properly written as a long-tailed n), as in southern English 'singing'.

Doubled consonants, which may appear at the beginning of a word as well as in the middle, have a heavy, almost explosive sound, contrasted with the normal very soft pronunciation. The distinction is often significant: thus Biggo and Bbigo are quite different places. Early writers, however, ignored it, or indicated it by diacriticals. Consequently the statesman and historian who has a central role in this book is referred to as 'Kaggwa' in the text but as 'Kagwa' (his own spelling) in the apparatus.

There are five vowels in Ganda and they have approximately continental (e.g. Italian) values. Doubled vowels are pronounced long. Again, however, early texts fail to mark this distinction, so that king Muteesa I was regularly called Mutesa (or M'tesa).

Abbreviations

AAR	*African Archaeological Review*
Annales ESC	*Annales, Economies, Sociétés, Civilisations*
CA	*Current Anthropology*
CSSH	*Comparative Studies in Society and History*
HA	*History in Africa*
IJAHS	*International Journal of African Historical Studies*
JAH	*Journal of African History*
J(R)AI	*Journal of the (Royal) Anthropological Institute*
UJ	*Uganda Journal*

1   Preamble

This book is about the stories of the past which have been recorded in the kingdom of Buganda, the original nucleus of what has become the Uganda Republic. Especially it is concerned with stories of old kings, or characters who were reputed to be such; for Buganda was an intensely monarchical society and the past that interested it was mainly the dynastic past, or one that had been given a dynastic form. These stories have intrigued me, on and off, for four decades; and though they have been analysed from various points of view by a number of scholars,[1] I believe there is still much more to be said about them.

Buganda was important to me, for it was the first African country that I got to know. It provided me with two of the best years of my life, and I have fond memories of the beauty of the land and the kindness of the people. But there are also less personal reasons for deeming its history worthy of detailed study. When it first came to the notice of literate observers, in the third quarter of the nineteenth century, it had all the appurtenances, except writing, of a state: courts, councils, armies, taxes, a complex hierarchy of ministers, provincial governors and local chiefs. That could be said of a number of other African polities, and even in East Africa, where units were generally small and loosely organised, Buganda was not the largest or most complex; that position certainly belonged to the extraordinary kingdom of Rwanda. It is, however, acknowledged to have been quite exceptionally centralised and autocratic, conforming more closely than almost any other system to the post-Renaissance European model of a state: an organisation possessing a monopoly of legitimate force within a clearly defined territory. As such it demands and has in fair measure received the attention of both political theorists and historians.

Buganda was also at one period important to Britain, and to some extent to the West as a whole, being a key pawn in the 'scramble' for control of eastern Africa. It owed this prominence partly to its geographical position at the headwaters of the Nile but also to its adaptability, its openness to new ideas and ways of doing things. These qualities were the more remarkable in that it belonged to one of the most secluded regions of Africa, last to

1

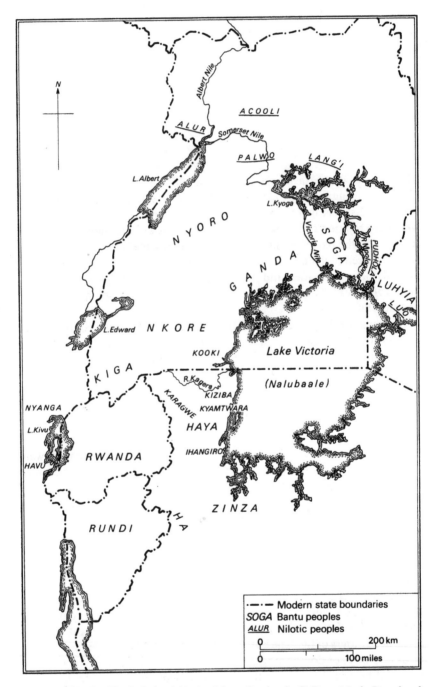

Map 1   The Lakeland (derived from Benjamin C. Ray, *Myth, Ritual and Kingship in Buganda*)

experience the influence of distant cultures and economies. As late as 1840 it was wholly unknown to and unknowing of the world beyond central equatorial Africa. Within the next decade Muslim merchants from the east coast appeared for the first time at the Ganda court, in search of ivory and, to a lesser extent, slaves, and in 1862 two British army officers, John Speke and James Grant, who had been given leave for African exploration, followed in their tracks.[2]

This reconnaissance had no immediate British sequel, but Muslim influence, cultural as well as commercial, grew apace. The reigning king, or *kabaka*, Muteesa I, himself learnt to write in the Arabic script and, though he avoided the decisive step of circumcision, he adopted many Muslim practices, such as the observance of Ramadan, and broke with many of the customs of his ancestors. So when Henry Morton Stanley, brilliant journalist and intrepid traveller, came to Buganda in 1875 on the first stage of his historic journey across Africa, the court was prepared for further innovation.[3] Stanley persuaded the king to invite Christian missionaries, and in 1877 a group selected by the Anglican Church Missionary Society reached Buganda, followed two years later by French Roman Catholic evangelists.[4] Though Muteesa certainly enjoyed theological discussions, that was not really why he welcomed these strangely gifted foreigners. First and foremost, he saw them as a counterpoise to the Egyptian power that had begun to threaten his independence; agents, themselves mostly Europeans, of the ambitious Khedive Ismail had already been active in the rival kingdom of Bunyoro to the north-west, and a Belgian officer, Linant de Bellefonds, was actually visiting Muteesa when Stanley arrived. Visitors who, like Stanley, Speke and Grant, came from the east coast, where power actually rested with the harmless Arab sultan of Zanzibar, seemed to be as innocuous as their technology was valuable.[5] Muteesa, of course, could not realise that the Egyptian 'empire' on the Nile was little more than a front for the advance of European power into Africa, and it was after his death in 1884 that the real menace became apparent.

Meanwhile the great revolt of the Mahdi in the Sudan in 1883 had cut all connections between Egypt and equatorial Africa, and the threat from the north had been removed. By then, however, the European powers were on the brink of the decision to take over direct control of Africa, no longer relying on local instruments such as Egypt or Zanzibar. In 1885–6 Britain and Germany divided the east coast between them and began to plan the penetration of the interior, Germany at first much more energetically than Britain. Thus the Christian presence in Buganda began to look like a Trojan horse. Under the new king, Mwanga, the position of the missionaries became very precarious, and that of their converts even more so. By this time the latter were a quite numerous body, and indeed it is perhaps the chief mark of Buganda's singularity that here and here only in East Africa Christianity, as well as Islam, made significant headway before the colonial conquest. The gains were made mainly among the younger generation of the ruling elite, most of all among the praetorian companies which had recently been equipped with imported firearms. The danger to the political establishment was manifest, and in 1886 some forty Christian 'readers' were rounded up and executed by burning.[6] A larger number of Muslim Ganda had suffered the same fate under Muteesa, when he found it politic to turn against Islam;[7] and there was a kind of precedent in the practice of *kiwendo*, the random slaughter carried out from time to time to ensure the health of king and kingdom. All the same it is remarkable that within a decade of the first preaching of the gospel so many youths should have been ready to die for the faith – for they had been given the chance to retract and reports say that they went singing to their death. The Catholics among them are now saints of the Church.

The 'readers' were not exterminated, however, and two years later the tensions within the kingdom erupted in a four-way armed conflict between Muslims, Catholic and Protestant Christians and the traditionalist or 'pagan' party. Into this turmoil, in the last days of 1890, came Captain Frederick Lugard, 'an officer of Her Majesty Queen Victoria' but employed at the time by the Imperial British East Africa Company, the instrument of those officials, businessmen, churchmen and military men who sought to push the British state into the heart of Africa. Buganda had just been assigned to the British 'sphere' as part of a general settlement of matters at issue between Britain and Germany, and the Company was eager to begin the exploitation of the ivory-rich and fertile Lake region in the far interior. Lugard's small force decided the internal conflict in favour of the Christians and, within the Christian party, in favour of the Protestant, or 'English', faction. Lugard then pushed through a remarkably successful scheme of power-sharing, which survived in essentials throughout the colonial era; the offices of state were divided nearly but not quite equally between Protestants and Catholics, with a small consolation prize for the Muslims. The Company was broken financially by the cost of Lugard's operations, and in 1894 a reluctant imperial government felt bound to take direct charge of the country, which was then known by the Swahili form of its name, Uganda.

The 'Uganda Protectorate' was at first supposed to be coterminous with the kingdom, but within months British-led mercenaries combined with the Christian Ganda army in an invasion of Bunyoro, half of whose territory was then transferred to Buganda. In the course of the next two decades British rule was extended over the miscellany of peoples who make up modern 'Uganda', and the authorities reverted to the proper vernacular name of 'Buganda' for the kingdom, which became one of the four provinces of the Protectorate.

The events of 1888–92 had left King Mwanga a virtual prisoner of the British and the collaborating Christian chiefs, and a last desperate effort to regain his independence in 1897 led to his defeat and eventual deportation. The kingship was, however, preserved in the person of his infant son, Daudi (David) Cwa. Soon afterwards the Sudanese mercenary troops, the main instruments of British power, broke into mutiny, and again the 'loyal' Ganda fought with great gallantry in support of their British patrons and protectors. The survivors were doubly rewarded. Individually the Christian leaders were confirmed as a privileged elite within the Ganda kingdom; and the kingdom itself not only survived as an entity under British colonial rule but enjoyed a privileged autonomy. Like other African peoples the Ganda lost their independence, but they extracted the maximum advantage from the new dispensation, in the form of security, territorial expansion, new knowledge and material progress. Above all their rights were enshrined in a formal agreement signed in 1900 by the Christian Regents and Sir Harry Johnston, a Special Commissioner of Her Majesty. They were thus able to believe that they had not submitted to superior power but had freely accepted British tutelage.[8]

In course of time the special status of Buganda within the colonial regime was gradually eroded, and foreign interest in its history and institutions declined. But as the time came for African dependencies to be converted into states there was a revival of interest, academic and practical, in those pre-colonial societies that had already proved themselves able to tackle the tasks of government. Buganda in particular was hailed as a shining example of a 'modernising despotism',[9] a term of unalloyed approval in the political science of the 1950s. Later, however, the theory to which that term belonged came to be seen in a sinister light, as the ideological cover for the American strategy of planting military and other repressive regimes around the Third World. Buganda thus lost its liberal admirers, and by 1985 it was being presented as a case-study in tyranny.[10] The change of term is very revealing: 'despots' may have their uses but no-one looks tolerantly on 'tyrants'.

Early visitors from Europe had admired the discipline and decorum of Ganda society and the lively intelligence of its elite, but they were also shocked by its cruel and arbitrary punishments and the casual ruthlessness of its apparently absolute ruler; and this ambivalence has persisted in more recent commentaries. In my own early writings about the country[11] admiration was evident; and in retrospect I find it strange that a peace-loving democrat should have responded even half-favourably to the aggressive despotism that nineteenth-century Buganda unquestionably was. I can only plead that I was reflecting the prejudices of the late 1950s and early 1960s. That was the time when new African nation-states were being launched to the hopeful applause of most spectators, so that almost anything could be forgiven to people who had proved the ability of Africans to build and operate recognisable states.

In the 1960s, however, luck and skill deserted the Ganda. They failed either to establish the kingdom as a separate state, as most of them would have preferred, or to integrate properly with the Uganda Republic created by the departing British; and their failure plunged the whole country into the abyss. In 1966 Milton Obote, a politician belonging to the north of Uganda, broke the kingdom by force and in the following year he formally abolished it as a political entity. But to achieve these ends he had to use the Uganda army, which in 1971 decided to dispense with him as well.[12] The horrors that followed are too painful to dwell on and too well known to need retelling. But there is one misconception that needs to be contradicted. Many people assume a continuity between the brutalities of ancient Buganda and the terrible events that took place in Uganda between 1971 and 1985. That is too simple, and more than a little unfair, since the Ganda were overwhelmingly victims of the atrocities, not perpetrators. Idi Amin and Milton Obote, whose second period of power from 1980 to 1985 was probably even bloodier than Amin's, came from traditional societies of a quite different kind; and in any case their tyrannies were a product of post-colonial stresses rather than a harking back to pre-colonial patterns of behaviour.

Conversely, though, I ought never to have let my pleasant experience of late colonial Buganda colour my assessment of the very different society that existed there in the nineteenth century. There was a time when it was perhaps necessary for foreign commentators to ignore or explain away the various ferocities of Africa, past and present, but that time is long past. In the century of Auschwitz, Dresden and Hiroshima no Westerner can possibly write from a position of moral superiority, but that is no reason for concealing the fact that nineteenth-century Buganda was a place of great cruelty and that the power of the kings rested on systematic violence, both internal and external. That, however, is not all that can be said about it. European reporters were fascinated as well as appalled, recognising also heroism, questing intelligence and a courtesy that was more than superficial. The state was in its own way an intricate work of art; and whatever value judgement may be passed on it, anyone who is interested in political evolution must dearly want to understand how it came to be.

The question is, however, whether understanding is possible. Until Speke and Grant sat down to compose their journals, no words had ever been written in Buganda, and twenty years earlier no literate person even knew that the place existed. Contemporary and near-contemporary documents, the normal raw material of the historian, are thus absolutely lacking for pre-nineteenth-century Buganda. Nor has much been learnt from material remains. One of the minor tragedies of Uganda's recent past is that, just at the time when funds for African archaeology were being greatly increased, the country became unworkable in. Investigations were resumed in 1985, but there has not yet been any systematic research in the core areas of the kingdom, and the fragments of ancient pottery that have come to light are without date or context. Work done on the periphery and in neighbouring countries, both before and after the disasters, provides a bare framework of knowledge about technical and economic change during the last two millennia; but in spite of the growing resources of archaeological science and the growing subtlety of its interpretations, its historical insights are at best limited and ambiguous. So for any real light on the origin and development of the Buganda kingdom we have to rely mainly on its elaborate corpus of orally transmitted traditions. In fact the book is at least as much about tradition as it is about Buganda. Like the foremost scholar of Africa's past, Jan Vansina, I hope to show 'how intricate, how rich, how revealing these messages from our forebears really are'.[13]

Two questions have to be confronted at once. First, is my material actually oral tradition? I must not delay what some will consider a damning admission: I have not myself collected traditions 'in the field' from living Ganda. I did long ago talk to many people in rural Buganda, but not about ancient history, in which my interest had not then developed. So I have to persuade myself that I was born too late to hear really authentic stories about the pre-colonial past, and that I can make a contribution by critically examining the stories arduously recorded by others when the old culture was still in more or less full vigour, before there had been two generations of colonial rule and of Western influences both obvious and subtle. Armchair study is perhaps more justifiable in Buganda than in most places. Vansina's most important precept for students of tradition, that they should collect as many different versions as possible, would be difficult to apply to this highly centralised society, which naturally had a centralised tradition. For most Ganda, in fact, 'tradition' has long meant the contents of a book published in 1901 as *Bakabaka b'e Buganda* (The Kings of Buganda) and republished as *Basekabaka b'e Buganda* (The Former Kings of Buganda) in 1912, 1927 and 1949. Its author was Apolo Kagwa (in modern spelling Kaggwa) who, besides being a prolific writer, was the dominant personality in early colonial Buganda, holding the office of 'prime minister' from 1889 to 1926. The present study is in the main an extended commentary on this work. There is an English translation with notes by M. S. M. Kiwanuka,[14] and unless there is special reason to use the Ganda text references will be to that edition, which appeared in 1971.

By the 1950s there were copies of Kaggwa's book in most villages, and it would have been hard for an outsider to go behind it or beyond it. After him, it is true, a number of other Ganda writers made significant contributions. In the 1950s a retired schoolteacher with antiquarian interests, Michael Nsimbi, compiled studies of place-names and personal names which are a mine of historical detail and often help to make Kaggwa's spare narrative more intelligible.[15] Earlier the Catholic journal *Munno* had given space to wide-ranging historical discussions, with valuable commentaries by Tobi Kizito and J. T. K. Gomotoka,[16] who both belonged to distant branches of the royal house. The history written by James Miti is very important for the study of late nineteenth-century events;[17] but these are not my present concern, and none of these writers questions the basic frame of Kaggwa's story of the kingdom. He himself, moreover, was clearly presenting what was already an authorised version, for the names of the kings and some of the most interesting stories had appeared in several publications a generation earlier (see below, pp. 29–30). The material I am trying to exploit, therefore, was once oral tradition, but it has been crystallised in print for over ninety years.

The second question is whether or to what extent this tradition is history. But before we can begin to answer it certain distinctions have to be made, and first of all the crucial but not always recognised distinction between oral tradition and oral history. Those who use the latter term properly are referring to the information provided by old people about the days of their youth. The search for such information has become a flourishing branch of academic history; and indeed, few historians, when studying that part of the past which is in living memory, would fail to make use of as many memories as they practicably can. But that is not 'tradition', which deals with times beyond the memory of any living person. There is, however, an intermediate category, which might be called either first-stage tradition or secondary reminiscence. It consists of the reported experiences of those who were old when today's elderly informants were young. For example, in 1975 my father told me (not for the first time) that his grandmother had told him how, when she was a little girl, a man came to their house in Lancashire and called up the stairs: 'They've ta'en Boney.' The generations in this case were unusually long (that being the point of the anecdote), and the period of 160 years from 1815 to 1975 must be close to the maximum limit of historical reminiscence, which cannot go beyond the late childhood of the oldest grandparent of the oldest living informant. For people do not usually have any motive to retain or repeat the personal memories of those they never knew. (I do repeat my father's testimony, but that is because I have a special interest in the past and because I know from other sources who Boney was and why his taking mattered.) So there is a fair measure of agreement that at about a century and a half before the time of first written record historical reminiscence ceases and 'tradition' takes over. Thus the classical historian Moses Finley pointed out some time ago that the Greeks of the time of Herodotus, the so-called father of history, around 450 BC, had no means of knowing what had really happened in their country before the sixth century.[18] For Africa, though he is more hopeful about the recovery of the distant past, Joseph Miller has agreed that there is a major break in the character of the evidence near the beginning of the second lifetime back.[19]

More than half of Apolo Kaggwa's *The Kings of Buganda* is oral history, much of it indeed the history of his own times, describing events in which he had been a prominent actor. He himself was still fairly young, but his informants included an aunt of King Muteesa, a lady whose memories would go back probably to the 1820s.[20] She in turn would have been able to draw on the reminiscences of people who were adolescent in the third quarter of the eighteenth century. It is significant that for her great-grandfather King Kyabaggu and his elder brother Namugala, but for no previous rulers, we have personal descriptions, clearly derived at no more than second hand from people who had actually known them. Namugala had a humped back and was a drunkard but (by the standards of the time) a man of mild disposition. His brother, who ousted him from the kingship, was a much fiercer character, and he was short, thickset and bald. Beyond Namugala we find ourselves in the domain of tradition, which corresponds to the history that we learn at school. That is to say, we are dealing with a past that is not remembered but taught, with what society has decided to believe about the way it came to be. And the question is then how far society, when unconstrained by documentary records, can be trusted to tell the truth – or indeed whether it has any means of knowing what the truth is.

The short answer is that it can't and it hasn't, and that, insofar as it appears to relate to periods before the middle of the eighteenth century, the Ganda tradition is not history. Since I am writing a book about it, I obviously do not believe that it is valueless, nor that understanding of the past cannot be extracted from it. But I am sure that its earlier 'chapters' cannot be taken at anything like face value as a record of historical events.

In these matters, as in most others, there are intellectual fashions, and it is important that in the 1950s and 1960s, when African history was becoming an academic sub-discipline, there was a very general disposition to believe in the truth of traditional narratives. The Iliad, written in the eighth century BC, was accepted as containing genuine memories of a war supposedly fought some four hundred years earlier, though the interval had been almost entirely non-literate. Academics as well as the general public were convinced that 'Arthur' was the name of a man who fought and governed in early sixth-century Britain, although, apart from one ambiguous reference, there is no written evidence of his existence until the eighth century, and very little even then. And biblical scholars, who agreed that there was no historical writing in Israel before the tenth century BC, were nevertheless confident that the Patriarchs were real people who had lived seven or eight hundred years before David and Solomon. In all these domains a more sceptical attitude is now evident. For Dark Age Britain, it is sufficient to contrast Leslie Alcock, *Arthur's Britain* (Harmondsworth, 1971) and John Morris, *The Age of Arthur* (Chichester, 1973) with Nicholas Higham, *Rome, Britain and the Anglo-Saxons* (London, 1992), in which Arthur is barely mentioned at all. In Old Testament history the deconstruction was accomplished by T. L. Thompson and J. van Seters in the mid-1970s.[21] On Troy, Moses Finley was always a sceptic, but by 1979 he could be confident of scholarly acceptance when he wrote that 'Homer's Trojan War . . . must be evicted from the history of the Greek Bronze Age'.[22]

Although Africanists sometimes proceeded as though no one had ever studied proto-literate history before, they can hardly have been uninfluenced by the prevailing climate of scholarly opinion. For them, however, there were special reasons for suspending disbelief. The rise of African history coincided with the transition from colonial rule to independence, and was very much a part of it. The new nations were perceived to need a past in order that they might have a future, and in areas such as Uganda only tradition could give that past any real depth of time. It is true that there were dangers in its study and promotion, in that it was the property of 'tribes', whose pride and self-awareness could pose a threat to the newly created 'nation-states', almost all of which were multi-tribal. However, it was hoped that by setting out the traditions of the separate tribes and showing their interrelationships scholars would be able to bring a national history to birth. The need was not just ideological but also immediately practical. It was clearly wrong that African schoolchildren should go on being fed the Tudors and Stuarts; they should be learning the history of their own people instead, or as well. But their teachers, African as well as expatriate, had grown up with the Tudors and Stuarts; and it was thus necessary that the new African history should as far as possible be of a familiar kind, a reasonably confident tale of political successions in an agreed chronological frame. Lists of the *kabakas* of Buganda, the *bakama* or Bunyoro and the *rwots* of the Payera Acholi were soon in print, complete with dates and ready to be learnt by rote. The dates, it is true, were only given as approximate, but Standard VII would obviously take little notice of plus-or-minus signs.

There was in fact a powerful incentive to blur the obvious and crucial distinction between history in literate and in non-literate societies, between textbook and tradition. It was often argued that the way in which history is taught to the young is always influenced by the prejudice and self-interest of the teachers and of those who direct them, with the implication that accounts of the past based on oral tradition are no more unreliable than any other. But that was to miss a vital point, which is that where there are written records invention and misrepresentation are subject to constraint. Students can in principle go behind teacher and textbook to look at the chronicles and other surviving materials for themselves. Of course chronicles are selective, usually biased, sometimes actually mendacious; but they tell us what their authors believed, or wished others to believe, soon after the events that they report. Traditions, on the other hand, are documents of the time at which they are reduced to writing, and there is no way that they can be verified. An exception must be made for societies in which they are preserved in verse or other patterned form and memorised verbatim, often with severe penalties for error, by hereditary professionals. There is, however, no reason to think that anything like that took place in Buganda, where there was no special guild of remembrancers. There were, it is true, shrines that were said to contain the remains of former kings, and at each shrine there was a woman who claimed to be the successor of the king's queen-sister and who could rehearse, with more or less picturesque detail, the deeds of his reign. How much credence should be given to this institution is a question that will need close scrutiny, but suffice it to say here that shrines are by no means always authentic. And without such special protection the chain of testimonies, of which oral tradition is composed, is vulnerable at every link; it may have been – probably was – tampered with to suit the interests of each succeeding generation. More than that, at the end of the chain there may be, not an original event, but an original fiction.

Tradition is not really a single category but a variable mixture of at least three different things: genealogy, saga and myth. Knowledge of genealogy is obviously vital in societies that, like most African ones, are structured by lineage, so that status, land rights and marriage possibilities depend on ancestry. By the same token, royal and chiefly pedigrees are the indispensable charters of authority and power. However, it has long been recognised that for that very reason they are commonly adjusted, if not fabricated outright, and not only in Africa. David Henige has used material from all over the world to show that royal descent lines of any length are more than likely to be false.[23] As a matter of fact I was made aware of this at an early age. My step-grandmother (and this will be the last family anecdote) was a keen adherent of the British–Israelite movement, and she possessed a chart showing that King George V was descended, by way of Kenneth McAlpin, founder of the kingdom of Scotland, from one of the last kings of Judah, who died in exile in Egypt. It followed that the British Empire was heir to the promise of world dominion that had been given to the seed of Abraham. Even at the age of twelve I could not but notice that the links between Egypt in the sixth century before Christ and Argyll in the ninth century after him were somewhat lacking in credibility. I did not then know that they had been forged by medieval Scottish propagandists before being re-used by twentieth-century eccentrics.

Comparative studies suggest a more basic objection: the names at or near the beginning of a traditional genealogy are usually – one may probably say always – those of gods, archetypal heroes and other imaginary characters, who give dignity to the lineage by tracing it to the beginning of the world. For British genealogists, kings of Judah were only links in the chain that took the ancestry of their royal patrons back to Genesis. So attempts to establish a chronology for the origins of a kingdom by counting the royal generations back to the alleged founders are almost certainly misconceived. We do not nowadays put a date to Adam or Noah, and not all scholars would try to put one to Abraham or Jacob; and the cut-off point between theology and political history is by no means easy to detect. This is not to say that all genealogical material is concocted or unreal, but none of it can be given automatic credence.

Another kind of traditional matter that may convey historical information is that which has to be called, for want of a better term, 'saga'. This word originally meant no more than 'saying', and the Norse stories so labelled include some that I would classify as myths. As the term is used here, however, sagas are long-repeated oral tales of violence and valour, rooted in real events though usually embellished and glamourised. They are told partly for their own sake, as entertainment and inspiration, partly to gratify the descendants of outstanding warriors and honour the polity they fought for. They may well outlive the five generations of primary and secondary reminiscence, and they are history of a kind. Indeed it may be said that the warrior is the beginning of history, for he is the first kind of person who has deeds to be remembered, as distinct from ritual acts to be rehearsed. The oldest passage in the Bible is probably the Song of Deborah, celebrating the victory of Barak (and Yahweh) over Sisera; and the text itself (Judges 5:11) tells us that, before it was put into writing, the battle was commemorated by 'the players striking up in the places where the women draw water'.

Now saga in this sense is not a common African literary form. In West Africa, it is true, there is the famous tale of Sundiata, the heroic thirteenth-century founder of the kingdom of Mali; but that comes from an area where Islamic influences, including the use of writing, have been operative for many centuries. East African 'heroic recitations'[24] rarely relate to events earlier than the late eighteenth century and most of them date from the late nineteenth century or even the twentieth, while the long Zairean narratives commonly described as 'epics' are really myths or romances, works of pure imagination.[25] The reason for the scarcity of warrior tales is simple: the warrior was not an African type of man. This may seem a strange statement to make about a continent not noted for non-violence. But, whereas every African male could expect to engage in potentially lethal combat at some times in his youth, few made fighting a permanent way of life, and certainly there were no warrior *classes* such as those for whom the Iliad and the Song of Roland were composed. The celebrated Tutsi aristocracy of Rwanda might seem to be an exception, yet they were considered cowards by their German conquerors, to whom they offered no resistance, and inspection shows that they owed their dominance to organisation and mystique rather than personal valour. By the same token, even Sundiata is celebrated as a magician and not only as a general. For the truth is that African societies were controlled not by fighting men but by intellectuals, wielders of symbols rather than of spears. (We shall see that Buganda was a qualified exception, but only in its latest phase.) Missionaries and other early witnesses knew that in Africa the 'witch-doctor' was the real power in the land. The intelligentsias and educated elites about whom so much was written in the late colonial and early post-colonial years were only superficially a new kind of ruling class, manipulating new kinds of symbol in a basically familiar way. And the characteristic discourse of intellectuals is not saga but myth.

In Buganda we have a tantalising reference to harpists who entertained people in the evenings by singing 'the legends and traditions of the country';[26] and there is little doubt that some saga-like material is embedded in the pre-reminiscence section of the tradition. Predominantly, however, this consists of stories of another kind. The distinction was recognised by the Cambridge scholars Henry and Nora Chadwick, who included Buganda in their great history of world literature.[27] They were especially interested in popular 'heroic' stories of the kind here called saga, and their appetite had been whetted by certain tales picked up by Stanley at Muteesa's court. But they were disappointed by the fuller versions of the dynastic tradition that were available a generation later. With the disappearance of the 'heroic court' warrior tales seemed also to have vanished, and there was now a predominance of 'mantic' stories, that is to say of matter of the kind that appealed to priests and prophets, roughly equivalent in my terminology to myth. But in this they appear mistaken. The court was still there, though under the British peace its heroic dignity

was certainly much diminished; but the whole religious structure of society
had been driven underground by the triumph of Christianity. Insofar as
Kaggwa's book, produced after the great changes, was a history of late
eighteenth- and nineteenth-century Buganda, it was as full of battle,
murder and sudden death as anyone could wish, whereas those of Stanley's
stories that were attached to more ancient kings were already of 'mantic'
character, more obviously mythical than they would appear in Kaggwa's
prosaic summaries.

A historian who proposes that a large part of African tradition is really
myth is bound to upset his colleagues, since he appears to be declaring their
efforts to be futile in advance; and in retaliation they are likely to accuse
him of being a 'structuralist'.[28] Being fascinated by the writings of Claude
Lévi-Strauss on mythology, and respectful of other structuralists such as
Georges Dumézil and the Africanist Luc de Heusch, I would take that label
as a compliment, but one that I would have to disclaim, since I find the
structuralist techniques of myth-analysis too difficult to use. In any case,
even before that term had been invented people managed to disbelieve in
Arthur and Robin Hood and Heracles and Noah, and I myself was writing
with innocent scepticism about Ganda and other African traditions at a
time when Lévi-Strauss had only just begun to turn his attention to myth.[29]
My thinking on these matters (more fully set out below, pp. 43–56) is in fact
eclectic, having been largely formed by earlier writers, especially by
ritualists such as Sir James Frazer, Jane Harrison, A. M. Hocart and Lord
Raglan, as well as the historian of religion Mircea Eliade (notably his
classic work *The Myth of the Eternal Return*) and those whose approach is
basically psychological such as Geza Róheim, A. E. Jensen and Joseph
Campbell. I have tried to make use of the insights of more recent writers –
including the structuralist perception that stories have a life of their own
and are not solely products of particular societies at a particular time – but
do not accept that older views have been wholly invalidated.

There is a general point here that may be worth making. In the natural
sciences there is decisive progress: the sun does not go round the earth;
there is no such thing as phlogiston. But in the study of literature, history
and anthropology there are no such total victories, and so-called paradigm
shifts are often not much more than changes in mood and fashion. Each
academic generation has its own priorities and perspectives, but however
fruitful its innovations may be they complement but do not abolish the
achievements of the past.

Another problem is that the word 'myth' seems to encounter a certain
resistance, especially from African scholars, who perhaps take it to be a
derogatory term, signifying something obsolete or childish, not suitable for
grown-up modern nations. If so, they are quite wrong. Like music, myth is

a fundamental mode of discourse, an essential mark of humanity, vital to psychic and social well-being. If there are peoples who lack a mythology, so much the worse for them. Contrary to a common belief, that is not true of Africans. But much of their mythical inheritance has been concealed behind a facade of political history; and the present work is partly one of restoration, aiming to strip away the plaster and disclose the antique carvings beneath.

Even those who most strongly insist that oral tradition is history generally accept that it is not only history, that it is one of the chief vehicles of a people's culture. Talk of the 'cultural values' expressed by traditional narratives, however, carries with it another danger. It may give countenance to the tribalism that bedevilled African studies for too long. Ganda tradition, in my view, would hardly be worth writing about if it were talking only to the Ganda and did not have something valuable to tell us all. It is here above all that I appeal to the authority of Lévi-Strauss, who has insisted that the context of a specific narrative, though it certainly includes its own natural and social environment, also comprises other stories, some of which may have been recorded in very distant and very different societies. Since he has demonstrated the intricate links that unite the myths of North and South America, I have no qualms about attempting to relate African traditions to Near Eastern, Greek, Celtic and occasionally to yet more distant mythologies. In particular I shall try to show that what the Ganda said about the past of their kingdom cannot be fully understood without reference to the great, ancient and still resonant myth of the sacred kingship.

To some, this will appear a dangerous evocation of the diffusionist heresy. During the last sixty years and more, the study of culture-history has been dominated by various kinds of processual thinking, which lead to a heavy bias in favour of convergent innovation and internally generated change, and against the idea that the similarity of widely separated ideas, stories and institutions could be due to ancient common origin.[30] And indeed that idea is not vital to my main argument, which is that much of the Ganda tradition is myth; and the parallels with distant cultures that will be adduced may, if the reader wishes, be taken merely as more or less interesting analogies, and not as the historically grounded homologies that I believe them to be. Yet diffusionism does have strong attraction for the historian, because it replaces the mechanical working out of developmental processes with a more interesting story of events, and because a vast amount of diffusion – of techniques, ideas, games, music, languages and institutions – is historically documented. Modern communications have of course made such transfers easier, but it is unreasonable to assume that none took place in the undocumented past. Diffusion is never a complete explanation of social and cultural phenomena, but it is often a necessary part of one.

Diffusionist hypotheses came to be rejected with especial vehemence in African studies because they were often linked with racist or at any rate elitist assumptions. Such links, however, are not essential. No theory of intrinsic superiority is needed to explain the fact, which is difficult to deny, that in particular eras certain corners of the world have been especially innovative and influential, and that one of these was the Middle East in the Neolithic period of pioneering food production and settled community life. To accept that tropical Africa, as well as Europe, owed much to that region and period, so far from devaluing African studies, would help to move them into the mainstream of humanistic enquiry. I have, it is true, an interest to declare at this point. By what right does a foreigner with an imperfect command of the language set out to interpret the traditions of an African people among whom he happened to reside for two years a long time ago? My answer would be that Europeans who have been given some kind of access to African culture, no less than Africans who have experienced the reverse process, have the necessary role of interpreters and builders of bridges. This does not imply support for the economic and political concept of 'Eurafrica', a neo-colonial enterprise for which I have no time at all. But it does mean inviting African intellectuals not to retreat into the shell of a peculiar 'Africanity', but rather to try to identify that which is distinctively African and that which is more nearly universal.

I must add that in spite of this portentous introduction the book is a particularist, indeed a tediously detailed study of an individual tradition. It will spend a long time on myth but will eventually return from myth to history and try to answer the original question: how did Buganda come to be? African traditions do have value as historical evidence, but this cannot be rightly assessed until they have been studied in their own right, as social artefacts, and some of them as products of poetic and religious imagination.

Finally, there is another possible question that I find harder to answer: in face of the multiple calamities of Africa at the present day, is it not a selfish indulgence to write about ancient history and myth – especially as I was originally hired in the hope that my work might be of some small and indirect material benefit to the Ganda people and others? I can only plead that I have nothing useful to offer by way of help or counsel. It is possible, indeed, that Africa has more than enough foreign counsellors already, and that the best ways for an Englishman to give practical help are to contribute to Oxfam (or similar) and to beg his own government to write off the debt.

As I crawled towards the end of the first draft of this book I found that I had suffered the just fate of the idle scholar: someone else had written it first, and better. At least, that was my initial reaction to the sight of Benjamin Ray's *Myth, Ritual and Kingship in Buganda*, which appeared in 1991. Closer inspection, however, showed that Ray has written his own book, an important and illuminating one which may just leave room for mine. He confronts the central puzzle of Ganda studies, the apparent contrast between the mystical implications of the elaborate royal ritual and the very secular reality of the nineteenth-century kingdom. In 1944 a Swedish scholar, Tor Irstam, drew on older ethnographic descriptions to present *The King of Ganda* as the archetype of the institution of divine or sacral kingship that had been exhaustively examined by Sir James Frazer in his *Golden Bough*. In that model the king appears as a hieratic figure, hedged about with divinity, whose business is not government but the magical assurance of the fertility of land and people. Yet the actual king of Ganda encountered by travellers and missionaries was the head of a military bureaucracy, a ruler of very real and terrifying authority; and personally he was a self-willed young man of clearly sceptical temper, enjoying the exercise of power but well aware of his human limitations. He still went through some of the ritual motions, for instance remaining closeted with his 'fetishes' on the day of the new moon, but it was obvious that he would much rather have been out hunting.[31] Theory, based on what people told enquirers about the customs of the kingship, seemed badly out of tune with the observed realities of Buganda. Above all, there was no sign of the ritual regicide that was the key component of the Frazerian system, the alleged practice of putting kings to death either at the end of a fixed term or when their vital energies began to fail. The last four pre-colonial *kabaka*s certainly died from natural causes, and while several earlier holders of the office were said to have been assassinated there was in each case a specific domestic or political motive and no clear evidence of a ritual imperative.

Sweden was in fact the last stronghold of Frazerian anthropology and 1944 was close to the time of its collapse. In the next generation divine kings were very much out of fashion. The mystery of kingship was now seen as mere mystique, sacrality as one of the 'resources' at the disposal of governments, helping them to secure obedience and hold the state together. Latterly this cynical interpretation has begun to be modified by a more sympathetic appreciation of the profound emotions that kingship can arouse.[32] Ray insists that, while the *kabaka* was in no sense a god, was known to be a man like others, his role was something more than that of a political executive. He was, he writes 'Buganda's supreme symbol of order and meaning'.[33] Later he quotes the dictum of another recent writer, Michael Kenny, that the kingship was 'the transcendental symbol of political identity'[34] and he himself describes the king as 'the centre of myth and history . . . of power, legitimacy and prosperity . . . and of civil religion'.[35] Centrality, moreover, is inherently sacred.

All this is certainly true and a great advance both on the naively magico-religious and the naively political concepts of Ganda and other kingships. Yet it is in the end unsatisfying, for it does not explain why the Ganda people should have made an individual man the focus of their lives in this totalitarian way. Many societies, alike in old Africa and in modern Europe, have managed to construct identities for themselves without the help of kings. Others, such as modern Britain, have drawn a clear line between the symbolic and the executive functions of government. Others again, such as the United States, have joined the two functions together but have made very sure that the resulting power is not arbitary or unfettered. So what went wrong in Buganda (and I will permit myself this value-judgement) to allow the *kabaka* such total dominance over both the political and the affective life of his people? The answer has to be sought in history.

Ray is a historian of religion, which means that he is somewhat closer to anthropologists than to other kinds of historian; and his work is an essentially static analysis of the nineteenth-century kingdom. Insofar as he considers its objective past he accepts the orthodox account given by the official tradition, stating roundly that 'it originated in the fourteenth century through the unification of the clans under a paramount leader called the Kabaka'.[36] I shall be trying to show that this assertion is insecurely founded and that Buganda was in one sense much older and in another sense much younger than the tradition seems to say.

Ray does not tell us how or why the clans were thus unified, nor does he allow for any really fundamental subsequent change until the impact of foreign influences in the second half of the nineteenth century. Yet without a historical dimension functional explanations of political institutions are in danger of becoming circular: things are as they are because if they were otherwise the system would not work as it does. It is not very difficult to describe the social–psychological and the residual constitutional functions of the present-day British monarchy, but these do not explain it; for if it were not given by history the same needs would have been met in other ways. Nor is the history of such institutions irrecoverable in the absence of documents. The formula of the Royal Assent to legislation would itself be proof that kings of England had once been true sovereigns, who did not necessarily approve the wishes of their servants and vassals, even when in Parliament assembled. Likewise the kingdom of Muteesa I cannot be fully understood except through the legacy of both its recent and its very ancient past.

The search for that past will necessarily lead beyond the frontiers of the kingdom. Ray not only dismisses the links that some scholars have seen between Buganda and Egypt of the Pharoahs,[37] but also pays little heed to its immediate neighbours. Yet Buganda was one of a numerous group of states that occupied the wide tract of fertile upland commonly known as the 'Interlacustrine' or 'Great Lakes' region of East Africa but hereinafter less cumbrously called 'the Lakeland'. Three of these units – Rwanda, Burundi and Bunyoro – were as large as or larger than Buganda, others were much smaller and some were minuscule, but almost all were monarchical in form; and though their institutions and ideologies showed quite radical differences there was an underlying family resemblance between them. How far this was due to a distant common origin and how far to 'peer polity interaction',[38] the accumulated mutual influence of neighbours, must be a matter for debate. But, either way, Buganda cannot properly be examined as an isolated system.

There is also a caveat to be entered about the political background of Ray's research, which he has himself described very fully and frankly.[39] When he arrived in Buganda to study traditional ritual Idi Amin had just come to power, and the Ganda briefly hoped for a restoration of the kingship which Milton Obote had overthrown. Ray quickly gained the confidence of the custodians of the royal shrines and other persons closely linked to the monarchy; and these people, who like many other Africans had an exaggerated notion of the power and influence of Western academics, obviously hoped they could promote their cause by persuading him of the pre-eminent value of the Ganda kingship. He was fully aware that he was being used, and if any bias did creep into his findings it was similar to my own. For in 1953 I had shared the indignation of the Ganda people at what seemed the high-handed action of the Governor in deporting the *kabaka* to London (an act which gave the institution a new lease of popular life), and was in some degree infected by a royalist sentiment normally alien to me. Both of us, in short, view the pre-colonial kingship partly through retinas imprinted with the image of a late colonial and post-colonial institution which was inevitably very different in style and function.

Except where I clearly signal otherwise, I have left the text as it was before I saw Ray's book, even where there is considerable overlap. I had already made use of his earlier and shorter writings on Buganda,[40] naturally with due acknowledgement.

Finally, it should be noted that in 1993 the book gained an unexpected topicality through the restoration of the monarchy in the person of *Kabaka* Mutebi II. I did not foresee this development and did not write in order to promote it, or to discourage it.

And now it is high time to consider what the Ganda tradition said.

2   The story and its making

Most versions of the story begin with Kintu, who came into the land from the north or from the east or from the sky and founded the kingdom of Buganda. Kintu was the First Man as well as the First King, and he brought with him the First Woman, Nambi, the sucker that gave rise to all banana trees and the first cow. After a while, as a result of the first sin, Kintu disappeared, leaving the realm to his son Cwa. Another son, Wunyi or Winyi, is said to have become king of Bunyoro, Buganda's north-western neighbour, which claimed greater antiquity and had certainly at one time been more extensive and powerful.

Little is told of Cwa, except that he sent his delinquent son Kalemeera to stay with his uncle in Bunyoro, where he promptly seduced his host's wife Wannyana and left her carrying the child who would become Kimera the third king, or K.3. (In this notation, introduced by Martin Southwold, K. conveniently stands for 'king', for the Ganda title *kabaka* and for Kaggwa, to whose list it refers.) Cwa disappeared in his turn and Kalemeera died on the way home; and so, after a period of regency, the chiefs, who had somehow become aware of Kimera's existence, sent to fetch him to his kingdom.

The (Ba-)Nyoro, it need hardly be said, knew nothing of this story, and when some of them read it in Kaggwa's book they professed outrage at the idea that a king's wife could be seduced by anyone, let alone a foreigner.[1] For their part they identify Kimera (or sometimes Kintu) with one Kato, the junior twin of their dynastic founder, thus putting the upstart kingdom of Buganda in its proper place. And neutral commentators have generally seen the story of Kimera's parentage as a transparent fiction, the reality being the foundation or re-foundation of Buganda as an offshoot or dependency of the Nyoro power. We shall see that there is more than this to Kimera's advent, and will have to consider what historical basis it may have had and whether Buganda is to be explained (or explained away) as a 'secondary' or 'conquest' state. It is at any rate clear that Kimera was the original beginning of the dynastic tradition and that the Adamic figure of Kintu is concerned with the origin, not of a particular kingdom, but of

Generation

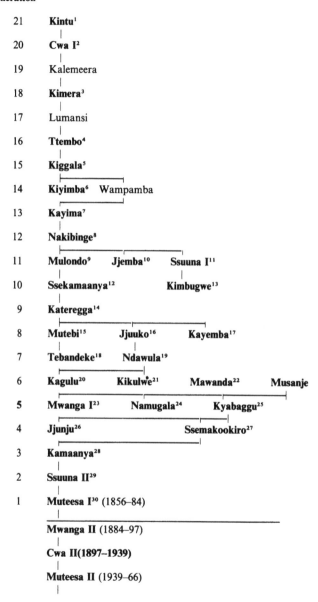

As presented in Kagwa, *The Kings of Buganda*, and Roscoe, *The Baganda*.
Reigning monarchs are shown in bold type.

Fig. 1   The dynasty

human society. The very first reporter, John Speke, was told that a hunter (or as he characteristically described him a 'sportsman') came down the Katonga valley from the west and made himself master of the land. He was originally called Buganda, like the country, but changed his name to Kimera.[2] A later commentator, the scholarly diplomat Sir Harry Johnston, decided that 'the first real king of Uganda (sc. Buganda) was this Kimera'.[3] Cwa and Kalemeera then appear as rather awkward links between the mythological prologue and the dynastic story proper.

After the arrival of Kimera there is a series of incidents which seem to have more to do with family relationships than with politics. He himself was murdered by his young grandson Ttembo, who held him responsible for the early death of his father Lumansi. Ttembo went mad with guilt and in spite of elaborate and bloodstained 'cures' he died young. His son Kiggala lay with his sister, who gave birth to the twin branches of the Mayanja river, and he ended up blind and impotent and mocked by his young wives. Kiggala's son Wampamba married his mother's brother's daughter, also an incestuous act according to Ganda custom, and was therefore excluded from the succession, though the offspring of the union, Kayima, was allowed to become king.

With Kayima's son Nakibinge (K.8) we come to the most vividly narrated episode in the whole story. The succession was disputed by a cousin, who enlisted the help of Bunyoro. Nakibinge won some victories in the ensuing war but in the end, despite supernatural help from Ssese, the island home of the gods, he was slain. In spite of this disaster his son Mulondo, though still a little boy, was able to inherit the kingdom, and no more is heard of the Nyoro for several generations.

There followed a series of kings about whose deeds, as H. M. Stanley put it, 'tradition, fable and history are alike silent'.[4] Kaggwa does tell a little about them but nothing of any obvious consequence. The mists only begin to clear with the accession of Kateregga (K.14), whose name was reverberant for nineteenth-century Buganda, being one of the few that were mentioned to Speke. But here is a problem. It is clear from the narrative that Kateregga was at first the ruler of a very small territory in the central 'county' of Busiro and that he began an expansion to the west that was continued by his successor Mutebi.[5] Between them these two kings incorporated the western counties of Mawokota, Butambala, Gomba and Busujju, with part of the great north-western march of Ssingo. Now Kateregga was in the ninth generation back from the beginning of the colonial era in 1890 (hereafter 'Generation Nine' or G.9);[6] and on the commonly accepted and reasonable allowance of twenty-seven years to each royal generation his reign would have to be dated to around the middle of the seventeenth century. Yet Kimera, G.18, thus late fourteenth or early fifteenth century, and before him Kintu, G.21, were presented as rulers of a state essentially similar to nineteenth-century Buganda. It is of course possible that Buganda was from its beginning a considerable state, that it was reduced to a small remnant in Nakibinge's reign and that Kateregga started a new process of recovery and expansion. But it is simpler to suppose that the traditions of Kintu and Kimera project the later greatness of the kingdom into a distant and imaginary past and that Kateregga's reign marks the true beginning of Buganda as a significant power.

After Mutebi the story again becomes very confused, brothers and cousins following one another on the throne with much attendant violence, some of it fantastically narrated. A fundamental change is indicated by the accession of Namugala (K.24), for whom an entirely new and elaborate installation rite was conducted on Buddo hill in southern Busiro, thereafter the ritual heart of the kingdom. The normal habit of tradition is to insist that all basic institutions go back to the beginning of things; so when it acknowledges innovation it must be supposed to be telling the truth. In fact we have now reached Generation Five and the era of remembered history, and from now on we can be confident at least about the main sequence of events. Namugala was deposed, but not killed, by his more dynamic brother Kyabaggu, who in turn suffered revolts by sons of a former king and more disastrously by his own sons, who then fought against one another. The eventual victor was Ssemakookiro, probably the ablest and most ruthless of all Buganda's rulers, whose reforms ensured that the succession would thenceforward pass more or less smoothly from father to son.

The instability of the eighteenth century did not prevent, and must be suspected of causing, the rapid expansion and elaboration of the state. King Mawanda (K.22, G.6) pushed the borders far to the north and the east, and is credited with a great increase in the role of centrally appointed chiefs at the expense of local power-holders. He probably began and Kyabaggu (K.25) continued the destructive raiding of Busoga, the country on the eastern side of the Nile. His successor Jjunju overran the south-western province of Buddu, hitherto in the orbit of Bunyoro, and won a decisive victory over the Nyoro army. This was the last major annexation, and thereafter Buganda settled down to consolidate its gains and to enjoy internal peace and regional hegemony. This it did until the great crisis of the 1880s and 1890s, when it was shaken to its foundations, but not destroyed, by European culture, trade and military power.

That, in summary, was the story that Apolo Kaggwa presented in 1901. He did so with authority, for he was close to the centre of power from his youth

up. Great-grandson of a prominent provincial chief, he was a 'page' at
Muteesa's court and graduated under Mwanga to be the troop commander
in charge of the Ggwanika, the treasury and more especially the royal
armoury. Like others of his kind he was drawn to the society and
instruction of the missionaries, and he became the leader of the 'English'
faction, but unlike some he did not perish on the pyre of 1886, being let off
with a severe beating. After the Christian triumph of 1889 he was appointed
katikkiro, chief minister, and held that powerful office until 1926. As a
reward for helping the British to control the country he became Sir Apolo,
member of an order of knighthood normally reserved for ambassadors and
colonial governors, and he was also a great landowner and generous
patron. Few Ganda were likely to dispute his version of the kingdom's past,
except in detail. But the question before us – one of the questions anyway –
is how far that version was historically true.

Clearly it was not history in the modern sense, for it contained no
analysis of social and economic structures or of the dynamics of political
change. Later scholars have sought to remedy these deficiencies but they
have felt obliged to rely on the data he provided and to take it more or less
at face value. One of the earliest of these was Bishop Julien Gorju whose
work, published in 1920, was an intriguing mixture of prejudice and insight,
drawing on the information provided by those most knowledgeable
witnesses, the Catholic clergy.[7] More influential among anglophone
readers was an article on 'The early history of Buganda' written in 1935 by
Sir John Gray, a colonial official who served in Uganda and became Chief
Justice of Zanzibar.[8] History was the passion of Gray's life and he wrote
copiously on many aspects of East Africa's past. He was a very scholarly
man, but his scholarship was of a conventional kind, and he wrote about
Buganda as though it were medieval England; the facts, that is to say, were
known, barring a few doubtful points, and the historian's task was to
present them in a rational and ordered way. The academics who have
discussed the history of the kingdom from the 1950s onwards have treated
it with more sophistication but with a similar basic credulity. Kintu, they
agree, is not likely to have been a historical personage (though they
sometimes write as though he were), but the 'Kintu figure' has something to
tell us about real events. For the rest, there is little questioning of the outline
of the received tradition. Martin Southwold, in an elegant study of the
system of royal succession, felt justified in accepting that kings did follow
one another as Kaggwa said they did, because the given sequence enabled
him to construct an intelligible pattern of change.[9] Matthias Kiwanuka,
whose edition of Kaggwa's *The Kings of Buganda* earned him a London
doctorate, added a good deal of marginal information and critical
comment but did not dispute the historicity of the narrative, which

provided the frame for his own *History of Buganda*. As a Ganda patriot he was upset by the suggestion that his country started life as a Nyoro colony, but that led him to put his own gloss on the story of Bunyoro-born Kimera, not to dismiss it from history (see below, pp. 194–5).

It must be said that there is a good case for credulity, since the story is butttressed by much circumstantial detail and by material evidence scattered about the land. For each reign we are given the names of the king's principal wives and their fathers, the names and clan affiliation of his principal officers, the location of his capitals and of his corporeal remains.[10] It must be appreciated, however, that political life in recent pre-colonial Buganda was in part a competition between the commoner clans, whose claims to ancient connections with the kingship have therefore to be viewed with some reserve. The evidence of the royal shrines carries rather greater weight. When a king died the cadaver was placed in a sealed hut and left to dry out. The skull was then removed and the jawbone, seat of the continuing spirit, was worked loose, wrapped in bark-cloth, decorated and bestowed in a *ssiro*, a shrine, usually at one of his former capitals. The rest of the body was stored separately, most often in a collective royal graveyard. The location of the cemeteries and the individual jawbone shrines was noted by Kaggwa. Most of them were visited and inspected by a colonial official in 1936 and a record made. In 1959 Professor Roland Oliver made a fresh survey, personally visiting most of the shrines and confirming in all cases that the sites were known to local people.[11] By then most of them had been rebuilt in more modern style as part of the royalist revival of that time. In 1972, after the fall of the monarchy, Benjamin Ray found them still functioning and made them the principal focus of his study.[12] Unlike Oliver he was allowed access to the inner precincts and given instruction in their meaning.

The shrines, concentrated in the central county of Bu-siro, which is by definition 'the land of shrines', were a crucial element in the structure of Ganda kingship, linking it both to the past and to the world of spirit. They were miniature courts where the dead kings, though transformed into *mizimu*, 'shades', continued to preside, each speaking through a medium and attended by a 'chief minister', by those of his widows who had not been immolated and by his queen-sister; and as these people died off they were replaced by successors coached in the data of his reign. They were the scene of regular festivals on the day after the new moon, and were periodically visited by the reigning king and by others who 'paid court' in the hope of help and counsel. But for our purpose their chief significance is a historical one. 'The jawbone shrines', Oliver wrote, 'were the real charters of Buganda's present dynasty', the chief source of the royal tradition and the guarantee of its truth. Oliver also argued that the distribution of the body tombs was consistent with the pattern of Kaggwa's history. The early kings, from Kimera (K.3) to Nakibinge (K.8), were buried at individual sites, three of them in an area just north of the Mayanja river, which was the northern border of Busiro. At this stage they were following the practice of Bunyoro, as was natural for a dynasty of assumed Nyoro origin. Nakibinge's campaign, though apparently ending in defeat, actually in Oliver's view secured Buganda's independence, and this was marked by a new mortuary custom giving first importance to the jawbone. From then on the bodies were consigned to collective cemeteries, first at a place called Gombe (singular of *magombe*, the underworld), also just north of the Busiro border, but from Tebandeke onwards at Merera in Busiro. The story is that this king (K.18) asked why he should have to pay the high fees demanded by the custodians of Gombe, and when his courtiers assured him that he was indeed being ripped off he sacked the place and established a new cemetery for himself and his heirs.[13] Finally Muteesa I, having learnt from his Arab friends that other potentates, such as the sultan of Zanzibar, were not mutilated after death, decreed that he himself should be buried whole. What is more, in 1869 he had the bodies of ten previous kings exhumed and reburied with their jawbones. And David Henige, a Wisconsin scholar whose learning and incisive mind brought a new rigour to the study of African tradition, seized on this episode to ask why only ten of Muteesa's twenty-nine predecessors received this treatment. Was it not likely that other graves and shrines did not then exist, but were fabricated later in order to enhance the kingdom's antiquity?[14] The bodies disinterred were those of the eight immediately preceding kings (spanning five generations), whose reality no one would wish to doubt, together with Kimera, who would obviously have to have a shrine whether he had lived or not, and, rather oddly, the obscure Ssuuna I (K.11). Henige also noted that Speke's enquiries in 1861–2 had yielded the names of only seven kings before Muteesa, and again implied that in the interval between his visit and Stanley's the genealogical fakers had been busy. Benjamin Ray, however, will have none of this.[15] He points out that Speke's informant was a man of no great authority, who was doubtless able to provide only a sample of the most recent and most famous names. His list, moreover did not correspond with Muteesa's reburials, including one (Kateregga) who was not exhumed and omitting five who were. He also sees little significance in the small number of the 1869 transfers. Perhaps Muteesa did not see the project through. Or maybe the tropical soils had already devoured the older skeletons.

We can probably dismiss the idea that Muteesa simply invented a long king-list to impress Stanley and other visitors and that numerous royal shrines were created between then and the end of the century in order to confirm the list. But that does not dispose of Henige's more general point, namely that monuments which serve as the charters of a state are automatically suspect. Even those scholars who believe in a historical King Arthur do not accept that the tomb discovered at Glastonbury in 1191 was really his. It is well known that the Norman and Angevin kings of England, members of a new and alien dynasty, did much to promote the legends of King Arthur who, besides high antiquity, had the great merit of being an anti-Saxon hero. Contemporary doubters would be silenced by the identification of his bodily remains, and the monks of Glastonbury obliged, thus greatly adding to their abbey's fame and wealth.[16] It is suggested that there was a close parallel in the complicity between the self-interest of Ganda shrine-keepers and the needs of a Ganda dynasty of no very great real antiquity.

It would be rash to claim that most of the Ganda shrines were imaginative constructions, but there is evidence that at least one was. Kaggwa stated that Kagulu (K.20) had neither grave nor jawbone shrine. He could not have had, since tradition tells us that, having been driven from the throne by rival princes, he was drowned in Lake Victoria.[17] Yet by the time of the 1936 survey he did have a shrine, which Oliver found to be one of the best preserved. Unless, therefore, Kaggwa's story was wholly false, any jawbone deposited at the shrine must have been inauthentic. It is true that his version of events was disputed by another authority, who claimed that Kagulu died of wounds and was secretly buried, to be exhumed at a later date.[18] This testimony is, however, suspect. Attempts were being made in the early colonial period to constitute the members of the royal patriline as a regular clan, which it had not been in the past. Very few sons of nineteenth-century kings survived that turbulent time (see below, pp. 225–8) and so it was necessary to secure recognition for as many distant branches as possible. Although Kagulu's sons were supposed to have been killed or disgraced, people claiming descent from him did gain official acceptance as princes in the early colonial period, and the shrine was clearly part of their rehabilitation.

Henige suggests that the number of kingly shrines may have been swollen by those belonging to other members of the royal house. But this may be taken further. The land of Buganda, especially its central area, was full of shrines, little enclosures invested with numinous authority, and by no means all even claimed connection with the kingship. Of similar power-houses in the southern Sudan it has been asserted that they were 'absolutely necessary for the continuation of life'.[19] In Buganda they were called masabo (singular ssabo, 'a place for praying at'). Some were the homes of nationally acknowledged ba-lubaale, eminent manifestations of divinity, and these were commonly distinguished as biggwa (singular kiggwa).Others belonged to *misambwa*, spirits with a merely local habitation and a name, linked with large trees, rocks, streams, snakes, anything that seemed to have more than its share of the life-force. Others again were regarded – but there is no clear dividing line – as ancestral figures from the distant past. Those who constructed pedigrees for nineteenth-century *kabakas* thus had a great stock of known potencies to draw on, as they sought to fill the void between the legendary founders, Kintu and Kimera, and the five or six remembered generations of the dynasty. (It is perhaps significant that Mgr Streicher, leader of the Catholic mission at the turn of the century, claimed to know of the shrines of thirty-eight rulers before Muteesa – nine *more* than the total usually recognised.[20]) Some of the shrines may really have contained relics of older rulers, forgotten or dimly reverberant in saga. Others however were probably local deities, whose communities had gained enough clout to secure them a place in the history of the ever more dominant state. But I shall try to show that most of the 'early' kings were neither individual rulers nor gods but representations of particular aspects of kingship, recurrent personae in the perennial royal drama. Ritual, in other words, did not provide a record of the dynastic past but itself generated the 'dynasty', being far older in its essential features than the state it helped to support.

The king-creating process is best illustrated by characters who did not quite achieve canonical status. Thus antiquarians in the colonial period provided Kintu, the First Man, with a voluminous pedigree, consisting of divinities and other shadowy personages, each with a specific location.[21] His father, according to one such account, was called 'Buganda', who figures in an earlier report as his son, and in Speke's version, earliest of all, was the alias of his great-grandson Kimera. The good sense of the orthodox tradition, however, rejected this shadowy personage, who was obviously derived from the name of the country and had no more historical reality than Britannia – and no more religious reality than the goddess Roma of the imperial cult. Yet 'Buganda' had a shrine that was still just extant in the 1950s, tended part-time by an old woman and dutifully kept in repair by the local chief, though he had no idea of its function.[22] Here in other words was a concept that narrowly failed to be translated into historical terms, and it is reasonable to suspect that there are others which narrowly succeeded.

On the holy mount of Buddo, where from the mid-eighteenth century onwards the kings have been ritually installed, there were four sacred houses.[23] One belonged to Buganda. Another was dedicated to the war-god Kibuuka, or rather to his 'twin', called Serutega. (The umbilical cord of every ritually important person in Buganda was regarded as his twin and carefully preserved.) The third house was that of Buddo, said to have been the adviser of King Namugala, the first to undergo the rite. Although visitors were shown something that was supposed to be Buddo's 'mummy', this claim cannot have been correct. No doubt the ritual had a designer, but he was not called Buddo, for that is the name of a locality, not a person. It signifies 'the grassy place', an ordinary name for what had once been an ordinary hill. Finally there was the house of Lumansi, who figures in the dynastic lists but is not reckoned a king, since he is said to have died before his father Kimera. So we have an abstract noun, a god and a hill. What is a long-dead non-regnant prince doing in this odd collection? Part of an answer is contained in his name: *Luma-nsi* is 'Bite-the-earth', presumably a snake. The identity is confirmed by Stanley's presentation of the name as 'Almass', which would have been a strange garbling of Lumansi but is explicable if it were given to him in the form 'Wa-lumansi'; for one function of the prefix *Wa* is to humanise the names of animals. (*Ngo* is a leopard but *Wa-ngo* is the Mr Leopard of the fables.) Snakes certainly featured in the Buddo ritual, and a curious tale is told about a young king – allegedly Muteesa – spending a night vigil there and confronting a mystical puff-adder.[24] We shall see, too (below p. 105) that a serpent king was the key figure in the myth that acted as the charter of the Buddo ritual, though his name was not Lumansi.

This is the kind of material that helped to fill the more distant sections of the dynastic tradition. Further doubts about its veracity arise from well-established methods of analysis: in the first place from source-criticism, which shows that in the nineteenth century the tradition was not as solid and invariant as it later became. At first sight, indeed, the sources are remarkably consistent. Kaggwa's 1901 king-list is practically the same as those recorded by three visitors to the Ganda court a quarter of a century earlier: H. M. Stanley in 1875; the German adventurer who called himself Emin Pasha and paid two calls on Muteesa in 1876 and 1877 on behalf of the Egyptian government; and the missionary Charles Wilson, who arrived in 1877 and with his colleague Robert Felkin wrote the first systematic account of the country.[25] The information was derived from Muteesa himself and may thus be said to have the highest possible authority. The argument is double-edged, however, for once the king had pronounced the names of his predecessors and their sequence it would be very difficult, given the nature of the Ganda state, for anyone to propose anything different.

It is all the more striking that an alternative version does exist.[26] In December 1890 a young German, Franz Stuhlmann, arrived at the capital at the moment when a young Englishman, Frederick Lugard, was trying to get the Ganda government to accept British suzerainty. In fact the matter had been settled by European diplomacy in the previous August, but the imperial agents in the field did not immediately abandon the great game, and Stuhlmann was certainly engaged in political intrigue. He was also, however, an indefatigable collector of knowledge, and he found time to write down a list of Ganda kings, which differed markedly from all the others.[27] His informant was Stanislas Mugwanya, a Christian convert like Kaggwa and head of the Catholic party in the state, which was also at that time the anti-English party. The Catholics were eventually reconciled to British over-rule and Mugwanya went on to become, like Kaggwa, a pillar of the colonial regime. More to the point, he was a son of the priest of the god Nende and had grown up at the great shrine at Bukeerere in eastern Buganda.[28] Nende was a war-oracle, in effect the department of military intelligence for the eastern front, and also had an important role in internal security, princesses being stationed there to keep an eye on things for their brother. The alternative king-list survived as late as 1900, when it was recorded with minor variations by Sir Harry Johnston, another polymath who, however, did not claim that his list was more accurate than any other 'rendering of floating traditions'.[29]

It is thus clear that only with the publication of Kaggwa's book did the 'Muteesa' version achieve the status of undisputed truth, and that previously there had not been total agreement on the dynastic history in the inner circles of the state. The names of the kings in the 'Mugwanya' list were almost the same as in the 'Muteesa' ones, but they appeared in a significantly different order. There was no dispute about the recent past, nor about the time of the foundations, but in the long middle stretches of the story it seems that names could be assembled almost at random. Certain sequences were fixed by narrative necessity; thus Kayemba (K.17) must always follow Jjuuko, because there was a well-known fantastical story about the enmity that cost Jjuuko his life, but the surrounding names were differently ordered. According to Mugwanya, Kateregga (K.14) comes after Mawanda (K.22) – as he did in Speke's much shorter list; Kalemeera, the non-regnant prince who fathered Kimera (K.3) appears immediately before Ndawula (K.19); there are two Nakibinges, one followed as in Kaggwa by Mulondo (K.9), the other by either Mutebi (K.15) or Wampamba who, according to Kaggwa, was Nakibinge's grandfather.

Now it is of course possible that the deviant list was simply erroneous. Perhaps history was badly taught at the Bukeerere shrine, or perhaps the young Mugwanya had not been an attentive student. But the existence of such discrepancies does introduce doubt. It could be that neither version was founded on historical knowledge, that Muteesa's formulation was in part an arbitrary ordering of hitherto free-floating names and that when writing began in Buganda there was a mass of traditional data but not yet a coherent history of the kind that Kaggwa would present.

It should be mentioned that about 1896 a priest of the Catholic mission,

	'Muteesa' Group			'Mugwanya' Group
Kagwa (1901)	*Stanley* (1878)	*Wilson* (1982)	*Stuhlmann* (1894)	*Johnston* (1902)
Kintu	Kintu	Kintu or Ham	1. Kintu	
Cwa	Chwa	Chwa	Buganda	
(Kalemeera)	Kamiera	Kalemera	2. Tshua	
Kimera	Kimera	Kimela	3. Kimera	Kimera
(Lumansi)	Almass	Rumaansi	4. Tembo	Tembo
Ttembo	Tembo	Tembo	5. Kigalla	Kigala
Kiggala	Kigara	Kigala	8. Nakibingo	Nakibingo I
Kiyimba	Wanpamba	Wampamba	15. Matebi	Wampamba or Matebe
(Wampamba)	Kaeema	Kaima	12. Ssekamanya	Kamanya I
Kayima	Nakivingi	Nachibinge	11. Ssunna I	Suna I
Nakibinge	Morondo	Mrondo	10. Yemba	Zemba
Mulondo	Sekamanya	Sekamanya	13. Kimbugwe	Kimbugwe
Jjemba	Jemba	Jemba	7. Kaima	Kaima
Ssuuna I	Suna I	Suna I	8. Nakiwinge	Nakibingo II
Ssekamaanya	Kimbugwe	Chimbugwe	9. Mlondo	Mulondo
Kimbugwe	Katerega	Katarega	18. Tewandeke	Tewandike
Kateregga	Ntewi	Mtebe	16. Djuko	Juko
Mutebi	Juko	Juko	17. Kahemba	Kaemba
Jjuuko	Kyemba	Kaemba	2/3. Kalemera	Kalemera
Kayemba	Tibandeke	Tibandeka	19. Daula	Ndaula
Tebandeke	Mdowra	Ndaula	20. Kagula	Kagala
Ndawula	Kaguru	Kagura	22. Mahanda	Mawanda
Kagulu	Kikuruwe	Chikurwe	23. Mwanga	Mwanga I
Kikulwe	Ma'anda	Mawaanda	14. Katerega	Katerega
Mawanda	Msangi	Msanje	24. Mugala	Namugala
(Musanje)	Namugara	Namgaba		
Mwanga				
Namugala	(From this king onwards all lists are in agreement.)			
Kyabaggu				
Jjunju				
Ssemakookiro				
Kamaanya				
Ssuuna I				
Muteesa I				

Non-regnant princes are bracketed in the Kagwa list. For sources see text.
Numbers show position of Stuhlmann's Kings in Kagwa list.

Fig. 2   The principal king-lists

Père Auguste Achte, composed a manuscript history of Buganda in French with a genealogy which conformed, not to the Mugwanya, but to the Muteesa pattern, differing from Kaggwa's in only one small particular.[30] Each king was provided with a narrative that is again very close to Kaggwa's, though generally abbreviated. Now in 1902 Kaggwa published a collection of tales, mostly humorous or didactic fables or novellas.[31] Six of these, including the celebrated tale of Kintu which will be discussed later (below, pp. 89–92), had previously appeared as specimen texts, with interlinear French translation, in a language manual produced by the Catholic mission, the second edition of which was printed in Switzerland in 1894;[32] and the wording of Kaggwa's version, though not identical, is so close that he must be presumed to have written with this work before him. Could he also have lifted his history from Achte? Since he could not read French, this suspicion can be dismissed. It is much more likely that Achte summarised an early draft of the *The Kings of Buganda*, which is known to have been almost complete by 1897. There are, however, a fair number of differences of detail, which may mean either that Achte had other sources or that Kaggwa altered and perhaps expanded his story before publication. In the latter case the authority of the final text is diminished.

The doubts raised by source-criticism are reinforced by the application of form-criticism, the analysis of the *Sitz im Leben* of narratives, the circumstances in which they were created and the needs they served. During the thirteen years that had elapsed between Speke's and Stanley's visits the court had had much contact with Muslim merchants and through them had gained some knowledge of the outer world. It was apparently the Muslims who had taught some Ganda to identify the culture-hero Kintu with Ham, the accursed son of Noah then commonly assumed, though on somewhat slender grounds, to have been the ancestor of the African race.[33] More fundamentally, some Ganda had acquired an inkling of the Jewish (rather than Greek) concept of history that underlies Muslim as well as Christian thinking about the past.

It was such considerations that led Henige to argue that the king-lists collected by foreigners from Stanley onwards were not an innocent African tradition spontaneously vouchsafed, but were instead produced in response to leading questions, and by people who had some idea of the kind of answer required.[34] The very notion of a list, it has been argued, does not belong to a truly non-literate culture. Nor can the data be divorced from the political context of the time. Stanley and other visitors were trying to sell central Africa to European states, businessmen and churches, and so were glad to believe that here in the heart of the continent was an ancient, surprisingly well-ordered kingdom with a pedigree stretching back to the European middle ages, one that had preserved some faint memory of Near Eastern civilisation and was now ready and able to receive the wisdom of the West. And for his part Muteesa, needing as we have seen European patronage to ward off the more imminent threat from Egypt, would have been responsive to a demand for numerous and impressive ancestors.

And yet it is hard to accept that the tradition was simply custom-made for European visitors in the 1870s, designed in conformity with Muslim and Christian models. It was far too elaborate to have been an entirely new creation. In fact, there is reason to believe that it had been composed in its main outlines two generations earlier, in the reign of Kamaanya the twenty-eighth king. The clearest indication is that much higher up the list there appears the name Ssekamaanya (K.12). The additional prefix *Sse-*, literally 'father', indicates 'the late Kamaanya', the one no longer with us. So, just as an English history book that refers to 'Queen Elizabeth the First' must have been published or re-edited later than 1951, the Ganda tradition that speaks of Sse-kamaanya cannot have reached a fixed form before the accession of Kamaanya (the Second). But in addition it must have crystallised before that ruler's death, for after it both Kamaanyas would have been equally entitled to the prefix *Sse-*. It seems therefore that the early nineteenth century provides the main historical context for the formation of the tradition. This was a time of political consolidation after at least three generations of growth and turmoil. Unity and peace had become supreme objectives and factional conflict was for the time being muted and controlled. The moment was thus right for the construction of an agreed history, which would cater for the interests of all parties in the state, though there remained a degree of latitude about the sequential arrangement of their contributions. And it is more than likely that such an expedient compilation would be largely fiction.

By the end of the century the intellectual as well as the political impact of the outer world had become far more direct than in Muteesa's time. Buganda had become part of a British dependency, Christianity had become virtually the religion of the state, literacy had become widespread and the Bible had been translated into the Ganda language. The full title of Kaggwa's history, the *Book of the Kings of Buganda*, carries an obvious biblical echo, and its format, a reign-by-reign chronicle with a list of each king's ministers, closely follows that of the annals of Israel and Judah. In considering the impact of literacy it is essential to realise that, as Michael Twaddle acutely pointed out, the Ganda 'were consorting with Christian missionaries, not Ionian philosophers'.[35] The rationality that accompanied the written word was of a particular kind, which did not include a critical approach to the study of history.

One of Kaggwa's mentors, however, was something of a philosopher, and he has an important role in the story. The Rev. John Roscoe, who arrived in Buganda in 1891, was a Cambridge graduate and was in touch with those Cambridge scholars, especially J. G. Frazer, whose interest in the roots of classical paganism was drawing them into the study of 'primitive' religion. The day of the professional field anthropologist had hardly begun, and Frazer relied on people such as Roscoe, whose work took them into far corners of the earth, to provide him with the materials for his great work on ritual kingship and related matters, *The Golden Bough*. So when Roscoe, a particularly close associate, embarked on a meticulous enquiry into Ganda institutions and culture he had definite themes to explore and questions to answer.[36] For his part he relied on his friend Apolo Kaggwa to provide the elderly respondents who could give him authoritative information. But Kaggwa did not merely bring the old chiefs and princesses to the capital; he (or his secretary) took notes of their discourse, and he then sat down with his most prized possession, a typewriter, to turn them into books: first *The Kings of Buganda*, then the *Tales*, then an ethnographic study, *The Customs of the Ganda*, and finally a collection of clan traditions.

Roscoe's own version of the material was published in two preliminary articles in 1901 and 1902[37] and comprehensively in 1911 in *The Baganda, Their Customs and Beliefs*, one of the most detailed and influential of the anthropological studies of African peoples to appear in the early colonial period. It includes a historical section which is a shorter version of Kaggwa's *The Kings of Buganda* (together with a genealogical chart), but otherwise it is an ethnography, written like most such works in a timeless present but actually attempting to portray Buganda as it was in the reign of King Ssuuna II and the early years of Muteesa. It covers much the same ground as Kaggwa's *Customs of the Ganda* and in much the same way; but as was demonstrated by Kaggwa's American editor, there are enough differences between the English and the Ganda versions to show that neither author was guilty of simple plagiarism. Similarities resulted from the use of the same informants and from similar assumptions, interests and methods. Here of course the leadership belonged to Roscoe, from whom Kaggwa derived the idea of ethnography, the format of the presentation and the choice of topics. His influence and, behind that, the influence of Frazer's theories were very evident, and led to overemphasis on the ritual aspects of the Ganda monarchy at the expense of government and war. But neither Frazer nor Roscoe was greatly interested in local history, and in that domain Kaggwa had a free hand. Even in the sphere of 'customs and beliefs', moreover, his control over the informants doubtless ensured that the Englishman learnt what the Ganda authorities wanted him to learn.

Kaggwa frankly stated that his purpose was to show that the Ganda had always been good at government,[38] and therefore deserved a high degree of autonomy within the colonial state. But apart from this it is difficult to detect overt bias in his writings, at any rate when he was not discussing his own times. He was a soldier and a politician, shrewd and quick-witted but not a profound thinker nor a subtle literary artist. His brisk matter-of-fact narrative contains few judgements or opinions, and nothing remotely like the ideology that informed his only model, the Old Testament. There is no reason to doubt that he presented the tradition essentially as he received it. Insofar as it was false, it was not he who falsified it.

It may be useful at this point to compare the Ganda tradition with those of its principal Lakeland neighbours.[39] Within that ecologically varied but mostly fertile region, which lies between Lake Victoria – its Ganda name is Nalubaale – and the string of lakes, Albert, Edward, Kivu and Tanganyika, that occupy the Western Rift Valley there were in the nineteenth century some seventy autonomous polities. Four of these were much larger than the rest: Buganda in the east had probably around three-quarters of a million people, Bunyoro in the north rather fewer, Rwanda and Burundi in the south-west well over a million each. (It must be understood that these figures cannot be better than guesses.) These 'great powers' had much in common, including quite closely related languages, yet in constitutional structure, in the internal distribution of power and (so far as such things can be defined) in social and cultural values they differed from one another at least as sharply as the historical states of Europe. The region could thus have been designed as a laboratory for the political scientist – and also for the student of oral tradition, since each kingdom generated a very different kind of historical discourse.

By the end of the nineteenth century, when it came under German rule, the kingdom of Rwanda had been expanding its territory and tightening its control for the previous 150 years.[40] Starting from a relatively small area in the centre of the country, it had absorbed similar kingdoms in the east – Ndorwa, Bugesera, Gisaka – and many tiny polities of an older kind in the west and south, and it was steadily intimidating and subjugating the independent hill communities of the north – a process halted only by the Partition, which left some of them on the British side of the frontier. The secret of the kingdom's success clearly lay in its structural arrangements, in the elaborate devices which persuaded the powerful to pursue their ambitions within the framework of the state, and not to break it up or undermine the royal supremacy. The warrior cattle-owners known as Tutsi formed an aristocratic order, almost a ruling caste, regarding the king as merely the most eminent of their members. Yet aristocracy did not here mitigate autocracy but, as in Tsarist Russia, reinforced it. The state established ultimate control over cattle, the only important transferable resource and the passion of the Tutsi; and at the same time monarchical power maintained, extended and intensified the domination of the Tutsi as a class.

Crucial to the operation of this state were the people called *Ab-iru*. The word means 'servants' and in some other parts of the Lakeland it denoted the peasant masses; but here, like the European 'minister', it had the special meaning of royal servant, state executive. The *Ab-iru* formed a corporation, or network of corporations, which served as the brains of the kingdom. They are often called 'ritualists' in the ethnographic literature, and, though this term gives too narrow a view of their role, it rightly points to the manipulation of symbols, of myth and extraordinarily elaborate ritual, as the basis of their own power and that of the state they served. Their literary legacy, in particular, is very rich. It includes, in the first place, the *ubw-iru*, 'the matter of the *Abiru*', which has seen the light in two published versions.[41] It is of the essence of ritual that it should be performed correctly, but precision of detail is hard to maintain without written instructions. Here, however, the professional training of certain 'ministers' included the inerrant recitation of long programmes of ritual performance which, it is confidently claimed, were transmitted over the generations with little or no change. These are precious documents for the historian, and not only for the light they throw on the workings of the pre-colonial Rwanda kingdom. For the *Abiru* had both elaborated and conserved a structure of ritual kingship older than themselves, one found in broad outline in neighbouring kingdoms and even in certain small pre-Tutsi kingdoms that had been allowed a degree of autonomy within the Rwanda state – and one which, it will be contended, underlies the Buganda monarchy as well.

Rwanda's intelligentsia did not merely celebrate kingship as such, but also preserved knowledge of the names, relationships and deeds of individual kings, with whose memories the rights and duties of various components of the system, including their own, were inextricably linked. To this end they developed other literary genres, including genealogies, prose narratives and panegyrics which alluded to what was apparently an agreed dynastic history.[42] Scholarly Belgian priests, followed by their gifted pupil the Abbé Alexis Kagame, used these materials to construct a history of the kingdom that seemed to cover a thousand years.[43] More critical historians discarded much of this, but still accepted seventeen generations of authentic dynastic succession. Recently, however, David Newbury has re-examined the basis for this credulity and found it insecure.[44]

Most of the time the names of the kings followed in a prescribed sequence. After Yuhi came alternately Cyilima and Mutara, then Kigeri, then Mibambwe, then another Yuhi and so on. Whatever the origin of this pattern (to which we shall be returning), it obviously confers on the kingdom and its institutions a comforting rhythm of repetitive change that signifies perpetuity.

The kingdom of Burundi, next to Rwanda, was of similar nineteenth-century size; its people spoke the same language; it was structured by the same Tutsi domination. Yet its tradition was utterly different in character. The historian Jan Vansina came to Burundi after studies in Rwanda and in the Zairean Kuba kingdom, where too a long and detailed dynastic history could be recovered, and he was disconcerted by what he found, declaring the tradition to be a 'scandal'.[45] Here was a great mass of lively stories about the past but no sequential frame to set them in and so, to all intents and purposes, no history at all.

Here too the dynastic succession had a cyclical pattern, a recurrent sequence of four named kings who, as a French scholar has put it, 'were changed eternally – into themselves'.[46] There was, however, a crucial difference. The kings of Rwanda had personal as well as cyclical names, and they figure as distinct individuals in the dynastic poems and other historical sources, which show the cycle revolving four times by the end of the nineteenth century; but in Burundi there is only a repetitive blur of stories about indistinguishable bearers of the names Mwezi, Mutaaga, Mwambutsa and (most often) Ntare. Narratives that probably refer to nineteenth-century events are hard to separate from myths of the origins; and insofar as the history of Burundi has been reconstructed it is because the names of its rulers are sometimes mentioned in Rwandan sagas.

When a king of Burundi was carried to his resting-place in the northern mountains, to the necropolis which has been well described as 'a State of Dead Kings, a Kingdom of the Beyond, an Other-Burundi',[47] he entered the shrine of his namesake in the fourth generation back, who then effectively ceased to be. The royal persona counted for more than individual personality, myth for more than history and ritual for more than government. There were *Abiru* in Burundi too, but they confined themselves to ceremonial and ideology and did not develop an executive apparatus like that of Rwanda. And so, although Burundi went through a period of rapid expansion in the first part of the nineteenth century, ritual function was not permanently translated into political power. Neither the ramifying royal clan, the Ganwa, nor the Tutsi as a whole were effectively subordinated to the monarchy. Rival princes held sway in some of the provinces and in others the people were at the mercy of the local Tutsi, who were behaving like robber barons. The difference between the two kingdoms, both of which were conserved by the colonial power (Germany until 1915, then Belgium) was tragically illustrated at the beginning of the independence era. In both countries the precipitate withdrawal of Belgian control was accompanied by republican revolutions. In Rwanda the end of the monarchy meant also the downfall of the Tutsi and the death of many of them. But in Burundi aristocratic power was less dependent on the kingship and survived its fall. Attempts by the Hutu majority to assert democratic rights were answered with genocidal brutality, and the Tutsi remained in control of the state.

In Burundi, history was submerged by fictions illustrating the timeless role of kings. There were similar tales in Rwanda too, but there they were subordinate to a narrative sequence which for some three centuries had been growing with events. In Bunyoro, by contrast, the tradition that found its way into print at the beginning of the twentieth century was a work of art, in which both myth and history were woven into a formal design of great imaginative power. The circumstances of its recording were rather unusual. At the end of 1894 a combined British–Ganda force invaded Bunyoro and quickly overran it, though guerrilla warfare continued until the capture of King Kabarega in 1899. Half the country was then annexed to Buganda and the rump was partly administered by Ganda chiefs. The mood of Nyoro intellectuals at the turn of the century was thus understandably elegiac.

In the wake of the conquerors came the Rev. A. B. Fisher and his wife Ruth, both servants of the Anglican Church Missionary Society, which was by then well established in Buganda. Ruth was moved to carry out research into Bunyoro's culture, and to this end she got the newly literate kings of Bunyoro and Toro (the latter a recent breakaway with a common past) to write its traditional history. These young colonial protégés knew little of such matters themselves, and wrote to the dictation of the 'witch-doctors', 'withered skin-clad ancients' who had been assembled for the purpose. She then collated the two royal accounts, edited and translated them and presented the result as the core of a book published in 1912.[48] In the surrounding chapters, part personal memoir and part ethnography, she displayed the prejudices of her time and kind; clearly she had no great opinion of the Nyoro people or their pagan culture. Yet, almost despite herself, she treated the tradition with evident respect, using a heightened English such as would have been thought suitable for Greek or Norse mythology. And it was indeed a remarkable work, which set out the whole story from the Creation to the British conquest, much as the Jewish history traced a thread from Adam to the fall of Jerusalem. It must be assumed that among the 'witch-doctors' was a man, probably a court priest, who had pondered deeply on the fate of his country and of mankind.

There have been, he said, three ages of the world, each ending in a cataclysm. Twice there has been a new beginning that has not quite restored the splendour of the past. First there was the world that was made by Ruhanga, the 'Great Artificer', at the request of his brother Nkya ('Dawn') and for the benefit of Nkya's children, who are mankind. Nkya's son Kantu, 'Human being', is the archetype of our fallen nature, the origin of death and evil, and his insolence caused the Creator to withdraw into the sky. From his brother Kakama ('King' – also called Itware, 'Government') there descended the First Dynasty. Sometimes called the Batembuzi, 'Pioneers', these 'kings' consist of names and attributes of God, and the first age was aptly described by Fisher as the reign of the gods. The last of this line, Isaza, made the mistake of quarrelling with the King of the Land of Shadows and was lured into the darkness from which he was unable to return. That was the first great disaster.

Since it is said that his deputy Kwezi, 'Moon', rose into the upper world, it is obvious that Isaza is the sun. But the story is not of course simply a nature-myth (as I may have implied when I first discussed it long ago);[49] the sunset is a metaphor of mortality. In fact we hear no more of Kwezi, and the throne of the world was occupied by Bukuku, formerly the keeper of the gate. The usurper, whose name is 'Meanness', had an only child, a daughter called Nyinamwiru, and, being fearful of a grandson who would supplant him, he cut off one of her breasts (and by some accounts one of everything else) so that no man would desire her, and to make doubly sure kept her in a doorless hut. But a bold hunter called Isimbwa made his way in through the roof, stayed there five months and then, irresponsible male that he was, went on his way, leaving her carrying the child who would be Ndahura, first ruler of the second dynasty.

There is no doubt that this was once an independent myth of genesis, describing the first encounter of man and woman, the meeting of Siegfried and Brunnhilde, the beginning of human life. (Do not ask how Bukuku came to have a daughter – myth does not abide such questions.) But our priestly author has skilfully placed it in his grand design, identifying the feckless hunter with the son born to Isaza and the daughter of the King of the Shades. The device established continuity in spite of catastrophic change. Bukuku was an illegitimate ruler, and his reign was a liminal interlude, separating but also linking the age of God and the second age, which belongs to the descendants of Isimbwa.

The beginning of that age is described in the classic terms of hero-myth. Having failed to prevent the birth of the dreaded grandson, Bukuku tried to cut his existence short. And so, like countless other heroes, the infant Ndahura was cast into the water, to be providentially rescued, in this case by a potter who found the basket snagged on the bank where he had gone to dig his clay. Fostered in secret, he was soon tending cows like other boys, and one day he got into a quarrel with the king's herdsmen at the watering-place, and when Bukuku himself intervened the precocious boy slew him and sat upon his throne. He thus restored the world that had ended with the passing of Isaza, but the renewal was only partial; the primal glory was forever lost.

Nevertheless Ndahura and his kinsmen and comrades, collectively called the Ba-Cwezi, lived for a time in great felicity on the rich lands between the lakes and did marvellous things. They are the 'Demi-gods' (as Mrs Fisher called them), the powers that ruled the lives of the Nyoro-speaking peoples under the general authority of the high god.[50] Nowadays they inhabit the spirit world and are known to human beings only through the mediums, the men and women they have chosen as conduits for their healing and oracular energies. In the second age they still lived in middle-earth, but their stay was not to last. Like Isaza, Ndahura was captured by the King of Eternal Darkness. He returned on the third day but did not resume the kingship, leaving it to his son Wamara. In his time omens and misfortunes multiplied, and the Ba-Cwezi suffered the worst of all fates for rulers: they lost authority, and in the end even their women mocked them. That was not to be borne, so Wamara led them into the waters of a lake and thence into the world of spirit. Wamara is the ruler of the dead, and his passing from middle-earth was the beginning of mortality. In this existential sense the stories of the doom of the Ba-Cwezi were told all over the central part of the Lakeland, but the conception of them as a dynasty of kings of long ago seems to have been an innovation of our Nyoro priest, who gave the theme a structural significance. For him it was the second great disaster.

Again, however, not everything was lost. Away to the east of the Nile there were twin boys, who had been fathered by one of the Cwezi on a barbarian woman, and the elder, variously called Isingoma, Mpuga and Rukidi, was now summoned to take over the vacant kingship. And so the third age began, the age of human kings, the Ba-Bito, putative descendants of Rukidi, whose line would continue until 1967. The accounts of his reign and those of his immediate successors are still full of symbol and fantasy, but the story of the kingdom's vicissitudes becomes steadily more realistic as it approaches the era of secondary and then primary reminiscence. It culminates in the British-led invasion and the capture of King Kabarega, which was the third great disaster and for the author the end of the Nyoro story. The fourth age would belong to the British.

This is philosophical history, the past conceived according to a tragic design. Its dialectic follows a downward spiral; for each age is less glorious than the one before and space contracts with time. The first dynasty were lords of the cosmos; the Cwezi held sway over the civilised world; the mortal Bito kings ruled the historical kingdom of Bunyoro; and now there is only a truncated remnant, in which a puppet king and demoralised chiefs must defer to British and even to Ganda overlords. The purpose is clearly therapeutic, giving meaning to defeat by placing it in an artistic sequence and dignity to political ruin by relating it to the larger tragedy of mankind. Its story somewhat recalls the Jewish history, which in its present form was put together after the kingdoms of Israel and Judah had been destroyed. Both were the work of priests whose political order had collapsed, leaving them in sole control of the tradition, which therefore took on a strongly theological cast. For the Nyoro, however, the divine kingdom lay not in the future, which was both gloomy and opaque, but in the distant past.

Even before its downfall Bunyoro had been a rather loosely joined state.

Power was diffused among the members of the ramifying royal clan and the centre held on to the provinces with difficulty at best.[51] No doubt for that reason there was little agreement about the names and sequence of the Bito kings. It seems to have been more important to assert the divine antecedents of the Bito as a group than to remember individual rulers or their deeds.[52]

Bunyoro and Buganda were closely related in culture and their histories were undoubtedly interwoven, yet the presentation of the tradition in the two countries could hardly have been more different. Whereas Bunyoro's past was artistic in form but uncertain in detail, the Ganda story contained masses of apparently agreed data but no visible form at all. Very occasionally the names of kings were repeated, but not in any set pattern. The Ganda worshipped deities, the *ba-lubaale*, some of whom were also Cwezi, but they were not the ancestors of the kings and the stories about them were only feeble anecdotes purporting to explain their names or characters. Kintu, the reputed ancestor of the kings, was certainly an imaginary being but not in the ordinary sense a god. The tales of him are plainly myths; but the deeds of his successors, though mildly bizarre, do not actually compel disbelief.

It is this very disorderliness of the Ganda tradition that has made most students accept it as a genuine history, which does not always tell the whole truth but is nevertheless a record of real events, of invasion and resistance, intrigue and fratricide, conquest and conflict and consolidation. Such themes are indeed present, but I shall try to show that the appearance of realism is in part illusory, that the Ganda tradition is no less a construction than that of Bunyoro or of any other Lakeland kingdom. But whereas Rwanda's history was created by a kind of corporate intelligentsia, Burundi's by independent story-tellers and Bunyoro's by an individual poet-priest, the history of Buganda was the work of a committee. It was a compromise between the claims of the several contending groups that came together in the course of the seventeenth and eighteenth centuries to make the Ganda state. It was vital to each section that its heroes and ancestors should find a place within the 'national' history; but until Europeans started asking for lists the precise sequence of names and stories was not important, and different arrangements of the material were possible. The consolidated tradition thus contained material from a variety of sources. Some of it was saga, referring to real events; some of it was authentic genealogy; but internal and comparative study shows that much of it was myth. It is not merely that the stories of the early kings contained imaginative matter: originally they had not been talking about politics at all. And until they have been fully examined in their own mythical right we cannot begin to ask what they may be able to tell us about the real past.

So there are some preliminary tasks to be undertaken. It is necessary to consider the meaning of myth and its relationship with history; to become better acquainted with the end product of the history, the mid-nineteenth-century kingdom, on which there is abundant information; and to locate it as best we can in its prehistoric setting, using the evidence of archaeology and language about the past that lies beyond the furthest reach of tradition.

3   Introduction to myth

The relationship between history and myth has been a sensitive one for Westerners, since a fusion, or confusion, of these two categories lies at the root of our culture, the classically mythical themes of the Incarnation and the Resurrection having been attached to the memory of a man who undoubtedly said and did some of the things that are reported of him and very probably was indeed crucified under Pontius Pilate. In itself, such an attachment was not uncommon; but Christians assert that *their* myths are true, that the whole story must be taken as historical reality. That position was not reached easily, and the effort underlies the great doctrinal controversies of the early Christian centuries. But gradually the divergent heresies of the Arians, for whom Christ was wholly human (that is, historical), and of the Monophysites, for whom he was wholly mythical (that is, divine), were repressed or marginalised and the Catholic synthesis prevailed. The balance was, however, disturbed by the Reformation. For although the Protestants did not challenge trinitarian orthodoxy they sought with varying degrees of urgency to divest Christianity of its more obviously mythical accretions (as they saw them), such as Christmas and the doctrine of transsubstantiation, in order to stress the redemptive history.

By the end of the nineteenth century the old heresies had reappeared on the frontier between radical Protestantism and unbelief. Rationalists now questioned whether Jesus had been anything other than a man, while the 'Christ-myth' advocates doubted whether he had ever been a man at all. (Similar ideas gave rise to fierce disputes over Greek mythology, some scholars holding that most or all of the heroes had been living men while others declared them to be faded gods.) In the inter-war years biblical studies were dominated by the so-called form-critical school, which set out to complete the Protestant mission of 'demythologising' the scriptures and at the same time went far towards emptying them of history as well. These critics sought to show that each episode of the biblical story reflected its 'situation in life', the circumstances in which it had been produced in writing. The gospels were documents of the Christian communities in the late first century; and when, for example, they show Jesus tangling with the Pharisees we are not to infer that he had really been at odds with that sect but that the church was. Almost nothing, in fact, could be said about the actual life of Christ. This historical scepticism by no means excluded faith in the Christian message, the *kerygma*. The leading form-critics were German Evangelicals, who said more or less openly that the point about the biblical documents was not whether they were factually true but whether they 'worked' for the preacher.[1]

This approach had something in common with the functionalist school of social anthropology, which dominated African studies in the years before the Second World War and for some time afterwards.[2] In its perspective, traditional narratives were 'mythical charters', which served not to preserve the real past but to validate present-day social relations, by asserting that they had existed from the beginning of things and were thus part of the natural order. As the links between anthropologists and colonial governments grew closer the accent was placed more and more on the political aspect of social systems: for stories that buttressed the authority of African chiefs were also functional for their colonial overlords.[3] Anthropologists of this era, with few exceptions, were little interested in the existential aspect of myth; and their attitude to history was not so much sceptical as indifferent. As one of the most distinguished later remarked, it had hardly occurred to them to 'try to relate tribal traditions to a possible actual sequence of historical events';[4] the point was the part that the reports played in the maintenance of society and, for the scholar, the light they threw on the way the society worked.

In the 1950s the influence of this kind of thinking waned, both in theology and in African studies. Functionalist exercises that showed how myth was manipulated for political ends began to seem tediously repetitive and scholars began to ask just why the public relations officers of dynasties should think that their masters' interests would be served by often bizarre and unbelievable stories about the remote past. Some came to see that stories have a life of their own and a meaning not wholly determined by ephemeral political calculations. So one reaction was a revival of historical interest and self-confidence. It became legitimate once more to write the life of Jesus and to correlate the stories of the Patriarchs with the archaeology of the Middle Bronze Age. Even within the functionalist paradigm, 'mythical charters' tended to be replaced by 'historical charters', with the implication that traditions might be not only useful but true, as nationalists and their neo-colonial patrons were very anxious to believe.

The study of traditions as history was taken up with somewhat uncritical enthusiasm in the very active school of history that flourished in and around Makerere University in Uganda in the late 1960s,[5] when every name of divinity, even that of God himself, was taken to be a datable royal ancestor.[6] As Steven Feierman has commented, attempts to translate oral narratives directly into academic discourse resulted in 'a creolisation of history rather than a bilingual account'.[7] During the 1970s he and other American scholars developed much more sophisticated approaches to African traditions. Even so, Joseph C. Miller still maintained that 'traditions relating to remote phases of . . . political history have nearly attained the form and status of a creation myth'.[8] It seems more natural to assume that stories that look like creation myths *are* creation myths and do not refer to political history in any direct way.

While one result of the decline of functionalism was a new credulity about traditional history, another development pointed in a completely different direction. The rise of structuralist studies did not take long to make its influence felt in both the biblical and the African scholarly fields. Anthropologists of that school can be even more radically anti-historical than their predecessors; for they assume that, in principle at any rate, an entire cultural tradition such as the Hebrew scriptures, or even the whole Christian Bible, can be treated as a seamless synchronic sphere, such that the interpreter can disregard the chronology of composition and work in any direction he chooses. Lévi-Strauss himself declined to apply his method to the Bible, but others have been less cautious, most notably the late Sir Edmund Leach, in his essays on Genesis and on the story of Solomon's succession in II Samuel and I Kings.[9] In the latter he used structuralist techniques (or tricks, as some would say) to support a quite old-fashioned functionalist analysis, trying to show that the historical books of the Old Testament reflected, in general and in detail, the interests and policies of the Jewish theocracy of the fourth century BC, when the canonical writings, which included documents of widely different age and purpose, were collated and edited. His later work, however, was quite mystical in its determination to transcend time and weld Old and New Testament into a single semantic whole.[10] In both works he insisted that histories, being products of the human mind, are structured in the same way as myths, from which they cannot meaningfully be distinguished. Though he did not write from a Christian position he was in practice reaffirming the traditional doctrine.

I happen to believe, on the contrary, that the future of religion depends on the dismantling of the Christian synthesis, so that history and myth can each be granted its proper rights. But it is not necessary to press that larger programme here. Christians insist that *only* their myths are true; so it is possible to set that unique convergence on one side and assert that elsewhere myth and history inhabit separate domains. This does not mean that each section of a traditional narrative must carry one label or the other. There is always a large territory in which myth and history interpenetrate; but it is easier to identify their respective contributions when they are recognised as being conceptually distinct.

Perhaps the most crucial difference is that myth deals with regularities, patterns, constants, whereas history belongs to the domain of the particular and the contingent. Leach was not wrong: histories are indeed products of the human mind, which does ceaselessly strive to impose order on the flux of experience. But their special characteristic is that they submit their structuring activity to the discipline of what Lévi-Strauss has called 'the powerful inanity of events'.[11] Historians may indeed be said to have invented chaos theory long before physicists began to recognise it; and the more orderly their product appears the further it has departed from the laws of its own being. They can never tell the whole truth even about single small series of events, and they are capable of selections and suppressions that amount to falsehood. But they are committed in principle to telling things as they actually were, and their narratives are based on evidence – unreliable perhaps, incomplete, one-sided, but nevertheless evidence. Myths by contrast are speculations, which set out, as Lévi-Strauss puts it, to 'explain why, though different at the beginning, things have become what they are, and why they cannot be otherwise'.[12] They describe, in other words, not what did happen, but what 'must have' happened.

By the same token, though both kinds of discourse are concerned with the past, they do not use the same kind of time. History is a constant flow, but the time of myth is discontinuous. An African theologian has used Swahili words to draw a distinction between Sasa, 'Now', the time of the living and the living-dead, those still personally remembered by name, and Zamani, the undifferentiated Past.[13] In Sasa, which is roughly our period of primary and secondary reminiscence, the world is that of everyday experience. But Zamani is the time of myth, the time of the foundations, when the familiar world took shape, having been altogether other. Some Africans identify the Past as the time before the white man, whose coming, however, is not much more than a metaphor for a more fundamental discontinuity. For the procedure of myth is to postulate a world in which things were not as they are now and then to recount the happening that turned it into the world we know. Adam accepted the apple – and so we cannot live at ease in the garden of eternal youth. There is a sense in which all myths are myths of genesis, of the fatal beginnings. To call them timeless would be incorrect, for in a timeless world there would be no happenings, and so no stories. Rather, myths stand at the intersection of timelessness and time, like the Big Bang of modern cosmology.

Myths, then, are imaginative stories, as the common use of the term implies; but of course not all fictions are myths. The novel is in many ways a polar opposite, resembling history in that it deals with particulars rather than with universals. It is a reproach to a novelist to say that his characters are (merely) types, but the characters of myth are types by definition: *the* Hero, the King, the Old Woman, the Serpent. Yet there are intermediate forms, such as the early 'novels' of William Golding, and medieval romances and modern thrillers, which draw heavily on the themes and patterns of myth. More traditional kinds of fiction – folk-tales, fables, fairy-tales – have a great deal in common with myths, but there are some important differences. Whereas myths belong to the Past, folk-tales and the like are set in a kind of indefinite present. We have to suspend disbelief in order to enter their world, but it is not the opposite of our own. Also, they tend to be socially didactic in a rather simple way, while the messages of myth are both more oblique and more serious. However, as Lévi-Strauss points out (and most of the Amerindian 'myths' he uses would be classed by others as folk-tales or fables) there is no hard-and-fast distinction. For example, Aesop's famous story about the Hare and the Tortoise appears merely to convey elementary lessons to children – 'concentrate on the job in hand', and 'never give up' – while also no doubt offering encouragement to the ungifted. But in a very similar modern African story, with Frog and Chameleon as the ill-matched racers, the outcome was nothing less than the doom of men. For Frog had said, 'Let Man die and come to life again', but Chameleon wanted him to die for ever, and they had agreed to settle the matter by a race. Frog should have won easily, of course, but he turned aside three times to eat termites, and it was when Chameleon swayed past the winning post that our fate was sealed. There are countless African variations on this theme,[14] conveying the strangely comforting message that the imperfections of the world are the result of some accident or minor malfeasance at the beginning of time. They are more than fables, but still not quite myths; for they amount to saying: 'If you ask a silly question – such as "Why do we have to die?" – you will get a silly answer.' True myths treat such questions with more respect.

It seems clear in fact that folk-tales and fables are edited myths, designed to be told to children or to general audiences that may include children as well as women. Myths themselves, on the other hand, were directed at adolescents, their original setting having been the initiation camp, where boys at the age of puberty were instructed in the facts of life, in the broadest sense of that term, partly by cruel ritual and partly in symbolic expositions. The stories associated with that intense experience, whereby the whole business of growing up was compressed into a few extremely demanding months, naturally carried a very powerful charge, which enabled them to escape long ago from their primary context. (If they had not done so we would not know them, since the camp instruction was secret.) A great many societies, of course, including Buganda, do not practise puberty initiation and have not done so within our knowledge. But the rites are so widely distributed around the world that they must be assumed to belong to the most ancient era of human society. It is thus likely that the myths that went with them began to be told quite soon after there were words to tell them with. That is to say, while the memory of events is short in the absence of writing, stories are very long-lived, and those relating to basic human concerns are practically immortal.

The most important of the facts of life is of course death, which is the essential subject of myth, as Lévi-Strauss finally made clear. Through almost the whole of his great work, the *Mythologiques*, he had denied any ultimate meaning to myths, maintaining that their significance lay only in the logical relationships that could be found within and between them. But on the penultimate page of the fourth and last volume he dropped this mystification and revealed, in a peroration of great eloquence, that in the last resort all myths are about mortality.[15] All the other oppositions he had so ingeniously laid bare – between raw and cooked, high and low, wet and dry, discrete and continuous – are metaphors or disguises of the great contradiction, which is between being and not being – or more accurately between being and no-longer-being.

If that were all, historians could be forgiven for concluding that myth was no professional concern of theirs. They would be wrong, for there is no more significant feature of any culture than the ways it has found of expressing itself about death. But of course it is not all. The universal preoccupation serves as a kind of carrier wave for messages that may be related to many other human concerns, to anything in fact that causes perplexity or stress, whether it be natural or social, moral or political, universal or local. Myths can thus be classified in an ascending order of particularity. In the first category are those that deal with the basic dilemmas of human existence, with the origins of love and death, together with themes of almost equal universality such as the incest taboos, the subordination of women or the necessity of work. Attempts to resolve or evade these dilemmas, as Lévi-Strauss has brilliantly shown, are regularly linked to questions about culture, to explanations of the origin of fire, hunting, farming. Second, there are essays on the origin of a particular society and of its basic institutions, its internal structure and its relations with other societies. Finally, there are stories that account for the pre-eminence of a specific lineage, for the privileges of lesser office-holders and priests and for arcane customs, ceremonies and even place-names.

The two latter classes can well be lumped together as 'charter' myths in opposition to the 'genesis' myths of the first category; and this distinction is crucial. The one attempt to apply the structuralist method to the Ganda tradition, by Ronald Atkinson, unfortunately derived more from Leach than from Lévi-Strauss and, unlike Leach, failed to distinguish between 'Solomon' myths, which deal with politics, and 'Genesis' myths, which are concerned with death and sex.[16] Jürgen Jensen, who has written very interestingly about the traditions of people on the fringe of Buganda, does recognise the distinction and prefers to reserve the term 'myth' for stories of the genesis type, describing stories with a clear political reference as 'historical legends'.[17] For him, the word 'historical' does not imply much confidence in their veracity. But often they have been taken as schematised and romanticised records of a real past. After all, it is argued, myths may be imaginative stories, but imagination has to have something to work on and, when the subject matter is political and social relations, what could that be but actual historical experience? Vested interests can hardly get away with pure invention.

These points are indisputable, yet caution is still needed, because the distinctions drawn above, though valid in principle, are rarely clear in practice. Many myths (and legends) belong to more than one category, referring simultaneously to the fundamentals of existence and also to questions of power and status in a particular society. In the book of Genesis itself, for example, commentators usually draw a line at chapter 11 verse 10 or 27, to separate genesis myths proper from the stories of the Patriarchs, which are classed as charter myths or historical legends. Yet Genesis 4, the story of Cain and Abel, is both a myth about the origin of human violence and a quite particularist reference to the itinerant metal-workers of early Palestine, the Cain-ites or Kenites, justifying their miserable condition, as it appeared to the settled population, and showing why people who were both vulnerable and indispensable had to be placed under special divine protection. Conversely, we shall see (pp. 72, 126–8) that some of the patriarchal stories were really genesis myths of the purest kind.

Mythical traditions are thus rather like textbooks (of law or medicine rather than history) which are being constantly re-edited to reflect new knowledge and interests yet keep the basic shape given them by their original authors. Or, perhaps better, they are palimpsests, in which successive texts are partly but not totally obscured by more recent over-writing. The task of the analyst is thus exceedingly complicated, for he has to distinguish, not just between original composition and present text, but between many layers of text, each expressing the needs of its own time within a frame laid down by its predecessors. But the difficulty is also an opportunity. In principle, it may be possible to identify the contribution made by each succeeding age and so to arrive at a cultural history more interesting and more authentic than the political narrative given by a simple presentation of the tradition as it now stands.

The beginning of the tradition may be distant indeed. Lévi-Strauss has pointed to apparent connections between his American materials and Japanese, and even Greek, mythology; and if, as seems likely, they are the result neither of chance nor of recent diffusion the common prototype must have emerged very early in the global dispersal of Speaking Man or, as he is more usually labelled, *Homo sapiens*, who on present evidence seems to have evolved in Africa between one and four hundred thousand years ago. As noted earlier, however, I venture to discern a clearer line of descent from a great complex of myth and ritual that developed in the Middle East in the neolithic period and lies at the base of both 'Western' and African culture. My reasons, it must be admitted, are partly subjective. From my first acquaintance with East African traditions I had a curious sense of familiarity, such as I do not experience when I read about Amerindian or Melanesian or even Indian mythology. Surely I had met these gods and heroes before? Over time this vague recognition has hardened into the conviction that many of the stories told at various places in the western half of the Old World do have a common pattern that is not due to chance or to universal propensities of the human mind but to a shared historical origin, at a time level that is remote, certainly, but still a long way above the beginnings of language.

Those who postulate such links have of course to show, at the least, that the necessary movement of people or ideas or both could have taken place. And here again recent intellectual discourse has been mostly unfavourable. The most plausible context would be the diffusion of food-producing and associated technologies from an original centre in the Middle East to Europe, on the one hand, and tropical Africa, on the other. But for some time now prehistorians have been sedulously deconstructing 'neolithic culture' and trying to show that food production developed independently in many different parts of the world. Yet in relation to Africa completely autonomous invention is not a reasonable thesis. Tropical Africans share with West Asians, North Africans and Europeans the peculiar practice of symbiosis with animals belonging to the same three genera: cattle, sheep and goats. And they could not have arrived at the idea by themselves, because wild ancestors of those animals did not live in tropical Africa. (Cattle could have been domesticated in Mediterranean Africa but sheep and goats were at home only in Asia.) With agriculture the case is not quite so clear. Wheat and barley, the basic crop plants of western Asia, Europe and North Africa, cannot easily be grown in the tropics, where local grasses had to be substituted. But it is still almost certain that the idea of re-sowing the seeds of certain cereals was not indigenous. For when cultivation did begin in sub-Saharan Africa it was on the northern fringe of the region, near Khartoum, and not on the ecologically similar savannas of the south;

the date was around 4500 BC, considerably later than in western Asia; and the crop plants were accompanied from the start by livestock of northern origin. So it is fairly clear that the main elements of the revolutionary food-producing or 'neolithic' economy arrived in Black Africa as an already assembled package.[18] And it is not credible that the package should have included economic innovations only, without associated institutions and beliefs. Not long ago Igor Kopytoff revived the idea of 'ancestral pan-African culture patterns' which, he proposed, took shape in what is now the Saharan–Sahelian region during the neolithic, 'often under frontier conditions and in contact with the kindred patterns of the pre-Islamic Near East'.[19]

It is one thing to show that traditions found in central Africa could be historically related to those of the ancient Mediterranean world, but quite another to prove that they actually are. Similarities of course are not enough, for they could be explained in different ways. The simplest explanation is convergence or coincidence, the operation of the laws of chance on the limited resources of the human imagination. Another possibility is diffusion, in the sense of the relatively recent spread of tales and bits of tales by itinerant story-tellers or along chains of cultural intercourse, especially perhaps through fairs and markets, where people from different societies have convivial meetings. It is unquestionable that stories have travelled long distances in this manner; and in particular David Henige has shown that the influence of the Bible has been felt in every corner of the world,[20] not only through missionary teaching in recent times but also indirectly by way of Islam and perhaps through Ethiopia and the medieval Christian kingdoms of Nubia. But not all resemblances can be thus dismissed. It is here that the structural method of analysis can sometimes be decisive, eliminating hypotheses of chance and recent diffusion and leaving remote common origin as the only reasonable explanation. For whereas individual motifs, themes and even whole stories may well be supposed to have been created independently in different lands, or to have wandered from one land to another, neither of these things can be plausibly predicated of whole sets of intricately related myths. Indeed, at the beginning of the *Mythologiques* Lévi-Strauss declared roundly that when he had demonstrated the presence of such a set in different regions a historical link between the peoples concerned was proven, and it was up to historians and ethnologists to work out the when and how of the connection.[21] Later he retreated somewhat from that position, making a distinction between historically related and logically related sets and admitting more scope for recent diffusions;[22] yet he clearly continued to believe that much of Amerindian mythology goes back to the original peopling of the New World.

But what is a set and how can it be recognised? The proofs offered by Lévi-Strauss are often exceedingly complicated, but for most purposes a simple test suffices. Owing to lapse of time, movement of people and adjustment to changing social needs, a myth is likely to lose some of its components and so become less intelligible; but the missing parts can often be replaced from elsewhere. So when two or more stories that have been reported from different times and places illumine one another, when they make better sense together than apart, they must be deemed to have a common source, which had fuller significance than any version now extant. Elsewhere I have exploited the structuralist analysis of certain Zairean stories by Luc de Heusch in order to point out that they throw new light on the story of Noah: two episodes, the Flood and the Curse of Ham, which in the biblical text appear to be arbitrarily juxtaposed, actually belong together.[23] Deeper meaning is also added to the conclusion of the Flood story, when the rainbow is set in the sky as token of alternance; the seasons would henceforth follow in due measure and mankind would not be destroyed by either flood or drought. But there is a price to pay. Periodicity means time, and time means death. As was plainly stated in the prologue (Genesis 6:1–4), mankind would continue but individual men must have a finite life.

A simpler example (by way of preparation for the stories discussed in the body of the book) is provided by the Nilotic-speaking Alur people of north-west Uganda, who tell how Man (Acunga, 'the Erect') won dominion over the animals.[24] When the (unnamed) old chief lay dying he wanted to make Lion his successor, but Dog went to Acunga and persuaded him to secure the nomination for himself. This he did by the simple expedient of roaring outside the chief's hut, so that the words of installation were pronounced in his favour. This is not much of a story in itself, but commentators have been reminded of the biblical tale (Genesis 27) in which Jacob tricked Isaac into making him his heir in place of his brother Esau. It will be recalled that Esau – a hunter, whereas Jacob was a stay-at-home – was an unusually hairy man. So Jacob prepared a goat stew for his father, as a substitute for the venison that Esau had promised him, and before serving it he put the goat's skin over his hands. Isaac, who had gone blind, felt the hair, accepted that the server was Esau and spoke the irrevocable blessing.

Now in theory it is possible that the Hebrew story has actually reached the Alur in very recent or less recent times; unmistakable versions of it, complete with the name of Isaac, do indeed occur in East Africa. It is also conceivable that the Israelites and the Alur devised similar tales of deception in complete independence. But what puts both these explanations out of court is that the Alur story gives meaning to what, if it were not holy writ, would be admitted to be a rather silly anecdote; however hirsute a man's hand might be, it could hardly be confused with a beast's paw. But now at last we can see the point. Esau was not really a human hunter. He was Lion, the natural ruler of the animal kingdom. The biblical text comes close to admitting this, telling us that when he came out of the womb he was red, and hairy all over – in other words, a lion cub. And later on, when Jacob had become rich in flocks and children, he met Esau again in the wild, spoke humbly to him and made him a present of part of his wealth. He promised to follow on with the rest of his flocks, but then turned back to Succoth ('the Camp') (Genesis 33). When Man encounters Lion, if he has any sense, he lets him have a goat or two and makes off back to base as fast as he can go! The story is thus revealed as a myth of the primal age, a common variant on the theme of the Fall, the loss of innocence. Once upon a time man was an animal among others, but somehow – the circumstances are not important, nor does it matter whether his enterprise was wise or foolish, admirable or wicked – he acquired the special privileges and burdens of his humanity.

In both its provinces the story of Lion's ousting has been given a functional gloss, used for local political purposes. Acunga stands at the head of some Alur chiefly pedigrees, while the Hebrew version accounts for Israel's ascendancy over the Edomites, children of Esau, who had to live in the dry south and be slaughtered by David's troops. But as a charter myth it is singularly inept, since Israel's rights are made to derive from a piece of chicanery practised on a blind and dying father. Moreover, while the culture-hero Jacob was identified with 'Israel' at an early stage, the association of Esau with the Edomites was an innovation: 'Esau, who is Edom', explains the editor (Genesis 36:1), making an equation that was evidently new to his readers. The political message has been tacked onto an ontological myth, and that myth must have been the common ancestor of the extant Hebrew and African texts. The only way to avoid that conclusion would be to postulate a modern Alur genius who could extract from the Bible the original meaning that has eluded countless learned Jewish and Christian commentators.

That (as Lévi-Strauss is fond of saying) is not all. The Alur tale, like many African myths, features Dog in the mediating role proper to the anomalous creature who is both a dumb beast and a marginal member of human society. In Genesis 27, where it is Jacob's mother who puts him up to the trick, Dog is absent. (Rebekah is Gazelle, who was no doubt under the illusion that Man would be less of a danger to her than Lion.) Consider, however, the story in Genesis 25:27–34, in which Esau sells his birthright for some lentil soup. In its context the anecdote is redundant, for if Jacob had already bought the inheritance he had no need to resort to fraud. In origin it must have been a different story, and 'Esau' is here the mask for a different animal, the hungry hunter who came in from the wild and gave up his birthright of freedom for a securer food supply. Thus the entire cast of the Alur myth reappears in the stories of Jacob and Esau, though the roles have been partly rearranged.

So these African and Hebrew stories did belong to the same set, which must have been constructed before the early first millennium BC, when the primary documents of the Pentateuch were compiled. Its origin, however, does not lie in remotest prehistory, since it must be later than the emergence of heritable authority and the domestication of the dog.

Africans did not, of course, merely reiterate ancient myths, nor were they solely concerned to illustrate existential truths. They adapted and readapted the stories under the combined influence of historical circumstance and creative imagination. But to look only at the political dimensions of their traditions is to undervalue them. In their eagerness to equip Africa with a history, scholars have taken the risk, not only of getting the history wrong, but also of denying it a religion and a literature. For it is within the frame of a historical tradition that Africans have deposited the most valuable parts of their religious speculation and of their imaginative fiction.

This is not, to repeat, to deny tradition all historical content. Not only do its later layers obliquely reflect social, political and cultural change, but the presence of mythical themes does not automatically exclude a narrative from history. It has often been pointed out that, if there were not contemporary proof of their reality, the popular traditions of Alexander, Attila and Richard Coeur de Lion, among others, would have caused most scholars to dismiss them as purely imaginary figures.[25] From West Africa the story of Anyo Asema is a salutary corrective to over-scepticism. Nearly everything now reported of this character seems to make him a typical hero of genesis myth; yet there is the testimony of seventeenth-century European merchants to confirm that he really lived.[26] Nevertheless, it must not be inferred that there is always historical wheat within the mythical chaff; and above all, the alleged historical residue must not be offered to the public without any indication of the way it has been sifted.

For example, there is a Ganda tradition, to be discussed in more detail later, which tells us that once upon a time the land was ruled by Bemba Omusota, that is, Scaly the Serpent.[27] He was an oppressive ruler, who got his comeuppance through the cunning of Wanfudu, 'Tortoise'; and the way was thus made clear for the culture-hero Kintu to found a human kingdom. Obviously this is a myth or fable, yet scholars have been loath to deny it a place in past reality. Thus Sir John Gray referred to Bemba as 'a petty king . . . whom legend has converted into a snake',[28] without explaining why legend should have behaved in such a peculiar way. But in the authoritative

UNESCO *General History of Africa* Bemba's reptilian character disappears altogether, as does Tortoise, and we are told that Kintu encountered various difficulties in setting up the Buganda kingdom, in particular that 'a more serious threat was posed by King Bemba of Buddu'.[29] The story is thus transferred from Buddo, the hill in central Buganda where the texts locate it, to the south-western province of Buddu which has nothing to do with it. But a much more important objection is that readers are given no idea of what the tradition actually said.

It must be admitted that in Buganda the rationalisation of mythical traditions began early, with the work of what may be called pre-academic historians. The Christian converts and their successors who compiled and commented on the traditions had considerable knowledge of the Bible and, largely through the Bible, some idea of what history means to Westerners. The authors of the written tradition also saw, as members of a governing elite, that a long history of political success could serve as a charter for the autonomy they enjoyed under the British Protectorate and their special relationship with the protecting power. They were well aware that a tradition consisting largely of myths – or, as one of them put it, of 'jokes and fables'[30] – would not impress their overlords. They did not, however, invent the history, and to their credit they did not suppress its more imaginative features. But they apologised for them, and usually offered a more historical-seeming alternative version as well.

However, the conversion of myth into pseudo-history had clearly gone quite a long way even before the colonial period. Apart from those of Kintu, the reputed founder, the stories of the early kings, though odd, inconsequent and improbable, are not immediately recognisable as myths, and the gods of Buganda are not the subjects of anything remotely like the rich mythology that surrounds the Ba-Cwezi deities of the Nyoro and related peoples on their western borders.

The contrast between these two neighbouring African cultures strongly recalls a much more famous one. It is well known that the native gods of ancient Rome were strictly functional and its mythology was almost entirely a literary borrowing from the immense Greek store. Georges Dumézil has explained that Rome did have myths of its own but had concealed them in the 'history' of the early kings: 'In practice, it is in the first two books of Livy that one must look for the equivalent of the theologies and cosmologies of other Indo-European peoples.'[31] Like Rome, Buganda was a military state and it too had historicised its myths, depriving the gods of their biographies and society of any structure other than the dynastic one. Its adult male citizens were overwhelmingly preoccupied by politics and war and had little time for poetic invention or religious speculation. Thus, whereas in the region of the Ba-Cwezi scholarship has been trying to extract some history from a tradition that is in large part self-evidently mythical, in Buganda it is myth that has to be dug for in what appears to be a mundane political history. Part of the reward for the excavation, however, should be a better understanding of the history, through the uncovering of earlier societies very different from the aggressively dynamic nineteenth-century kingdom of Buganda.

4   Introduction to Buganda

The explorers who claimed to have discovered the interior of East Africa during the third quarter of the nineteenth century were following routes that were already familiar to Muslim (Arab and Swahili) merchants from the coast, and before that had been trodden by a great many parties of Africans taking ivory and slaves to sell there. So the journey of Captains Speke and Grant to Buganda in 1861–2 took them along the great caravan trail that led through the middle of what is now Tanzania and then north-west to the kingdom of Karagwe in the far corner of the modern state. It was a roundabout route, but for several generations Karagwe had been the entrepôt for the trade of the rich region between the Lakes. It was there that King Muteesa's great-grandfather had arranged the sale of his country's ivory in exchange for dark blue Indian cloth, though it was not until his father's time, in the late 1840s, that the first Arab merchants passed through on their way to the Ganda court, bringing back to the coast, and thus to Europe, news of a powerful monarch whose favour could unlock the commerce of a region rich in ivory and perhaps in much else besides. It was this road that the British travellers were following, though for them the immediate attraction of Buganda was that they believed it to hold the key to the mystery of the Nile source.[1]

The cool green uplands of Karagwe were a welcome contrast to the semi-arid scrublands of central Tanzania through which the travellers had passed. Also, having had to deal with a long series of petty chiefs, some little more than brigands, who haggled and blustered over their tolls, they were glad to find a well-ordered country and a court where there was hospitality and intelligent conversation. Despite its commercial importance, however, Karagwe was only a middle-ranking state in the Lakeland system and in 1861 it lay within Buganda's sphere of influence; and when word of the strangers' presence reached King Muteesa he sent a military escort to fetch them to his court. This would have been a *kitongole*, one of the troops of young fighting men who made the king's will prevail throughout his domains. The travellers found them a lively crew, though they could not approve the way they cheerfully plundered every habitation on the road,

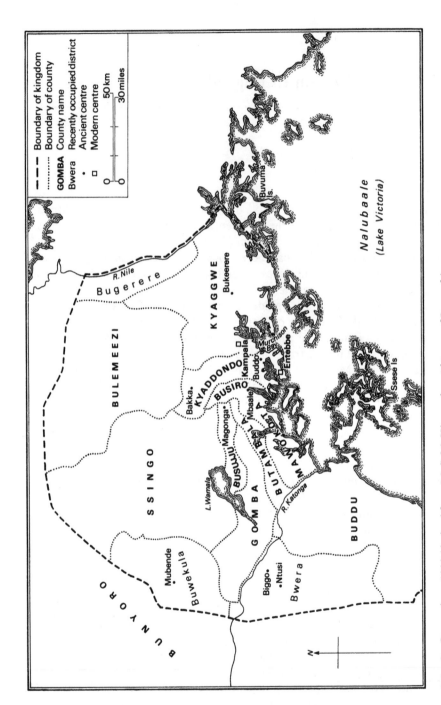

Map 2   Buganda, c. 1880 (derived from M. S. M. Kiwanuka, *A history of Buganda*)

Legend:
- Boundary of kingdom
- Boundary of county
- **GOMBA** County name
- Bwera Recently occupied district
- • Ancient centre
- □ Modern centre

50 km
30 miles

BUNYORO

Mubende
Buwekula

SSINGO

BULEMEEZI

Bugerere

R. Nile

Bakka.

KYADDONDO

KYAGGWE

Bukeerere

L. Wamala

BUSUJJU

Magonga

Mbaale

BUSIRO

Kampala

Murchison Bay

Buddo

Entebbe

GOMBA

BUTAMBO

Biggo.

.Ntusi

Bwera

R. Katonga

BUDDU

MAWO...

Buvuma Is.

Nalubaale
(Lake Victoria)

Ssese Is.

N

until they were back within the king's domain. One of the first things that impressed visitors to Buganda was that a road was what they found themselves walking on – not a winding track from one village to the next, but a wide well-maintained thoroughfare with causeways over the many swamps. All such roads led to the capital, which at this time was at a place called Bandabalogo just to the east of modern Kampala. Here, quite exceptionally in the interior of East Africa, was an undoubted town, a well-laid-out mass of thatched huts that housed palace officials, soldiers, artisans, the scores of royal wives and the thousands of other women who kept the court supplied and served, as well as a floating population of corvée labourers and of provincial chiefs, who were required to spend part of their time under the king's eye.

To greet his mysterious guests the king sat in state on a raised platform of earth covered with cloths and animal skins. (The sacred stool Namulondo, in which the essence of the kingship resided, was brought out only on very special ritual occasions.) Round him were gathered the members of his *lukiiko*, a body which the British would constitute as a council of the realm and eventually as a representative assembly, but which then had a much looser structure. Among those present were the chief officers and courtiers and a selection of the provincial chiefs currently in attendance; also certain people who would find no place in the colonial system – fantastically garbed 'sorceresses', really mediums of the spiritual powers, and probably other counsellors known as 'doctors' or 'diviners'. And on the fringe were the *bambowa*, the Binders or Enforcers, who stood ready with their cords to seize and drag away anyone who awoke the king's displeasure.

Muteesa's realm stretched in a broad arc round the north-west corner of Lake Victoria, from the Nile outflow in the east to the Kagera inflow in the south, some 30,000 square kilometres in all. It was a rich country, the most favoured part of the Lakeland, which is the most favoured part of Africa. Thanks to the great inland sea that the Ganda call Nalubaale, 'Mother of the gods', it enjoys a very reliable supply of rain. There are two official seasons of precipitation, the long rains from March through June and the shorter but fiercer rains, often accompanied by thunderstorms of extraordinary violence, in October–November; but few months are wholly rainless and prolonged drought is unknown. Being on the Equator it is warm all the year round, but as it is around 4,000 feet above sea-level it is never oppressively hot. And if climate has been kind, geology has been even kinder. Buganda is a land of small green hills, each rising some 200–400 feet above the valley floor. Many are flat-topped; for the land was once a plateau that has mostly crumbled away. As a result, while the hilltops support only a thin grass cover and the bottoms are infertile even when they are not waterlogged, the long slopes are covered with soils that are young by the standards of this primeval continent and well supplied with plant nutrients. Deep, well structured, not easily eroded, they support a lush vegetation of which the characteristic feature is ten-foot-tall elephant grass (*Pennisetum purpureum*). Once upon a time the whole country was forested, but habitation and cultivation have destroyed all but some 'galleries' fringing the streams and a large remnant, the Mabira, in the eastern march. Deforestation, however, has not had its usual consequence; soil fertility has remained high.

Into this hospitable land there came, at a time still to be determined, the banana plant, which provided and still provides the staple food of the Ganda people and also, usually fermented, the staple drink. In most ways bananas are the ideal food plant. In yield of calories per unit of area they are excelled only by cassava (manioc), which is less palatable and less vitaminous. Still more encouraging is the yield per unit of labour. The initial clearing and planting of a two-acre grove, sufficient to feed a large family, is a considerable investment; but once that is done the only work required is the splitting of dead stems to make a carpet round the plants. By this means moisture is conserved, weed growth suppressed and the organic content of the soil maintained. Banana 'trees' are really herbaceous plants that reproduce by suckering. They repeatedly throw up tall, hollow, fruit-bearing stems from the proliferating 'stool'. In a mature grove there will at any one time be plants in every stage of development from sucker to growing stem to flower to fruit; and if the grove is well kept the process will go on, if not for ever, certainly for longer than a human generation.[2]

Cultivation is thus simple in Buganda, and food preparation is even simpler. Bunches are cut down while still green, peeled, steamed for a couple of hours and served with whatever meat or vegetables the household can provide. Alternatively, some common varieties can be put in a trough with some grains of sorghum and converted in a period of days to the thick sweet liquid called *mwenge*, or banana wine. Neither cooking nor brewing is preceded by the laborious pounding required by cereals or by roots and tubers such as cassava and yams. Freed of that chore, women were able to take over nearly all the labour of food production apart from the clearance of land. Men therefore could devote themselves to other activities. Hunting and fishing provided occupation for many; hut-building and maintenance were recurrent chores; unusually in Bantu Africa, the making of pots was a masculine activity; and so was the onerous chore of clothing manufacture. The Ganda were careful, even prudish, about the covering of the body; and cotton cloth, though known since the end of the eighteenth century, was a great rarity until about 1870 and did not become general until the colonial period. Some use was made of animal skins, but the preferred form of dress was bark-cloth, which also had other uses such as bedding and wrapping of goods. Most mature homesteads were dominated by a tall, smooth-stemmed ficus tree, a *mutuba*, the bark of which could be removed in large pieces without harm. It was then for the head of the household to spend several hours hitting it with grooved mallets to turn it into soft and flexible, though rather drab, apparel.

These occupations, however, did not add up to full-time employment as the term was understood by European or Asian peasants or by African men in lands of cereal-growing and animal husbandry. Much of the surplus time was undoubtedly devoted to socialising over beer, whether at informal neighbourly gatherings, at feasts given by the powerful to their clients or at communal ceremonies, especially funerals and the 'second funerals' where death was 'driven out' of the society. But there was also a great deal of energy left over for politics and war.

Bananas cannot easily be stored, and though they survive the two short dry seasons of Buganda they do not fruit at those times. Most households therefore cultivated small patches of sweet potatoes as a reserve against temporary pauses in the output of the groves, and also for occasional variation in a diet which, however, the Ganda do not seem to find unduly monotonous. Other sources of carbohydrate included various species of yam, finger-millet, sorghum, maize, sugar-cane and cocoyam (or taro). None of these was individually of much importance but the overall result was that the people were as well secured against famine as any in Africa.

It is crucially significant that of the plants listed only finger-millet and sorghum, with one kind of yam, are of African origin. Sweet potatoes, like maize, came from the New World, bananas, with cocoyam and some species of yam, from southern Asia. When they arrived in this area, and what the inhabitants ate beforehand, are the most important questions in the history of Buganda and the most difficult to answer.

The other main demerit of bananas is that, unlike cereals, they contain almost no protein, which therefore had to be supplied from other sources. Cattle do not greatly thrive in the over-lush vegetation of Buganda, and one of the main themes of the country's history is their acquisition from the drier grasslands to the west and their subsequent distribution to a population hungry for meat and milk. Sheep also were fairly rare, but goats were ubiquitous and so were chickens. These were killed on special occasions, which occurred fairly frequently but not frequently enough to meet the whole dietary need. Vegetable protein partly filled the gap, derived from leguminous plants such as beans, groundnuts and pigeon peas. Beans and groundnuts are also American plants and must be of fairly recent, though pre-colonial, introduction, but they clearly took the place of African cultigens, especially the cowpea and the so-called Bambara groundnut or earthpea. For the rest, hunting certainly played a part, but the country has for a long time been too densely populated for game to be really abundant; and a more important contribution certainly came from the water – to some extent from the rivers but above all from the great lake. The trade in dried fish made a major contribution to Buganda's diet and perhaps also to its political evolution.

It is difficult to say how completely these expedients added up to a solution of the protein problem. Buganda was one of the places where the children's sickness known by its Ghanaian name of *kwashiorkor* was first identified as a condition of protein deficiency. The malaise, however, is not and probably never has been really general; and for adults at least nutrition appears to have been adequate, for the Ganda impressed both early and later observers as a robust and vigorous people. Yet all was clearly not well with them. For while the land was certainly quite densely settled it was not as crowded as its exceptional quality would have led one to expect. Whatever the reasons for this, and they clearly need investigation, the consequence was that no citizen of Buganda lacked land to till.

Like most East Africans, the Ganda did not live in nucleated villages but in homesteads scattered about the countryside, often irregularly strung out along a path that traversed the side of a hill. These were dwellings of the *ba-kopi*, a term usually rendered as 'peasants' but more suitably as 'commoners' or 'ordinary people'. Strictly speaking, everyone was a *mu-kopi* who was not a *mu-langira*, a member of the royal line; but the term had come to be regularly opposed to *mwami*, 'chief'. That word designated the great kings of Rwanda and Burundi; but in Buganda it was the generic term for an office-holder other than the king. A *mu-kopi*, then, was one who was not a chief, who held no position of authority. He lived with probably a single wife in a small hut made of poles and mud with a conical roof of thatch extending almost to ground level, a low door and no windows. In front there would be a carefully swept courtyard and on the other three sides a banana grove, the whole forming a *kibanja*, a homestead held from a superior in return for whatever services he might require. Humble though his position might be, the *mu-kopi* was master in his own house. For Buganda was an emphatically patriarchal society, in which children were strictly disciplined and women could not speak to their husbands or to any other man except in a kneeling position.

At intervals there were somewhat larger groups of huts, including one that was bigger and better built than the rest. Here lived a chief, with his several wives, servants and hangers-on, sometimes known as the 'people of the reed fence', this being the feature that most clearly distinguished the home of a *mwami*. Some of his male retainers, and most of his women, would be slaves, either captured or purchased or occasionally acquired as pawns. But the outlying homesteaders would also be called 'his men', sharing in the feasts that helped to bind them to his service. Free-born Ganda were not serfs; they could attach themselves to any superior they chose. The process was described by the verb *ku-senga*, which in languages not far away meant simply to 'settle, clear new land' but in Buganda, where it was not possible to live and farm without a lord, was used in a transitive sense, 'to do homage to, accept the patronage of', a man of power. In theory the subordinate had the option to *-senguka*, 'to unsettle', to end his service, but it was a right not always easy or safe to exercise. The relationship was repeated right up the ladder, so that everyone except the king was in effect the client of someone else. Political advancement required courage in war, intelligence in counsel, but most of all the art of making oneself agreeable to a superior. Complementary to this was the art of making one's rivals disagreeable by the processes summed up in the verb *ku-lopa*, 'to slander, grass on, finger'.

By such means an ambitious man could hope to graduate from a merely local reed fence to an *m-buga*, the court of a district chief, a *mukungu*, and thence to the *ki-buga*, the 'great *m-buga*', the royal capital, the fount of all wealth and honour. Alternatively, he might have been sent there by his father or patron as a boy. Early travellers were impressed by the flying 'pages', young lads who scudded around the capital bearing messages and generally making themselves useful. From these, in the main, were recruited the next generation of the ruling elite. A youth who had survived the rigorous palace schooling and had displayed aptitude and fidelity would graduate to the captaincy of a *ki-tongole* troop. That is, he would become a *mu-tongole*, in theory the lowest kind of chief though some such people wielded considerable power. Some troops were of course maintained at the capital but others were stationed in the provinces, where they had small estates forming enclaves in the territory of a district chief, a *mukungu*. The *mutongole* remained directly responsible to the *kabaka* and his role was in effect to keep an eye on the chief. On occasion he would be ordered to seize the chief's property and take his place, or a *mutongole* would be sent from the capital for the same purpose. He was then established in the administrative hierarchy. This was a complex structure with many gradations. At the highest level, apart from the *katikkiro*, the chief minister and judge, and the *kimbugwe* or keeper of the king's umbilical cord, were the chiefs of the ten *ssazas*, literally 'divisions' but conventionally Englished as 'counties'. These were not all of the same kind. The most important were the four marcher provinces: Buddu in the south-west, Ssingo in the north-west, Bulemeezi in the north and Kyaggwe in the east. In the west-centre of the country were four smaller counties: Mawokota on the coast, Butambala, Gomba, and Busujju further inland. That left the two central counties of Busiro and Kyaddondo, which were a patchwork of domains belonging to ritual officiants, members of the royal family and shrine priests, nominally presided over by the sacred office-holders called the Mugema and the Kaggo. Within each county was an array of lesser *ba-kungu*, ranked in a conventional order.

The structure of power was further complicated by the presence of a parallel hierarchy, in which the idiom was that of kinship and the criterion for office was the approval of clan and lineage elders, the *bataka* or 'men of the land'. This structure also extended to the summit, for one of the most sacred titles of the king was *Ssa-bataka*, 'Chief of the clan heads' or 'Supreme man of the land'; and the revival of this title was the first step towards the restoration of the kingship in 1993. The clans, exogamous units defined by a relation of avoidance to an animal or plant species, survived the apparent demise of the kingship and were a crucial complement to it in all phases of Buganda's known history. Similar structures were found in all the Lakes kingdoms, and indeed many clans transcended political boundaries; but Buganda was unique in the strict correspondence between clan and 'totem'. Elsewhere a clan was a named grouping, and it often recognised more than one avoidance, while one avoidance might be shared by several clans. The Ganda units, by contrast, were identified only by their unique emblem, the *muziro*, together with an equally unique secondary avoidance called its *kabbiro* or 'secret'. Although the word for a clan, *ki-ka*, is derived from 'home', the clans were by no means localised. Each had a central place, where the senior *mu-taka*, successor to the founding ancestor, had his *bu-taka* or estate. But there were also numerous sub-divisions, each with its own *bu-taka*, and these were scattered far and wide. There is in fact reason to think that dispersal is inherent in this kind of totemic system. For the whole point of avoidances and other distinctive food customs is group identification, as kosher meat identifies Jews and the Friday fast Catholics; and they imply large, mobile, complex societies where individuals would be defenceless and lost without group support. People of the Lakes kingdoms could travel quite long distances and still be confident of finding fellow-clansmen to offer hospitality and protection. So, whether or not the large Lakeland clans had originally some basis in real kinship, they had become functional bodies, organisations of mutual succour in societies that were far removed from self-contained villages and real kinship obligations.[3] And in Buganda the succour provided was above all political in character. There was a relation of mutual dependence between the kingship and the clans, which are best seen as corporations competing for power and privilege within the framework of the state. The origins of these entities were probably diverse. Some had clearly been independent ruling lineages, but the common notion that Buganda originated as a confederation of autonomous clan-communities is too simple. Some of the emblems belonged to groups that, so far as can be discovered, had always been integrated into the kingdom, and others appear to have been primarily religious societies. In the course of time, however, the state had imposed a common pattern of subordination. All the clans, and many of the constituent lineages, had their own special duties towards the king and in return were guaranteed a share of its wealth and security. And though a new clan head was chosen from the members of the senior lineage by the elders, his appointment had to be confirmed by the *kabaka*. Thus the clans in no way acted as a brake on the growth of despotic power, which manipulated their competition just as it manipulated the individual ambitions of appointed officials.

Buganda was peculiar in that the members of the royal patriline, the *balangira*, did not constitute a clan and recognised no totem apart from those of their mothers. They were moreover systematically debarred (with only two or three remembered exceptions) from provincial chiefships or other subordinate political offices; and the king's own brothers were kept under close guard, when they were not actually liquidated. So with royalty excluded from government except at the very top, the rich slopes of power and privilege were occupied by ambitious commoners, whose upward striving was the stuff of Ganda politics. The higher the climb, the greater the peril; Apolo Kaggwa devoted a long section of his ethnographic work to a description of the various unpleasant ways in which the lives of those who had displeased the sovereign were brought to an end.[4] Yet most Ganda seem to have enjoyed the great game of politics, even apart from the rich rewards it could bring in terms of women and power, wine and meat and adulation. Even for the simple *bakopi*, who were not playing the game in any serious way, there was the same mix of peril and opportunity. Lives and limbs were at mercy of superiors, but there was secure enjoyment of fertile land, and also the possibility of additional wives and the certainty of eating meat provided by the chief from his surplus livestock and drinking wine from the bananas grown by his ample household.

Perhaps the main point about the political system was that it was to be a large extent self-lubricating, being highly productive of plunder and tribute. The state organisation was able to assemble large numbers of disciplined fighting men, for all free Ganda males belonged to a frequently mobilised militia, and so was able to steal women, goats and cattle from its neighbours, or terrify them into regular payment.

By the nineteenth century territorial expansion had virtually stopped. Further annexations might well have strained Buganda's military and administrative resources, but there was also probably a half-conscious calculation that there would be too many subjects to claim a share in the spoils and too few foreigners within reach of despoilment. So by the middle of the century Buganda was distinguished above all by its territorial clarity. Most African kingdoms have ill-defined frontiers, a wide borderland where the king's commands may or may not be obeyed, but Buganda, as has been well said, had 'sharp edges; one was either in it or outside it'.[5] Royal power was exercised close to the border not much less effectively than within a mile of the palace. Beyond the border there was a wide domain of influence and depredation but not government. Kings Kamaanya, Ssuuna and Muteesa launched regular raids into these areas, interfered in succession disputes so as to secure pliant rulers, sometimes exacted tribute, but did not incorporate them into their own system.

To the east lay Busoga, a geographical description for the country bounded by the Nile on the west, Lake Kioga, the Mpologoma swamp on the east, and Nalubaale. In the north and east of this area there were sizeable kingdoms, though not comparable to Buganda, but the polities in the south and west were minuscule and they were harried unmercifully by the Ganda from the late eighteenth century on. To the west there was dry short-grass country where large herds of long-horned cattle were not very effectively defended by the kingdom of Nkore (better known by its anglicised name, Ankole). South-west of the Buddu province, the little kingdom of Kkooki had become a virtual Ganda protectorate well before the beginning of the colonial period, when it was organised as a 'county'. To the south, strung out along the west coast of Nalubaale, were the small Haya states, where a Nyoro dialect was spoken: Kiziba, Kyamutwara (which split into three early in the nineteenth century) and Ihangiro, none of which could offer much resistance to Ganda attacks by land and sea. (Unlike Kkooki, these were cut off from Buganda by the Anglo-German Agreement of 1890, which created a straight and immovable frontier line along the first degree of latitude south of the Equator.) In the interior the somewhat larger kingdom of Karagwe, as we saw, accepted Buganda's superior power if not its actual suzerainty. On the north-west frontier lay the formerly great kingdom of Bunyoro, now very much on the defensive. Though Muteesa's boast that King Kamurasi paid tribute to him was probably ill-founded, the Nyoro were subjected to frequent raiding by Ganda armies, and it is not surprising that they called Buganda Mhwahwa, 'the land of wild dogs'. The Ganda also benefited from, if they did not engineer, the secession of the province of Toro in the south-west which, like Nkore and Karagwe, was of great strategic importance. What was at stake here was increasingly the control over the rapidly developing trade with the east coast of Africa and thus indirectly with the great markets of the West. The slave trade, which ravaged much of eastern Africa, remained on a modest scale in the Lakeland, where manpower and womanpower were too valuable to the kingdoms to be exported in large numbers and where the rulers were strong enough to prevent slave-dealers from becoming slave-raiders, as they did in much of Tanzania and eastern Zaire. Here the main quest was not for people but for ivory, and the chief object of Ganda policy was to make the *kabaka*'s court the centre of the ivory trade for the whole region, so that coastal traders would have to pay a monopoly price and the *kabaka* would have new means of rewarding his servants, in the much-coveted imported cloth, and new instruments of power in the imported firearms with which he began to equip his elite troops.

A story reported from the latter part of Muteesa's reign may convey the flavour of Ganda politics in the final decades of the kingdom's independence.[6] For several years before his death the king was a sick man, suffering from venereal complications; and he came to suspect that certain of his senior chiefs were plotting to place one of his sons on the throne. He therefore cunningly gave them his daughters in marriage, so that they could spy out the conspiracy. (It did not bother him that this was totally contrary to custom, inasmuch as princesses were not supposed to wed at all.) The information provided by his daughters allowed him to deploy his most faithful household troops and to round up the adult princes, placing them in a ditched enclosure. Muteesa then took his favourite son Kalema out of the stockade, provided him with a gun and sent him back to shoot his brother Mawanda, who had emerged as leader of the malcontents, promising him immunity and the eventual succession. The assassin was duly brought to trial but Muteesa blandly professed that he could not bring himself to execute his son. When he died, however, the king-makers rejected Kalema as a man who had shown himself to be a killer.

Two points deserve special notice. One is that, in spite of the patriarchal set-up, women played a crucial role at court;[7] at the height of the crisis there is mention of a special 'council of the women', and in general the king's sisters, his principal wives and his daughters were his most trusted aides, while the queen-mother was a power in the land at least equal to her son. The other is that Mawanda was heard to complain that Muteesa's physical decline was 'making the kingdom old'. In other words, even in a time of hard-headed power struggles the older resonances of sacred kingship still retained some power.

There are clear signs that by the end of Muteesa's reign in 1884 the zenith of Buganda's wealth and power had passed; and since the system was one of dynamic equilibrium even a cessation of growth spelt crisis and possible collapse. But that did not happen, partly because the internal crisis merged with the external shock of Europe's direct intervention, but also because the institutions were resilient enough to emerge from the upheavals, profoundly transformed but structurally intact.

That, however, is another story. Here we are concerned with Buganda in the middle quarters of the nineteenth century: an intensely political society, dominated (at least in appearance) by the quest for rank and power; a predatory society, which systematically robbed its neighbours both of their capital (in livestock) and their means of reproduction; a quasi-urban society, unique in the interior of East Africa, where barbaric cruelty coexisted with genuine civility; above all an open society, with few impediments to the exercise of talent or the entry of new commodities and new thoughts. I shall try to show that this Buganda was a quite recent growth, but also that it had very deep roots. So it is now necessary to set out what can be known about the more distant past, which lies beyond the reach of explicit tradition.

5   The remoter past

The archaeology of the core area of Buganda is very little known, but enough work has been done in neighbouring lands for faint outlines of the regional prehistory to be discernible. We know that hominids, members of the human family, lived in the Lakeland almost if not quite as early as in the lands of the East African Rift, and that it was in the mainstream of cultural evolution throughout the Pleistocene epoch. With the coming of the Holocene, however, some ten thousand years ago, the record becomes very sparse. The reason seems to be that, as rain returned to Africa after the great late Pleistocene drought, dense equatorial forest spread eastwards to the shores of Nalubaale, and was shunned by the hunter-gatherers of the Late Stone Age, who were mostly adapted to a savanna way of life. To the north, things were moving fast during the early Holocene. From the expanded lakes of northern Kenya right across to Lake Chad and the middle Niger fishing communities became settled enough to make earthenware vessels to hold their stews, developing the art of pottery in apparent independence.[1] By the end of the fifth millennium BC, as noted earlier, some settlements on the middle Nile, just downstream from Khartoum, had acquired domestic animals from further north and were probably experimenting with the northern practice of sowing selected cereal grains. The southward spread of this new, 'neolithic' economy seems to have been slow but, by the end of the second millennium BC at the latest, pastoral and perhaps marginally agricultural communities were established in the highlands of Kenya and north-central Tanzania.[2] Meanwhile, over in West Africa some peoples had apparently developed a different system of food production based on the protection of yams, oil-palms and various legumes.

None of this activity, however, had reached the Lakeland, which is separated from the middle Nile region, and from Ethiopia, by inhospitable lands of swamp and arid steppe; the river itself does not provide a thoroughfare, being blocked in the southern Sudan by masses of floating vegetation. So for all or nearly all of the last eight thousand years before Christ Buganda with the rest of the Lakeland seems to have been inhabited only by a few bands of stone-using forest hunters, and to have remained beyond the furthest ripples from the economic, cultural and political transformations in the Middle East and northern Africa. During the Pharaonic period, say from 3000 to 500 BC, the distance between the two ends of the Nile Valley was probably greater than ever before or since. But then a surprising new chapter opened. On the shores of Nalubaale and across in Rwanda and Burundi there are numerous sites yielding pottery of a very distinctive kind, commonly known as Urewe ware. Apart from a few sherds that are probably outliers from the quite different ceramic tradition of the eastern highlands, this was the earliest pottery in the Lakeland, and it was not crude, as might have been expected, but highly accomplished, consisting mainly of well-made bowls with elaborate incised decoration and other frills. What is more, the same sites often produced clear evidence of iron-working, and this too was of a high standard; it has been argued that these central African metallurgists had even found out how to make a kind of steel – although there was no preceding regional Bronze or Copper Age.[3]

The origins of this 'Early Iron Age' culture are something of a mystery. It is hardly credible that it could have sprung fully formed out of the Lakeland – and for technical reasons the local invention of iron-working is especially difficult to imagine – but there are no obvious antecedents for it in the lands to the north. The problem is compounded by great uncertainty over the time of its inception. Of the many radio-carbon dates derived from the sites the great majority are within the first four centuries of our era, but a fair number straggle back through the first millennium BC and even into the second. Some experts are prepared to accept some or all of these early dates, and with them the hypothesis of independent invention, since there is no possible external source for iron-working before about 500 BC. Others hold that the readings must be erroneous or misleading. There is no obvious change in the pottery over time, and so a shorter chronology seems more plausible, allowing the technology to have been derived from the north, most probably from Carthage by way of Nigeria.[4]

However that may be, the point for us is that quite advanced ceramic and metallurgical activities were established in the Lakeland, including Buganda, by the beginning of the Christian era and perhaps a few centuries earlier. Moreover, although nothing is yet known about the agricultural support for the iron-smelters and potters, it is hardly possible that they did not have any. So the development of settled, organised, technically proficient societies in this region goes back to a time far beyond the reach of the most optimistically interpreted oral traditions; and it needs to be held in mind that the social and political formations of recent centuries have behind them a much longer history than might be suggested by the thirty (or so) kings of dynastic memory. The Urewe cultural complex seems to have disintegrated around the middle of the first millennium. Few of the carbon dates referred to it are later than AD 500 and only one or two doubtful ones are later than 700. The second half of the first millennium is in fact something of a dark age in the Lakeland, and when the record becomes fuller again after AD 1000 it discloses a different kind of society. However, though there seems to have been some loss of creativity, and perhaps of population, the Urewe people certainly did not disappear, and the continuity of institutional life was never completely broken. One of the most striking things about the Early Iron Age pots and smelting furnaces is that some of them were discovered at sites that the local people still associate with royalty.[5] And still more significant is the continuity of language.

Inferences from language, like those from material remains, are for the most part a matter of probability and human judgement, and the respect that historians, like other laymen, accord to the expert witness should always be a wary one. Nevertheless, on some points relevant to Buganda there is now an informed consensus.[6] Nearly all the people of the Lakeland speak languages belonging to the Bantu family, one of the world's most remarkable linguistic groupings. Over four hundred languages, occupying between them much the greater part of the continent south of a line drawn eastward from the West African Hinge, are so closely related that their common origin is evident to the naked eye of the amateur observer. In the great majority, for example, *bantu* or something very like it is the word for 'people'; and there are also many similarities in the ways that words are constructed and arranged. Within the Bantu territory, the widest diversity of languages is found in the north-west quadrant, roughly corresponding to the equatorial rain forest; and both the immediate and the distant relatives of the family are found in West Africa. It is agreed, therefore, that the first Bantu speakers lived in the southern part of the Cameroon–Nigeria borderlands, and a simple explanation suggests itself for their vast expansion. They were on the left flank of a southward drift of West African fishermen and farmers, doubtless impelled ultimately by the drying of the Sahara after 3000 BC; and whereas all the others were halted by the ocean they were able to pass round the Hinge. They then found themselves in a sub-continent that was mostly inhabited by sparse bands of hunter-gatherers, whom they gradually absorbed or reduced to a kind of subservient symbiosis.[7]

The Bantu family of languages cannot be divided neatly into sub-groups, as the Indo-European family is divided into Indo-Iranian, Celtic and so on. Nevertheless linguists recognise a 'Great Lakes' group and reasonably assume that its common parent was spoken by the pioneers of Early Iron

Age settlement in this region.[8] However, it is clear that the present uniform Bantu-ness of the Lakeland is misleading and that several other peoples, speaking languages unrelated (or only very distantly related) to Bantu, converged on this highly attractive region in the period between about 500 BC and AD 500. The modern languages contain unmistakable traces of vocabulary drawn from Central Sudanic languages, such as are now spoken in parts of north-west Uganda, north-east Zaire, south-west Sudan and Chad, and there is some reason to think that members of this speech community may have mediated iron technology to the Bantu, and perhaps also cereal food plants.[9] One scholar, David Schoenbrun, has detected also the presence of an Eastern Sudanic element nowadays represented by a few remnant communities in north-east Uganda.[10] Most important is the evidence for an intrusion of Cushitic-speaking pastoralists; but here we tread on treacherous ground.

As all Africanists are aware, colonial writers had a very simple explanation for the state-building achievements of the Lakeland: the native peoples had been conquered by 'Hamites', brown-skinned, narrow-nosed intruders from north-east Africa who were sometimes described as 'Caucasoid' and who, precursors of the true Caucasian conquerors, imposed their enlightened rule on the black majority. The tall, 'ethiopoid' Tutsi cattle-owners of Rwanda and Burundi, with the similar herdfolk called Ba-Hima or Ba-Huma who lived on the grasslands of the central Lakeland, appeared to be living evidence of this creative invasion – a theory reinforced by an idea deeply planted in the European mind, that people who control animals are intrinsically nobler than those who merely till the soil.

As the colonial system waned, so did its preferred mode of historical interpretation, and it is a long time since the Hamitic theory, with its obviously racist connotations, was academically respectable. Indeed it became improper to suggest any kind of distant northern influence on tropical Africa. Yet cattle were unquestionably brought there from the north, and it is not really racist to point out that their original owners must have been 'Hamites', since no other kind of man ever lived in their homelands. Now the term 'Hamitic' was also, and more correctly, used in a linguistic sense, to define the speakers of the African branches of the Hamito-Semitic (or as it is now called Afro-asiatic) phylum: ancient Egyptian, Berber, the Chadic languages (of which the best known is Hausa) and the Omotic and Cushitic languages of Ethiopia and Somalia. And it was reasonable to suppose that the pioneers of pastoral economy in the Lakeland would be Hamitic in that sense too, since no other kind of language was ever spoken in the north-east African homeland. Yet the Tutsi and Hima spoke just the same Bantu languages as the peasant cultivators among whom they lived, and colonial scholars found no plausible 'Hamitic' etymology for any words in those languages. Intrusive minorities often lose their original language, but they do not usually lose it without a trace. More recently, however, such traces have been discovered. In and around the Eastern Rift Valley in northern Tanzania there are a few languages classed as Southern Cushitic, a distant offshoot of the Cushitic family of Ethiopia, itself a branch of the Afro-asiatic phylum – and thus in the old terminology Hamitic. It is generally accepted that Southern Cushitic pioneers were responsible for the 'Pastoral Neolithic' sites which testify to the arrival of domestic livestock in the Rift Valley region by the end of the second millennium BC. It would be surprising if in the course of the next two millennia some of these herdfolk had not found their way round the south shore of Nalubaale to the rich upland pastures that lay beyond it. And Christopher Ehret and his students have found linguistic evidence that they did just that: a handful of words in the Lakeland Bantu languages, including those for 'lion' and 'blood' that are of special interest to herdsmen, can be traced to Southern Cushitic.[11] Thus the pioneers of pastoralism, and perhaps also of cereal agriculture in the Lakeland, were, after all, linguistically Hamites of a sort. Racially, if this question is of any interest, they were neither stereotypical Negroes nor in any meaningful sense 'Caucasoids', but a type of human being that had been evolving in eastern Africa for many millennia. It is not to be supposed that the modern Hima and Tutsi are in any simple way the lineal successors of the Southern Cushitic herdfolk, for they are the (by no means identical) products of a long and complex historical evolution, which we shall have to explore briefly as part of the background to Buganda.

The Hamitic theory, it must be said, was always at its weakest in relation to Buganda, where Ba-Hima were not state-builders but simple herdfolk living on the fringes of the kingdom, often in the service of Ganda chiefs, and ethiopoid features could be discerned in the ruling classes only by the eye of racist faith. Indirectly, however, the arrival of the Cushites in the Lakeland may have been a formative influence.

Some time after the waning of Urewe civilisation a new impetus made itself felt, most obviously at the large settlement known to recent locals as Ntusi, 'the Mounds', some way to the west of the Lake in south-west Uganda.[12] The site was within the expanded colonial boundaries of Buganda, but in the nineteenth century it was in Bwera, the 'white' or 'holy land', a thinly populated no-man's-land between Buganda, Bunyoro, Nkore and the little kingdom of Kkooki to the south. Recent investigations have shown that Ntusi was first occupied in the eleventh or perhaps the tenth century, and by the thirteenth had become a town with a population of something like

5,000. Numerous cattle bones attest its wealth in herds; in valleys nearby there were artificial ponds for the watering of stock; and a few miles to the north, on the bank of the Katonga river, an extensive system of earthworks, the Biggo or 'Strongholds', was clearly designed for their safe-keeping.[13] Yet this was not strictly speaking a pastoral society; for there is evidence of agriculture as well, and it would be hard to see how such an agglomeration could have lived by animal husbandry alone. All the same, there had obviously been a marked change in the pattern of economic life. Unlike the Early Iron Age sites, Ntusi and Biggo are set in the driest section of the Lakeland, where cattle and cereals (sorghum and eleusine millet) do better than the yams and other moisture-loving plants that were probably the basis of the Early Iron Age diet.

Archaeologically speaking, these sites are set off from their Early Iron Age predecessors not only by size and complexity but also by their pottery. This was generally much cruder, though there were a few fine wares, and in place of elaborate incised patterns the decoration, if any, consisted of rouletting, made by wrapping twisted or knotted fibres round the wet clay.[14] The first appearance of this technique in the Lakeland was in Rwanda in the eighth or ninth century AD. It also turned up a little later in the Kenya Highlands, and was common in north-central Africa – but did not occur south of the Lakeland. A northern cultural influence thus seems certain, and a northern immigration has to be considered.

Relevant here is yet another ingredient in the regional linguistic brew: Nilotic. Unlike that of Central Sudanic and Cushitic, the presence of this kind of speech is not solely an inference from putative loan-words; for on the left bank of the Nile in northern Bunyoro there are still a few thousand non-Bantu people known to the Nyoro as Ba-chope and to themselves as Jo-pa-Lwo, 'the people of Lwo'. Speakers of Lwo dialects, generally recognising that name, are very widely spread in the areas to the north and east of the Lakeland. The Alur, Acooli, and Lang'i form a continuous bloc across northern Uganda; there are offshoots in eastern Uganda, and one of these, conventionally known as Luo, passed round the north-east corner of the Lake and absorbed great numbers of Bantu and other communities to become one of the two largest ethnic groups in Kenya. There are also scattered Lwo speakers in the southern Sudan, such as the Bor, Pari and Anywak and more importantly the Shilluk, whose dialect probably rates as a distinct language. Together with the Dinka and Nuer who, like the Shilluk, live in Sudan close to the confluence of the White Nile and the Bahr-al-Ghazal, and with some smaller groups further north, the Lwo form the Western, or 'River-Lake' branch of the Nilotic family; the Eastern and Southern branches are widely extended in Kenya and northern Tanzania, their best-known representatives being the Maasai and the

Kalenjin. Taken as a whole, the Nilotic peoples display a strong bias towards cattle-keeping; but the exclusive pastoralism of the Maasai was untypical. All other groups cultivated cereals as well, and, as the term 'River-lake' implies, fishing was a basic part of the Western Nilotic economy.

Historians have long assigned a major role to Nilotic speakers in the Lakeland – or rather, two distinct roles.[15] Originally, they were alleged to have immigrated from the north in the fifteenth century, destroyed the Ntusi–Biggo system, which was seen as an 'empire' ruled by the mysterious 'Ba-Cwezi' people, and then developed the successor states of Bunyoro and Buganda in the north of the region. (There was an almost explicit analogy with the rise of the barbarian kingdoms of western Europe out of the ruins of the Roman Empire.) But it has also been claimed that they had created the 'Bacwezi' system in the first place, and perhaps much else as well. It is not clear whether this first wave of state-builders is supposed to have been specifically Lwo or to have spoken some other variety of Nilotic language. Either way, Nilotic invaders are historically expedient, since they make it possible to preserve the conquest theory of state-formation while discarding the obnoxious Hamitic hypothesis, which required builders and rulers to have been a specially endowed group, in some sense not really African. There is no doubt about the Africanness of the Nilotic people of northern Uganda and southern Sudan, who indeed tend to be blacker as well as taller and leaner than the mass of the Lakeland population.

A few words of clearly Nilotic origin have found their way into the Ganda language and rather more into Nyoro, where Lwo influence is particularly noticeable in the terminology of kingship. One key word, moreover, ki-kali, which denotes the royal courtyard and is derived from Lwo kal, 'fenced enclosure', occurs also in Nkore and Rwanda. So it is possible that Lwo immigrants not only introduced a new pottery style but acted as catalyst for the profounder economic and political changes that clearly took place in the Lakeland about the end of the first millennium. Though not the first cattle-keepers in the region, they may well have helped to develop the mixed agro-pastoral economy that took shape on the central grasslands and the social relations that went with it. But Ntusi and Biggo need to be set in a wider perspective, which will show that they were manifestations of a general process of African development and cannot be explained solely by any local ethnic movement, however far-reaching. Far to the south, in and near what is now Zimbabwe, strikingly similar changes were taking place at exactly the same time, culminating in the thirteenth and fourteenth century with the building of the famous stone structures that have given the modern state its name. Here too, and in many other places, the tenth and eleventh centuries saw a marked change in the style of pottery; rouletting was not used but, as in the Lakeland, the new wares were on the whole simpler and cruder than those of the Early Iron Age, implying new social priorities, not general retrogression. Indeed, for sub-Saharan Africa as a whole the period from about AD 900 to 1400 was one of rapid demographic and economic growth, with a big increase in the number and size of settlements, the formation of trading networks, the appearance of central places and of specialised production centres (for salt, copper, gold), often a new emphasis on cattle-keeping, and signs of a growing concentration of wealth and power. Though documentary evidence is still very sparse, and for the Lakeland non-existent, there is a sense in which prehistory is over in Africa by the first half of the present millennium. In particular, we can often be confident that we are now dealing, not with the faceless 'cultures' or 'traditions' of archaeology, but with familiar ethnic entities such as Hausa, Yoruba and Igbo in Nigeria, Shona in Zimbabwe and Luba in south-eastern Zaire. And with Ganda?

The beginnings of an answer to that question have to be linguistic, since one definition of 'Ganda' is 'the people who speak the Ganda language'. The initial Bantu settlement of the Lakeland will have produced long chains of intercommunicating dialects. In time these ceased to be mutually comprehensible and separate languages emerged, which in turn would gradually diversify into new dialect clusters. At certain times and places, however, one particular dialect would achieve a wide ascendancy, counter-acting the usual tendency to fission. It is a striking fact that, while there were some seventy autonomous communities in the Lakeland, there were, with minor exceptions disregarded here, only three languages: in the south-west, 'West Highlands' or Rwanda-Rundi-Ha; in the central zone, 'Rutara' or 'Nyoroan', comprising the Nyoro, Nkore, Haya, Kerebe and Zinza dialects; in the east, spread along the north shore of the Lake, Ganda, Soga and Gwere, forming the 'Gandan' or 'North Nyanza' cluster. (*Nyanza* is the Swahili for 'lake' and was at one time used as the name of Victoria/Nalubaale.) All three are fairly closely related, the latter two more closely than the first, and it is reasonable to try to relate their internal configuration to Later Iron Age history.[16]

Lexico-statisticians discover the relative distances between different pairs of languages, and some believe that it is possible to go beyond this and estimate the absolute date at which speakers of the parent language parted company. The assumption is that languages have a half-life, that basic vocabularies decay at a roughly constant rate. No practitioner of 'glottochronology' pretends that words behave with the regularity of radiocarbon atoms; but experiments with languages having a long documented history have persuaded many of them that the results are at any rate better than total ignorance. It is generally reckoned, for example, that after about five hundred years without sustained contact dialects cross the threshold of mutual comprehension and become distinct languages. Now it is remarkable that the south-western kingdoms of Rwanda and Burundi, together with the fragmented kingdoms of Buha, share a 'West Highlands' language in which dialect variation is minimal. Such wide uniformity could only have been imposed and sustained by a political authority that was established some time well within the last half-millennium. We need not postulate a single government, but should rather envisage closely related groups securing power throughout the south-western Lakeland. This is in fact the 'Tutsi conquest' deduced by early ethnographers from the prevailing social structures, but on the linguistic evidence it took place more recently than historians have usually allowed.

Recent calculations suggest that 'Rutara' and 'North Nyanza' began to diverge from one another about a thousand years ago, at the time when some people were moving out from the Early Iron Age settlements on the Lake shore to colonise the grasslands to the west.[17] The divisions between the Rutaran dialects are deeper than in the West Highlands group and betoken a separation that began some five or six centuries ago, when the Ntusi system seems to have been dissolving. It seems likely, therefore, that in the heyday of that system, roughly between AD 1000 and 1400, a single dialect was spoken all over the lands between Nalubaale and the Ruwenzori mountains in the west and northward to the shores of Lake Albert. There is thus some linguistic support for the concept of an 'empire of Kitara' that many commentators have deduced from the remains at Ntusi and Biggo and from an interpretation of some traditions current in the area. ('Rutara' is a recently invented term intended to signify 'the language of Kitara'.) Words such as 'empire' or even 'state' are almost certainly overblown, and the term 'Kitara' probably has a different and more recent reference (see below, p. 200), but the influence of Ntusi does appear to have been wide ranging. Carbon dates obtained from the Biggo earthworks, though not conclusive, suggest that it flourished a little later than Ntusi, probably from the fourteenth to the sixteenth century,[18] and the dialect spoken there is likely to have been the one ancestral to modern Nyoro and Nkore, which are distinctly closer to one another than to the more southerly Rutaran dialects.

The distance between the North Nyanza dialects (Ganda, Soga and Gwere) is slightly greater than in Rutara, and the common ancestor was probably spoken in the first centuries of this millennium. There is, however, no sign of an ancient central place comparable with Ntusi, so that an early concentration of political power is very improbable. Within the Buganda kingdom linguistic uniformity is total; but that is just one manifestation of the powerful centralising forces at work in the nineteenth century and tells us nothing about the kingdom's antiquity.

In sum, the messages conveyed by the regional prehistory to the student of Buganda seem to be the following. First, there was here a confluence of two very different cultural traditions. One, enshrined above all in Bantu speech, is western, a culture of the rain forest and its margins, an offshoot of the 'Western Bantu tradition' analysed by Jan Vansina.[19] This was to all intents and purposes an indigenous African creation, the goat being the only certain ancestral indicator of distant contacts with North Africa and ultimately with western Asia. The other tradition belongs to the Nile valley. At base it too was the creation of African communities, the ancient fishing peoples of the great valley, but it received more substantial inputs from the neolithic culture of the Near East. It may be presumed to have been mediated to the Lakeland both by Nilotic and by earlier Central Sudanic and possibly also Eastern Sudanic immigrants, and indirectly by Southern Cushites.

Second, settled communities, skilled in metallurgy and able to indulge a taste for well-made earthenware, were present at least two thousand years ago. Among the few archaeological finds in the Ganda heartland is a pottery model of a human head discovered at Entebbe. Plastic art of any kind was rare in eastern Africa, and the only comparable artefacts were the heads found at Lydenburg in South Africa and dated there to the fifth century AD.

Third, new and more complex economic and political formations began to take shape in the Lakes region about the end of the first millennium, perhaps stimulated in part by the arrival of Nilotic people from further north. It is unlikely that Buganda was fully integrated into the system that was probably not called Kitara. Its language is distinct from 'Rutara', and the directors of the Ntusi and Biggo systems would not have had much interest in a land that was not really suited to cattle-rearing. But there is reason to think that in the early part of this millennium change was in motion along the north shores of Nalubaale as well; and though oral tradition cannot, in my view, be used to chart the events of that period directly, we are getting near to the time at which the Ganda people's own view of the past begins to be relevant. Like other peoples, however, they start the story, not with local politics, but with the beginning of the world.

6   Genesis

Sun and moon

Thanks to a slight northward tilt of the plateau, nearly all the waters of
Buganda actually flow away from the great Lake, in slow papyrus-choked
streams which wind their way towards the Nile as it turns westward
through Lake Kyoga. Only the Nile itself, to the east of the ancient
kingdom, has breached the line of hills fringing the northern coast of
Nalubaale. It is not surprising that many of the key places in Buganda's
history should lie on this narrow watershed between the Lake shore and its
hinterland. The moving capitals of the nineteenth-century kings were
always on one or other of the hills overlooking Murchison Bay, within the
boundaries of modern Kampala or not far away. A few miles just south of
west is Buddo where, since the middle of the eighteenth century, the rites of
the king's installation have been performed. Further to the west, near the
end of a long swampy finger of the Lake, the shrine of the war-god Kibuuka
at Mbaale, 'the Rock', was a major focus of patriotic sentiment.

However, there is reason to think that the most ancient nucleus of the
realm was further away from the Lake, in the lands lying almost encircled
by the two branches of the upper Mayanja river, which have their sources
close together just north of Kampala. This was Busiro, 'the land of tombs'.
The modern county of that name extends southward to the Lake shore,
including Buddo and the seat of British and later governments at Entebbe;
but the name properly belongs only to the northern area, containing all the
shrines in which the decorated jawbones of the early kings were preserved.
This area was also, as we shall see (below, pp. 149–54), the scene of the most
archaic royal rituals. In its centre, some fourteen miles directly north-west
of Kampala, is the hill of Bakka, at 4,371 feet the highest point for miles
around. And here, in the reign of Jjuuko the sixteenth king, the sun fell out
of the sky and there was darkness over the earth, until a magician called
Wanga managed to fix it back in its place.[1]

This story has usually been taken to be the report of an eclipse; and
indeed a solar eclipse visible in the latitude of Buganda did occur in

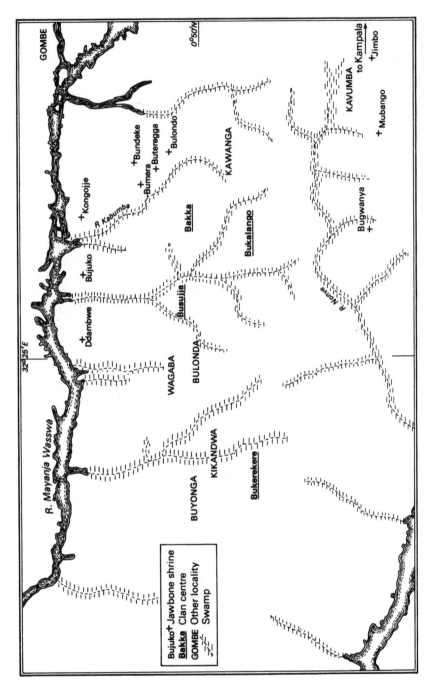

Map 3   Busiro, land of tombs (derived from part of DOS 26 (Y732), sheet 70/11 (Kakiri))

AD 1680, about the time that generation-dating would assign to Jjuuko (G.8). However, there are signs that astronomical history, though probably contributing to the way the story is presented, is not what it was really about. It would perhaps be a quibble to remark that the sun does not 'fall' in an eclipse but dies or is swallowed up; but it is impossible to ignore the name Wanga. For this did not belong to any mere magician, but to the Creator, who in earlier tellings was surely fixing the sun in the sky for the first time.

It is still conventional to describe African religion as 'animism', implying a foolish belief in the personality of natural phenomena. Alternatively, it is depicted as consisting in equal parts of witchcraft and the cult of ancestors. So it is necessary to insist that almost all Africans have always believed in God, as most of them still do. Anthropologists and some other commentators have been reluctant to apply this term, redolent as it is of Christian and Islamic ideology, to the creator and sustainer of the African cosmos, preferring to write of 'Spirit', 'Divinity', 'the most eminent mystical agency' and the like; but this seems an unnecessary caution. True, Africans were not monotheists; their religious thought left room for many other spiritual potencies. But then, so did St Paul's.[2] True, they sometimes fragmented the divine being, so that for some East Africans the singular God, Mu-lungu, could coexist with a plurality of *mi-lungu* sprites. But then the Hebrew word for God, 'Elohim', was also plural in form. Africa's God was not the partisan vigilante of the Judaeo-Christian tradition, nor was he constantly changing the disposition of the cosmos to suit his worshippers. But it is an exaggeration to describe him as 'withdrawn' from the world he made, and he was far from being 'otiose', as some theorists have suggested. He was the shaper and organiser of the universe, the artist who gave structure to the flux of appearances, the ultimate guarantor of the natural and moral order.

God was known to the Bantu-speaking peoples by innumerable praise-names and titles, illustrating various aspects of his sovereign activity.[3] In the Lakeland he was often referred to as Ru-gaba (or I-gaba or Kye-ba-gaba), 'the Apportioner' (of roles and destinies). But his creative function most commonly made him appear in the guise of an artisan. Sometimes, like the Egyptian Khnum, he was the Potter, Bumba or Ru-bumbi, but more often the Joiner or Fixer, who put the world together as a man hafts a tool or sets up the frame of a hut. The two names that have the widest distribution in east-central and west-central Africa respectively, Mu-lungu and Ka-lunga, are both derived from the ancestral Bantu verb-root *-lung-* (or *-dung-*), signifying 'lash together' (see Notes on language, p. xii above).[4] From this notion probably comes the Ganda (and Nyoro) adjective -*lungi*, meaning 'well constructed', hence both 'beautiful' and 'good'. African thought is at once realist and optimistic: God is the maker of things as they are, but on the whole he has done his work well.

Other names of God current in the area just to the south of Nalubaale, Katabi (Katai) and Ngasa (Nyangasa, Mugasa), contains verbs with a very similar concrete meaning. But the appellations of the Creator in the Lakeland itself mostly derive from the verb *-panga*, which seems to have meant 'to haft'. By regular processes of phonetic change the original Bantu word had become -hanga in the Nyoro language and -wanga in Ganda. So the Nyoro generally called God Ru-hanga, Hangi or Nya-mu-hanga, while the usual Ganda forms were Mu-wanga or (Sse-)-r-wanga. It is, however, one of the prerogatives of the High God that he alone can dispense with a grammatical prefix; and so Wanga is revealed as the basic form of his Ganda name.

If this was not immediately obvious, even to writers and story-tellers at the beginning of the century, it was because less attention was paid to the Creator in Buganda than in most other places. Perhaps the *kabaka* was reluctant to acknowledge any superior power – though in the equally monarchical society of Rwanda the supreme deity, there called Imana, was omnipresent and served to reinforce rather than weaken the royal authority. But whatever the reason, the centre of the religious stage was occupied by the polytheistic *lubaale* cult, whose mediums offered more practical help and solace.[5] Many of the 'spirits' in whose names the mediums spoke were in fact titles or attributes of the High God, who had, so to speak, been broken up in order that he might be more effectual. When the missionaries enquired about the concept of divinity they were supplied with the name Katonda, which does mean 'creator' but seems to have belonged to a minor cult figure before it was used to translate the Christian 'God'. The same applied to the various derivatives of the -*wanga* stem. Thus a Nyoro scholar noted with surprise and some contempt that 'the Ganda call Ruhanga "Muwanga" and are possessed by him'.[6] (For him, the High God should have been above the vulgar practices of mediumship.) The simple form of the name, Wanga, was included in the *lubaale* family (sometimes as the 'father' of Muwanga!), but was much less well known. And so it was possible for storytellers to come up with the idea of Wanga as a human wonder-worker and to reuse the myth of the Creation in the context of an eclipse.

Other traces of the story's true meaning survive in the bare anecdotal version that found its way into Kaggwa's typescript. When the sun fell at Bakka King Jjuuko was staying at Wagaba, a high ridge across the valley to the west. The name Wa-gaba is based on the same stem as the alternative divine name Ru-gaba or Kye-ba-gaba, and can thus be rendered as 'the hill of God'. And Jjuuko himself may not always have been the seventeenth-century king that a literal reading of the official history would make him.

We have seen that the (Nilotic) Lwo language has contributed to the formation of the Ganda vocabulary. Now the Lwo term for divinity is Juok, and that would easily become Jjuuko on the lips of Bantu speakers, who must have a vowel at the end of every word. Later it will be shown that there is also a quite different explanation for the name of Jjuuko, and this may help to explain why the story of the Creation should have been located in the middle of Buganda's history and not at its beginning.

Meanwhile we have to ask why the world should have begun at Bakka, a place of no special importance in nineteenth-century Buganda. It was then the home of Walusimbi, chief and father of the Civet-cat clan, one of the more prominent of the totemic groupings but not one that had any special status or recent royal associations. However, members of this clan are recorded as having held the office of *katikkiro*, chief minister, in many of the early reigns; and in particular Walusimbi himself – that is to say, a bearer of that hereditary title – was *katikkiro* to the second king, Cwa, who was himself significantly surnamed Na-bakka, 'lord of Bakka'. Walusimbi acted as regent for a time after Cwa had 'disappeared'; and some authorities go further and identify him with the shadowy figure called Ntege who is said to have ruled in Buganda before the coming of the kings. According to Michael Nsimbi, 'the ancestor of the Civet clan is Buganda-Ntege-Walusimbi . . . They say that when Kintu came to Buganda Walusimbi was on his hill at Bakka and ruled all the clan chiefs who were in Buganda.'[7]

There is also a story that God (Kyebagaba) sent the Moon to inspect and report on Walusimbi's government. Jealous of this commission, the Sun followed him down and a fight ensued, in which the Moon got the bruises or mud splashes that still disfigure him.[8] As it stands, this cannot be a primordial tale, for it assumes a hierarchical administration such as that of nineteenth-century Buganda, with the Moon playing the part of a *mutongole* in the celestial service. But it is all the more striking that it features a local clan chief, not the *kabaka*, as God's viceroy on earth. We have to suppose that it had been adapted from an earlier tale, which, moreover, was firmly linked with Walusimbi's domain. For the name Bakka means 'they go down', a clear allusion to the visitation of the sun and the moon.

Taken together, the two cosmic fantasies show that there were minds in Buganda that were prepared to speculate imaginatively about the origins of heaven and earth, but also that such genesis myths were not told in a historical vacuum. They betray an awareness that Bakka was the oldest centre of kingship in the country, or the one that had the best claim to have been the nucleus of the historic Ganda state. They thus help us to redefine the main historical problem: how and when did kingship pass from Bakka, or how and when did the holder of the Walusimbi title cease to be the ruler of the land? But first we must ask what kind of polity he may have presided over.

Let us anticipate later discussion and assert that, to judge from the distribution of ritual locations and the neighbourhood of other, apparently separate systems, it was a quite tiny country, bounded by the Mayanja Wasswa on the north and east, the stream Nonve on the south and the district called Bukerekere on the west: something like twenty square miles in all. Even many centuries ago there could have been fifty to a hundred people to the square mile in this rich land, which in the present century has supported several times as many. And a population of between one and two thousand would have been enough to provide a surplus for the king and his family and a few attendants. The French anthropologist J.-C. Muller has described the 'divine kings' of Nigerian villages with populations ranging down from two thousand to fifty persons.[9] Some will probably find it absurd that such entities should be called 'kingdoms'. Surely they were chiefdoms at the most? But that depends on what one thinks a king is for.

Luc de Heusch, penetrating analyst of Bantu myth and ritual, has pointed out that much discussion of African history has been vitiated by failure to notice the difference between 'state' and 'kingship'.[10] Behind this error is the prevalent schema of political evolution that makes human societies progress at varying speeds from 'tribe' through 'chiefdom' to the culminating glory of a 'state', of which 'kingdoms' are a rather primitive form. But a king is not in reality a man of power and kingship is far older than organised government – even of the sort of government which is headed by a 'chief'. We in late twentieth-century Britain have almost daily notice of a monarchy whose real meaning does not lie in its residual constitutional functions but in the performance of very basic rituals – coronations, weddings, jubilees, funerals – which give shape and meaning to the people's own amorphous lives and assure them that they are part of a continuing story. And it is well understood that the survival, or rather the revival, of 'sacred' kingship in Britain is a function of the electronic media, which give the population of a large state the illusion of participation in royal events.* Before the invention of these devices, a kingdom not only might be but had to be extremely small; for it could not work unless most of the people were present at the rituals that were the reason for its existence.

* I have let stand these words from a draft of 1990, though it has since become clear that the mass media, which created twentieth-century kingship, will also destroy it. For the essence of the institution is that the sacred persons are secluded from view except on the great ritual occasions, but the British public now insists on observing them day by day, and night by night.

The great Lakeland states, as scholars have long recognised, grew out of much smaller 'toparchies', such as survived between them, on their edges and even inside them into the present century. Within Rwanda, for example, there were several semi-autonomous kinglets, of which the best known was the 'ruler' of Busozo, described by the White Fathers as a 'a living relic', a 'fossilised puppet', kept in aseptic seclusion until the time came for his son to assume the burdens of sacrality.[11] Yet in these 'obsolete and rustic' courts, centres for a few thousand people, it was easy to recognise the ritual and ideology of the great military state of Rwanda with its million or more subjects and its complex hierarchies of power. The 'mascot' king of Busozo bore the same title, *mwami*, as his mighty overlord. The term recurs in the small communities on the further side of the Western Rift, and along with it there is sometimes the title *mu-bake*, a simple variant of the Ganda *ka-baka*.[12] Some of these peoples of eastern Zaire are closely related to the Rwanda in language and culture; others, such as the Nyanga, have a markedly different kind of Bantu speech. Yet it is, as we shall see (pp. 131–5), the Nyanga, a people numbering some 30,000 in the 1950s but divided among several kingdoms, who have preserved the most elaborate and illuminating of all myths of kingship.

On the opposite, eastern fringe of the Lakeland complex there were similar, though even less imposing, expressions of the monarchical idea. The fragmented Luyia-speaking Bantu communities of western Kenya are usually described as 'acephalous' or 'chiefless'; yet in most of the little local groups there was a man set apart, treated with deference, distinguished by a fly-whisk, by a copper bracelet and often by a decorated headdress known as a *lu-simbi*.[13] Similar adornments, with a related name, *n-shembe*, occurred among the people of the western fringe; and they are clearly the origin of the Ganda title Wa-lu-simbi. (Wa- is an additional prefix, conveying the notions of personality and special status.) In modern Ganda *n-simbi* are cowrie shells (and by extension money). And since these occur only on the shores of the Indian Ocean and were not thought to have been introduced to the Lakeland until the nineteenth century, it has been assumed that the title of Walusimbi (though not his office) must be a recent invention. In fact, a few cowries have now been found in archaeological sites dated to the first half of the millennium. More important, the word really denoted shells in general, as witness the Rwandan mountain Ka-ri-simbi, named for the fossil shells, residue of an ancient lake shore, that litter its base. Indeed the word may have had the still wider meaning of 'ornament', embracing beads and feathers as well.

The wide distribution of such words and features suggests that small-scale ritual kingship was very old in and around the Lakeland, as scholars had already sensed in the 1930s. How old it was they had no means of knowing; but there is now powerful reason to believe that it goes back to the beginning of the Early Iron Age, at least two thousand years ago and possibly more. The pottery of the distinctive kind produced in that era has been found in sites traditionally linked with kings – in fact with kings hitherto thought to have reigned only a few generations ago.[14] And the quality of the ceramic output, as of the associated metallurgy, indicates that it was made by specialist craftsmen, not for common use but at the behest of privileged people. Linguistic evidence points in the same direction. There is at least one word for a holder of politico-religious office, (*mu*)*kumu*, that certainly goes back to the beginning of Bantu speech, and others such as *mw-ami* and *mu-langira* that are shared by quite distant members of the Bantu family. Thus the monarchical institution appears to have been part of the cultural package that came to eastern, central and southern Africa along with Bantu linguistic forms. Indeed the chief, as Europeans generally preferred to call him, was a normal feature of recent pre-colonial Bantu societies, as he was not among the speakers of Nilotic or Sudanic languages. However narrow and feeble it might be, his authority was rarely absent, and only some mountain-dwellers near the northern edge of the Bantu domain, such as the Kikuyu, the Gisu of Mt Elgon and the Kiga to the north of Rwanda had been able to escape from it or to dispense with it altogether.

It is commonly suggested that the precursors of states in the Lakeland and elsewhere in Bantu Africa were 'clan-chiefdoms', which were persuaded or coerced into forming larger unions under a single head. The term implies a community consisting wholly or mainly of kinsfolk, the chief being simply the senior lineage elder; and there is again an evolutionist assumption of normal progress from kinship politics to proper politics. This model does not fit the postulated ancient kingdom of Bakka. Walusimbi, it is true, was the head of a clan; but at least three other clans – Mushroom, Colobus Monkey and Frog – had their principal estates nearby and played crucial roles in the royal ritual.[15] Small though it was, the kingdom was already complex in structure. Indeed, it is essential to the concept of the sacred king that he should stand above and outside the ordinary ties of kinship.

Ritual, it is here maintained, was the beginning of kingship, but at an early date other functions were attached to it. The very sacredness of the king made him a suitable performer of varied social roles, as the micro-polities on the recent fringes of the Lakeland show. These little entities were not states, for the people at their head possessed no significant coercive powers. Some did act as war leaders, but only in the sense that they gave the signal for campaigns and perhaps magically ensured their successful outcome. Some made rain for their people – or, as was sometimes needful in these humid countries, stopped it. But the role most commonly ascribed to them is that of judge, or rather arbiter or, still better, mediator of disputes. Some early kings (not in Buganda) are said to have identified themselves in childhood by being good at settling their play-mates' quarrels. East of the Lake, some Luyia and Gisu communities which had dispensed with hereditary heads selected a boy with that kind of character to be their nominal leader. Often they called him the *mu-gasa*, 'the fixer', elsewhere a title of God but here signifying the architect of the consensus that was always Africa's political ideal.

There is reason to think that economic uses were also found for the sacred person. Jacques Maquet has persuasively argued, for example, that the kings and chiefs of the savanna were above all controllers of the granaries,[16] organisers of the reserve food stocks which, as in Joseph's Egypt, gave the people a chance of survival when the rains failed. It is easy to see that this role at the centre of communal exchange could in some circumstances give the king opportunities for exploitation, especially when long-distance trade brought in new commodities that he could distribute or withhold. Many, indeed, have seen foreign commerce as the principal catalyst of state formation, inasmuch as a strategically placed ruler could either organise exports himself or levy toll on merchants, and so could acquire the resources with which to hire servants and enforcers. Very few doubt that the export of gold had something to do with the rise of Great Zimbabwe. The theory is very plausible, but if it purports to explain the origin of power, and not merely its expansion, it contains an obvious flaw: it presupposes that people with some kind of power already existed. The original source, it is suggested, can only have been ritual performance; and so the 'religion' and 'trade' theories of African state-building[17] are not opposed but complementary.

The Lakeland never had any gold to speak of, but it did have abundant supplies of ivory, the second most valuable of the pre-colonial exports from eastern Africa. And work done recently at Ntusi has revealed an ivory workshop and imported glass and cowrie beads, which prove trading contacts with the coast in the thirteenth century.[18] But whether the exchanges were large enough in volume or early enough in date to explain the apparent concentration of power at Ntusi and Bigo remains very uncertain. On the other hand the accumulative role of kings is amply attested. It might have been supposed that in the fertile and well-watered Lakeland, and especially in Buganda, there would have been little need for a royal store-keeper, at any rate after the coming of the banana. And yet the titles of Lakeland kings point clearly to this as the most important of their early roles. The verb *-gaba*, 'distribute' or 'apportion', which we have seen to yield names of God, also gave rise to *mu-gabe*, title of the king of Nkore, and *mu-gabe-kazi*, 'female king', the queen-mother of Rwanda. But more often the allusion is to the other aspect of the social exchange process. Mukama, title of the king of Bunyoro, means or could mean 'the Milker', and has been taken to refer to pastoral domination of the agricultural masses. Much more likely, however, it implies that the king is the one who 'milks' his people. Even this indirect allusion to cattle-keeping may not have been present originally, for *-kama* meant 'squeeze' in general before it was specialised to the squeezing of udders. The more widespread term *mw-ami* is similar, for it probably derives from *-ama*, 'suck' – which is no doubt related to *-kama* in the prehistory of the language. And the Ganda title *kabaka* belongs to the same set of ideas. It has often been linked with *mu-baka*, 'envoy' and used to support the hypothesis that Buganda began its career as a province or client of Bunyoro. The hypothesis, as we shall see, may not be entirely false, but etymology does not support it. *Mu-baka* and *ka-baka* do both derive from *-baka*, to 'grab' or 'grasp'. But whereas a *mubaka* is one who grips the message staff, the *kabaka* is he who grabs his people's wealth, as the *sa-ka-baka*, the sparrowhawk, seizes its prey. Many proverbs in and around Buganda compare the king with the queen bee or the queen ant, whose accumulation is the sole object of their subjects' lives. Such things were not said in a revolutionary spirit, but with a kind of wry acceptance. Government is expensive but it is also necessary. That, however, is the philosophy of the large state. In the little 'mascot' kingdoms, and we may fairly assume in their Early Iron Age predecessors, exchange was less one-sided; and such tribute as the king received from his people was paid for with very onerous obligations, the nature of which will become clearer as the analysis of myth proceeds.

Meanwhile the brief account of Wanga's miracle has shown, not that a king called Jjuuko ruled Buganda in AD 1680 (or that he did not), but more interestingly that a *kabaka*, a man whose ritual headdress set him apart from his people, probably lived on the slopes of Bakka hill in the first millennium of our era, and conceivably in the first millennium BC.

There are perhaps much longer vistas even than that. At Kadero just north of Khartoum Polish archaeologists have discovered a cemetery belonging to the people who lived there before 4000 BC and were, on present showing, the earliest food producers in sub-Saharan Africa, certainly tending cattle and goats and probably experimenting with the cultivation of various cereals. Most of the graves were plain and poor but a few, set apart from the rest, were richly furnished, with decorated potsherds, a porphyry mace-head – surely an emblem of authority – and a diadem of marine shells.[19] The gulf of space and time that separates these finds even from the Early Iron Age of the Lakeland is enormous and almost empty of evidence, and to suggest any connection is to defy the current scholarly paradigm, which insists on autochthonous processes of development. Yet it cannot be ignored that here, six thousand years ago, midway between Buganda and the Egyptian and Near Eastern centres of Neolithic culture, there was a *Walusimbi*, Lord of the Shells.

Man and Woman

After the Creation comes the Fall, or so one would expect. But Genesis 3 is older in fact than Genesis 1; and the most ancient and highly charged question is not how the natural world came into being but why human life is what it is. The answer always takes a historical form: life was once otherwise, but there was a primal event that converted it into the laborious and finite existence that we know. For some Lakeland priests and poets, this event was literally a fall out of heaven,[20] but more commonly the process was reversed. It is God who retreated to the sky, leaving humankind to its own devices. It comes to the same thing, of course. The first happening causes disjunction and polarity. Earth and sky, man and God, the mortal and immortal realms are irreversibly sundered and set apart. In a real sense the Creation and the Fall are one and the same event.

The first story to come out of Buganda in written form, recorded by H. M. Stanley in 1875, seemed to combine both these themes; for it told how the 'patriarch' Kintu first came into the world and then left it, being disgusted by the drunken violence of his descendants.[21] In this tale Kintu is the familiar African character called 'the withdrawn High God', and there is even another account of how he appointed Sun and Moon to their offices in the cosmic state.[22] Now this is odd, for, to judge by his name Kintu is not God but Man, in the sense of human person. There has been much confusion over this point, because Ganda has a common noun *kintu* which means 'thing' in most of the English senses of the word, and commentators have struggled to explain why the founder of Buganda should have been so named. But the prefix *ki-*, which often introduces the names of material objects, has other functions as well, and one is to give an honorific or generalising meaning to the idea contained in the stem, corresponding in some ways to the use of an initial capital in English. Thus it is often found in the titles of office-holders, such as Ki-tunzi, Ki-baale, Ki-ambalango (the Wearer of the Leopard-skin) and in the names of divinities. *Mu-wanuka*, if there were such a word, would be simply 'one who descends' but Ki-wanuka is 'He Who Descends', the power manifest in the lightning. So whereas *mu-ntu* is a human being Ki-ntu is the archetype of the human condition.

To Europeans it is anomalous that Kintu should be depicted as God (and

English missionary versions of the tale about his celestial government replaced him with Gulu, 'Heaven' or 'the Lord of all'.[23] African religious thought, however, being profoundly humanistic, did not consistently distinguish between the Creator and the First Man. It does not really matter whether the character who ends up in the now inaccessible land beyond the sky is called God or Man, provided that he is finally separated from us who have to live below. All the same, it is appropriate that the best-known Ganda version of the story of Man should have reversed the sequence, causing him to visit the sky but return in the end to middle-earth. This tale has often been discussed, most perceptively by Benjamin Ray;[24] but it is such a crucial piece of Ganda mythology that it must figure prominently here as well – and a good story can always bear retelling. It was a very popular tale in late nineteenth-century Buganda, and several versions got into print. It was published in a fragmentary form by the missionaries Wilson and Felkin in 1882,[25] more fully by Sir Harry Johnston in 1902[26] and three times by Canon Roscoe between 1901 and 1911,[27] as well as by other missionaries.[28] Apolo Kaggwa referred to it only briefly in his historical book but placed it at the head of his collection of Ganda tales or legends, *Ngero za Baganda*. However, as noted earlier, verbal echoes show that he derived it, not directly from tradition, but from a Catholic language manual.[29] It is this story that will be presented here, as fully as is necessary to convey its real character.

Kintu, it tells us, came into this land (*mu nsi muno*, which could also be rendered, 'into this world') and lived here utterly alone. He had one cow with him, and he ate its dung and drank its urine, and that was how he lived. (This statement caused some difficulty for British reporters. Roscoe wrote discreetly that 'he lived on what the cow provided him with', but Johnston bowdlerised it further, saying that he drank the cow's milk, and thus removed much of the story's meaning. At this stage, being without society, the hero was a non-person, not yet truly Ki-ntu, and therefore ate non-food.) But then Nambi, daughter of Heaven, came down with her brothers and they saw the man (*musajja*, man as distinct from woman) and they asked him where he came from and he said he had no idea. Then Nambi said to her brothers: 'I'm in love with this man and I want to marry him.' Her brothers exclaimed: 'You're in love with him! How do you know he's a man [*muntu*, man as distinct from beast]'? Nambi replied: 'I'm sure he's human. Does an animal build a house?' So she went straight up to Kintu and announced that she meant to marry him.

Her uninhibited wooing would have been highly improper in the real world of Buganda, but even in myth the woman has to get her father's consent, and this was not at first forthcoming. Gulu ('Heaven') ruled that Kintu must first be tested to see if he could live without his cow, and so the sky-children were sent down to steal it while he was asleep. Nambi was loud in protest: 'You can't do this to my darling Kintu! How will he live? He will die of hunger and thirst! You may not like him but I do!' So she went down again, found him subsisting on bark and brought him up to the sky-country. There he had to satisfy his prospective father-in-law by performing a series of impossible tasks – consuming enormous quantities of food, splitting rocks with a copper axe, filling a jar with dew, finally picking out his cow from Gulu's countless herd. All this he managed to do, by trickery and with the help of friendly creatures. Eventually father-Sky had to concede both the cow and his daughter, but warned them to go quickly, before her brother Walumbe got to know about it. So the couple set off for earth very early in the morning, taking also goats and fowls and a banana sucker; but when they were halfway down they found they had forgotten the millet-seed for the chickens, and Kintu had to go back for it.

Something is clearly wrong here. Chickens in Buganda fend for themselves and certainly do not have sacks of precious grain humped about for them. The story has evidently been refracted through the European mind of the priest-recorder. That Kaggwa should have echoed the statement is an example of the potency of writing; once a story has become a text it is likely to be repeated by Africans as it stands, complete with obvious errors. What the story really said, of course, was that Kintu and Nambi brought millet seeds from the sky in order to sow them. Lévi-Strauss has shown that myths of the transition from nature to culture normally have an alimentary code: eating proper food – cooked or cultivated or both – is an essential part of becoming human. Now that he has ceased to be solitary Kintu will no longer eat dung and drink urine. It is a commonplace of Lakeland mythology that the hero learns from a woman to drink milk, which had hitherto been unknown or repugnant to him; and although it is not spelt out in this tale we may assume that Nambi taught Kintu what cows, as well as women, were really for. The theft of the cow signified that Kintu, the developing human male, was being freed from dependence on his mother in order that he might acquire a wife. He was a boy in the limbo of latency, no longer having access to the breast but not yet fit for the adult kind of access to a woman, and so still undeserving of his name. To become 'Kintu' is to grow up, for in African thought children, being asexual, are not truly human beings. So Kintu's progress from urine to milk is one of a series of equivalent transitions, which also take him from innocence to sexuality and from isolation to society.

The Ganda, however, did not drink much milk, and Nambi would have had to provide him with vegetable food as well. Now millet (*Eleusine coracana*, known to the Ganda as *bulo*) also played a rather minor part in their diet in recent times. So the story must have taken shape either before the coming of the banana or in another country.[30] Close variants of it do occur in Bunyoro and Nkore, where millet was a staple food.[31] On the other hand the evidence of folk-tales suggests that millet fields were once a standard feature in Buganda too.[32] In the extant tale the couple brought bananas as well as millet from the sky. This does not mean that the Ganda remember the introduction of this exotic plant any more than stories of the origin of cows or of milk-drinking supply clues to the origin of Lakeland pastoralism. It signifies on the contrary that they cannot imagine civilised life without the groves, all descended from the one celestial root.

For civilised life and for adulthood there is a price to pay. When Kintu got back to his father-in-law's home Walumbe was indeed waiting for him and did insist on accompanying him to earth. And Wa-lumbe is none other than Death, for which the ordinary word is (o)lumbe. So Kintu returned from heaven with his bride and his cow and his inescapable affine, and life on earth began. Crops grew, children were born. But Death asked for one to be his servant, and when Kintu refused he said that he would kill them. Kintu did not know what he meant, but soon his children began to sicken and die, as the children of man have been doing ever since.

That was really the end of the story, but most versions add a kind of epilogue. Nambi complained bitterly about Walumbe to her father, who sent his elder son Kayiikuzi to arrest him. But Death, once established on earth, could not so easily be removed. He took refuge in some deep shafts (probably old gypsum workings) at a place called Ttanda or Ntanda, which was thought to be the entrance to the underworld. Kayiikuzi ('the Digger') prepared to drive him out and ordered everyone to stay indoors and keep quiet. Despite this, some children were allowed out to play, and when the terrible figure emerged from the pit they cried out in fear, and he went underground again and the chance was lost. Kayiikuzi then said he was exhausted and could do no more. And Kintu replied: 'Very well, go home. Let Death go on killing my children if he must. I, Man, will go on begetting them, and never will he be able to make an end of us.' In that famous affirmation (echoed in the popular saying, 'Kintu's children did not all perish') 'Man' includes 'Woman' and the word rendered as 'beget' also means 'give birth'. What is celebrated is the vitality of the human species.

Kaggwa, who recognised the parallel with Adam and Eve, blamed Nambi for the carelessness that brought death into the world, and Roscoe went further, accusing her of being the 'source of all evil, sickness and death'.[33] But, as Ray points out, this anti-feminine message seems to be absent from the earliest version, in which the couple share the responsibility for the forgotten millet and it is Kintu, not Nambi, who returns, against orders, to the sky and so gives Death his chance. Nevertheless Kaggwa's version does accord with countless African tales, which in one way or

another attribute our mortality to the malice, carelessness or inquisitive-
ness of a woman.[34] But the tone of voice in which this was said is not the
Christian one. It was St Paul who first took seriously what had hitherto
been a purely formal possibility, namely that Adam could have refused the
apple and that his descendants could still do so.[35] True, if Nambi had not
forgotten the millet seed we would not have had to die; but she did, and we
do. Such stories were really a kind of joke – as the story of Eden is now
treated by most people. 'You know what women are like' (boys were told) –
'forgetful, nosey, sometime spiteful creatures. But they have redeeming
features and we cannot do without them.' If men could do without women
they would not be mortal, but if they were not mortal they would be lonely
dung-eating creatures unworthy of the name of Kintu. Neither in the
African myths nor, I believe, in the Hebrew one is there any suggestion that
the conduct of our first ancestors was avoidably sinful, or even really to be
regretted.

There is also an early version that ignores Nambi altogether.[36] Kintu, it
says, was a regular visitor to heaven, where he was well entertained and sent
away with a guest-gift, as the rules of Ganda hospitality require. He was,
however, strictly forbidden to return without an invitation. But one day the
hospitality was too lavish and he staggered off to earth without his gift, a
maize-cob. (This particular version is thus dated to the early or middle
nineteenth century, when maize was a new introduction and a great rarity.)
When he went back next day to collect it God was furious and appointed
Death to be his constant companion and custodian.

Between the story of Kintu and Nambi and that of Adam and Eve there
is only a general resemblance of theme and message. The Ganda myth is
actually more closely related to another Hebrew tale (Genesis 29–31),
featuring Jacob the father of the people of Israel, whom we last saw
cheating Lion out of his rightful kingship. After that dubious victory we
find him alone in the heart of Israel, and there 'he dreamt that he saw a
ladder, which rested on the ground with its top reaching to heaven'. Those
who compiled the biblical texts used this tradition as a cue for political and
theological pronouncements, and it is to the editors that we should ascribe
the literary device of the dream, a common way of dismissing mythical data
no longer understood. In the old tale the ladder really stood before Jacob
and he climbed it – what else would he do? – and so came, not to
Paddan-Aram as the rationalisers had it, but to the fields of heaven. There
he saw his cousin Rachel and at once performed an impossible task, rolling
the stone from the mouth of the well, a feat that had required the combined
strength of all the shepherds. Thereafter the duties laid on him were
mundane services; but the upshot was that he was at last able to set out for
home, accompanied by Rachel and also by the Cow – for that was the

meaning of Leah, the name of the dull-eyed woman he was obliged to take along with the beloved Rachel (meaning Ewe).

Before he left there was the curious episode of the division of his father-in-law's flocks. The account of this is rather confused, but the point is that Jacob ended up with striped and speckled and brindled sheep and goats, that is with animals that were both white and black. Laban, 'the White', had tried to reserve for himself 'all that had any white on them' but Jacob had foiled him, in one version with God's help and in another by magic. Now black is universally the colour of death.[37] In Sumer, for example, mortal men were regularly described by the gods as 'the black-headed people'. In Africa the symbolism preceded and had nothing to do with racist stereotypes. There, where all known men were naturally black, gods and other beings exempt from death were white (so that Europeans were initially regarded as undead spirits). But boys returning from the initiation camp were painted partly white, to show that they had passed through the valley of the shadow and were allowed to live, though not for ever. By the same token Jacob's ambiguous flocks tell us that his visit to the sky, like Kintu's, had won for mankind the gift of real though not everlasting life. The same symbolism accounts for the curious anomaly that Nambi, daughter of Heaven, is also described as a woman of the Colobus Monkey clan, a group of no other special distinction. The black and white fur of the colobus, a much-prized accoutrement, was also an apt emblem of our mortal life.

As the Esau story showed, Jacob was the ancestor of us all, not just of the tribes of Israel. And Rachel, the First Woman, naturally committed the primal fault. When she left her father's house she stole the sacred objects called the teraphim, thus ensuring that Laban would pursue them, as Death pursued Nambi. When he caught up with them she hid the objects by sitting on them and excused herself from rising on the plea that she was indisposed. Her misdeed had brought on her the Curse, the first of those monthly flows that Lévi-Strauss has shown to be the model for all periodicities and the beginning of human time.[38] The denouement was the same as in the Ganda tale: humankind was excluded for ever from the immortal realm. For Laban now marked the boundary between earth and heaven by a great stone that even Jacob would not be able to roll away. Some say that the stone has since been moved, but that is another story, belonging to a different mode of thought. For Africans, as for the ancient Hebrews, there could be no return to the sky-country that the first ancestors had left. In both cultures the Fall is the essential myth of genesis, establishing the most basic of all binary discriminations, which is between male and female. It was by this distinction that time was set in motion and the real world of hunger and work and death was brought into being.

Few people have ever seriously believed that the Garden of Eden existed in space and time. Jacob, however, was appropriated by Israelite patriots and made into a key figure of the national ideology; and it therefore became necessary to believe in his historical existence. As a result his ontological role was obscured, and Adam was probably introduced to perform it in his stead. In much the same way the Ganda, or some of them, came to think of Kintu not only as First Man but also and primarily as First King, founder of the state, progenitor not of all men but of the ruling lineage. But historians who are tempted to think that there must be some basis for that claim should heed the comment made by the eminent folklorist Sidney Hartland in 1912: 'It is obvious that [the story of Kintu and Walumbe] is a tradition of the beginning of things; and though the Baganda may have identified Kintu as their earliest king and assigned his wife to the Colobus Monkey clan, to accept such a rationalisation is hardly in the spirit of modern science.'[39] And in case it may be thought that science has changed its mind since Hartland's day, appeal may be made to a more recent authority, Georges Dumézil, whose remarks on the Roman diety Janus are very much to the point. Janus is the god of beginnings. As such, he appears in myth as the oldest of the gods; in ritual he presides over the opening of the day, the month, the year and the age; and in 'history' he assumes the guise of the first king of Latium. And Dumézil complains that 'from the mass of "firsts" that surround and illumine him the historicists extract the one "first" that . . . is couched in the reassuring language of their speciality and confer on it the privileged position of historical evidence'.[40]

Kintu stands at the intersection between popular storytelling and dynastic tradition, but it is to the former that he properly belongs. That much is clear from the provenance of the tales. Stanley heard about him through his Swahili caravan-leader Uledi, who had been listening to an 'old sweeper' during their stay at the capital. Johnston's version was one of a number of tales purchased from 'a peasant' at a rupee apiece. The content of the tales points in the same direction. Visits to the sky are common in the traditional literature of many lands, the English tale of Jacob and the Beanstalk being just one example. The Ganda version, moreover, makes use of themes well known to folklorists as 'the Giant's Daughter', 'the Impossible Tasks' and 'the Helpful Animals', which are also combined in the medieval Welsh tale of Kulhwch, the young kinsman of King Arthur, whose desire for the hand of Olwen, daughter of Ysbaddaden the Chief Giant, led him to essay a whole series of fantastic tasks with a great array of helpers.[41] Parallels of this sort are often treated dismissively by students of Africa. 'Folktale' elements', 'narrative clichés', '*Wandersagen*' are said to have infiltrated the tradition, decorating it with fantasy but without detriment to its basically historical character. But such themes and motifs cannot be treated as though they were detachable components devoid of serious meaning. The tale of Kintu puts the impossible tasks into their proper ontogenetic context, among the ways in which the hero is shown to have escaped from childhood. Indeed, the motif is probably derived from actual procedures of puberty initiation, in which the boys were ordered to do absurd things and then shown the tricks by which they could pretend to do them. By virtue of its better-preserved structure the African tale gives point and purpose to stories which in their biblical and European 'folklore' versions had become trivial and unmeaning, and it must therefore be closer to a very ancient prototype. Kintu's folk-tale traits were intrinsic to him and cannot be subtracted.

Moreover, Kintu and Nambi were by no means the exclusive property of Buganda but belonged to a ramifying network of African myths that could undoubtedly be subjected, by those who have the skill, to a rewarding structuralist analysis. Here only a few of the simplest linkages can be pointed out.

Kayiikuzi is not identified in the Ganda tale, but in other Lakeland accounts of the hunting of Death, which are many, the not-quite-successful pursuer is the Lightning.[42] And in a vast number of stories, African and other, the adversary of the Lightning is the Rainbow, conceived as a monstrous serpent that rears out of the waters of the earth.[43] According to some of the Mundang people of Chad a python lives under the royal granary and when it shows itself in the courtyard the king is about to die.[44] It is thus likely that Walumbe, who emerges from his underground lair to seize the children of Man, was originally pictured by the Ganda as a python, as he certainly was next door in Busoga.[45] Na-mbi took her name from ancient African words related to motherhood; and she has close kinswomen in Mumbi the great mother of the Kikuyu and in Mumbi Mukasa, the goddess or ancestress of the Bemba people in Zambia. What is more, Mumbi Mukasa is said to have had elephant's ears,[46] and this peculiar trait has echoes in Buganda. Nambi herself has the odd nickname Na-ntuttululu, 'Lady of the earhole', and in one version of the story Kintu's wife is called simply Matu, 'Ears'.[47] Now there are variants that show Kintu not as a solitary herdsman, but as a solitary hunter. That was how he came to have animal helpers, whom he had been kind enough to set free from his traps. And some say that the great change in his life came when he found that he had ensnared a much stranger creature, the woman who would be his bride.[48] This version supplies a link with another tale which does not name Kintu or Nambi at all. It concerns a hunter who finds in his trap a woman with enormous ears. She promises him that if he will take her home he will have wealth beyond his dreams, provided only that he never mentions her peculiarity. Sure enough, his herds multiply overnight and a splendid house springs up and is filled with servants. But there comes a day when one of his sons is provoked into being rude about the woman's ears. At once she vanishes and so do all his cattle and all his other goods, and the poor man is back where he began.[49]

This group of tales is in turn transformed by another, about a man whose cows breed incessantly although he has no bull, the secret being that a star comes down at night to serve them. But one of his wives is curious and spies on the bull-star at its work. Immediately the cows scatter over the horizon and normal poverty returns.[50] Clearly these groups are structural inversions. In one, the source of prosperity is a woman who is not of middle-earth and the ruinous fault is committed by a man. In the other the celestial benefactor is male and woman reverts to her usual role of inquisitive destroyer. The message is one and the same. The fatal secret is the truth about the real world. In the old time a man might have a star in the cowshed and a goddess in the kitchen, but easy abundance is not now the lot of humankind. As Lévi-Strauss has shown, it matters little whether a story describes the adventures of a mortal man in the sky or of an immortal woman on the earth, whether the sons of God mate with the daughters of men (as in Genesis 6:1–2) or the daughter of heaven with the earthly man. The point is that such things happened before the Flood but cannot happen now.

Kintu returns under his own name but in an unfamiliar role in a story that belongs to the great 'Cwezi' mythological cycle and was recorded by Père Césard in Ihangiro, a small kingdom on the west side of Nalubaale.[51] One night a jackal ran through the court of King Wamara and in the morning he went out to hunt it with his chiefs Irungu and Mugasa, members of the Cwezi pantheon hardly less prominent than himself. This prelude strikingly recalls the opening scene of an Arthurian romance,[52] and the sequel reveals the country into which the knights' quests really led them. The hunters followed the animal into a tunnel and found themselves in a strange land, the realm of Kintu, who impounded their dogs but received them kindly and sent them home laden with gifts. Mugasa (who is the god of the Lake, provider of rain and patron of cultivators) thus acquired crop plants (it seems that the Cwezi had lived by the chase alone) and Wamara received cattle, including a very special white cow. Kintu stipulated that a return gift should be sent to him, but when he got home Wamara forgot this obligation. At last Kintu sent Death, here called Rufu, to claim his due. Received by Wamara with violence, the emissary took refuge in an inner room, where a servant-girl saved him. The good Father Césard tells us that at this point his pen refused to write, but from other tales of the hunting of Death we know that she hid him in her body, so that thereafter all who came out from there would bear Death's mark. So Rufu escaped, seized the white cow and drove it into a swamp; and the king, mad with grief, plunged in after it, followed by all his people. This is perhaps the best of the many tales told in south-west Uganda and north-west Tanzania to explain why the Cwezi gods, like the High God before them, have disappeared from middle-earth. Wamara and his kinsmen were never seen again as living beings, but from time to time they return in spirit to possess their chosen vessels.

The story is by now a familiar one, showing once again that the price of food and culture is mortality. The white cow is lent, not given, and in the end must return whence it came. To this is added the usual wry comment that death might nevertheless have been eliminated if it had not been for the treachery of woman, who binds men to the cycle of generation and decay. But there is one rather strange innovation: Wamara, who figures in cosmology as the lord of the underworld, here enacts the role of mortal man, while 'Man' is presented as the king of the land of the dead. A variant, recorded close by in Kiziba, allots the roles in more normal fashion. Here it is a son of Kintu whose quest leads him below the earth and the ruler he meets there is Rugaba, God himself. Kintu's greed is inflamed by the cows and the millet that his son brings back as guest-gifts, so he invades Rugaba's country and carries off his herd by force; and it is because of that outrage by our first parent that sickness and death have been the lot of the children of Man.[53] However, the Ihangiro tale is a proper mythical inversion. It shows how the king of darkness, like the Walumbe of the Ganda, came to take up his permanent abode; and symmetry requires that Man should take his place in the land of fleeting light.

Finally, the Ganda have a tale about a lad called Mpoobe who pursued a cane-rat into a burrow and so came into the land of death. He was allowed to go home laden with possessions on condition that he told no one of their source. But he did tell his mother (the person of all others who should have been left in the dark) and Death came to claim him. He pleaded successfully that he should first be allowed to enjoy his wealth. Several times Death returned and went away, but at last everything had been consumed and Mpoobe had to depart into the darkness.[54]

Mpoobe is the hero of a *lugero*, a mere tale, and he makes no pretension to historical existence. But Kintu does, and we shall have to ask why and when he came to make it and what he may yet be able to tell us about Buganda's real past. But the condition of that enquiry is that his mythical personality be examined in its own right; and that task is not yet complete.

Man and beast

Kintu settled with Nambi at Magonga in Busujju county, where the priest Mwanje would keep his shrine in later times. But after a while he decided to go on a tour of his dominion, leaving his deputy Kisolo in charge of what had now become a royal household. When he returned he found that Kisolo had invented agriculture, turning inedible wild bananas into proper bananas and useless legumes into other familiar food crops. (Do not object that Kintu and Nambi had brought a banana plant and millet seed from the sky; that was a different story.) But it appeared that the deputy had been busy in other ways as well, for Kintu saw that Nambi 'had a womb that he had not left her with', and when he questioned her she referred him to 'the old man'. So he asked Kisolo: 'Why didn't you tell me about this when I came home last night?' Kisolo replied: 'I didn't want to trouble you when you were tired.' It is clear that, just as in the previous tale Kintu had not known what Death was on about, so now he did not understand what had happened. How could he when it was the first time that it had ever happened? All the same he was angered by what seemed an evasive answer, so he picked up a spear and wounded Kisolo in the foot. And this was the first time that anything like *that* had happened. The chiefs in council rebuked him for his primal violence, and he sent messengers to conciliate his aggrieved deputy, who had fled from the court. Kisolo at first agreed to come back, but then, seeing the smoke of bush-burnings in the distance, he inferred that Kintu still meant to kill him, and so he gave his escort the slip and limped off into the bush.[55]

And there, in the bush, he still remains. For the name Ki-solo stands in the same relation to the common noun *n-solo*, meaning 'wild animal', as Ki-ntu to *mu-ntu*, 'human being'. Only this explanation makes sense of the motif of the bush fires, which are lit partly to drive the game for the hunters to kill. So the outcome of the story, as of the tales of Acunga and Esau, was the estrangement of men and beasts. It informs us about the end of the age of innocence, when man could live with nature in amity and peace – and without death. Kisolo cursed his master, saying: 'For as much as you have struck me without cause, you will look for me and not see me [a euphemism for death] and you too will not remain long in this land.' And soon afterwards Kintu vanished from the world.

None of this meaning was apparent to Apolo Kaggwa, who rehearsed the story briefly in *The Kings of Buganda* and more fully in his *Bika bya Buganda*, his history of the clans of Buganda. He presented it simply as a scandalous incident in the early history of the royal house, and probably as an example to kings of how not to behave to their chief ministers. (In one version he described Kisolo not as *musigire*, 'deputy', but as *katikkiro*, like himself.) But any such political interpretation was only a trivial gloss on what was really a version of the universal myth, showing that agriculture, procreation, violence and death came into the world together. In his first brief account Kaggwa suggested that Nambi had been guilty of misconduct, but in the fuller version it became clear that her pregnancy, the first of all pregnancies, was supernaturally contrived. Kisolo thus appears as the originator of fecundity, both vegetal and human. He was indeed also called Muwanga, 'the Creator', so that his disappearance can be seen as another way of talking about the withdrawal of the High God.

Nor was his activity confined to Buganda. Henry and Nora Chadwick noticed more than half a century ago that the Ganda stories of Kintu are echoed in the traditions of a geographically distant Bantu-speaking people, the Ila of Zambia.[56] In this rather meagrely recorded tale[57] a certain Mungalo came into the Ila country from the east with his daughter Chintu and his son Malumbe, a formidable magician who struck terror into the hearts of the people. That was hardly surprising, for, prefixes apart, Ma-lumbe is the same as the Ganda Wa-lumbe, who is Death; and 'Chintu' is pronounced almost exactly like the 'Kintu' of the Ganda. Now it is particularly remembered that Malumbe played *chisolo* (the African board-game) with a local chief called Munyama, after which he plunged into a pool. Like pit-shafts, pools are entrances to the land of the shades, so that the story ends with Malumbe, like his Ganda counterpart, taking up his permanent residence. Further, the name Mu-nyama is precisely analogous to Ki-solo, being a personalised form of the Ila word for (wild) animal, *nyama*. Thus the personnel of *both* the Ganda tales of Kintu were known to the Ila; and it follows that the tales were fragments of a single mythical complex.

There is something more. Chisolo, the Ila word for the board-game, is simply a variant spelling of Kisolo. Now animals are called *n-solo* by the Ganda and their immediate neighbours, but the word does not occur with this meaning in other Bantu languages; most of them, like the Ila, use the word *nyama* (or similar), the primary meaning of which is 'meat'. On the other hand, with the meaning of 'board-game' words based on the stem *-solo* (or *-soro*) are very widespread, and they are easily explained as deriving from the verb *-sora* (*-cod-*), meaning to 'pick out' or 'choose'. (The game consists of picking up seeds or pebbles from one compartment of the board and moving them to others, according to complicated rules, in such a way as to capture the opponent's pieces.) It appears, therefore, that the Kisolo of the Ganda myth did not get his name from an existing common noun *nsolo*. Instead, the Ganda began to call animals *nsolo* in allusion to their prototype Kisolo, 'the board-game player'. Myth, in other words, was once so much part of the life of the Ganda people that it had altered their everyday speech.

Clearly the board-game has a crucial place in the scheme of things, and it is not surprising that it should figure prominently in other Lakeland myths. It was for lack of skill at the game that Ryangombe, the great cult-deity of Rwanda, nearly lost the kingship of the spirits to a mysterious rival, being saved at the last by the precocious advice of his mysteriously begotten son Binego.[58] More to our present purpose, it was the occasion in Bunyoro for the separation of earth and heaven. The boy Kantu, son of Nkya (Dawn), was angry with his uncle Ruhanga, the Creator, because his three younger brothers had been given real names – Peasant, Herdsman, Ruler – while he had been left simply with a diminutive form of Kintu or Muntu, Man. So he set out to 'spoil things'; and to begin with he invented the game, got Ruhanga (the Artificer) to make the first board and challenged him to a contest. He cheated and won, and when his (unnamed) mother took his part in the ensuing quarrel Ruhanga climbed angrily to heaven, kicking away the posts that held the world together, so that the sky floated far away.[59] Thereafter Kantu is said to have 'come to' successive rulers of the land and caused them too to disappear.

Putting the Nyoro, Ganda and Ila myths together, as the philological and other links allow, we discover three propositions which are clearly meant to be related if not identical: Man defeats God at the *chisolo* game, and by implication brings about his own mortality; Man wounds Beast, the *chisolo*-player, with the same result; Death, the brother of Woman, defeats Beast at *chisolo*. It is clear that the actors fall into two camps. Man is on the side of Death; Beast, as we have already noted in Buganda, is equated with God. That was only proper, because animals, lacking the individual self-knowledge that is the distinctive human burden, have the apparent immortality of their species. The duck that swims on the lake this autumn may not be the one that was there last year, or a thousand years ago, but it might just as well be. The heroes of Amerindian and of Greek myths can usually escape from their dilemmas by turning into animals or stars, but Africans, like Hebrews, do not seem to have allowed themselves this recourse. Their myths show – in existential, not evolutionary terms – how Man separated himself from the immortal beasts.

The third term in these conflicts, their object or context, is either Woman or the *chisolo* game; and it is tentatively suggested that these concepts are also closely linked. For it would probably be agreed that games of skill or chance for two people are, among other things, symbols of or substitutes for sexual encounter. There is for example a remarkable Nigerian bronze sculpture that shows a man and woman sitting at the board-game, and behind them a strange beast which, according to the commentator, 'resembles Thurber's seal, but is probably a leopard'.[60] However, the artist was both naturalistic and highly skilled, and if he had wanted to show us a leopard he would have shown one. In fact his beast (like Thurber's seal) is a lightly disguised figuration of lust. The man, intent on his game, is pushing it away with a backward movement of his hand. It appears that the couple, who are not in their first youth, are using the game to fend off or to delay the onset of passion.

It has in fact been asserted that the African board-game, taken as a whole, 'is an allusion to marriage'.[61] If this equivalence is granted, the theme of sexuality is seen to be as salient in the 'Kisolo' set of tales as it is in the 'Nambi' set. This is again the capacity that deprives human beings of permanence. In Rwanda too Ryangombe won the game only by begetting a son, and the next episode in his mythical biography would show that he had thereby become mortal.

Kisolo of the Ganda still has more to tell us. It is curious that he who represents the animal kingdom as a whole is also held to be specifically the ancestor of the Otter clan, who in fact were responsible for preserving his story. Kintu for his part is claimed as ancestor by the Leopard clan; and that too is an anomaly, for as First Man he should be the progenitor of all the Ganda, while as First King he should be the ancestor only of the royal patriline, which stood outside the totemic system. His Leopard associations, as we shall see, are an important historical clue, but for the present it is their symbolic meaning that must concern us. The Leopard and the Otter clans both had their headquarters near the shrine of Kintu at Magonga, and the priest who tended it was chosen from the Leopard folk. The pairing of these totems is clearly not accidental. Otters are also swift, sinuous carnivores, and the local species, *lutra (hydrictis) maculicollis*, has spots on its neck and chest. It is thus a water-leopard, and a leopard is a land-otter. Now Kisolo is one of a large class of water-divinities who have suffered a wound in the lower limb. One of these lives close at hand. In the Cwezi mythology it is told how Mugasa (or Mukasa as the Ganda call him) was attacked by the young warrior-deity Kagoro and received a spear-wound in the knee, so that he has ever afterwards been lame.[62] It is clearly relevant that the otters of the Lake, which are numerous, sometimes have a white patch on the knee; also that Captain Grant was told in 1862 about a king of all the otters who lived in the Lake and was white[63] – in other words a deity. Mukasa, moreover, is the provider of both agricultural and human fertility, supplying children as well as rain to the people of the Lakeland; it is even said that, like Kisolo, he 'gave the human race the power of bearing offspring'.[64] Though it would be wrong to identify him with Kisolo the Otter there is obviously some connexion or overlap between these two mythical personages. And both have been wounded, one in the foot and the other in the knee.

The fight between Kagoro and Mugasa, which recurs in another mythical context, has some distant resonances. Since Kagoro is, on one level, the lightning and Mugasa is manifested in the storm-clouds, the anecdote can be seen as a simple nature-myth. We now know, however, that meteorology is only one of the codes in which a myth can express itself and enjoys no special privilege. We have also learnt that individual myths can be fully understood only as members of a set, and that to assemble the set it may be necessary to travel far afield.

Outside the domain of Bantu language, the fate of Kisolo–Mugasa also overtook the rain-god of the South African Khoi, Tsu'i-Goab, who was attacked by Gaunab, 'the Destroyer', and speared in the knee.[65] This was clearly the central event in the deity's career, for 'Wounded knee' is what the name Tsu'i-Goab means. It should not be inferred that the Khoi, or some of them, had migrated south from the Lakes region, or that the story is a mere *Wandersage*, a fragment of folklore spread by casual diffusion in fairly recent times; but rather that the Nyoro and the Khoi, and the Ganda, have preserved a mytheme older than themselves. For the injured deity is not even confined to Africa. The Welsh sea-god Bran had been wounded in the foot;[66] and that most mysterious figure of European literature, the Fisher King, who came out of the mists of the native mythology into the polished verses of Chrétien de Troyes, suffered eternally from a spear-thrust in the thigh, which had somehow caused the land to be made waste and the people desolate.[67] It is obvious enough, moreover, that this king of fishers, with his sable cloak and his cap of dark fur, who entertained young heroes in his house by the river, was really an otter – that is to say, he had been an otter until the demands of literary quasi-naturalism caused him to take on human form. And in Norse tradition the killing of Otter (here quite undisguised) by Loki was the beginning of an endless chain of violence and suffering for gods and men.[68] There seems to be a very widespread recurrent theme: the killing or wounding of an otter was the dolorous stroke.

The quarrel between Man and Beast recurs in a somewhat different form in the origin-myth of Kiziba, the little kingdom on the southern border of nineteenth-century Buganda. Here it was told[69] that the hunter Kibi came south from Bunyoro and struck up a friendship with the young prince Kanyamaishwa, who had been exposed on the borders because of his abnormal dentition and had grown up in the wild. They went on together into Kiziba, and Kibi attracted a large following by his generosity with the game-meat that his skill supplied him with. Before long, he was strong enough to carry out a treacherous coup, assassinate the reigning king, and install Kanyamaishwa in his place. The story then seems to be building up to the further murder of Kanyamaishwa; but nothing happens, and it peters out with power uneasily shared between the hunter and his royal protégé. It must be suspected, however, that the recorded versions are not complete, for it is from Kibi that the recent rulers of Kiziba claimed descent. Though the story has thus been grafted onto the dynastic history, a political interpretation would be plainly inadequate even if not wholly wrong, for it leaves nine-tenths of the story unexplained. Its real meaning is evident from the names of the chief characters: *Ki-bi* is straightforwardly 'Evil' or 'the Evil One' and *Ka-nyamaishwa* is 'Little Beast', and his teeth were beyond the human range.

This is one of a class of tales that is widespread in Africa and especially in the lands of Bantu speech, where it has become perhaps the commonest of all narrative clichés. Nearly every Bantu royal or chiefly lineage traces its descent from a hunter who came from outside and seduced people from their previous allegiance with his gifts of meat. The theme is represented in Buganda by Mulanga, said to have been a son of Kintu, who introduced iron weapons and made himself very popular by lending out property and then assuring people that 'here in Bu-langa there is no such thing as a debt'.[70] But although Mu-langa is clearly the eponym of the royal lineage, the *ba-langira*, he did not finally establish himself in the official tradition. He is rarely mentioned elsewhere than in Kaggwa's *The Kings of Buganda*, and even there his story is left in mid-air; the dynasty does not descend from him but from another son of Kintu. On the other hand, when Kaggwa briefly reported the traditions of Bunyoro he applied the 'seditious hunter' motif to Rukidi, the founder of the Bito dynasty,[71] whose advent is described by the Nyoro themselves in quite different terms.

The immigrant hunter is thus clearly a conventional figure, not to be taken literally in any of his numerous appearances. It is possible that it is derived, in part, from historical experience; for it is likely that the pioneers of Early Iron Age technology and culture did use their presumably still scarce iron-tipped weapons to build up surpluses of game meat, with which they would be able to purchase power. But as John Boston remarked of similar traditions in West Africa: 'The hunter legends are nevertheless unsatisfactory as historical records. There is something in their make-up which resists a literal interpretation and tends to bring historical enquiry to a full stop.'[72]

There is of course a simple and universally valid political interpretation of these tales: the function of government is to deliver the goods. Gorbachev's Soviet Union did not survive the failure of *perestroika* to fill the shops, and to the dismay of ideologues of both left and right Western electorates notoriously vote according to the recent and immediately prospective trend of their incomes. African political behaviour is perhaps even more straightforwardly materialistic; people do not object to politicians 'eating' so long as some of the spoils accrue to them as well. To ignore such pragmatism would be sentimental, but it would be equally perverse to deny a profounder meaning to the hunter cliché, on which light is thrown by a modern English myth, William Golding's *Lord of the Flies*. In that imaginative tale, it will be recalled, Ralph the Good King, owner of the sacred conch, wielder of legitimate authority, is overthrown by Jack the Hunter, who wins over the other boys by holding a barbecue. Ralph completes his own defeat by accepting a piece of roast pork himself. Golding is no doubt saying something anthropological about authority and power, but he is also saying something religious about the human condition. Jack's victory is nothing less than the Fall of Man, and his killing of the first pig brings horror into the island paradise. As in Genesis and in Lévi-Strauss's *The Raw and the Cooked*, eating is knowledge and death; but for Golding the forbidden food is meat, the food that has first to be deprived of life. The theme recurs in the murder of the innocent Neanderthalers by the *sapiens Inheritors* and in the 'eating' metaphor that runs through the terrible saga of *Pincher Martin*.

An existential interpretation of the African hunter tales is thus seen to be a necessary complement to the political-historical ones. Like the 'Kisolo' myths of which they are a variant, they convey the simple message of the primal disaster: when he first took up a spear to kill a fellow-creature Man broke the rules of the game, separated himself from God and forfeited immortality. Golding repeats this ancient African theme but gives it a subtly different inflection. No Africans have ever been vegetarians, except by necessity; and in their view it is no more possible for men to abstain from violence, at any rate against animals, than to abstain from women. But if they do not quite speak with Golding's accent, neither do they speak with Robert Ardrey's. There is no pride in the violence of our fallen nature, simply acceptance. It has been reported of African hunters that they apologise to their victims, and there is no question but that the words are sincere. For if Man were not Kibi, the evil hunter, he would not have to die.

But he cannot avoid being Kibi. And because Africans acquiesced in the human limitations they never had to contemplate, as Golding did in the visionary epilogue to *Pincher Martin*, the last setting of the sun, the death of Man himself. It is the people of the Christian West who, acquiescing in nothing, have strained the fabric of human life to breaking-point. Sentimental about animals, they have come near to exterminating all that do not serve their immediate purposes. Shocked by violence, they have professed a willingness to use weapons that might put an end to human life, to Africans a crime beyond comprehension.

Snake and Tortoise

In the third principal myth of Kintu the hero stays in the background and the active parts are played by characters of a different kind. The story is set in the time before time, when the kingship was held by Bemba Omusota, that is, Scaly the Snake. He was an oppressive ruler, and at last Tortoise, Wa-nfudu, prompted by his friend or master Pangolin (Ki-gave or Lu-gave, the scaly ant-eater) bravely took on the task of tyrannicide. Introducing himself at the court he tempted the king, saying: 'You know that tortoises live for ever, or nearly, and I will tell you our secret. Every night we cut our heads off and in the morning we are as good as new.' He then showed himself in the evening with his head retracted into his shell, and poked it out again just before dawn. Thus convinced, Bemba and all his snake-retinue agreed to have their heads cut off, that they too might have everlasting youth; and the way was thus made clear for Kintu to found the line of human kings.[73]

If it had not been for this final statement, which gives the story a dubious place in the dynastic history, it would have appeared to be a simple animal fable, one of the many in eastern Africa that celebrate the cunning of the Tortoise. Its inclusion in the Kintu corpus has in fact embarrassed educated Ganda narrators, for whom their first king belongs to political history and should not have anything to do with fables, and their responses provide a fine example of creolised history. Kaggwa himself protested: 'The story of Bemba cannot be true. How could a mere snake be the ruler of a country? It is possible that Bemba and others were real human beings.' He did not, however, suppress or distort the story he received, but others were less scrupulous. One pretended that Kintu's agent in the attack on Bemba was a soldier who just happened to be called Tortoise, perhaps because he used a tortoiseshell as a helmet.[74] More usually, Tortoise was simply eliminated from the story and Kintu himself was credited with despatching Bemba, in one account beheading him with a sword, *kitala*.[75] This served to explain the place-name Kitala, which is actually a variant form of *mu-tala*, a hill or tract of land. The Ganda did not have swords, the word *kitala* being a recent loan from Swahili, and the writer suggested that Kintu had purchased one from the Maasai before starting his journey to Buganda. (By then it had become accepted that his starting-point was not the sky but somewhere in the east.) And even sophisticated scholars, as we saw, have not been able to resist seeking a historical character behind Bemba's reptilian mask.

But rationalisations of that kind simply will not do. Bemba really was a snake, or rather he really is the Serpent; and Wanfudu is Tortoise, Mr Tortoise, Brer Tortoise – that is, the name consists of the ordinary word for a tortoise, *n-fudu*, with the humanising prefix *Wa-*. It is therefore within the conventions of fable that the story must be discussed. Now we have already established that fables are myths, stories set in that impossible epoch when animals were still human and people were still animals, before Acunga roared or Jacob lied or Kintu took up his spear to wound Kisolo. But they are myths that have been edited so that they may serve primarily for the entertainment and instruction of children. It is these versions that were most readily accessible to colonial searchers, and in published collections of African 'mythology' they therefore gained a disproportionate prominence, which both reflected and reinforced the colonial conception of Africans as a child race. In fact, animal fables are not confined to Africa, and they are not as childish or as simple as they may appear.

The tale of Bemba and Wanfudu embodies the concept of the trickster, which provides the theme of a vast number of African and other fables, the hero being most commonly Hare (the ancestor of Brer Rabbit) but also quite often Tortoise, as here. In a sense there is no mystery about the popularity of this kind of tale. Most of us are childish enough to have a sneaking admiration for really clever con-men; and children, for obvious reasons, delight in stories that show a small creature getting the better of much larger or fiercer beasts. In one typical example, Tortoise challenges both Elephant and Hippo to a tug-of-war, then tricks them into pulling against one another, so that they are amazed by the strength of his resistance. In many recent versions, especially those featuring Ananse, the spider-man of the Akan peoples, the trickster is a more subtle kind of anti-hero, coping with the frustrations and impotences of Africa under colonial rule and post-colonial depression. But he has also an older and more august role. As the Norse Loki, as Esu of the Yoruba, as the North American Coyote he is revealed as 'demiurge', not exactly the Creator, nor yet Satan, but author of life as it so imperfectly is. Likewise Prometheus, who moulded men out of clay and endowed them with fire, also tricked the Olympians into accepting only bones and fat as their share of the sacrifice, a deception for which we are still paying the price.

We must suspect, therefore, that Wanfudu is a more ominous figure than he seems. And indeed the Ganda make no bones about it: the story lays bare the illusion of eternal life. Very similar in form and message is the Greek tale of Medea, 'the Trickster-woman', who conjured a live lamb out of a cauldron of mutton and so persuaded the daughters of old King Pelias to cut him up and stew him, with the result that Jason was able to take over the kingship. Here too is the deceptive promise of immortality leading in reality to dismemberment and death. The Ganda tale, however, is clearly superior and probably closer to the original; for by making Tortoise the deceiver it can exploit both his notorious longevity and his natural ability to conceal his head, whereas the Greek tellers had to fall back on magic, and by casting Snake as the victim it arrives at a beautiful irony. Snakes, which periodically renew their skins, are very widely believed to live for ever – unless of course they have their heads cut off. So in foolishly seeking immortality Bemba discovered the only way in which he could have lost it.

The Greeks did not make this point explicitly, but we can be sure that Pelias too was not mortal until his daughters killed him.

Scaly the Snake is also featured in the best-known of all myths of the origin of death, and again his role in Eden is made more intelligible by the Ganda version. It is widely recognised that the story is partly deformed in the extant Hebrew text, and both Sir James Frazer and Sir Edmund Leach have in rather different ways reconstructed its true shape.[76] What really happened was that Adam (that is, 'Man', Kintu) was tricked into eating the fruit of the tree of knowledge in the belief that it was the fruit of life, which the serpent craftily reserved for his own use. Likewise the Mesopotamian hero Gilgamesh had made a heroic journey to the end of the universe and had been granted the plant of life, only to have it stolen from him by the serpent on the way back to middle-earth.[77] In the real world snakes may be able to live for ever, but men are not. The Genesis tale, moreover, hints openly at the reason for their incapacity. It hardly needed Freud to tell us that the snake, besides being self-renewing, is an emblem of male lust, or that the knowledge eaten by Adam and Eve was carnal knowledge. And here again is the irony: Adam had no need to eat from the tree of life. Made in the image of God, he possessed immortality already, and only by tasting the fruit of knowledge could he possibly have cast it away. He had in fact acquired the snake's phallic nature in exchange for the power of renewal that had previously been his.

The Hebrew myth thus introduces the theme of sexuality, which is hidden in the tale of Bemba but salient in the two other Kintu myths and essential to the entire complex. Young people used everywhere to be taught the necessary connection between sex and death at the time when they were becoming aware of the necessity of sex; and it is therefore to be suspected that the original scene of the confrontation of Snake and Tortoise was the initiation camp. That context becomes more evident when we consider a fragment of western European mythology, which is in some ways closer to the Ganda tale than those already considered. Among the ancient stories that found their way into European literature there is the one known as the beheading game, which surfaces most notably in the Irish collection called *Bricriu's Feast*, the Franco-Breton romance of Caradoc Short-Arm and the beautiful north-English poem *Sir Gawain and the Green Knight*.[78] A strange being – giant or sorcerer or green-hued horseman – appears at the king's court and issues a challenge: let someone strike his head off now, and allow him next day, or next year, to return the blow. The young hero – Cuchulainn, Caradoc or Gawain – duly wields the axe but to his horror the stranger picks up his head and makes off with it. What seemed to be some kind of game has become a terrible reality. In honour bound, the hero presents himself at the appointed time, but the ogre merely feints to strike, perhaps making a small gash in his neck, and the ordeal is over.

That this is an initiatory test is manifest at many points, especially in the story of Gawain who, like adolescent boys doing their 'walkabout' in primitive societies, had to endure a lone journey in the wild country before he was deemed ready for the final test of his manhood. And, while the Ganda tale discloses the point and purpose of the beheading game, the recognition of mortality, the European tales hint at the nature of the ritual act that gave rise to it. Decapitation, they make clear, was threatened but did not actually occur. The allusion, I believe, was to circumcision, the ancient rite whereby adolescent boys were admitted to sexuality and forewarned of death. That was the wound in the 'neck' that Gawain suffered in lieu of beheading.

Since neither Europeans nor Ganda, so far as the records go, ever practised circumcision, or indeed any form of general puberty initiation, this may seem an over-bold hypothesis. However, initiation ritual lies at the very base of human society, and operations on the penis are so widely spread around the world that they must be assumed to be part of the prehistory of every culture. The rite, moreover, was so traumatic that it left an enduring residue in myth. Behind all these stories of feigned beheading we can discern the symbolic castration recognised by Freud. 'Come now,' says the Deceiver, as Tortoise said to Snake, 'let me cut off your "head" and then you can live peacefully for ever.' After that terrifying menace the actual operation would come as a great relief, as it did to Gawain – even though the cut that left him a sexual being also failed to free him from his mortal condition. The Ganda myth likewise alludes not too obscurely to the liberating wound that is circumcision. Ronald Atkinson has acutely observed that its four characters form a kind of evolutionary series.[79] First there is the writhing Snake; then Tortoise, the reptile with inefficient legs and partial scaly cover; then his companion Pangolin (*Manis tricuspis* or *Manis gigantea*), the clumsy, anomalous scaly mammal that sometimes stands on its hind legs; and finally erect-walking, scale-free Man. The inference from this progression is unmistakable. By the removal of his last scale the quasi-reptilian boy becomes fully human, licensed for sexual action and destined to a finite life.

Relevant here are two short stories recorded in Rwanda early in this century.[80] They are simple encounters of boy and girl, adorned with some elementary symbolism: in one the girl is at first a calabash, in the other the boy is for part of the time a snake. But the conclusion of both is the same: 'They came to grips, and so passed out of *buzimu* into *buntu*.' The missionary compiler rendered this as 'from darkness into light', but that is clearly not correct. *Bu-zimu* is the land of spirits or the condition of being a spirit (*mu-zimu*); *bu-ntu* is not 'light' but the condition of being human (*mu-ntu*). And so we see that the mediators Tortoise and Pangolin have helped Bemba to become Kintu. The ritual beheading converts the snake-boy, with his raw sexual potential, into a human being, who has left the spirit world of childhood finally behind him.

Kintu, then, was the vehicle for very basic ontological and ontogenetic statements about love and death and becoming an adult person. The rudiments of the thought and even some of its expression go back to the beginnings of mankind. Some of the development, however, is characteristically African; some appears to have been achieved by early bearers of Bantu speech, and some again is proper to the Ganda people; the vivid and moving tale of Nambi, her lover and her brother clearly owes much to an individual narrator. It is also noticeable that the social context of the three Kintu stories is not the same. In the first, he is at the beginning alone in the land and even at the end is the head of a single household, with no subjects that he has not himself begotten. In the tale of Kisolo, by contrast, he has become a king, with a royal capital, a steward belonging to another clan, a council of chiefs and a territory to tour. As for the story of Bemba and Wanfudu, analysis may have shown that it is really about something else altogether, but what is overtly at stake is the kingship; and despite its fanciful content it purports to describe the foundation of the dynasty that was still ruling at the time of the colonial conquest. Thus Benjamin Ray, who dismisses my 'folkloristic' interpretation (which was first proposed, very briefly, in 1958)[81] and stresses the relation of the story to the ritual of royal accession, has an undoubted point.[82] But he fails to address the problem inherent in functionalist exegesis: why should the majesty of Ganda kingship have been enhanced by the telling of a silly story about a tortoise and a snake? The answer is that the story, which in its basic elements is far older than any specifically Ganda ritual or institution, is not really silly. It signifies puberty initiation and its painful lessons, and by relating these to the Ganda monarchy gives it a dignity it would not otherwise have had. Kingship is 'sacred' because and insofar as it carries an emotional charge generated by the profoundest human experiences.

Nevertheless, each of the Kintu myths does have a kind of historical context and may contain clues to the actual history of Ganda society. Before these can be deciphered, however, a lot of colonial clutter will have to be cleared away.

Man and his history

When the first witness, John Speke, enquired about ancient history he was told nothing about Kintu, and his list of kings began with Kimera, alias Buganda, who would later be identified as his great-grandson and third holder of the kingly office. That does not mean that the concept of Kintu did not exist in 1862, but it does show that he had not then established himself as a historic king or reference-point for the dynasty. Thirteen years later, however, he dominated the traditions reported by Stanley who, with his journalist's eye for a good story, was much intrigued by the 'blameless patriarch'. He did not hear any of the tales we have been discussing but he did recount another one, to which we shall return in due course, wherein Kintu, having withdrawn from the sinful world, was briefly rediscovered by a much later king, only to be lost forever.[83]

Stanley recognised him as a genesis figure comparable, he suggested, to Adam or Noah. But then he remembered that links between African barbarism and divine revelation would not be acceptable to his readers; so he recanted these 'wild and vain fancies' and settled for describing the Kintu story as 'a simple tradition of central Africa'.[84] The next step in the incorporation was taken by two of the missionaries summoned by Stanley to Buganda, Charles Wilson and Robert Felkin. They found Kintu firmly established at the head of the royal genealogy and, taking a cue from Muslim residents, blandly identified him with Ham,[85] the delinquent son of Noah who was supposed to have wandered off to central Africa bearing his father's curse. They were not, it seems, deterred by the obvious difficulty that, if both the biblical and the Ganda traditions were taken literally, Ham would have lived over three thousand years before Kintu. But the unsophisticated speculation was very significant, because it showed that foreigners were already adding arbitrary glosses of their own to Ganda tradition and using it as a vehicle for their ideological pretensions. The Curse of Ham, punishment for a deed so dark that the biblical text can only hint at it, had originally justified the Israelites in reducing the masses of Palestine, children of Canaan son of Ham, to a servile condition. But it was sometimes claimed in the nineteenth century – and Afrikaner fundamentalists continued to believe this in the twentieth – that Europeans, descendants of the virtuous Japhet, had a similar right to the services of Africans. Were not Kush and Misraim – Nubia and Egypt – also sons of Ham? In fact there was nothing specifically African about the 'Hamites', who included everyone the Israelites chose to regard as radically alien. Although 'Kush' did designate the Napatan kingdom in the northern Sudan the Bible makes this hero the father of the Mesopotamian peoples rather than of black Africans.

In any case missionaries were somewhat behind the intellectual times. By the 1880s biology had superseded the scriptures as the most popular source of charters for European supremacy, and in this new climate the myth of Ham was turned upside-down.[86] The term 'Hamite', as we have seen, was now reserved for the brown-skinned natives of north-eastern Africa, to whose influence all the cultural and organisational achievements of the continent were routinely credited. Commentators who still wanted to use scriptural authority now had to class black Africans either as 'pre-Adamites', products of an earlier and less successful creation on which the Bible is silent, or as 'antediluvians', people who in their dark corner of the earth had escaped the Flood. Ham might be accursed but as a son of Noah he was still entitled to dominion over such benighted folk, at any rate until the sons of Shem and Japhet, Arabs and Europeans, were in a position to take over. However, the more intellectual European observers no longer bothered with the scriptures. It was their genetic deficiencies, or their isolation from the civilised world, not ancestral iniquity, that doomed black Africans to be subjugated, first by quasi-Europeans and then by real ones.

Signs of a 'Hamitic' presence were thus eagerly sought for in Buganda. As we saw, they were not very easy to discover; but it was hard for Englishmen of the early twentieth century to forgo the belief that the good order and courtesy, the administrative skills and the intellectual receptiveness that they found in that country must have been the result of a civilising impulse from far away. And Kintu now had a key role to play. The human archetype became a historic state-constructor, and he who had lived in the land before there were any other people came to be depicted as an alien intruder. In Christian circles, where the religious and moral value of the myths was recognised, he was thought of as a proto-missionary, probably an adventurous Copt, who had managed to sow some seeds of truth among the heathen long ago. A typical speculation was that 'a knowledge of the locality of Tanda and of the earthly career of Walumbe would throw light on the migration of patriarchs who taught their children to hold fast by the eternal hope'.[87] ('Tanda' is in fact in Ssingo county.) Stanley himself had conjectured that he was 'probably a priest of some old and long-forgotten order'. But it was political skills, the techniques of government, that were above all credited to Kintu during colonial times. The British had admired the organisation of the Ganda state and not only preserved it intact but used Ganda to help them administer other parts of the Protectorate. To justify this favoured treatment of a particular African people they needed to believe that history had made it an exception, that its leaders were not Africans in the ordinary sense. In 1893, when Stanley's companion Mountney Jephson retold his version of the Kintu myth (in a book designed for children and patronisingly titled *Stories Told in an African Forest, by Grown-up Children of Africa*), his illustrator portrayed Kintu and his wife as Caucasians. Sir Harry Johnston, negotiator of the deal with the Ganda chiefs and an intellectual whose liberal sympathies coexisted with a virulent theoretical racism, was more specific. Following a hint supplied by Speke, he concluded that 'Kintu may be a personification of the influential immigrants from Galla countries who first gave impetus to civilisation in Unyoro [Bunyoro]'.[88] The Ganda themselves pretended that their founding hero had also, as an afterthought, created the rival kingdom; and this made it easier for Johnston to reverse the process, treating Buganda as an offshoot of Bunyoro, where people of possible Ethiopian origin were easier to find.

It was the missionary anthropologist John Roscoe who set the seal on the new, historical interpretation of Kintu, asserting that he came 'either from the east or the north-east' and 'was a powerful ruler who invaded and conquered the land and who by his superior skills incorporated the clans into one nation under his government'.[89] That statement articulated all the ruling preconceptions of the early twentieth century: the evolutionist belief that clans always precede states, the diffusionist assumption that the transition could only have been effected from outside; and the colonialist conviction that the historic function of British rule was to enlarge political scale. For Kintu's creation of Buganda, spectacular in its own day, was clearly a prefiguring of the integration of that kingdom into a much larger system – not 'Uganda', whose independence was not yet on the horizon of thought, but the British Empire.

In myth-making as in other matters the Christian Ganda elite collaborated eagerly with the British. For, as Michael Twaddle has shown,[90] the idea of Kintu as an immigrant state-builder was even more useful to them than it was to the British. Their privileges, personal and national, rested on the British belief that they possessed a tradition of government that set them apart from other Africans, and they had a better chance of sustaining that belief if they were seen as heirs of an Ethiopian conqueror. So the inconvenient myths were hurriedly pushed aside or rationalised to make way for the historic hero, creator of the unique institutions of Buganda. It could not be denied that tradition brought Kintu from the sky, when it did not make him simply autocthonous, but the idea was dismissed as *lugero bugero*,[91] 'a mere myth' or 'just a story'. One writer remarked that 'no-one has ever come from heaven except our Lord Jesus Christ'.[92] Another said drily that he felt bound to set the hypothesis aside, since he did not have a long enough ladder to interrogate the inhabitants of the sky.[93] He could, however, question knowledgeable Nyoro, and so came up with the idea that Kintu was the brother of their dynastic founder Rukidi, who had come from Bukedi, the wild lands beyond the Nile – though the Nyoro themselves more usually identified this character with Kimera.

This was not a completely new idea. Stanley had reported that he came from 'the north' and Felkin had specified Foweira, a known place on the banks of the Somerset Nile, in the Lwo-speaking area of northern Bunyoro. Kaggwa too, after a brief reference to the sky story, had given what he claimed to be the real history of Kintu, which took him by a circuitous route from a place called Podi to his final capital at Magonga; and in the second edition of *The Kings of Buganda* he added that Podi was 'in Bunyoro'. Both Foweira (Pawiir) and Podi are names of Lwo origin. 'Bukedi' (or Bukidi) properly referred to the country of the Lwo-speaking Lang'i people to the east of Bunyoro; but the term came to be used loosely for the general area of northern and eastern Uganda; and the opinion later gained ground that Kintu had come to Buganda not from the north but from the east, beyond Mt Elgon, and this theory has more recently won some scholarly endorsement.

The Ganda Adam, in other words, had been transferred from the domain of ontological myth, the realm of absolute beginnings, to serve as the hero of a different kind of genesis tale, one that identified and validated a particular political society. Was there, however, a genuine historical tradition embedded in the Kintu myth? Most students of Buganda have assumed that there was, that stories of the Man did allude to some ancient migration or political transformation as well as to the timeless truths we have been discussing hitherto. Thus David Cohen's massive investigations of local traditions in Busoga led him to much the same conclusion as had been reached by less sophisticated Ganda enquirers, namely that 'Kintu' represented a current of migration which has passed westward through the land some seven centuries ago.[94] However, there is nothing surprising about the prevalence of Kintu stories and a Kintu cult in Busoga, especially in the southern chiefdoms. We have after all discovered him, or her, as far afield as Zambia; and in part the stories derive from a widespread common heritage of myth. They also undoubtedly reflect the political domination of the area in the nineteenth century. The principal shrine of Kintu in Busoga – with a shrine of Walumbe nearby – is in an area where Ganda colonists are known to have settled. Just as the Ganda and the Nyoro powers competed for ascendancy in the politically fragmented Soga region, so did Kintu compete as ancestor, god and miracle-worker with 'Mukama', a character derived from the Nyoro word for 'king'. Cohen's researches have abundantly shown that there was much coming and going along the northern coastlands of Nalubaale. They do not attest an ancient 'heroic' migration from east to west such as could give historical substance to the myths of Kintu. In fact, Michael Twaddle has shown very clearly how the idea of Kintu's advent from the east arose.[95] It was not a 'tradition' but an ethnological speculation on the part of Ganda who went to work in the Eastern Province of Uganda as clerks, traders and administrators in the early colonial period, and were surprised to find that 'their' Kintu was well known to the Soga and even (in the simpler form Muntu) to the Gisu of Mt

Elgon. They inferred that he must have lived in those parts before he came to Buganda, his chosen land.[96] To this conclusion they were undoubtedly predisposed by a very widespread mythical convention. As Wyatt MacGaffey has pointed out,[97] founding heroes in Africa come with great regularity from the east, and this 'orientation' is a matter not of historical fact but of symbolic compulsion. The land of sunrise and moonrise has to be the place of all beginnings.

The 'northern' hypothesis is older and at first sight more persuasive; and at one time I was inclined to accept that the myth of Kintu had been conflated with some real tradition of immigration from the north – perhaps that fifteenth-century Nilotic invasion which some historians have seen as the key event in the history of the Lakeland. There is, however, another and simpler explanation. During the third quarter of the nineteenth century the banks of the Somerset Nile held stations of the Arab merchants who were promoting the export of ivory and slaves, and it was from these bases that visitors of strange aspect and alarming powers had descended on Buganda, as well as Bunyoro, in the 1870s. When these intruders, including the missionary Felkin, asked the Ganda where Kintu came from, it was natural for them to reply: 'No doubt from the same direction as you.' As a man of the mythical past, he too was a strange and powerful being, and as a deity of a kind he was often thought of as white. The 'tradition', in other words, was a new one, elicited by European questioning and nineteenth-century experiences.

Not all Ganda, however, were happy with the idea of Kintu as an immigrant. For one thing, as Twaddle notes, it dawned on some of them that he might set a precedent for European settlement, which Uganda had so far avoided. Prestigious origins certainly buttress political claims, but authochtony may be even better. Hence there was a strong counter-assertion that he was in fact a native[98] – perhaps not of Buganda proper but of the nearby Ssese islands. Towards the end of the colonial period a synthesis was finally achieved. Kintu, it was said, was the scion of an old indigenous dynasty, but as a child he was sent either to Ssese or to the Elgon area to protect him from his wicked brother Bemba, and returned later to take the kingship.[99] This enabled the Ganda to have it both ways, much like the Israelites who claimed the land of Canaan both by right of conquest and (through the Patriarchs) by right of ancient occupation, as well as by the gift of God.

Ganda intellectuals had also to wrestle with the problem that Kintu as First Man was father of all the people but as founder of a dynasty his descendance had to be restricted to the royal patriline. Advocates of the *balangira* 'clan' argued with some success that he was not the ancestor of the other clans, which were descended either from his clients or from aboriginals who had lived a primitive existence before the advent of the great civiliser.[100] Yet in the end the older view prevailed. The Ganda nationalists of the 1940s and 1950s have often been slightingly described as neo-traditionalists, because the 'nation' they worked for was not the new multi-ethnic state of Uganda that the British authorities were preparing for them but the existing homogeneous kingdom of Buganda which, they hoped, would resume the independence it had formerly enjoyed. To give resonance to this programme they began to describe the Ganda people, the subjects of the *kabaka*, as *abaana ba Kintu*, 'the children of Kintu'. That designation, however, had once belonged to all mankind, but the symbol of common humanity had finally become an ethnic signifier.

Kintu does have a history, but not one that can be directly reconstructed from the traditional narratives. When David Cohen used these to plot the movement of 'heroic migrating families' across Busoga he was well aware that he was dealing with an 'Adamic' figure, but the intellectual climate of the time encouraged him to believe that genesis myths had somehow been superposed on genuine memories of distant, roughly thirteenth-century political events. Yet such historical speculations fall under the ban of redundancy, since the mythological interpretations are self-sufficient, leaving no loose ends. It seems preferable, therefore, to reverse the process, taking the genesis myths as the starting point and trying to see how and when political ideas were grafted onto them. And the first step is to use the social geography of the tales, each of which has a location and a context.

Kintu's sky-bride, it will be recalled, was assigned to the Colobus Monkey clan. The same emblem served to unite and distinguish a number of ordinary descent-groups, and one of these supplied the priest who kept the shrine at Ttanda where Death took refuge from the Lightning; it was there presumably that the tale of Nambi, or at any rate its epilogue, took its extant form. Another Colobus lineage, which claimed seniority, was based at Bu-sujja a mile or so to the west of Bakka, where the sun fell, and its chief, Ka-sujja, had a role in the archaic ritual of nuclear Buganda (see below, p. 151). It might be inferred that the myth was part of the ancestral culture of the little kingdom of Walusimbi, perhaps going back to the Early Iron Age; but that may not be correct. In essentials, of course, it was far older still, but there are signs that in its extant form it was a more recent construction. Death could not have taken up his abode at Ttanda until the quarries had been long disused, nor could Ttanda figure in a Ganda myth until it was part of Ganda territory, thus probably not until the late seventeenth century. Nambi is the daughter of Heaven, but she is also assigned a human father, Bakazirwendo Ssemmandwa, who disputed the headship of the Colobus clan with Kasujja. His first name, meaning

'Women-are-a-disaster', cynically summarised a possible message of the myth. The second signifies 'Chief (or father) of the *mmandwa*', the deities of the spirit-possession cult and their mediums. It will be argued later that this specialised form of religion did not take hold in Buganda until the eighteenth century; and it seems likely that the ancient myth of the Fall was, so to speak, issued in a new edition as part of the ideological ferment of that time.

Kintu himself is associated above all with Magonga, a locality just to the west of the Mayanja Kato in the country of Busujju (not to be confused with the Busujj*a* of the Colobus folk). It was here that he had his fatal quarrel with Kisolo, whose heir, the head of the Otter clan, lives close by, as does the Leopard clan chief who claims to be in a special sense Kintu's heir. Busujju lies outside the probable orbit of ancient Bakka, and there is a circumstantial tradition that it was incorporated into the growing Ganda state in the reign of Mutebi the fifteenth king, who belongs to Generation Eight. The local ruler who was then dispossessed belonged not to the Leopard clan but to the Grasshoppers, and the chief who was installed in his place, taking the title of Ka-sujju, was a Pangolin. Nevertheless Magonga, or more precisely the plot called Nnono, the 'kernel' of the world, was one of the most sacred places in Buganda. There in a secret wood was the tomb of Kintu, tended by a hereditary priest of the Leopard folk, and there in the first seven days of each moon elaborate rituals were performed for the good of king and kingdom.[101]

The story that so intrigued Stanley concerned the twenty-second king, Mawanda, who was told that his long-lost ancestor Kintu had summoned him to his presence. So he went to Magonga with the queen-mother (or in another version his sister) and began to take counsel with this hero of the elder days. But the *katikkiro* (or a lesser chief called Namutwe, or a certain Ssenkoma, who would become a local river) had secretly followed him, and just as Kintu began to speak the king became aware of him and struck him in anger – as Kintu had once struck Kisolo. Dismayed by this violence, Kintu broke off the audience, and since then he has never been seen or heard by any mortal man.[102]

Mawanda lived in Generation Six, on the edge of the period of secondary reminiscence, and there is no reasonable doubt that he did really live. He was in fact one of the greatest of the kings, but he was in origin a usurper, and so he would need all the legitimising sanction he could get; and with this object he seems to have secured the help of the shrine-priests at Magonga. Though there is some doubt about his real parentage, he claimed to be the son of a former king by a woman of the Leopard clan, daughter of the hereditary chief Ssegirinya, whose lineage had important duties in connection with the Kintu cult. There is thus reason to think that around the middle of the eighteenth century the ancient myths of Kintu were harnessed to political interests and used as part of the charter of the expanding Ganda state.

For this to happen, of course, the Magonga shrine must have been already in being and enjoying some degree of popular authority, and must have already given currency to the myth of Man and Beast, Kintu and Kisolo. Moreover, it was clearly part of a wider organisation. The Leopard clan has estates in various parts of Buganda, including those at Mangira in Kyaggwe and Buvu on the Busiro coast which were said to have been temporary homes of Kintu; and Cohen found many traces of mobile groups in Busoga and further east which made use of this totem. So it could be that in this sense, as the patron of a cult organisation, 'Kintu' did come to Buganda from the east. On the other hand he appears also in the mythology of the Haya and other peoples to the west and south. All that can really be inferred at this stage is that shrine-priests played a larger role in the political evolution of the area than has usually been suspected.

A great light was cast for me on these matters when I became belatedly acquainted with the work of Matthew Schoffeleers on the mythology of the Maravi peoples.[103] This features a place called Kaphiri-ntiwa, 'the little flat-topped hill', in a mountainous area of central Malawi, where God, people and animals dwelt together before the beginning of time. The primeval felicity was of course brought to an end, in this case by man's invention of fire, which caused God and the animals to flee. The echoes of the Ganda tale of Man and Beast are very clear, but the Promethean theme gives it new meaning, showing just why the smoke of bush-burnings, which help the hunters to drive game, caused the final estrangement of Kisolo, who was also God, from our first ancestor. Yet another name associated with Kisolo was Sse-byoto, 'Father of Hearths', suggesting that he was indeed the Ganda Prometheus, giver of fire to men. Now Schoffeleers explains that the myth served as the charter of the *nyau* dance societies, which had a central role in the social and religious life of many Malawian communities.[104] The dancers wore elaborate masks, mostly of animals, and among other things they celebrated the coming of the rains, when hunting was in abeyance and the enmity of men and beasts was for a time suspended. When the dry season returned the bush was set ablaze, the dancers became people again and the animals fled from them. The illusion of paradise was set aside and mortal life resumed.

The word *nyau*, originally *ngabo*, is etymologically related to the names of cults widely distributed in central Africa, such as the *mi-ngab* of Kasai in Zaire and the *migawo* and *myaoo* of western Tanzania. So it is not wildly improbable that a similar organisation once flourished among the Ganda. It is true that their recent ethnography knows nothing of masked dances, but these were still practised by their southern neighbours the Haya;[105] and the place-name Magonga is itself revealing, being related to the reflexive verb *-egonga*, which in modern Ganda means 'to make faces' – in other words, to put on a mask. Moreover Kintu's council, which tried to make peace between him and Kisolo, clearly consisted of animals. Fifteen of Buganda's clans had representatives permanently stationed at or near Magonga, and some of the names openly disclose their bestial character. The Grey Monkey's ambassador at Kintu's ghostly court was Bwoya, 'Fur', and the Elephant clan's was called both Ssessanga, 'Tusker', and Nyininsiko, 'Lord of the forest', while Ka-yimbye-obutega of the Oribi Antelope folk seems to be 'He who causes the traps to sing'. The Leopard, which presided at Magonga, is the most formidable of forest beasts and has often been (as in medieval England) an emblem of royal power.[106] But it is perhaps more to the point that for some Bantu peoples it was associated with the earth and its fertility,[107] and was thus naturally both paired with and opposed to the Otter, the king of the waters.

So it is a reasonable conjecture that at some time in the past the primordial tragedy was regularly re-enacted at Magonga, and that, as the Delphic oracle and the cult of Apollo helped to promote the unity of Hellas, so the shrine and myth of Kintu had an ancient and wide-ranging integrative role, giving some sense of common identity to the tiny kingdoms of the eastern Lakeland before the rise of Buganda or any other major state. Just how ancient this ritual complex may have been is difficult to say. Since Leopard centres were spread along the north shore of the Lake, it could be that the cult was responsible for the 'North Nyanza' or 'Gandan' linguistic uniformity early in the millennium. On the other hand, Magonga was on or near the frontier between the Gandan and Nyoroan territories, and at least three of the clans prominent in the ritual – Bushbuck, Grasshopper and Buffalo – have strong Nyoroan associations. So the florescence of the cult may go back to a time before the linguistic separation – or alternatively may have arisen to mitigate its consequences.

At some point the system lost its autonomy, the dances ceased, and the myth of Kintu, with what what was left of the Magonga ritual, was harnessed to the Buganda state. The story of Mawanda's visit obviously refers to this process, though not necessarily to its beginnings. Now that king's eventful reign came to an abrupt end when he was assassinated by his praetorian troops, who transferred the kingship to another set of princes, sons of a Sheep woman. (The Sheep clan was one of those that had no role at Magonga.) It was no doubt because he failed to found his own line that Mawanda's interview with Kintu was said to have been abortive. But the legitimising sanction of the great Ancestor had evidently become an essential part of the apparatus of state. After the very brief reign of

Mwanga I, his brother Namugala instituted an elaborate ritual that would
be carried out at the beginning of every subsequent reign on the hill of
Buddo in *southern* Busiro, more precisely at the place called Naggalabi,
'where evil is shut out'. Ritual was as usual reinforced by myth. For it was
now said that the reign of Man himself had begun at Buddo, this having
been the scene of Tortoise's victory over Bemba, whereby Kintu was able to
become king. That tale was clearly the special property of the Pangolin
clan, whose ancestor Mukiibi, a client of Kintu, commissioned Tortoise to
destroy the reptilian tyrant. The people who took the pangolin as their
emblem are reputed to be among the oldest inhabitants of Buganda, but
they first became prominent in the reign of Mutebi in Generation Eight,
and seem to have given support to the new regime of Namugala, being
accorded a significant role in the Buddo ritual. The pangolin is a creature
that has commonly been regarded by Africans with a kind of wary respect.
An animal that is clothed in scales yet suckles its young does not belong to
any of the proper categories, and such anomalies, it has been persuasively
argued by Mary Douglas, have a mediating power that is the essence of
sacredness.[108] She has memorably described the 'Pangolin society' which
exploited this sentiment among the Lele of central Zaire; and others have
noted the role played by the creature in the circumcision rites of eastern
Zaire.[109] It seems possible, therefore, that the Ganda Pangolins were in
origin a cult-group with an initiation rite modelled on puberty ordeals, and
that the linked myth was adapted to the legitimisation of the reconstituted
kingdom around the middle of the eighteenth century.

Some glimmerings of history do thus emerge from the genesis myths of
Buganda, but only when they have first been given their full mythical value.
History, in its usual sense of past politics, is an accretion to the existential
myth, not the other way round. And it will have become apparent that
traditions cannot usefully be presented in straightforward linear succession, because they are not static but are constantly being adapted and
revised – without, however, losing their earlier lineaments altogether. Our
quest for Ganda genesis began in what is now the middle of the tradition,
with King Jjuuko of Generation Eight. It then took us back to the
beginning, not of the Ganda state, which remains so far hidden, but of time
itself. Then, since the character who inaugurated human life had new
functions to perform in colonial and even post-colonial Buganda, we had
to move forward almost to the present day, only to end up nearly but not
quite where we began, with an as yet hazy outline of political change in
Generations Six and Five.

Those vague outlines we shall try to sharpen and fill in, not without hope
of being able to go further back in real time. It must not be thought,
however, that with Kintu out of the way orthodox historical analysis can at

once begin. On the contrary, the most interesting (and controversial) parts of Ganda mythology have yet to be unveiled. Kintu and Nambi, like Adam and Eve, Jacob and Rachel, set time in motion. But time did not then move forward in the linear manner that historians are used to. Instead it was bent into the more pleasing form of a circle, so that its end is also its beginning. After the myths of genesis come the myths of the perpetual return.

7　The cycle of the kings

The child and the dancers

Like his father, Kintu, the second king, Cwa Nabakka, is said to have
disappeared from the land, and the dynastic history starts again with the
coming of his grandson, Kimera. The claim that the newcomer, though
born in Bunyoro, had been begotten there by Cwa's son Kalemeera has
been dismissed by critical historians as an attempt to mask the arrival of a
new dynasty of Nyoro origin. Some have, in addition, detected a second
break in continuity after the reign of King Nakibinge, who is assigned to
the sixth generation after Kimera and the twelfth before the colonial era.
In his days the kingdom was invaded by a Nyoro army, brought in by a
rival prince; and at the last he was left to face them alone, supported only
by his heroic wife Nannono, who sharpened reeds for him to throw when
he had run out of spears. After his death she acted as regent for a time, and
if the child she was carrying had been male he would have been given the
kingship; but when she gave birth to a girl the kingmakers turned
elsewhere. When the campaign started, Nakibinge had sent his other wives
and their children to a hiding-place on the eastern border; and although
the oldest of his sons, Mulondo, was only a small child he was now
brought back and installed as king.[1] It seems strange that the Nyoro
should have permitted a peaceful succession, especially of a child, and the
borderland refuge story looks suspiciously like another cover for a foreign
usurper. I myself formerly adopted a historical interpretation of
Mulondo, though not of Kimera; but I have come to see that this was to
misunderstand the language of tradition and that both stories are more
fully and more interestingly explicable as myths. It will be simpler to start
with Mulondo.

　　The associations of this king, it must be noted, imply that he was as
indigenous as any in the entire tradition. His reputed capital and tomb were
at Bu-londo, which is barely a mile to the east of Bakka hill. His mother,
known only as Na-mulondo, was a daughter of the Mushroom clan, whose
chief, Ggunju, resides at the southern foot of Bakka.[2] It appears therefore

that he belonged to the most ancient core of the kingdom. Can we then take the tradition at face value and assume that some time in the sixteenth century the chances of history did produce a child ruler for this little state?

Martin Southwold, who did make this assumption, noted that up to this point the kingship had regularly passed to a son or grandson, but that after Mulondo the succession was usually fraternal (often fratricidal) until the filial rule was restored at the beginning of the nineteenth century. He suggested that the obvious unsuitability of a child king in a time of national crisis had caused the constitution to be changed.[3] But it is hard to believe that the kingmakers would even have thought of putting the government into the hands of a small boy at such a time. Whatever the rules have said, some older kinsman would surely have been preferred. So whatever the meaning of Mulondo's juvenility it is unlikely to have been the result of a dynastic accident.

Was it perhaps a pure invention, a reflection of political conditions at the time of recording? In 1901, when Kaggwa produced his *The Kings of Buganda*, the *kabaka* was in fact a little boy, Daudi Cwa, who had been installed four years earlier at the age of two, after his father Mwanga had unsuccessfully revolted against British rule. Kaggwa himself was the senior regent, and it was he and his colleagues who had persuaded the British not to abolish the monarchy but to preserve it in the symbolic person of the infant prince – the only surviving member of the royal house who was not unacceptable to them. In these very different circumstances a child king was no longer an anomaly – was indeed the best possible kind of king from the point of view of the Protectorate authorities and the collaborating chiefs. It is thus tempting to surmise that the story of the infant Mulondo was meant to supply a precedent for the role of the young Cwa. Though Mulondo had figured in earlier king-lists than Kaggwa's as the successor of Nakibinge he had been a name only, and no previous mention of his extreme youth had been recorded.

However, this interpretation cannot be more than a half-truth. If the story had been derived from the politics of Kaggwa's time a prominent role would surely have been assigned to Mulondo's regent, but no such person is even mentioned. Moreover, Kaggwa was not an imaginative man, and he could not possibly have invented the strange details that surround and emphasise the legendary king's youthful state. It is told for instance that the royal stool Namulondo (signifying 'Mulondo's mother') which remained ever afterwards the most sacred object in Buganda, the heart and soul of the kingdom, was originally made for the little boy to sit or stand on so that his people could get a proper view of him. It was carved by his maternal kinsmen of the Mushroom clan, whose descendants had in historic times the honour of guarding it and bringing it out on ceremonial occasions. That was how they acquired their emblem, for a mushroom (as gnomes are well aware) is itself a stool, and a particular kind was called *namulondo*.[4]

This was the name, not only of a legendary queen-mother, but also of a goddess,[5] and the association brings to mind an ancient precedent: Isis, queen of heaven, wife of the god Osiris, mother of the god Horus, is believed to have been originally the throne of Egypt.[6] Though the theology and mythology of Osiris were very complex there is no doubt that he was among other things the immortal counterpart of the dead pharaoh, as his son Horus was the divine aspect of the living king. This part of Egyptian religion, in other words, was a projection of the sacred kingship, not vice versa; and the whole concept of Isis springs from the picture of the young king sitting on the throne as though upon his mother's lap. It becomes hard to resist the conclusion that Ganda mythology preserved a glimpse of this imagery, which was doubtless old when the pyramids were young. Mulondo, in other words, is Horus, neither god nor man but the ideal persona of kings at the beginning of their reigns.

'Mulondo' was indeed a title of royalty in several tiny polities to the east of Buganda, including the north-eastern district called Bu-londo-ganyi ('the realm of Mulondo among the Lwo-speakers'), which was administered in colonial times by a Ganda sub-chief bearing that locally traditional title. It derives from the passive form of the verb -*londa*, which means 'to choose' and also 'to find'; from other Bantu languages it appears that the basic meaning was 'to track down'. A Mu-londo is thus both a chosen one and a foundling.

It is characteristic of sacred kings that they have to be ritually discovered before they can assume their office. This was true of the king of Janjero,[7] one of those formerly independent states in south-west Ethiopia that show a rather strong family resemblance to the Lakeland kingdoms. Within the Lakes region the custom is embedded in myth, most strongly perhaps in the conservative kingdom of Burundi, where the 'type' king Ntare is said to have been a child found by hunters in a cave, or sitting in a forest glade wearing the skin of a lion he had killed, a creature of the wild distinguished from the beasts only by the brightness of his eye.[8] The great King Mahe of Kyamutwara, whose reputed capital has been identified as a site of Early Iron Age industry, was captured by hunters in the wild country after his grandfather's death had left the throne vacant; his advent put an end to a famine, so that he was called Rugomora, 'Giver of plenty'.[9] Rukidi the Piebald, founder of the Bito dynasty of Bunyoro, was summoned by a wizard from his home in the wild lands beyond the Nile.[10] In fact, as Jean-Pierre Chrétien has finely said with reference to the south-western Lakeland states: 'A *mwami* [king] is by definition a strange being who arises on the frontier, comes out of the wild, emerges from a river or a swamp, manifests himself in the guise of a wandering hunter or a common charcoal-burner.' It is absurd, he argues, to use such themes to reconstruct migration-routes or support hypotheses of recent conquest.[11] Likewise the god Dionysus was discovered in November by the priestesses of Delphi in a winnowing-basket;[12] King David was found by Samuel among the sheep; and his descendant was both the Lamb found by the shepherds in a manger and the King tracked down by the Wise Men. The same ritual act has given rise to the countless 'lost heirs' of European fiction, from Oedipus to Tarzan; and the reason why the heirs were lost will shortly become evident.

All these foundlings were children, if not infants; and there is clear evidence that in the Lakes region the Child King had at one time been neither an occasional accident nor a figment of mythology but a routine ritual reality. The best example is the *mwami* of Busozo, the little kingdom in the south-west which has already been noted as an indicative fossil. According to the White Fathers who visited it before its extinction in 1925, the *mwami* was a 'hieratic figure' who lived in seclusion, hedged about by his divinity. But when his son, 'having reached his seventh year, has given proof of his survival, he is freed from the network of prohibitions and it is the child who is subjected to them in his turn'.[13] Canon de Lacger, whose words these are, perceived that there were here to be seen in miniature, or in germ, the main features of the great monarchies of Rwanda and Burundi. But in Burundi at least the institution of the Child King persisted into modern times. The last king to be installed there without European supervision was Mwambutsa (later officially called the Fourth), who succeeded in 1915, during the German–Belgian interregnum, and he was then about three years old. Nor was this an exception, for according to the knowledgeable official E. Simons the king at the time of his accession was always a minor.[14] An earlier witness, the German H. Meyer, had said that to be eligible he had to be unmarried and have both parents living,[15] which has much the same implication. The very long reigns credited to the nineteenth-century kings Ntare and Mwezi tend to confirm this claim.

At first sight there is nothing in the recent history and ethnography of Buganda to suggest any similar practice. King Mwanga II is known to have been about eighteen when he came to the throne in 1884 under the eye of European missionaries, and Muteesa I had probably been about the same age. It is true that his father Ssuuna II had been appointed at the age of twelve, according to Kaggwa's informants, or sixteen according to Stanley's, but he was a precocious lad who had already been on campaign, and there is nothing to show that any of the previous three or four kings, whose historical existence is certain, had not been at least adolescent when their reigns began. There are, however, normative statements that contradict the recent facts and suggest, as does much else, that nineteenth-century

Buganda was radically innovative. The most definite is that of Franz Stuhlmann, who was there in 1890: 'The new king must always be still a child, and during his minority his mother conducts the government together with the chiefs.'[16] This is almost word for word what was said about Burundi, and it has partial support from two earlier testimonies. Speke had reported that the queen-mother 'remained until the end of his minority the virtual ruler of the land',[17] and Felkin confirmed that 'the queen-regent exercises practically the same rights as a king until her son ascends the throne'.[18] The decisive evidence, however, that the kings of Buganda were ideally and ritually children is the fact that some years after their accession, as we shall see (pp. 147–54), they had to go through elaborate initiatory rites known as the *okukula kwa kabaka*, 'the king's growing up'.

Mulondo, then, can be recognised as the Child King, a figure who in the perhaps distant prehistory of Buganda had been accustomed to reappear at the proper time in the recurrent drama of kingship. He came, inevitably, from the east. The refuge to which Nakibinge had sent his children is said to have been Kyajjinja, a locality in the far east of the modern kingdom. However, since this name is simply 'the place of the rock', it could have been almost anywhere; and there is reason to think that the discovery of the heir took place much nearer to the ancient centre, in the district just to the east of the Mayanja Wasswa that gave its name to the modern county of Kyaddondo. For that name must be analysed as *kya-i-londo*, 'the (place) of the thing that is found'. The use of a 'neuter' prefix in place of the personal *mu-* is appropriate, for until he had been ritually inducted and socialised the wild boy was more thing than person.

Kings of this 'Mulondo' sort could well be children, since it was not their role to govern or wage war. Not only that: they had to be children, because that was the essence of their actual role. We cannot in fact begin to understand dynastic traditions until we have got to closer grips with the question: what is a king?

In Sir James Frazer's *Golden Bough* and in the works that were written in its vast shadow a clear answer was given. Ancient kings, in Africa and elsewhere but especially in Africa, served as mediators between their people and the forces of nature, presided over the agricultural cycle and kept it moving, were hedged about with taboos, above all were killed or took their own lives, either after a fixed term or when their vital energies had begun to wane, lest their weakness should infect society and land. By the later colonial period, however, the focus of intellectual interest in Africa had shifted from religion and magic to politics and administration. Even the use of the word 'king' was officially discouraged, even in relation to the pre-colonial past. The proper function of African chiefs was now to help the colonial authorities to collect taxes and maintain order. They were no longer required to promote good harvests or an abundance of children, for these were matters that could be left to the technical departments. Traditional ritual might still be licensed, provided it was purged of human sacrifices and other unacceptable practices and made to appear a quaint parody of the ceremonial of imperial Britain. In this atmosphere the whole concept of 'divine kingship' was questioned and the sacrality of African monarchy radically belittled. It was even denied that ritual regicide had any basis in real custom. Anthropologists working under the aegis of colonial governments, which would have treated the killing or forced suicide of a king as murder, did not hesitate to disbelieve or explain away the reports of such killings that had been submitted by witnesses when the kingdoms were still living systems.[19] Even scholars such as G. P. Murdock, or Roland Oliver and John Fage in their earlier writings, who still accepted the idea of 'African kingship' as a historically related complex, treated it as primarily a mode of government, not as a religious or intellectual construction.[20] And to the political sociologists who were moving into Africa in the 1950s and 1960s belief in the sacredness of kings was merely one of the 'resources' at the disposal of those who operated the political system. It was rarely asked whether the belief had any other function or just how it worked as an instrument of power.

With the passing of the colonial era it became possible to take African royalty seriously again. And that should be especially easy for British observers, who have found their own royalty, until very recently, taken very seriously indeed. To ask what kings and queens are for is to ask why the weddings of not very remarkable young men should have engrossed the British nation throughout recent summer days – or for that matter why their marital difficulties should be regarded as matters of consuming public interest. Sociologists of course have their answer, which may be pronounced with a conservative accent, approvingly, or with an angry radical intonation: it is the monarchy that has held British society together in a time of uncertainty and change. The statement is obviously part of the truth, but not the whole of it. For it fails to explain why the integrative mechanism should have taken this peculiar form. Moreover, it is well known that the life-crises of British royalty are watched with a kind of compulsive interest by foreigners who have not preserved a similar ritual complex.

Here surely is the point: it is the personal life-crises of royalty that have been the focus of popular emotion. The function of kings is to be born, to come of age, to marry, to procreate and to die – in other words, to do what all men do, but to do it with special solemnity and drama. These were their first tasks, long before the enlargement of social scale made government possible and needful; and thanks to the scale-reducing power of television these are their last tasks, after government has passed to other hands. In the beginning a king was a boy chosen and set apart before the start of his active life, in order that he might enact the great transitions on behalf of all the people. Whereas particular myths of kings derive from ancient royal ritual, the kingship was itself a myth, one of the most effective and enduring of humanity's attempts to give order and meaning to the flux of time. Frazer was thus fundamentally right. He erred, however, in seeing as magical what was really symbolic: the king did not ensure continuity but rather assured it. Frazer also gave undue prominence to the king's agrarian role, which was only one of the codes in which the myth expressed itself. It has been well said with reference to *The Golden Bough* that '"the priest who slew the slayer and shall himself be slain" is the personification of the life-cycle',[21] and with reference to medieval England that 'the body politic of kingship . . . represents, like the angels, the Immutable within Time'.[22]

We can now return to the details of the story of the foundling king of Buganda. The youths of the Mushroom clan, who made a throne for their little nephew, also entertained him with performances known as the *ama-zina ama-gunju*, the Ggunju dances, after the title of the clan head. That these were more than recreational is clear from a story about the discovery and bestowal of the late king's remains.[23] Since the Ganda army had scattered before Nakibinge was slain, no one knew where the body lay. Eventually a peasant came upon the bones by chance and made off with the spear that was lying beside them. Then he heard the drums beating for the Ggunju dance and went to watch it. The royal spear was recognised and he was arrested, but saved himself by quoting the legal maxim *omu-lonzi tattibwa*, 'a finder is not put to death'. He then led the officers to the remains, which could at last be given ritual burial, thus making Mulondo truly king. This funerary association of the dance is not accidental, for the head of the Mushroom clan was the hereditary royal mortician. Ggunju is in fact the marsh mongoose, *Atilax paludinosus*, who gropes with his long fingers in the banks of Buganda's swamps and prises frogs and suchlike from their watery holes; and it was the grim task of his human counterpart to burrow into the closed hut where the royal cadaver had been drying out and detach the skull, so that the jawbone could be extracted and separately bestowed. The Ggunju dances, Michael Nsimbi reports,[24] were exceptionally vigorous, with much leaping and tumbling. They were also very noisy, being accompanied by drums large and small and the jingling of many bells worn by the dancers. He records also the songs that went with them in recent times. These do not seem very interesting, consisting of conventional praise of the *kabaka* and impudent demands for money from the spectators. Away on the east coast of Africa, however, and a century earlier Bishop Steere of Zanzibar recorded two specimens of a Swahili verse-form called Gungu songs.[25] First there were charming verses in praise of the poet's wife, clearly derived from Arabic models and not relevant here. The second song begins: 'Mother, take me to see the decorated tower [?] and the children dressed up, wearing bracelets and necklets, holding up swords and shields. One is astonished to see them.' It goes on to talk about defence against the Galla and Comorian raiders who harried the coast towns in the early nineteenth century.

As always, the first step is to discard the adventitious context and focus on the central image. Forget Mulondo's position in the Ganda genealogy and the Nyoro invasion that is supposed to have preceded his accession. Forget also the coastal raiders, introduced by a modern poet who could not make sense of the picture he had inherited. (Real tribesmen and pirates would not have been deterred by boys in ritual finery.) The scene is this: a child with his mother watches a dance performed by older boys round some object that is doubtfully rendered as a decorated tower, but which may reasonably be conjectured to have been a throne.

To a European brought up, like myself, in the classical tradition there is another picture which could complete the set. It is the one that inspired the great Hellenist Jane Harrison with the inspiration for her work of creative scholarship, *Themis*. The infant Zeus, having been born (some said) in a Cretan cave, was taken away from his mother by the Kouretes, a band of 'young men who perform armed movements accompanied by dancing'. Above all they made frightening noises, with flutes and timbrels and clashing arms. (The function of the dancers' weapons, in Crete and Zanzibar, was clearly to be struck together.) In the myth, the Kouretes were trying to drown the cries of the new-born god as they spirited him away from his murderous father Kronos. And in real life, it seems, Cretan youths long continued to leap before the altar of Zeus as they sang for crops and children and for Themis, the right ordering of society and cosmos. With brilliant intuition Harrison related these fragments of Greek myth and popular culture to African and other 'primitive' initiation rites. She perceived too that the noisy dance around the divine child was not the immediate prelude to puberty initiation but belonged to an earlier rite such as the 'birth from the goat' that was enacted by Kikuyu boys of ten years or fewer and that the clangour was a deliberately frightening experience designed to force them out of the security of early childhood.[26] The original instrument of terror was the bullroarer, as it still is (or recently was) for the Malinke of Guinée, according to Camara Laye's beautiful description of an ordeal he went through some years before the greater trial of circumcision.[27] The Kouretes were the makers of kouroi, that is of boys who, having given proof of survival, were able to leave the nursery and take the first steps towards manhood.

A similar band called the Korybantes surrounded the child-god Dionysus, whose name may have meant 'the infant Zeus'. As is well known, Dionysus was the god of passion and disturbance, of transformations and transitions, patron of drama, lord of the vine, who emerged each spring from the swamp at the foot of the Acropolis to make his entry into the city of Athens. His career is perhaps best displayed in figure 6 on page 60 of *Themis*, which reproduces a pictorial sequence on an ivory relief from Milan. Though it belongs to the Roman period, far removed in time from the prehistoric culture of the Mediterranean, it preserves the structure of the myth with special clarity. First the newborn child is being taken from his mother by the midwives. Then the boy is shown sitting on a throne, with a high-peaked crown about his head, his arms raised in blessing, and two mail-clad warriors dance round him holding up spear and shield. Moving on, we find the prince riding on a he-goat, while goat-legged Pan marches in front and Silenus steadies him from behind. In the final scene, now a tall youth, he is mounting a chariot drawn by two leopards. The relief sketched for *Themis* (or a very similar one) is reproduced by photograph in Kerenyi's *Dionysos* (plates 66 A–E) and is there given the caption: 'Scenes from the life of Dionysos: birth, enthronement, the boy riding away on a he-goat, and the youth driving a team of panthers to his marriage with Ariadne.'

If the fourth scene depicts the hero's marriage, the one that precedes it must allude to the previous rite of passage, which is initiation into manhood. That this should have included goat-riding is not very surprising, for to Greeks especially the he-goat, *tragos*, a creature of roughly human size but with a much larger member, was the prime symbol of male sexuality. Boys whose voices were breaking were said to *trag-izein*, 'play the goat',[28] and the 'goat-songs' that went with their initiations gave rise in time to the celebrated literary creations known as trag-edies. Rather less obvious, because not linked with a sudden physiological change, is the crisis that was represented in the second scene of the Dionysus sequence. Yet it is still familiar to us in the child's first day at school – insofar as the abruptness of the transition has not been blurred by crèche and play-school. In some African societies, as we have noted, it was marked by formal ritual; and in ordinary life it was the time when boys began to run half-wild, learning the elements of herding and hunting, scrounging food instead of being wholly provisioned by their mothers. But for the boy who was chosen it was the time of his epiphany, when he came out of his secret refuge to assume the duties of kingship.

In classical Greece, where the sacred kingship had long ceased to be a functioning reality, the sequence of the boy's transitions – birth, installation, initiation, marriage – had been transferred to an imaginary being. It is very clear, however, that the god Dionysus was a surrogate for the human king. Each spring, when he came again to the city of Athens, he was reunited with the 'queen', the wife of the *archon basileus*, the 'royal ruler', the powerless civic official who preserved the last memories of kingship in that sophisticated republican society.[29] In Buganda, too, though the king was very much in evidence in the nineteenth century, his office had been rather thoroughly secularised, and only confused and fragmented echoes of the old system of ritual and myth were preserved in the tradition. Some of their neighbours were more conservative, however; and the best of all paradigms of kingship is found in a remarkable document called The Mwindo Epic,[30] to which we must digress before we can take the Ganda tradition further.

The four journeys of the king

The Nyanga people, some 30,000 of them in the 1950s, live in the forested hills to the west of the Western Rift. Though their (Bantu) language stands rather apart from those of the Lakeland group they share with it many cultural features and institutions and, having a very secluded homeland, can plausibly be regarded as a specially conservative member, providing evidence of what societies such as Buganda may have been like a thousand or even two thousand years ago. They are great tellers of tales, and the published stories of Mwindo are only the *chef d'oeuvre* of a considerable oral literature.[31] We owe these precious documents to the bards who were active thirty years ago, to the enterprising anthropologist Daniel Biebuyck who persuaded them to recite their work to the tape-recorder and to the educated Nyanga who helped him with his meticulous transcription and translation.

The term 'epic' used by Biebuyck could give a rather misleading impression of the Mwindo story. It is indeed a long and eventful narrative, in prose with some passages of chanted verse. But it is not a tale of martial valour, and its central figure has more in common with heroes of myth such as Perseus and Heracles, or of romance such as Lancelot and Perceval, than with the warriors of the Iliad or the Song of Roland.

In the first published version, that of the bard Candi Rureke, it begins with the classic formula 'Once upon a time there was a king', who built a royal village called Tubondo, with seven entrances and seven meeting-places of the people, and lived there with his seven wives. And he ordered them not to give birth to male children but to girls only. All seven quickly conceived and six were duly delivered of daughters. But the birth of the seventh child was long delayed, and when at last it came forth, by way of its mother's middle finger, it was seen to be a boy, Mwindo. His wails were heard in the king's house and his councillors asked what child was born. The midwives made no answer, but a cricket betrayed the arrival of a son. The king, who is named only as She-mwindo, 'Mwindo's father', did his best to kill his unwelcome heir, but found him to be indestructible by ordinary means and so had him put inside a drum and thrown into the river. The prodigious infant (who is also called Ka-butwa-kenda, 'he who walked as soon as he was born') was not at all dismayed but set off upstream, seeking his father's sister Iyangura, who had married a water-spirit. It was quite common (Biebuyck explains) for Nyanga women to marry such spirits, this being a way of saying that bride-price was not paid for them and their children would be assigned to their own patrilineage. But Mwindo lived in a myth, and his aunt's husband was no mere legal fiction but a real live water-monster called Mukiti, who shook heaven and earth when he stirred in his pool. (Mukiti is the phonetic equivalent of the Ganda Musisi, the name of the god of earthquake, and Mwindo's sister Musoka clearly corresponds to the Ganda rainbow divinity Musoke.) His reception of his nephew was not at first a friendly one, and Mwindo had many perils to overcome before he was established in Iyangura's house. But Hedgehog tunnelled a way for him, Spider built a bridge over the staked pit that had been dug for him, and Lightning, summoned by his enemies, fell harmlessly around him and thereafter became his ally and protector.

Plans were now laid for the boy's return to Tubondo; friendly forces of all sorts were mustered, and in yet another interpretation of the Ggunju dance theme Mwindo was 'forged' in preparation for the battle by his mother's brothers, who were bats. The avenging army was at first thrown back by Shemwindo's supporters, but Lightning fell seven times on the royal village and destroyed it with all its people – save only the king, who escaped into the underworld by way of a fern's roots. Having revived his uncles, who had fallen in the battle, Mwindo went down in search of his father, while Iyangura stood above, like Ariadne at the entrance to the labyrinth, holding the end of a rope which he had tied round his waist.

So the hero came into the world of ash, and there he encountered the goddess Kahindo, whose body was covered in yaws. He endured her embrace and, in return for guidance to the house of her father Muisa, washed her clean of her affliction. When he arrived at Muisa's house he was received with apparent courtesy and offered a stool to sit on, banana paste to eat and beer to drink; but, forewarned by Kahindo, he politely declined all these things. That was wise of him, for those who eat or drink in the land of the dead do not return; and it was Muisa (so another tale tells) who brought death into the world. The hero performed the impossible tasks that were then set him and slew his treacherous host (temporarily) with a blow from his magic fly-swatter, which was in his hand when he was born and was the source of all his powers. Then he went on to the home of Ntumba the Aardvark, whither his father had fled. Ntumba, the long-snouted, deep-burrowing, night-wandering ant-eater *Orycteropus afer*, is an even more sinister personage than Muisa. The Egyptians long ago knew him as Seth,[32] chief of the powers of evil, enemy of the falcon Horus, who is the sun as well as the young king. The Nyanga, too, tell how he once hid the sun, releasing it only under pressure from all other creatures.[33] He lives in the northern sky, in the heart of darkness, in the form of the seven stars that Europeans, being ignorant of him, absurdly call the Great Bear. (It is curious that when Englishmen did make his acquaintance they called him an ant-bear.) The hero overcame this monster also, only to find that Shemwindo had escaped again, this time to the home of the supreme divinity, Sheburungu. Here Mwindo was challenged to a gambling game, with his father as the prize. He won, though not until he had staked the fly-swatter, that is to say his very existence, and returned to the upper world carrying his father, whom he had now forgiven. He then brought all the people of Tubondo back to life, and amid great rejoicing the old king and his son were enthroned together, one on each side of the queen Iyangura.

Mwindo now began to marry wives, and it seemed that the happy ending had been reached; but it was not so. Feeling a craving for pork, he sent his hunters into the forest to procure it. They quickly tracked down a pig, but as soon as they had killed it the seven-headed monster Kirimu, who lived in the depth of the forest, appeared and devoured two of them. The third escaped and brought the dire news to his master. So Mwindo had to leave Tubondo for the third time and go into the forest and despatch Kirimu with his fly-swatter sceptre. The monster was carried home and cut up, and all the people he had eaten came out alive and whole.

But still the hero had no peace; for his protector Lightning had made a blood-pact with Kirimu and was greatly angered by his death. So now he was carried into the regions of the sky to be afflicted by Rain and Sun and Moon and Star, who warned him on pain of death never again to take the life of any creature. Hitherto his behaviour had been boastful and aggressive and thus (Biebuyck tells us) offensive to Nyanga values; but now he was chastened and he returned to Tubondo for the last time to rule his people with moderation and justice.

This story, of which a bare summary cannot convey the vitality and beauty, has, as its editor points out, a very clear formal structure. Four times the hero goes out from his birth-place to undergo trials and adventures, and four times he returns with greater power and wisdom. Now Biebuyck subsequently published three other versions, obtained from different bards; and in these, though most of the same incidents recur, they do so in other combinations and sequences.[34] It is conceivable, therefore, that the pattern so evident in the Rureke version is not ancient or intrinsic but local and recent, that a creative genius among the Nyanga – Rureke himself, or his teacher perhaps – used miscellaneous free-floating conventional story themes as the material for an artistic edifice of his own devising. Certainly the individual incidents are mostly of a familiar sort and might be regarded as mythological commonplaces. Countless heroes have begun their careers by being cast into the waters, to be providentially discovered among the reeds or carried across the sea in a box or to emerge from the depths of the lake when the time was ripe.[35] They include gods such as Dionysus, figures of myth or romance such as Perseus or Odysseus or Theseus or Tristan or Lancelot or Noah, fictions such as Tom the water-baby, supposedly historical characters such as Moses, undoubtedly real potentates such as Sargon of Akkad or Cyrus or Pope Gregory the Great. Many return like Mwindo to take vengeance on the father or grandfather who had rejected or tried to kill them. Even more obligatory for the hero of myth is the harrowing of hell, whether the land of the dead is openly recognised, as it was for Orpheus or Heracles or Aeneas, or is lightly disguised as a Cretan labyrinth or as one of the sinister hostelries of Irish myth. Dragons, of course, have been slain with great regularity, and quite often they have had seven heads. The journey to the sky, even when modified as the climbing of a high mountain, is not quite so common an adventure; but there is a striking parallel to Mwindo's fourth journey in the story of Moses, summoned to the sky by the lightning-god, ascending by the storm-girt slopes of Sinai and returning with the laws that hold society together.

Yet it is not easy to see Rureke's construction as a mere spatching together of independent stories and motifs. Its integrity of design is too evident for that, since it moves in orderly sequence from the hero's birth as a king's son to his conclusion as a perfected king. So I shall pursue a more fertile hypothesis, namely, that it is the true and original form of the Nyanga royal myth, preserving in the heart of Africa an ancient and meaningful schema that survives elsewhere in more opaque and fragmented guises. It is surely significant, to begin with, that the pictorial biography of Dionysus shares the same four-stage pattern, though it has no similarly explicit text.

The four-part myth of Mwindo has a spatial as well as a temporal dimension. The royal hero's journeys take him successively into the four outer sectors of the Nyanga cosmos – water, hell, forest, heaven – that impinge upon Tubondo and its gardens, the human centre of the world. This topography was not an arbitrary invention of the Nyanga. The theologians of the Haya people, Buganda's south-western neighbours, divided the universe into the same four provinces, each governed by a different divinity under the sovereignty of the High God: Mugasa the master of waters, Wamara lord of the underworld, Irungu the ruler of the wild earth and Kazoba the sun, king of heaven.[36] And the double ordering of space and time achieved by the Nyanga can be shown to be repeated in one of the oldest of all recorded myths.

Nearly sixty years ago the excavators of the ancient city of Ugarit in northern Syria came upon a mass of broken clay tablets covered in cuneiform inscriptions from which, by a great feat of sustained collaborative scholarship, there has been pieced together, deciphered and translated a remarkable piece of literature generally called 'the Ba'al epic'. The document is incomplete and there is still much uncertainty about the meaning and sequence of the text, but the outlines are tolerably clear.[37] It was evidently the script of a kind of drama or series of charades, probably intended for performance at the dedication of a new temple of Ba'al in or about the fifteenth century BC; but it is generally agreed that the story itself was even older. The first scene shows the young Ba'al being handed over by his father El, the High God of the West Semites, to Yamm, the sea, who appears to have married the goddess Athtart (Ishtar, Astarte). Ba'al, however, has been equipped with two clubs, one of which is thought to represent the lightning, and with this he lays the monster low. He returns to the city of the gods in triumph and has his own palace built. But then he is challenged by a new enemy, Mot – that is, 'Death' – who either swallows him or persuades him to enter his underground realm by opening a door in the mountain side. Eventually he is brought to life again and is once more feasting among the gods.

So far the sequence of events is certain, and it precisely parallels the first half of the Mwindo story, with the successive victories over the lords of water and of the underworld. The rest of the drama is badly fragmented. At some stage, however, Ba'al slays the seven-headed serpent Lotan (the biblical Leviathan). He is also seen going out into the 'cane-brakes', the land of wild cattle, where he mates with his sister the formidable Anath. Finally he ascends to the summit of Saphon, the holy mountain, and Anath proclaims the birth of 'a bull for Ba'al, a wild ox for the Rider of the Clouds'. Ba'al's father is regularly called 'Bull El'; he himself is presented as a steer and Anath as a heifer (it is likely that for the performance they wore bovine masks); and so the new-born calf is really the young god who starts once more to run his everlasting course. The Dionysus–Mwindo cycle is here looked at from a slightly different angle, so that birth appears as the end instead of the beginning. Otherwise all three are identical, and Ba'al repeats the four journeys of Mwindo, triumphing in the realm of water, in the underground kingdom of death, in the wilderness and on the sky-touching mountain. It is also clear that his adventures correspond with the four life-crises of the sacred king: installation, initiation into manhood, marriage and the procreation of his heir. In other words the stories of Dionysus, Mwindo and Ba'al all project into the domain of fantasy an ancient ritual cycle that is also attested in part at least by the ethnography and tradition of the greater Lakeland states, most clearly in Rwanda and Burundi. Or, it would be equally valid to say, at the beginning of this century it was still remembered that the kings of these countries had enacted, or were supposed to enact, the myth of Mwindo–Dionysus–Ba'al.

The first recurrent crisis of kingship is of course the birth of the future king, and this was followed by a withdrawal as swift and dramatic, if not as romantic, as that of Mwindo. The chosen infant, identified as such by being born with seeds of millet clutched in his tiny fist, was taken away from the palace by his mother and brought up in secret somewhere on the edge of the kingdom.[38] When the time was ripe he was escorted back to the capital to claim his inheritance. It is said that from time to time the king's bow was sent to the hidden child, until he had the strength to bend it. Alternatively, or in addition, the boy was made to stand in a basket of flour, which was then taken to the king. When he saw that his son's footprint was the equal of his own he knew that it was time to take a draught of poisoned mead and leave the kingdom to the new power.[39] And now it becomes evident why princes have to be hidden and why so many fictional heirs were lost: if he had the chance the king would destroy his future supplanter, as Kronos, Herod, Arthur and Shemwindo all tried to do. No one supposes that in real life any significant number of fathers, royal or other, European or African, have had murderous intentions towards their sons. But the myth brings into the open and so renders harmless the profound ambivalence with which men regard the birth and growth of the boys who are both the promise of their continuance and the sign of their extinction. The Nyanga story preaches to Mwindo's father, showing him that in trying to prevent the conception, birth and survival of his heir he was both wicked and doomed to fail. Its message is essentially that of *King Lear*. Men must be willing to retire, to let time move on, to retreat before the hungry generations' tread. To resist this necessity is to cause great and needless evil.

Other Lakeland myths proclaim the same truth in rather different ways, some of them explaining that it is not the son but the grandson whose advent brings kings and other men close to the shadows. We have seen that in Bunyoro a king of the old time tried to prevent the conception, and thereafter the survival, of the grandson who would found the glorious dynasty of the Ba-Cwezi. Likewise King Kalemera of Kyamutwara had his only son Chiume blinded and imprisoned so that the line could not be continued.[40] (It is only in myth, which deals in the opposites of reality, that an African could have made Kalemera's monstrous pronouncement: 'Posterity is not desirable.') Strangely enough, he allowed Chiume a female attendant, and the result was the boy who would be Mahe the Giver of Plenty. (The story makes sense only on the assumption that, as is hinted in other contexts, blinding is a euphemism for castration and the sentence had not been carried out.) Learning later of Mahe's existence, Kalemera summoned him to court with other ten-year-olds, intending to kill him; but the boy escaped into Nalubaale, where he encountered Mugasa the master of waters and so, having passed the necessary tests, acquired the fertilizing powers he would make good use of when he became king, as of course in due time he did.

Rwanda mythology, with its recurrent four-term cycle of royal names, provides yet another variant on this theme. Since a similar pattern was found in Burundi, in the fragmented kingdoms of Buha, and among the Hunde to the west of the Rift, and since there are traces of it in several of the small kingdoms recently absorbed by the expanding Rwanda state, the cycle must be presumed to go far back into the past of at least the south-western part of the Lakeland; and it is immediately tempting to assume that the recurrent names denoted, not successive kings, but successive stages in the royal life-cycle, that at the right time Cyilima *became* Kigeri, and so on until the cycle began again. This, it must be said, was not what happened in recent times. Kigeri Rwabugiri, who ruled Rwanda for at least thirty years in the later nineteenth century, never, while king, bore any title other than Kigeri. But it is proposed that the naming of the kings was a legacy from an old drama of monarchy; and that though the recent kings lived out their individual lives under their own names they still wore one of the old cyclical masks and accepted the roles that went with them. Thus 'Yuhi' and 'Cyilima' were called 'pastoral' kings and were supposed to live at peace, whereas 'Kigeri' and 'Mibambwe' were kings of war. This pattern was also embedded in the mythical tradition.

Rwandan historians recognise four royal cycles, of which the last three (ending with the Yuhi Musinga who died in 1959) were undoubtedly real; this state, as we noted, had exceptional mechanisms for the preservation of the dynastic past. But the narratives of the First Cycle in Rwanda – and nearly all those of the timeless tradition of Burundi – do not belong to history but, like the Mwindo romance though in a different way, constitute a model of the sacred kingship.

The cycle is in a sense skewed, for Yuhi, who appears to close it, is really the new beginning,[41] as his story shows beyond doubt.[42] It begins thus: 'Mibambwe the public king was in his palace at Remera in Kaninya . . . and in the night, towards cockcrow, he heard a child crying.' No one else could hear it, save for his servant Mugunga who was inspecting the royal herds at the further end of the kingdom. The kings of Burundi and Ndorwa heard it too, but no one else. This is unmistakably the opening of a fairy-tale, and it continues in the same vein. The inconsolable child was tracked down by Mugunga in the far country of Buha, where her father (or grandfather) was king. She wept because she had lost her favourite bead. A hen had pecked it up and a cat had eaten the hen and a dog had devoured the cat, and so on, until the precious thing had come to rest in the belly of an elephant, which the men of Buha were afraid to tackle. Mugunga slew the beast and recovered the bead, and so delivered the child from her sorrow and Buha from her incessant wailing. In recompense he claimed her as his ward, and when she was of age he arranged for her to be secretly married to his master the king of Rwanda. In due course a son, Yuhi, was born and was kept in seclusion on the confines of the kingdom. The years passed, and word came to Mibambwe that the boy was grown. So he took the poisoned drink, leaving the kingdom to one of his acknowledged sons but charging the chiefs not to fight for him with weapons of iron but only with papyrus stalks. Thus when Yuhi came to the capital with his escort there was only a mimed resistance and the pretender was at once deposed.

Here we have the myth that describes and validates the transition from a Mibambwe to a Yuhi reign, which is also the crucial transition from one cycle and generation to the next. But comparison with the story of Mwindo shows that it has undergone elaboration, no doubt in the interests of those who held the Mugunga office. It is obvious that the wails that disturbed Mibambwe in the night did not really come from a far country but from the women's quarters of his own palace, nor were they uttered by a little girl but by his new-born son. They were in fact the sign of his doom, which would be delayed only until the boy was old enough to take the throne.

Yuhi, then, was the Child King, as indicated by the name itself, which not only has no meaning but is not a proper nominal form at all. It can only be an ideophone, an expressive word, mimicking an infant's cries, or perhaps the call of a herdboy to his beasts; the first, mythical Yuhi had the additional name Gahima, 'Little herder'. Once established in his kingdom a Yuhi king was required to remain, like Mulondo, between the rivers, in the central province of Nduga, which is nearly encircled by the upper branches of the Kagera, perhaps more precisely in the district called Bwanamukali, 'the place of the child in the inner court'. His successor Cyilima (or Mutara) would cross the river eastwards and take up his residence in Bwanacyambwe, 'the place of the child's crossing', after an extraordinarily elaborate ritual called 'the way of the pools',[43] which must surely represent the royal initiation into manhood. He then becomes Kigeri, type of the young warrior, slayer of the monster Murinda, whose name is 'Seven', from whose clutches he delivers his sister-bride. By the end of the 'Kigeri' phase the king of Rwanda was married, but it was as 'Mibambwe' that he closed the cycle by bringing the next generation into being.

Having begotten his heir the king has completed his prescribed course, and there remains for him only the final transition which is death. The tale of Yuhi's advent is one expression of this necessity; but it is also asserted, rather contradictorily, that the first Mibambwe gave his life to rid the land of Nyoro invaders. The assumption that this was historical information gave rise to much difficulty, for evidence from other parts of the region made it unlikely that a Nyoro army could have reached Rwanda as early as Generation Fourteen, to which the first Mibambwe would have to be assigned.[44] The problem is resolved by realising that the First Cycle is not a historical narrative but an ideal paradigm, and that 'Nyoro' was a later label for a mythical and originally nameless enemy. This Mibambwe bore the name Mutabaazi, 'the Campaigner', a term which had a very special significance in Rwanda. A *mutabaazi* was a king or prince who allowed his blood to be shed by the enemy, preferably on their own soil, because thereby he would magically procure victory for his people. (Early twentieth-century Rwanda had no hesitation in bestowing the title on Christ the Saviour.) So, one way or another, the path of the new generation was opened up by the passing of the king whose time had come, so that the endless cycle could begin again.

The young shoot

In Buganda there was no regular cycle of royal names and the tradition showed no obvious sign of mythical system. Yet the excursion into other cultures was strictly necessary, for the 'early chapters' of the Ganda history do consist largely of the debris of such a system, and it is only by piecing it together that they can be made intelligible. The task is all the more difficult because the tradition is a composite one, containing the residues of more than one version of the kingship myth, so that some of the cyclical roles are duplicated or even triplicated. Thus Mulondo, son of the throne-goddess, nephew of the Mongoose dancers, is not the only Child King to be commemorated in Buganda.

It will be recalled that Kintu's successor Cwa had a wayward son called Kalemeera, and the story goes[45] that the old chief Walusimbi, who figures here as Cwa's *katikkiro*, came to the king and accused the boy of adultery with his wife. Whether the charge was true is left uncertain, but Cwa

Generation

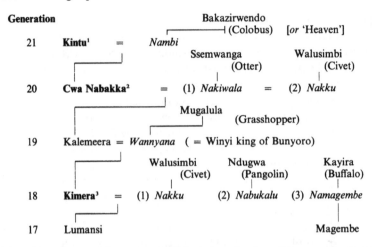

Note: Dynastic generations are counted back from the time of first record, with Muteesa I (1856–84) as Generation 1. Names of kings are in **bold** type, with superscript numbers showing their position in the dynastic list. Names of females are in *italics*, and their father's clan is shown in brackets.

Fig. 3   The beginnings

thought it best to get his son out of the way by sending him on a foreign business trip. So he gave him bark-cloth and other goods to trade in Bunyoro, where his uncle Winyi was the king. But Kalemeera had no sooner arrived at the Nyoro court than he seduced his host's wife, Wannyana, and got her with child. The irresponsible prince then set out for home but died on the road. In so doing he performed two valuable functions. In the first place he provided an explanation for the ancient practice of extracting royal jawbones; it was claimed that the precedent had been set by Kalemeera's escort, who brought the bone home as token of what had happened and to ensure that one part of the cadaver could be given proper bestowal. In the second place, he removed himself from the scene so that the heir to the kingdom could be his son, who would conform to the proper model of the hidden king.

When king Winyi learnt of his queen's betrayal he decreed that her child should be destroyed as soon as it was born. So the infant Kimera was put in a basket and thrown into a river, or some say into a flooded clay pit. Either way, he began his life, like a true royal hero, in the water, and was rescued by a potter who had come to the pit or the bank to dig clay and took him home for his wife to foster. Before long Kimera was herding cows like other small boys, and one day he let them stray into a plot of finger-millet (the *bulo* that Kintu and Nambi disastrously forgot). The field was the queen's property, and her servants wanted to drive the beasts out, but she forbade them saying: 'The millet is Wannyana's but the cows are Wannyana's also. Leave them alone, let them eat.' For she had learnt of her son's survival and had sent the potter cows for his sustenance.

Meanwhile in Buganda King Cwa had died, or as some say had disappeared, and the land was without a king. For a time Walusimbi acted as regent (we have seen that in reality the bearers of this title had long been kings in their own right) but then he was deposed and Ssebwana of the Pangolin clan was appointed in his stead. But this was no real solution to the absence of an authentic king, and eventually the chiefs, who had somehow become aware of Kimera's existence, sent a delegation to Bunyoro to summon him home. So the boy set off with his mother to claim the kingship that was his and his alone by right. It is remembered that, despite his youth, he was already a mighty hunter, and he displayed his prowess along the way, killing among others a buffalo, most dangerous of beasts. And this was clearly an old and integral feature of the tradition. It was as a hunter that he was described to Speke, and Stanley, who recorded the first extended version of the tale,[46] could give the names of the hero's two dogs, one white and the other black, apt symbols of the kingship that was both mortal and immortal. So it might be thought that the tradition was about to use the routine motif of the immigrant hunter who wins power by distributing the spoils of his chase, but it veers away from that familiar theme. Instead, in one version, Kimera arrives in the guise of a trader in salt. As in most of tropical Africa, mineral salt was very scarce in Buganda, and the produce of Bunyoro, extracted from the shores of Lake Albert, was always in great demand. So it was quite realistic to imagine that Ssebwana, having been sent an advance sample of the stranger's wares, should prepare to give him a royal welcome – though he did not realise quite how royal it would be. And now we are told of a curious conspiracy.

A woman called Nakku, daughter of Walusimbi, widow of King Cwa, and now apparently Ssebwana's consort, instructed his servants that when he sent them to bring in food and wine for the entertainment of his visitor they should go but not come back. So as Kimera drew near the regent stood on the *kiwu*, the royal carpet made of the skins of leopards and antelopes, waiting impatiently for his staff to bring in the feast. One messenger after another was sent to hurry them up, but they too failed to return. At last he lost patience and went off himself to see what was amiss. This was the cue for Kimera to step forward onto the carpet. The drums boomed out in welcome and all the people acclaimed him as their king. A line of women now came into view, each carrying a jar of banana wine, and behind them walked Ssebwana; but as he saw what had happened he dropped his own jar and fled away. And so began, or was re-established, the long line of Buganda's kings.

This would be a strange charade to be played by the leader of an invading army; and it was clear to me long ago that what has been preserved here is not the reminiscence of a historic conquest or dynastic upheaval, but the report of a many-times-repeated ritual progress, a dramatic presentation of the advent of a new king.[47] What I did not see until more recently is that it is the script of a very particular play, better known in its Greek version, the *Choephoroe* of Aeschylus (the Libation-bearers), second part of the great *Oresteia* trilogy. The assumption is that the dramas composed in Athens in the fifth century BC derived from, and could not have been created without, a ritual model that was already thousands of years old; and that the same model, or a nearly related one, was still productive in the African Lakeland at the close of the last century.

This claim may seem extravagant, yet the similarities are too striking to be ignored. The first play of the Greek trilogy, the *Agamemnon*, had shown how the king of Argos, returning in triumph from the siege of Troy, was treacherously done to death by Clytaemnestra his embittered wife in collusion with her lover Aegisthus. Years have passed, and now Agamemnon's daughter Electra comes to his tomb with the Chorus of slave-women to pour libations to his angry spirit. There she finds two young strangers, one of whom reveals himself as her brother Orestes, who was sent abroad, to Phocis, for safe-keeping (a familiar theme), and has now returned to seek vengeance on his father's slayers and to claim his royal rights. Together they plan and execute the killing not only of Aegisthus but also of their own mother. It is again the central image that betrays the kinship of the Greek and African dramas. We must set aside the rather silly story designed by some recent Ganda narrator to explain a scene he could not understand. What has come down through the millennia is the scene itself: a file of women carrying jars of wine, linked with the seizure of kingship by a young stranger whose right it is. The Greek story also includes some very specific echoes – not indeed of Kimera but of Mwindo. Phocis, for instance, where Orestes spent his infancy, was a district of western Greece, but it was also by etymology 'the country of the seals', in other words the sea. And its king, his host and fosterer, was called Strophios, 'the coiled one', and was thus a water-serpent like the Nyanga Mukiti, who is shown to us lying 'coiled in his pool'.[48] What is more, he was the husband of Orestes's father's sister, which is exactly the relationship of Mukiti to Mwindo. It is also clear that this is the regular role of the master of waters, who in Greece was better known by his other epithet Posei-don, that is to say Husband (*posis*) of the goddess Danu or Don. Thus Orestes can be seen as the boy who comes out of the waters to assume his kingship.

The title of the *Choephoroe*, middle play of the trilogy, alludes to the Choes, the Libations, the middle day of the three-day early-spring festival called the Anthesteria, of which Orestes was the legendary founder.[49] And it was on that day that the young god Dionysus, one of whose myriad mythical equivalents was Orestes, came out of sea or swamp to renew the year for the people of Athens. The Choes was a children's festival and Dionysus was a child god, who had taken over the role of the child king. Some doubt is thus cast on the report that he entered into ritual union with the queen (see above, p. 131). For the boy king naturally has his mother with him, and it had really been no sin for Oedipus to share the palace with Jocasta, though there came a time when she, like Clytaemnestra (and, it is suspected, many African queen-mothers) would have to die.

The Anthesteria was a rite of spring; and it was fitting that the god who presided over it, and over the theatre, should have been known also as Bacchus, 'the new shoot' – not of the vine only but of all reawakened vegetation. On the Equator, of course, there is no spring, but there are seasons of growth, and they belong to Ki-mera, whose name is derived from *ku-mera*, 'to sprout'. As I noted long ago, the boy found by the women in the millet-field is a clear image of the springing corn. This does not mean that he was a mere 'corn-spirit'. Agriculture is only one of the myth's many codes, and it would be at least equally true to say the green blades of the millet symbolised the strong-growing boy. More exactly, the image fuses two powerful emotions: the joy of cultivators (who were women) in the promise of the new crop and the joy of mothers in the thriving of their sons, and especially – for this is a myth of kingship – in the thriving of the chosen boy by whose growth the future of the whole community will be made secure.

Dionysus was often imagined as a bull, and so too was Kimera, whose mother's name Wa-nnyana makes her '(the Mother) of the Calf' (*nnyana*). It is remembered that Kimera wore a calf-skin when he came to Buganda, and it can be taken for granted that the skin was entire, showing that he brought to his people the strength and vigour of the young bull, immature still but holding the promise of more than human force.

When Kimera claimed the kingship, it was at the expense of the regent Ssebwana. Officially this man was a commoner and no kin of Kimera at all. In recent times the name belonged to the head of one branch of the Pangolin clan, and under colonial rule it became the title of the appointed chief of Busiro county. But this, like much else in Buganda, was clearly antiquarian opportunism, and does nothing to explain the role played by Ssebwana in the Kimera ritual. Perhaps he was a 'mock king' such as the boy who in Rwanda was placed on the throne to deceive the evil powers and then driven away after a ritual combat with the supporters of the true heir.

The name, 'Chief of infants', might support such an interpretation. It is, however, ambiguous, for it could also mean 'Father of infants' and imply a different role, which is endorsed by a curious passage in the otherwise fairly orthodox version of Le Veux's *Manuel*. In this case Kimera is invited to seat himself on the throne, but he draws back. How, he protests, could he, a mere child (*mwana muto*), seize the place that belonged to a senior? The word used here is *ssebo*, literally 'father' but also more generally a man of higher status. But then, the story goes on, 'his father' (and this time the word is *kitaawe*, a quite unambiguous term) 'lifted him up and set him on the throne'. This statement, which confirms that Kimera was indeed a child, is in obvious conflict with previous assertions that Kalemeera was long dead and that Ssebwana had left the scene. Clearly there were radically different versions of the Kimera myth, one of which, normally suppressed, has momentarily surfaced in the narrative of Le Veux's informant. It presents the crucial transition in its most ideal form, in which the father not only accepts but formally enacts his own supersession, and it implies that he is required only to abdicate, not to die. No version of the Kimera myth, indeed, makes any direct mention of killing. However, according to Kaggwa, when Ssebwana fled from the presence of the new king, he dropped the wine-jar he was holding, and the shattering of a vessel is usually a token of death.

Even more enigmatic than Ssebwana is the figure of Nakku, the woman who stage-managed the transfer of the kingship to Kimera. When Stanley recorded the story he portrayed her as a faithless wife who had fallen in love with the handsome young stranger.[50] That, however, was to interpret the myth by the alien conventions of European romantic fiction. If we are right about Kimera's extreme youth, any such motivation is of course out of the question; and the Catholic text more plausibly describes her as carrying out the commands of an oracle. Nevertheless, according to Kaggwa she did become Kimera's queen. She had previously been Cwa's, and she was also the wife of Kimera's double, Mulondo, and 'later', in terms of the official genealogy, of King Kayemba. Needless to say, Nakku is not the name of a historical individual but a recurrently acted persona in the drama of kingship. Indeed the holder of the Nakku office was included among the wives of every king. It was she who brought to a close the period of his mourning, taking up her hoe again and calling on the woman of Buganda to resume the labours that had been ritually suspended.[51] This function accords well with the role assigned to her in myth, which is to ensure the continuity of the kingship by contriving the transition from one generation to the next.

'Kimera' was the name of the chief actor in an immemorial drama, which had been performed in many lands long before the earliest beginnings of

Buganda: neither god nor king, he was the model of the human male in the first phases of his life and reign. But he was not simply a fossil, any more than Orestes had been in the time of Aeschylus. The solemn formula, 'You are Kimera', with which the latest of the *kabakas* was greeted at his accession, shows that the name had special power for the Ganda to the end of the nineteenth century and beyond. And while it is quite wrong to treat the story primarily as a narrative of conquest and state-formation that can be dated by means of the official genealogy, it would be equally misguided to ignore the signs that, like the myths of Kintu, the story of Kimera's advent does have something to tell us about local political change. There is the curious redundancy of Kimera and Mulondo, who both appear to play the same mythical role. Were these simply alternative names of the Child King, used perhaps in different ritual contexts? Or may they have belonged to different components of Ganda society, and be indirect evidence of the way that it was put together? And there is the simple fact that Kimera is said to have been born in Bunyoro. Ritual requires that the new king should come from outside – actually from the borderlands but apparently from beyond them – but does not specify his place of origin. Like most characters of his sort, Mulondo comes to Buganda from the east, as is symbolically proper. But Kimera comes from the north-west, and there is no symbolic compulsion about that. There is thus an initial presumption that the myth of the young shoot does cover a historical intervention from that quarter.

Here is perhaps the most difficult question about African pre-colonial history. Practically without exception, politically dominant groups in Africa affirm that their ancestors came from somewhere else and established control over an indigenous population, usually displacing former rulers. Often some commoner groups also claim a foreign origin, leaving the true natives, 'those found here', as a small minority. Historians in the colonial period generally accepted these claims without question – after all, they provided a kind of precedent for the colonial conquest – and the result was that African history was presented as little more than 'the unrewarding gyrations of barbarian tribes', in Lord Dacre's famously dismissive phrase.[52] Stung by this taunt, Africanists have spent much of the last quarter of a century either denying the gyrations or trying to make them rewarding by incorporating them into a developmental model. Yet there is no doubt that African populations were in fact very mobile or that political structures were fluid and often ephemeral.

The causes of the movements need more examination than they have usually been given. In particular, 'population pressure' has too often been invoked as a facile and complete explanation. In fact, there is no numerical information about densities or birth and death rates in east Africa before the twentieth century, and we do not know whether population was growing or not. It is entirely possible that epidemic and endemic diseases and periodic famines kept it broadly stable; and even if, as is likely, there was a secular upward trend it was too slow to enforce constant migrations. Nor would the adoption of agriculture, or of new crops or production techniques, automatically promote expansion. On the contrary, the point of such innovations was to increase the carrying capacity of the land and so to *reduce* the incentive to migrate. In fact it was the very absence of population pressure, especially on the eastern and southern savannas, where agricultural settlement is probably no more than two thousand years old and often much less, that generated mobility, in the simple sense that people had elbow room. They might wander off to seek better land, or much more often to escape from the pressures of kin and the exactions of the powerful. Indeed the abundance of land has been recognised as the chief brake on the development of complex economies and polities. But migrants were not always fleeing from power; sometimes they were seeking it. Polygamy ensured that there were always more young men who believed themselves born to high status than could actually enjoy it; and the response of the losers was often to move out and find someone else to dominate. And if they moved into a less highly structured society they had a good chance of being successful. They might simply have enough followers to bully people into submission. They might also have the techniques of command, the habit of authority. And there is reason to think that a foreign arbiter, one standing outside the local factions, would sometimes be actually welcome.

The foreign founder is thus not necessarily a mere cliché. On the other hand, the origin-stories of dynasties follow a suspiciously common pattern, suggesting that they are generated by structural needs rather than historical events. The uniquely skilled and generous hunter is one very widespread theme, but there are others. In some places it is combined with the true genesis myth about the being who comes out of the water to mate with the daughters of men. Or it may be claimed that the founding hero brought a knowledge of iron-working to people who did not have it. And, if that might be thought to be a distant reminiscence of the Early Iron Age, the indigenes are sometimes said to have been ignorant of fire as well; in other words, the formation of the dynasty is merged with the transition from nature to culture. It seems therefore that the advent of the Stranger, or the migration of the Rulers, serves to give primary myths a spatial dimension. As the past was divided into Sasa, real time, and Zamani, the time of myth, so was space divided into here and elsewhere; the crossing of the frontier was the beginning of proper human life.[53]

The ruling lineages of the little kingdoms west of the Western Rift mostly justify their dominance by an anecdote very similar to that of Kimera.[54]

Their ancestor, they say, came as a guest to the home of the aboriginal chief and tricked him into relinquishing his stool, or was given the seat in courtesy and refused to leave it. They trace their origin to the forest country in the west; and, though language and culture seem to link them rather with the Lakeland to the east, the historians who have studied the traditions in detail are disposed to find truth in this claim. The Kimera story, however, is more complex. The Ganda agree that Kimera came from Bunyoro, but assert that he was nevertheless really one of theirs. Scepticism is of course in order; patriots have obviously been trying to make the fact of Nyoro dominion more palatable. Indeed in Nigeria we can actually see a 'Kalemeera' being inserted into the traditions of an Edo-speaking community in what became Bendel state.[55] Earlier versions simply followed a pattern universal in south-west Nigeria: the dynasty-founder came from the Yoruba city of Ife, whose antiquity and wide influence are beyond any doubt. A more recent version, concordant with contemporary political needs, adds: 'Ah, but his father had actually been an Edo visitor!' This transparent invention warns against the assumption that, whereas Kimera's Ganda parentage is false, his Nyoro origin is true. For there is a time in the rise of new states when patriots actively seek a foreign origin, needing the cachet of a more illustrious society. A well-known example is the medieval Brutus legend, which allowed the rulers of the peripheral kingdom of England to pretend that they were the true heirs of Rome. Likewise, wherever Islam became influential in sub-Saharan Africa the local rulers added Arabian ancestors to their pedigrees.

In face of these conflicting considerations the only possible stance is a provisional agnosticism. Without further evidence we cannot certainly tell what historical basis the story of Kimera may have had. As we shall see later, other evidence tends to confirm that it concealed a political process in which the kingdom of Bunyoro played a real part. But now we must complete Kimera's mythical biography and explore its sequel.

The frog's nephew

Kimera reigned for some years in bliss and splendour, but his end was tragic. His marriage to the ill-omened Nakku resulted in only one offspring, the serpent Lumansi. Our texts, being determined to present these stories as history, naturally treat Lumansi as a human prince, who was sent by his father on an expedition such as became routine in the nineteenth century, a cattle raid into Busoga. They say, however, that he died on the way (Lumansi is also the name of a serpentine river that rises in eastern Buganda) and that his young son Ttembo, holding his grandfather responsible for the death, plotted a terrible vengeance. Urged on by Nakku,

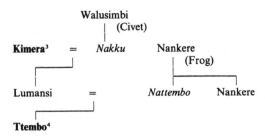

Note: Names of reigning kings are in **bold** type, names of females in *italics*.

Fig. 4   The frog's nephew

he treacherously struck Kimera down with a club during a hunt, and took his place on the throne.[56]

Nakku's strange malignance is easily explained; once again she is helping to bring about a transition, this time the most crucial of all, the one that leads from childhood to adolescence. Like most Lakeland peoples the Ganda bestowed a new name and persona on the royal hero for each phase of his career; and in due course the new name became a new king, who had to be fitted into the genealogical scheme. There was thus created an illusion of historical succession, not present in obviously timeless myths such as the Nyanga story of Mwindo, who went through the whole cycle of development with the same identity. At the same time the device precluded certain kinds of literary and intellectual by-product. Ganda culture, for example, could not easily have produced biographies or novels of psychological development. Whereas Mwindo grew in strength and wisdom with every adventure, in Buganda each transition produced a new person. At his accession as a child, the king was Kimera (or Mulondo); at his initiation a few years later he had become his 'grandson', Ttembo.

Like Orestes, Ttembo was driven mad by the guilt of parricide; in fact 'Madness' is what the name Ttembo means. And his doctors prescribed a drastic cure: an elaborate nine-day sequence of rituals and journeys attended by much killing, the central act taking place at the home of a chief called Nankere to the west of Bakka. All subsequent kings, until recent times, would have to go through this experience, which was explicitly called *okukula kwa kabaka*, 'the king's growing up'. The very full descriptions recorded by both Kaggwa and Roscoe, and later by educated descendants of key officiants,[57] are among the most precious documents in African ethnography, for they preserve the memory of what was manifestly a very archaic royal ritual. Professor Kiwanuka appeared to believe that it had been superseded by the new accession ceremonies performed for Namugala and his successors at Buddo.[58] This can hardly have been so, since the procedures were still remembered in detail six generations later; and in fact it was Ssuuna II, Muteesa's father, who put an end to the custom a century after Namugala.

In any case, the *okukula* had never been an accession rite. Roscoe made it clear that a considerable time – not less than two years, probably more – elapsed between the king's installation and what he described as his 'visit to Nankere for the purpose of prolonging his life'.[59] Benjamin Ray rejects this information, and asserts that the ritual instituted by Ttembo was the final part of the installation process, whereby the indigenous clan heads 'confirmed (*kukula*) the king's accession to the throne'.[60] But (*o*)*kukula* does not mean 'to confirm'; it means 'to grow, become older', and Kiwanuka correctly identifies the ritual as being one of 'maturation'. It is only by analogy with the Christian initiation rite that the King's Growing can be described as a 'ceremony of confirmation'; and there is no valid reason to doubt that installation and initiation were successive acts, not alternatives.

The first day of the *okukula* took the young king to Bukoto, now a northern suburb of Kampala. From there he travelled northwards to the home of Jjita, head of the Seed clan, where he spent the night. In the morning Jjita gave him his daughter Nalunga to be his first wife (though some say she was the daughter of a neighbouring chief), and he then turned westwards, past the rock Kkungu and across the Mayanja Wasswa, passing from Kyaddondo to Busiro county. Here he was received by Nakuni of the Civet clan and taken to Kongojje, a mile or so north of the hill of Bakka. Then he crossed the Kabumba stream to the home of Ka-londa, 'the Finder', who explained: '*Nnonze! Omulonzi tattibwa*' (I have found [him]! The finder is not put to death). (That, it may be remembered, was the plea of the man who found Nakibinge's spear and brought it to Mulondo, 'the Foundling'). And so ended the third day.

So far, the theme is the familiar one of the Child King coming across the river from the east and being 'discovered' by the kingmakers. It appears that although the drama has puberty initiation at its centre it encompasses the whole regnal cycle, beginning with the king as a small boy. The place-name Kongojje, for instance, gets its name from -*kongojja*, 'to carry on the back'. It is true that the king, even when adult, was always carried on a man's back, lest the sacred feet should come into contact with the earth; but the allusion here is surely to a specific ritual, such as was observed in Burundi in 1915, when the new King Mwambutsa, who was actually a child of only three years, was carried across a stream with joyful acclamation after a strange ritual murder.[61] The journey from Jjita's to Kalonda's would be something like twenty miles, which seems to make a long day for a child. It is likely in fact that the range of the king's progress was extended with the growth of his realm, and that the original river of transition was the brook that flows past Kongojje. Kyaddondo, 'the place of the finding', would then have been not the modern county of that name but the country immediately to the east of Bakka. From now on, at any rate, the king's journeys would be confined within Walusimbi's ancient realm.

The fourth day brought the king to the climactic rite. Kalonda's home was probably Bu-londa, a couple of miles west of Bakka; and from there he moved to Bukerekere, another two miles or so to the west, home of chief Nankere of the Lungfish clan, who greeted him in midstream, armed with copper spear and dagger, with his hair decorated in an ancient mode. Ttembo's mother, who is remembered only as Na-ttembo, was the daughter of a Nankere and presumably the sister of his successor. Ttembo was thus Nankere's nephew, and that, it must be presumed, was always the ritual relationship, no matter what the king's maternal clan might actually be. It is then a little easier to understand what followed. The king and Nankere entered his house from opposite sides and exchanged drinking vessels. Nankere proclaimed the boy to have come of age and to be truly king and then, turning to the queen-mother, he forbade her to set eyes on her son ever again. She too was a 'king' (*kabaka*) and they must thereafter live apart, she in a palace to be newly built for her. The king then went out through one door and turned back east to spend another night at Kalonda's. His mother and Nankere left in the other direction, and she would not in fact see her son again. In historical times she had her own court, close to the royal palace but separated from it by flowing water; and it was not until late in his life that Muteesa broke the prohibition, as he broke most other ancient rules. As for Nankere, being the king's mother's brother he would have held the regency during the king's minority, and so he was enacting his own ritual supersession.

The rite certainly enabled the young king to take effective grasp of the reins of power, but that was not the sole purpose of the encounter. While he was in the house of Nankere a macabre performance, having no obvious reference to a mere change of government, was going on nearby. One of the chief's sons was seized and men pounded his back with their fists until he died; and his dorsal sinews were then cut out to be made into anklets for the king to wear. The account published in 1959 by members of Nankere's lineage attempts, not altogether convincingly, to modify the horror, saying that the king himself punched the victim once in the chest and he died without a groan.

The journey to the underworld, the usual mythical counterpart of initiation ritual, is not here as openly described as it is in the tale of Mwindo or of many others, but the allusions to it are nonetheless unmistakable. Nankere's home lies in the west, the direction of sunset and endings.

Nearby is a locality called Bu-yonga, 'soot-land', a common designation of the country of the shades. And there is another, more oblique indication. Nankere, it was mentioned above, belonged to the Lungfish clan, but that was probably a recent political adjustment. The large Lungfish group is known to have been historically composite, and members of its major branches were not forbidden to intermarry. Nankere's people had their own distinctive *kabbiro* or 'second totem', which was the Frog, *ki-kere*. Both Na-n-kere and Bu-kere-kere are derived from the same root, so that the title of Ttembo's uncle could be rendered as 'Lord Frog of Frogland'. Now we know from the ancient comedy by Aristophanes that the Frogs dwell in the marshes that surround the Styx; and it is likely that the Ganda had the same idea. The swampy meres common in the country between the Great Lakes were often seen as entrances to the underworld; and we may hear the frogs of Buganda singing *kere-kere* to the young king as he crossed the swamps on his way to the land of shadows.

When he returned from the west to the house of Kalonda he had passed through the most crucial phase of his 'growing up', but his ritual progress was far from complete. The fifth day took him to Bu-sujja, home of the chief Ka-sujja, head of the Colobus Monkey clan. On the next day he played *oku-bonga*, a children's game in which large seeds are spun into collision, and came to the house of Nabitalo, a woman of the Civet clan, where he spent the night. The seventh day's programme was very crowded. First, Nabitalo and Kasujja took him to the top of the rock Nanfuka, so that he might survey his realm. This is an indication of how small the primary kingdom was, for the relief of Busiro does not allow long views even from a high place. However, there is an interesting echo from the Fipa country in western Tanzania, where the old king was visited by strange women, who invited him to show them the extent of his kingdom from a high place. A properly expansive gesture would have obliged him to reveal his underarm hair, so he described only a modest circle.[62] The history of the Fipa has therefore proceeded in a different direction from Buganda's. The old dynasty controls only a small central area and the rest of the country is divided between independent chiefs reputedly descended from the women.

The young *kabaka* was then brought by stages to the house of the mysterious Nakku at Kitoke, where he planted a banana tree (*kitoke*). From there Nakku took him to Ggunju, who conducted him into the presence of Walusimbi lord of Bakka. (Since descending from Nanfuka the party had been skirting the slopes of that central hill.) The encounter began badly, for the king had approached the house from the back and had to pay a heavy fine for his discourtesy. There followed an awkward duplication of the meeting with Nankere. Again the king went through the business of exchanging drinking vessels with his host, each standing on a royal carpet of lion and leopard skins, and Walusimbi repeated the edict of separation: 'You are grown up now, and you must never see your mother again.' He also told him to rule his people well.

The king spent the night with a son of Walusimbi called Kaweesa ('the Smith'), who next morning made three iron supports for a cooking-pot, in which the women Nabitalo and Nakku prepared a meal of finger-millet. The king then called for another game of spinning tops, but the attendant who rushed to bring the seeds was seized and put to death. Having drunk from the sacred well Na-bakka and planted a tree at Nsuka, he proceeded to a rock called Sse-mugema, where another curious charade was enacted. With the hereditary officials Mugema and Mbajja he amused himself by throwing shells into the fire, until another functionary called Nabugwamu, 'the Intruder', came and rebuked them for their profligacy. (Officious meddlers and killjoys were likely to be asked: 'Are you from Ssambwe?' – Nabugwamu's traditional home.) As with the spinning game, the point is at first sight that the grown-up king is no longer permitted to behave childishly. However, given the sexual associations of fire, the guess may be hazarded that the forbidden game was really masturbation.

The ninth and last day produced yet another grisly incident, when the attendants carrying the cooking-pots were accused of scattering soot in the king's path, and some of them were caught and killed. 'You black-faced people,' cried the officer Kawuuzuumo (of the Bird clan), 'have you painted the king black?' In Africa no less than in Europe black is the colour of death, and it is here acknowledged that the sacred being has not escaped the contagion of his people's mortality. But he was now given anklets made from the sinews of Nankere's son, which were supposed to ensure that his life, though not endless, would be long. (To this extent Roscoe's 'life-prolongation' description was justified.) He then went on to Kavumba, where he spent the night with Nakku, the supervisor of all royal transitions. By now he was on his way back to the Kampala area, and the ritual progress was at an end.

Obviously the scenario has been added to in the course of the centuries and some distortions have occurred. The latter part of the drama, after the return from Bukerekere, is not easy to interpret as a coherent whole. If, as seems certain, Walusimbi and the king were originally the same person, the arrival at Bakka would be the return to the capital and the conclusion of the journey. Political changes and the shifting of the kingdom's centre of gravity caused the action to be extended and its outlines blurred. However, it appears that the king's initiation included a kind of preview of his career. The night he spent in the house of Nabitalo would then represent the sacred marriage; and the climbing of the rock Nanfuka might be the equivalent of Mwindo's journey to the sky, the final stage in the perfection of kingship.

It cannot be concealed that the path of the young king was a bloodstained one and the implications have to be confronted. We have already seen that Buganda, especially its royal court, was notorious in the nineteenth century for its apparent carelessness of human life. It is likely that killings on the scale then practised were a novelty, reflecting the rapid rise of a successful but insecure military state in a troubled age, but there is no doubt that they had precedents in ancient custom. Tiny communities such as old Bakka could not have been so prodigal of manpower or so indifferent to their members' grief, but the principle and the value of sacrificial death were certainly unquestioned. The killings in the later part of the *okukula* somehow recall a children's game of forfeits, also the old army jokes that taught the basic maxim: never volunteer for anything! It is even possible that they were killings in play only, but rather more likely that our children's games carry an echo from a grim reality. Such sacrifices, unlike those enforced by military systems, did not reflect contempt for human life. On the contrary, they meant that life was so precious a thing that a high price had to be paid for its renewal. The association of puberty initiation with death was not purely symbolic. For one thing, in the absence of antisepsis circumcision, the usual centrepiece of the ritual, was dangerous as well as painful. But in addition, in most of the African societies that continued the practice of initiation into modern times there were rumours that at least one of the boys was deliberately killed in order to secure the survival of the rest.[63]

It is not, then, the murder of the Frog boy that is the heart of the enigma but its bizarre and brutal nature, to understand which we shall have to travel far afield. In so doing we shall hope to discover also why in the context of the king's initiation his maternal kinsmen were Frogs.

William of Malmesbury, an English writer of the twelfth century, made a brief report of a legend that had been preserved (and exploited) by the monks of Glastonbury. It told how Ider son of Nuth, a boy in the service of King Arthur, was given arms by the king and sent to prove himself by taking on 'three famous wicked giants'. He slew all three but fainted from exhaustion and was taken for dead by Arthur, who appointed twenty-four monks to pray for his soul at Glastonbury. Joel H. Grisward has demonstrated that behind the ecclesiastical accretions there is an ancient story that alludes to rituals of warrior initiation, having close analogues in the mythology of ancient India as well as in the early 'history' of Rome.[64] In particular, confrontation with a three-headed or triplicated antagonist was a feature of myths throughout the Indo-European world; and Cerberus, who had to be overcome by Greek heroes when they ventured into Hades, shows that the theme is linked with the initiatory journey into the land of the dead.

The triune opponent does not appear in Africa, but there is another, seemingly insignificant detail of the tale of Ider that strikes a familiar note: the adventure took place on the *mons ranarum*, the Hill of Frogs, which the text identifies as Brentecnol, that is Burnt Knoll near Glastonbury. Ider, it should be made clear, was not an ordinary knight but a king's son. Actually he had been the old British deity Edeyrn, whose father Nut (otherwise Nodons, Nuada, Lud) was the king of the gods. So we have a strange duplication. Both in Britain and in Buganda the ordeal of the young king's initiation took place in the country of the frogs. If the association was a historical one it must have been very ancient; if it was logical, the mytho-logic must be very compelling.

Light is cast on Bukerekere from a yet more distant source, the Sun Dance of the Plains Indians. At the heart of that great communal festivity was the ordeal of the young braves, who were tethered to posts by hooks inserted into the muscles of their backs and then had to dance until the hooks were torn out with the flesh. This was of course a test of the fortitude required of young men in those hard-living societies, but it was also something else. Lévi-Strauss has shown that it is intricately linked with a vast mythical complex concerning the *femme crampon*, the woman who clamps herself to a man's back, with strange and disastrous consequences.[65] In some manifestations she is the frog who jumped onto the moon and can still be seen clinging there. And so it becomes clear that the dancing braves were getting their frog-mothers off their backs. Physical torment both symbolised and masked the emotional anguish caused by the necessary loosening of the strongest of all bonds.

In Buganda, however, it was not all youths who were painfully inducted into manhood, but only the king, who went through this and other transitions on their behalf. And he in turn had delegated the suffering to another, who endured not only agony but death in order that the king and the people might live.

Whereas the stories of Kimera and even of Kintu may perhaps contain some allusion to historical events, there is no similar indication in the story of Ttembo, who belongs wholly to cyclical time. The ritual of which he is supposed to have been the first subject certainly goes back far beyond the reach of traditional memory. The murder of Kimera simply dramatises the basic truth, that grandsons by their mere existence proclaim their grandfathers' death; and the 'madness' that gave the hero his name, though rationalised as guilt, exaggerates the emotional disorder of adolescence, for which the cure anciently prescribed was the ordeal of initiation. When that has been completed, the reign of Ttembo is effectively over and the cycle moves on.

The father of the rivers

As in ritual, so in myth the second half of the royal cycle is less clearly preserved in Buganda than the first; and there is some reason to suspect that Kiggala, who follows Ttembo in the extant tradition, was not his original successor. Though he has a jawbone temple in the near neighbourhood of Bakka, he seems to belong to the coastal districts of Busiro, where most of his activities were located. Indeed he is also known as one of the *lubaale* deities, whose home was in the Ssese islands out in the Lake. According to Roscoe he was 'the spirit of deafness' (the name is derived from the verb -*ggala*, meaning to block, shut up). But there are signs that he had been much more than that. The second largest island in the Ssese group was called Bu-kasa, in allusion to the great god of the waters, Mu-kasa. The main island, however, was Bu-ggala, which by clear analogy should be 'the home of Ki-ggala', who is thus indicated as the greatest of the gods. (A closely related name, Mw-igara, belongs to a deity widely worshipped in the Nyoro-speaking lands to the west.) He seems to have been an inimical power, for he is given three other names: Ssewannaku, 'Father of sorrows', Mukaabya, 'Author of weeping' and Kungubu, 'Lamentation'. Perhaps that is why he yielded the first place among the gods to the kindly Mukasa.

At some stage this divinity was inserted into the royal genealogy – not right at the beginning, as might have been expected, but as the fifth of the kings. His placing, however, was not arbitrary, for the acts attributed to him are in some respects appropriate to Ttembo's successor. After initiation comes marriage, and Kiggala's most spectacular deed was a sexual one: before coming to the throne he lay with his sister Nazibanja, who gave birth to the twin Mayanja rivers.[66] These sluggish streams, which bear the names always given to male twins, Wasswa and Kato, rise close together just north of Kampala, then flow in almost opposite directions, but curve round to meet at the north-west corner of Busiro before moving away towards Bunyoro. They thus practically enclosed the Buganda heartland.

At first sight the story is just a piece of geographical fantasy; and indeed the Ganda were very fond of telling scandalous tales about hills and rivers, mostly without any historical or serious intent. But there is more to it than that. Incest is no light matter; it is one of the central themes of myth; and whatever his origin may have been Kiggala is presented to us as a king's son and a future king. It has to be asked how the Ganda could have admitted that he broke one of the fundamental laws of human society.

There is a dark feature of the sacred kingship that has been hinted at more than once but must now be brought into the open, namely that the woman who entered into marriage with the king, the maiden he had to

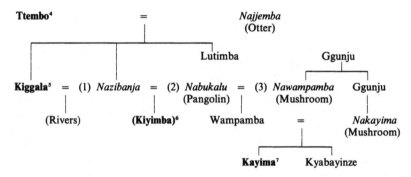

Note: Names of kings in **bold** type, with superscript number showing position in dynastic list. Names of females in *italics*, with father's clan in brackets.

Fig. 5   Father of the rivers

rescue from the seven-headed dragon, was his own sister. In Levantine myth, Ba'al was united with his sister the goddess Anath. In the ritual reality of dynastic Egypt the pharaoh's queen was regularly his father's daughter. So too was the *mumbo*, the consort of kings among the Hunde, neighbours of the Nyanga on the west side of Lake Kivu.[67] Elsewhere in Africa the custom had been generally suppressed, but there is ample evidence from ritual and myth to show that it had formerly been the rule throughout the vast domain of the kingship myth. The usual rationale was the need to ensure that the mystic energy of kingship was kept unweakened by alien blood, but the underlying thought was probably that the sacred one must prove his sacredness by an act that in profane life was most stringently forbidden. Whereas other men must go abroad to satisfy their desires, the king must return home when it is time for him to wed, and live secluded with the companion of his childhood. Indeed, it is tempting to speculate that the institution of marriage – that is to say, of holy matrimony, the ritual formation of an indissoluble bond between a man and a woman – was originally devised for the king alone, and was quite distinct from the ordinary exchanges of women between allied groups. It was by that means above all that the king was decisively set apart from ordinary humanity.

This exclusiveness was not easy to maintain indefinitely. In later pharaonic Egypt commoners began to copy the kings, not only contracting marriages but doing so with their sisters. In this respect as in others, however, Egypt was peculiar. In Europe and elsewhere the unions of both commoners and kings became sacramental but not incestuous. In most of Africa, on the other hand, royal marriage ceased to be a sacrament and the kings took part in the general system of marital exchange, though of course on privileged terms. (But there were societies in Zaire where the king, far from being polygamous, was required to be celibate, usually after a single ritual union on the night of his installation.) However, so radical a change left a large area of uncertainty behind it, and the dynastic mythology, in Europe and in Africa, reveals an uneasy discordance between its inherited data and recent real life. In classical Greece Electra could not be allowed to become the wife of Orestes, but she did the next best thing by marrying Pylades, his cousin and foster-brother. Medieval storytellers could not conceal that Arthur (who became the collecting-point for the debris of the kingship myth in north-west Europe) was guilty of incest, though they had to treat it as a sin for which he was ultimately punished. In central Africa, the Nyanga distanced the lady Iyangura to the furthest possible extent from the king her brother by having her successfully wooed by a water-monster. Nevertheless her relationship with Mwindo is consistently maternal (his actual mother disappears from the story after giving birth) and the cord that she holds while he explores the underworld would be recognised as umbilical even if it were not explicit that he had been born holding it. Some versions also acknowledge that Kahindo, the woman whom Mwindo embraced in the underworld, was both his sister and his bride. There is, however, a separate story which ingeniously splits the personality of the queen-sister; it features two unrelated heroines of the same name, one being of royal birth while the other is destined to marry royalty.[68] In recent Buganda the king was ritually married to one of his half-sisters, the *lu-buga*, mistress of the palace, *ki-buga*, who was enthroned alongside him and enjoyed power and dignity only a little inferior to the queen-mother's and his own. She did not, however, *become* the queen-mother and indeed was not supposed to have relations with the king at all. The long-abandoned custom of royal incest was embedded in the tradition but could survive there only in the guise of fantasy.

If Kiggala represents the archetypal king at the time of his marriage he should also be a slayer of the dragon, and Kaggwa's text duly conforms to the model. It tells how he was challenged by his brother Lu-timba, whose name conceals the common noun *t-timba*, meaning 'python'. Actually it was Kiggala's sons who went to war on his behalf. For two days the fighting was inconclusive, but on the third day the enemy forces, weakened by diarrhoea and red ants, were forced to flee. Lutimba himself died of stomach pains generated, it was thought, by Kiggala's fetish.

So the reign went on, but when the king felt himself to be growing old he handed the kingdom over to his son Kiyimba. Not for long, however. Something fell out of the sky and pierced Kiyimba's eye so that he died. Again it was generally supposed that the old king's fetish was at work. Anyway he resumed the kingship, and lived on and on, until at the last he mocked him, bringing their lovers to see him and pretending he had given them permission to remarry. And this was chiefly how he would be remembered; the medium at his shrine regularly mimed extreme decrepitude. Clearly the theme is again that of *Lear*: the half-hearted abdication, the disastrous clinging to youth and power, the refusal to die at the proper time. The story, in other words, shows how difficult is the discipline of the sacred kingship, and how necessary.

Further evidence that the dynastic story at this point has become a kind of miscellany comes from the name of the ill-fated Kiyimba. He is a figure who lurks in the background of Ganda traditions, being usually relegated to a kind of phantom prehistory before the coming of the kings. He is often linked with another shadowy figure in the formula: 'Buganda [the land] of Ntege and Kiyimba.' His location in the tradition as the sixth king, a ruler with no descendants, an interlude in the career of Kiggala, thus appears as an arbitrary way of lengthening the list of kings.

When Kiggala finally died, his surviving son Wampamba should have inherited the kingship, but his previous behaviour debarred him – though on the face of things it was less heinous than his father's. When he grew up he found that he was not begetting children, so he consulted the doctors and was advised to marry the daughter of his mother's brother, who was Ggunju of the Mushroom clan. He did so, and she duly bore him two sons, Kayima and Kyabayinze.[69]

Now the Ganda, like many patrilineal peoples, use the 'Iroquois' system of kinship, which makes clear distinctions between every kind of uncle and cousin. A man refers to his father's brother and his mother's sister simply as his 'father' and his 'mother', adding the qualification 'little' if necessary. For his father's sister and his mother's brother, however, there are distinctive terms, *senga* and *kojja*; and despite their gender the *senga* is a kind of father and the *kojja* a kind of mother. (One may even identify a man as a maternal uncle by saying '*Yanzaala*', 'he bore me'.) When it comes to the next generation the relationships are skewed. A man cannot marry his father's sister's daughter because she counts as his child (she is called *kazibwe*, 'the debarred one'), and by the same token he cannot marry his mother's brother's daughter, because she is the equivalent of his mother. Wampamba had therefore committed an abomination, as he acknowledged, saying that he had done very wrong to wed the woman *adda ku mange*, literally 'who goes back to my mother', perhaps 'follows' her, or 'refers to' her. However, when he took the boys to see their grandmother she said merely: 'You are Sse-mira-bikizzi, "Swallow-the-backbones"; what you swallow does not come back' – perhaps 'You certainly don't do things by halves!' or 'You have made your bed and must lie on it'? It is not easy to know what to make of this episode. On the face of it, the tradition seems to be running through the prohibited degrees: the king sleeps with his sister, his son marries the forbidden cousin. But again there may be more to it than that. In the 'alternative' king-list Wampamba figures as the successor of Nakibinge, a position held in the official version by the child-king Mulondo. His mother's name, moreover, is sometimes given as Na-mulondo. Perhaps he really is Mulondo, but a Mulondo who refuses to grow up, whose chosen woman is the nearest he can get to his mother? Be that as it may, it is very clear that in this section of the tradition the themes are domestic ones, not political, probing the dilemmas of the family rather than those of the state.

Kaggwa reports that Wampamba was not allowed to take the kingship, which passed, rather inconsistently one might think, to the product of his incest, the boy Kayima. Not very much is told of this king, whose chief function is to lead the story to its most dramatic and eventful episode, the reign of his son Nakibinge. The name Ka-yima signifies 'Little Mu-hima', or 'Herdboy' (the Ganda language has no *h*.) This does not mean that he belonged to the Ba-hima pastoralists of the western grasslands, but rather identifies him as yet another player of the role of Child King. The cognate form Ga-hima was the surname of the first of the Yuhi kings, who occupied that position in the Rwandan cycle. In historical times, however, Kayima was the title of the governor of the coastal county of Mawokota; and it is likely that 'King Kayima' survives from the traditions of a polity distinct from that of Bakka. His maritime origins are confirmed by the story of his death, which tells how his body was brought back by canoe after he had died on an expedition into Buddu, and also by the marriage alliance (further cemented by blood-brotherhood) that he contracted with Wampona, a Lungfish clan chief whose power-base was in the lake-shore districts of Buganda. From that alliance sprang the great warrior king Nakibinge, whose story closes the ritual cycle and simultaneously offers tantalising glimpses of historical events.

The death of the hero

Nakibinge son of Kayima, eighth of the Ganda kings, located by Kaggwa in Generation Twelve, had a hard time of it. As soon as he had 'eaten' the kingship he was challenged by his cousin Juma, son of Kayima's brother. There was a fluctuating struggle, but eventually Juma recruited an army from Bunyoro that enabled him to carry the day. It did him little good, however, for his 'man' Namunkululu, said by some to have been Kayima's *katikkiro*, procured his death and also that of his son Luyenje. The Nyoro

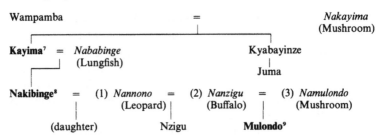

Note: Names of kings in **bold** type, with superscript number showing position in dynastic list. Names of females in *italics*, with father's clan in brackets.

Fig. 6   Death of the hero

then slew Namunkululu and took over the country themselves. Meanwhile Nakibinge had turned to his spiritual advisers, who directed him to the shrine of Kintu at Magonga. Kintu did not actually appear, as he would later do to Mawanda (K.22), but through the priest Bwoya he counselled the king to seek help from Ssese. So at least Kaggwa reports.[70] Le Veux's *Manuel*, which also includes the story, makes no mention of Kintu but has a picaresque tale of Nakibinge visiting an unnamed diviner with his *katikkiro* and then having to hide in the rafters while the man prophesied doom to the Nyoro leaders, who had come to him on the same errand.[71]

Anyway, the upshot was that Nakibinge took a canoe to Ssese and begged Wannema, the master of the islands, to lend him one of his warrior sons. He was first offered Mukasa but opted instead for the young god Kibuuka, also known as Kyobe. Now Kibuuka is 'the Flyer', and as soon as he arrived in Buganda he soared into the clouds and attacked the enemy from above, with devastating effect. But the victorious Ganda captured a beautiful Nyoro girl and offered her to Kibuuka who, disregarding all warnings, took her into his hut. Needless to say, she soon learnt his secret, then escaped and brought the intelligence to her people. So next day the Nyoro directed their arrows upwards and Kibuuka was shot down. His body came to rest in a tall tree at Mbaale in eastern Mawokota, and from there it was recovered by three locals belonging to the Sheep clan, who built a shrine to house it. The Ganda army was demoralised by this disaster and fled in disarray, leaving the king in the hands of the enemy, who slew him after a heroic final combat.

It is unlikely that this tale, which is full of circumstantial detail about the location of battles and the names of Nakibinge's supporters, has no reference to historical events. It is equally improbable that it can be taken as anything like straight history. Not only does it obviously draw a veil over the sequel but it conforms in part to a clear mythical pattern. In fact, the death of Nakibinge, leading to the accession of the infant Mulondo, is where we came in. It is the close of one regnal cycle and the beginning of the next.

The cyclical theme, however, is complicated by the first open intervention of the gods, the non-human powers known to the Ganda as *ba-lubaale*. Kaggwa, it is true, treated Wannema as though he were a secular ruler, but that is just part of his consistent policy of purging the history of its supernatural components. In fact the name, Wa-n-lema, was certainly one of the many that belonged to the High God, and he was sometimes also called Lubaale, a singular term for the Divinity that was more usually fragmented. The numinous islands lying just over the horizon in the midst of the great water that was Na-lubaale were a natural home for the gods, children and kinsfolk of Wannema, who mostly had their principal shrines on one or other of them.[72] Most powerful and popular of these was Mukasa, the force immanent in the Lake and in the storm-clouds that the Lake gives rise to, donor therefore of agricultural and of all other fertility. Mukasa was an independent potency with a sphere of influence that extended far beyond Buganda, but his 'brother' Kibuuka was a 'state' deity. He could be consulted by individual citizens but his fees were very high, and his main role was to preside over military operations, especially against Bunyoro, for which his enmity was undying. 'No man of Unyoro [Bunyoro]', a missionary reported, 'will pass Embale'[73] – Mbaale, the centre from which his influence radiated. The fourteen mediums who accompanied the god on campaigns acted as staff officers and political commissars and the shrine was probably an intelligence-gathering centre, as was that of Nende on the eastern front. At the beginning of the colonial era Mbaale was destroyed by iconoclasts – Canon Roscoe blamed Muslims but according to Kaggwa they were a Christian company, who told him that the shrine did not contain a body but only a long piece of dried meat.[74] Roscoe on the other hand purchased what he believed to be the shrine's contents and deposited them in the Ethnological Museum at Cambridge. There they remained until almost the end of colonial rule, when it was thought politic to send them home.[75] Besides weapons, a shield and a stool, they included human genitals, jawbone and umbilical cord, all in cases decorated with beads and cowrie shells. These remains do not of course prove that Kibuuka had ever been a human being, for shrine organisers would not have found such things unduly hard to come by. (Indeed, the cord and genitals could not possibly have belonged to a man who had been dead for over three hundred years.) Nor is it sensible to rationalise the dive-bombing by speculating about archers posted in trees.

There is in fact no reason to think that Kibuuka was anything other than a fictitious character. An identical story was told by people in western

Kenya, featuring the god of the Lake, there called Were, and his heroic brother Wambatsa, who fought off enemy raiders by the same means and came to the same end.[76] The Delilah theme at least is as old as the hills, a perennial expression of masculine distrust as well as a perennially useful excuse for martial failure. The Ganda version clearly served as the charter-myth of the Mbaale shrine, the most important in the country after Magonga, and its fantasies were probably woven round the reputation of a war-fetish, which slew the Nyoro from the air just as Kiggala's fetish had slain Kiyimba (above, p. 157). Other deities came to the Buganda mainland at the same time, among them Muwanga, who was found on the beach wrapped in a bundle as a fetish would be wrapped. The bundle, it is said, stood up and took the form of a young man.[77] It is striking testimony to the fluidity of Ganda theology that Muwanga was really the name of the Creator of the universe.

It is not the god but the king who presents the most difficult problems, for Nakibinge is a complex figure with several layers of meaning. In the first place he is the king whose function (like Arthur's) is to die; and the manner of his death is very significant. It will be recalled that the *mutabaazi* of Rwanda went out to let his blood be shed by foreigners on foreign soil so as to win victory and peace for his people, and that the prototype of these 'saviours' was the first, mythical holder of the Mibambwe title, who in other stories ceded the throne to his young son Yuhi. Likewise in the traditions of the great Lunda kingdom in southern Zaire there is a recurrent story about kings who were taken on campaign and then abandoned in the hands of the enemy. Sir James Frazer long ago perceived that this cliché preserved the reminiscence of a form of ritual regicide,[78] whereby the people got rid of a king whose mystical utility had come to an end, while casting the guilt of shedding royal blood upon foreigners, who would suffer for the impiety.

The details of the Lunda stories varied but the enemy were always people of the northern borderlands – just as for Mibambwe they were Nyoro. Now Nakibinge's final solitary combat was in Bulemeezi, the northern march of Buganda. Most of the modern county of that name was the former Nyoro province of Rugonjo, which was annexed by Buganda some time in the eighteenth century; but even the nuclear kingdom had included a small strip of land on the far side of the Mayanja Wasswa, and that was the original Bulemeezi. In it was Gombe, 'place of the dead', where the jawless bodies of the ancient kings had been buried, and of old it was believed that the king should not even look in the direction of Bulemeezi, lest he should at once sicken and die. Nakibinge is thus the Old King who must give up his life in order that the child Mulondo may renew the realm.

That, at least, is one of the themes that he evokes, but there are other resonances, which suggest not only that he was not a historical character, but that he had not originally been a cyclical persona either, but a protective deity like Kibuuka. His name is based on the verb -*binga*, meaning 'to drive away', and although that would certainly be apt for the hero who drove off invaders it occurs often in the Lakeland in a cultic context, referring to the warding off of evil. It is the base of Nya-bingi, name of a mysterious female figure at the centre of a pre-colonial politico-religious system in the borderlands of Rwanda and Uganda; of Ba-binga, reputed father of Ryangombe, the great cult-deity of Rwanda; and of Nya-binge, an Nkore divinity who was responsible for earthquakes – as, according to one early source, was Kibuuka.[79]

The ambiguities of Nakibinge are also reflected in the alternative king-list, in which his name appears twice: in eleventh position, where he is preceded by Kayima and followed by Mulondo, as in Kaggwa, but also in fifth position, directly after Kiggala, and there his successor is given as either Mutebi (K.14) or Wampamba.[80] It appears that nineteenth-century tradition-makers were determined to insert this name into the dynastic history but were not entirely sure where to put it.

Nakibinge's persistent praise-name is Omulwanya-mmuli, 'He who fights with reeds', and it evokes his last desperate battle. The story is that when he ran out of spears his wife Nannono, who alone stood by him, sharpened reeds for him to fling at the enemy. Now this in turn evokes the Rwandan tradition of the end of Mibambwe the *mutabaazi*. When he was told that the time had come for him to make way for the young Yuhi, he installed another son on the throne but told the guards not to defend him with spears but with reeds only, so that when Yuhi arrived at the capital he was met with a mere show of resistance.[81] The mock king, whose function was probably to deceive and deflect the forces of evil, was a recurrent feature of African ritual (we saw that that may have been the true role of Ssebwana, the 'regent' who gave way to the young Kimera) and so too is the mock fight. When, for instance, the new *kabaka* arrived at Buddo for the coronation ceremonies performed for Namugala (K.24) and his successors, his retinue exchanged blows of *birumbirumbi*, elephant-grass stalks, with the supporters of Ssemanobe, the priest and guardian of the sacred place.[82]

Also relevant is the ritual of the Shilluk kingdom on the middle Nile, just north of its confluence with the Bahr al Ghazal. That state is celebrated in the literature of anthropology, for it seems to have preserved more clearly than almost any other the lineaments of ancient kingship, especially the practice of ritual regicide. At one time the experts (engaged, as some have noted, in the assassination of their own Old King, Sir James Frazer) refused to believe in the reality of this, but recently scepticism has been in retreat. Certainly the picture was complicated by coups and politically motivated murders in the nineteenth century, when the Shilluk were caught up in the violence that enveloped the whole of the Sudan; but behind these the outline of older ritual can still be clearly seen. Indeed Douglas Johnson, the chief modern authority on religious behaviour in the southern Sudan, has declared that 'king-killing is common throughout the Nile valley'.[83] It is likely that until fairly recently the Shilluk *reth* was in truth, as early reporters claimed, shut up in a hut and left to starve in the company of a young woman. But it is what happens next that is really interesting.[84] As in the Lakeland, the royal corpse was sealed in a hut until it had dried out, and meanwhile his successor was chosen by the proper authorities. The dead king was then taken to his own village (like the jawbone of a dead *kabaka*) and buried under his own hut. For the next two or three days young men in war order, holding up shields and sticks, danced round the hut; often the spectators joined in and the mood was a strange mixture of panic and hilarity. Surely we can recognise again the Ggunju dancers, whose efforts helped to link the funeral of Nakibinge with the accession of his son? For now it was indeed time for the new *reth* to be installed.

In this process a central role was taken by Nyikang, reputed first king, ancestor of the Shilluk people, effective ruler of the Shilluk cosmos, in many ways a counterpart of Buganda's Kintu. He had shrines which, like Magonga, were oracles and theatres for ceremonies at the new moon. As at Magonga, milk and food were set out behind the shrine to nourish the unseen potency.[85] And, like Kintu, Nyikang is sometimes talked about as though he were God but is really Man raised to the highest power. It is said that he lived in Ukwa, 'the land of the ancestors' in the west, where there is no death, but that after a quarrel with the lord of the land, his kinsman Duwat, he set off to the Shilluk country with his wife and son. Duwat threw a stick after them, saying that they and all who came after them would be as dead wood. But Nyikang called back: 'We are not afraid. We will strive to procreate in abundance so as to spoil your curse.'[86] Allowance made for a stilted translation, this is almost word for word Kintu's famous defiance: 'Never will Death be able to make an end of us.'

Nyikang, grandson of the crocodile, who entered the country from the south, is certainly at one level the great river, giver of life to the Shilluk people. And when the king dies the spirit of Nyikang, which has dwelt in him, must be recovered from the water so that it can be transferred to his heir. For this purpose it becomes a figure of ambatch wood, cloth and ostrich feathers and is brought by its 'army' to Fashoda, the royal capital, from the north. At the same time the king-elect is captured and made to stand behind the effigy. He is then seated on the stool of the sovereignty and is filled by the spirit of Nyikang, so that he may be able to keep society and cosmos in due order. The king's retainers have deserted him and there is some suggestion that he was symbolically put to death. The scenario is not quite the same as in Buganda, but the themes of sacrificial death and mock combat, associated with the beginning of a new reign, are very similar.

The Shilluk live midway between Buganda and Egypt and their kingship has often been seen as a late flowering of an ancient Nile valley culture, which in the peculiar conditions of the lower river had long before given rise to the civilisation of the pharaohs. It is thus necessary to take a brief look at the long-debated question of the relationship between that civilisation and the cultures of Black Africa, especially those of the Lakeland.

Probably the majority opinion among scholars has always been that Egypt was a unique society, in Africa but not of it, owing nothing and contributing very little to the peoples beyond the desert. Its achievements have usually been credited partly to its unique environment and partly to stimuli from Asia, especially from Mesopotamia just before the emergence of the pharaohs around 3000 BC. There have always been dissidents, however. One of the greatest Egyptologists of the era before the First World War, E. A. Wallis Budge, ransacked the ethnography of Black Africa for parallels, and concluded that the Egyptian splendours arose from an essentially African (Nilotic or Sudanic) foundation.[87] In the next generation the most influential voice was that of C. G. Seligman, who took the opposite view: Egypt was the source of civilising influences that flowed out over Black Africa, partially redeeming it from eternal savagery.[88] He was one of the chief exponents of the 'Hamitic' theory, imagining Egyptian culture to have been mediated by light-skinned pastoralists who were 'quicker-witted' than 'the dark agricultural negroes', as well as being better armed. But his views must also be set in the context of the ultra-diffusionist theories that flourished in the 1920s, when some scholars saw Egypt as the fount of culture for virtually the whole world, distributing its missionaries from Nigeria to Peru and from Polynesia to Britain.

After the Second World War both racism and diffusionism were in disfavour, and the great liberal scholar Henri Frankfort reverted to the opinion of Wallis Budge, stressing the prehistoric African substratum that gave Egyptian civilisation its distinctive character.[89] Rather confusingly, he labelled this substratum 'Hamitic', but unlike Seligman he was not using the term in a racial sense; 'Hamitic' for him was opposed to 'Semitic', as 'African' to 'Asiatic'. When African and Black American scholars entered the debate they attempted a new synthesis. For them, as for Seligman, Egypt was the source of everything, but Egypt was authentically African.[90]

Mainstream (i.e. White) scholarship has mostly remained sceptical. In Budge's day knowledge of African cultures was superficial, and it has not been difficult for modern critics (including Benjamin Ray)[91] to show that many of the Egyptian parallels alleged by him, and even by Frankfort, were either erroneous or not significant. They also politely dismiss the attempts to annex pharaonic civilisation to the African nationalist cause. And, indeed, Egypt of the pharaohs cannot be seen as a purely indigenous creation. It is beyond doubt that an already developed West Asian economic complex, including wheat and barley, sheep and goats, was transplanted to Egypt soon after 5000 BC. (It is possible that at least one very important innovation, the milking of cattle, travelled in the opposite direction at about the same time or a little later.[92]) It is almost as certain that there was another major Asian input in the later fourth millennium, this time directly or indirectly from Mesopotamia, which had already pioneered irrigation and metallurgy, the wheel and the sail, and above all the idea of pictographic writing. Yet I believe that Budge and Frankfurt were right in principle: Egyptian civilisation was deeply rooted in African soil, and more particularly in the soil of the great valley. It was, however, a highly idiosyncratic flower. In the domain of myth I have found it much easier to link central Africa with western Asia and Europe than with Egypt. The reason is that all these cultures have a common ancestry in a neolithic, in certain respects perhaps even a pre-neolithic complex that was at least as much African as Asian and which flourished during the millennia while much of the Sahara was habitable and communication easy. The rise of the Old Kingdom in Egypt coincided with the final desiccation, and for nearly three thousand years, until the introduction of the camel, contact between north and south was reduced to the thin thread of the Nile as it wound its way through the Nubian desert. Egypt and sub-Saharan Africa thus went their own separate ways. Ganda culture does have some Egyptian affinities, but they are with the pre-dynastic infrastructure rather than the pharaonic edifice. In particular, while Nyikang of the Shilluk is clearly related on one side to Kintu of Buganda, he is on the other side a close kinsman of Osiris, who was certainly one of the most archaic members of the Egyptian pantheon, being both the great fertilising river and the power immanent in the kingship. Like the human pharaoh, he died, and then had to be recovered from the river, like Nyikang, and reconstituted so that he might beget Horus, the young power that would inhabit the old pharaoh's heir, sitting on the throne that was his mother Isis. In due time Horus would become Osiris, as Mulondo would become Nakibinge, and so the eternal cycle of life and death would continue to revolve.

The suggestion is that the story of the death of Nakibinge preserves the residues of a great drama that had been performed for thousands of years in the valley of the Nile, long before the formation of the Lwo or even of the Bantu language, that it discloses a knowledge, transmitted across the generations by who-knows-what channels of intellectual continuity, of the kind of things that ought to be done at the unmaking and making of kings. Yet the story also seems to tell us of a great historical crisis, of dynastic quarrel and foreign invasion, victory and defeat. The details are circumstantial and we shall see that they have some confirmation from the side of Bunyoro. The tradition, moreover, contains indications of real historical change.

There is, to begin with, a significant shift of geographical focus, from inland centres such as Magonga and Bakka to the coastlands and islands of Nalubaale. The Ssese islands and their deities now make their first appearance in the story (unless we count oblique references linked with King Kiggala); it is said to have been in the reign of Nakibinge that the *lubaale* gods came to the mainland and overran (literally, 'finished off') the country.[93] At this point, too, we are introduced to a new set of human actors. Nothing had been heard of the Sheep clan until they became the owners of the Kibuuka power, or of the Seed clan until they became Nakibinge's chief allies, or indeed of the Lungfish folk until their daughter Nababinge became his mother. Now the Sheep and the Lungfish were emblems of maritime groups widely dispersed along the northern coast of Nalubaale, which with its many inlets and offshore islands provided ideal conditions for a mobile, unattached way of life.[94] Somewhat like the Vikings, these people were fishermen in the first instance, then traders, and marauders where the opportunity arose. Their superb sewn-plank canoes were later described with some hyperbole as 'the finest in the whole savage world',[95] and they were inured to the hard and dangerous life of boatmen in crocodile-haunted and sometimes stormy waters. Those who played a part in Buganda's history were said to have come from Bumogera, a land vaguely located near the north-east corner of the Lake. The name signifies 'the country of the peepers', and is said to have been applied contemptuously by the Ganda to people in south-eastern Uganda who were unsporting enough to fight from behind prepared defences. However, Ganda raids into those parts did not begin until well into the nineteenth century, and the 'peeper' nickname is certainly older than that. Probably it originated in the sight of canoemen's heads appearing over the gunwales, and 'Bumogera' was the name given to such people's homeland.

The people of the Lungfish were the most powerful of these maritime groups. They had established a base in Ssese, and from there it was not difficult to develop landing places on the Buganda coast, mostly on the Entebbe peninsular and at Namubiru, the one point to the west where the shore gave access to open water, not choked with papyrus drifts.[96] But they were by no means restricted to Buganda. They were the largest element in the population of the Buvuma islands, just to the east,[97] and were prominent in Busoga and on the islands of the north-eastern Lake.[98] The advent of these maritime groups must be seen as one of the great formative events in Buganda's history.[99] It brought a hitherto land-facing, agrarian society into the vigorous, commercial, multicultural world of the great Lake. At the same time the canoes and seamanship of the newcomers made Buganda a maritime power, able to strike at will almost anywhere on the shores of Nalubaale. Though the kingdom in the nineteenth century made many plundering and tribute-gathering expeditions across its land frontiers, much of its wealth accrued from water-borne raids. For their part the 'Vikings' had much to gain from an alliance with, even incorporation into, a land-based political system, which would provide them with access to inland markets and strategic cover for their coastal and island bases.

The tradition of the Lungfish clan, taken at its face value, would make them present at the very beginning of the kingdom, since it claims that the clan 'ancestor' Mubiru became a client of 'King' Kintu.[100] But this must be seen as a formal statement of the relationship between the clan, represented by its patron divinity, and the Ganda state, for which 'Kintu' became the symbol. The actual forging of the relationship is more plausibly to be linked with the Lungfish nephew Nakibinge. And so, as Ronald Atkinson has argued, though on other grounds, that king appears to mark the transition from structure to history,[101] from cyclical to linear time. The transition cannot be a straightforward one, for with his successor Mulondo we are back at the beginning of the cycle. But it does seem clear that the ancient drama has been used as the medium for a discreet report of real events. The question is not whether there was dynastic dispute and foreign invasion, but when. That question, however, cannot be answered until we have examined the long central section of the tradition that stretches, in the official version, between Nakibinge and Namugala, the eighth king and the twenty-fourth.

8   Fragments of history

The kings who married many wives

After Mulondo there is an area of some obscurity and confusion, in which even the different strands within the orthodox tradition are not completely in agreement about the sequence of the kings. According to Kaggwa, Mulondo grew up but did not grow old, and he was followed on the throne by his two younger brothers, Jjemba and Ssuuna. Only after that generation was complete did his son Kamaanya (Sse-kamaanya, 'Kamaanya the First') secure the kingship. It then passed to Ssuuna's son Kimbugwe before reverting to Kateregga son of Kamaanya. Older authorities, on the other hand, had placed Kamaanya directly after Mulondo, and had said nothing about the genealogical relationships, while Father Achte made Ssekamaanya the son of Jjemba. Kaggwa's arrangement certainly seems the most plausible, since it implies a system of fraternal succession followed by rotation between two or more branches of the royal house, which commonly occurs in Africa. Kiwanuka maintains that since Mulondo, Jjemba and Ssuuna are all credited with reigns of some length they cannot all have been brothers and that Ssuuna at least probably belonged to a different generation. However, detailed argumentation is almost certainly pointless, since it is very unlikely that we are dealing, at this stage, with clearly remembered dynastic history. Mulondo, after all, was not a person but the mask of a particular phase of kingship, and his 'brothers' probably had no more individual reality.

Certainly very little is told of them. Of Jjemba we know only that he was especially devoted to his favourite wife, for whom he began the cemetery at Luggi in which all later childbearing royal wives would be buried. His successor, Ssuuna, is said to have raised a large mound at his capital, Jjimbo, and to have engaged in a wrestling bout with a prisoner, a little scarecrow of a man who nevertheless threw him; as a result he decreed that Jjimbo should be a place of asylum. It seems that these kings serve as carriers of explanatory tales accounting for minor features of the Ganda scene, together with the folk-tale theme about a king who comes down to

Generation

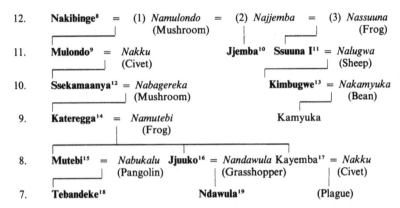

Note: Generations are counted back from the time of first record, Muteesa I (1856–84) being Generation 1. Names of kings are in **bold** type, with superscript numbers showing their position in the list. Names of females are in *italics*, with their father's clan shown in brackets.

Fig. 7   The middle kingdom

the level of his humblest subjects. Ssekamaanya (Kamaanya the First), reputed son of Mulondo and Nakku, is a little more interesting. His name signifies 'the Violent', and the chief incident of his biography shows how apt it was. When his son Kateregga was an adolescent Kamaanya took him to Bukerekere for the rite of 'growing up'. But Nankere, instead of producing one of his sons to be done to death for the young prince's benefit, merely sacrificed a bullock. When the king heard of this treasonable default he was exceeding wroth. Nankere was pursued into the forest and slain, and the villages round about were sacked.[1]

Here we do seem to be approaching the threshold of history, for the story implies a profound change in the nature of the kingship, when the old rituals were losing their power and those who conducted them were no longer sacrosanct. When Ssekamaanya gave the order for Nankere's death there were men who were willing and able to kill him. In other words, the king now possessed means of coercion and so had less need for religious sanctions, did not need to be bound by sacred laws. For Nankere's breach of custom was an excusable response to a greater sacrilege on the part of the king himself. The rite, after all, was the *okukula kwa kabaka*, 'the growing up of the *king*', not of the king's son. That is to say, when his son was of an age for initiation Ssekamaanya should not have been still alive, and certainly should not still have held the royal office. Like the celebrated

Ergamenes, king of Kush,[2] he had refused to depart at the appropriate time, and the consequences were momentous.

We have no means of telling whether this incident actually happened or was invented to dramatise a more gradual change. Certainly it was not the end of the *okukula* rite, which lasted well into the nineteenth century, and the office of Nankere still existed in colonial times and later. Moreover, the story is told in such a way as to leave no doubt that Ssekamaanya's action long continued to be seen as an outrage, not as a progressive revolutionary act. All that can be said is that if the event occurred, and if the official genealogy is to be relied on, major political change was on the horizon in the early part of the seventeenth century. And the sequel, without confirming the date, shows how the process begun by Ssekamaanya was developed in the next generation.

When Ssekamaanya finally died, the throne passed to his cousin Kimbugwe, not to his son. Not long afterwards Kateregga became the father of twins by a woman of the Monkey clan. Now Africans, being generally reluctant to use the concept of chance, did not accept that a child could be made by one sexual encounter, or even by several encounters of a tepid kind, but only by repeated strenuous exertion. It followed that the energies going into the production of twins were assumed to have been prodigious, and were both admired as heroic and rejected as uncanny. Where the latter reaction dominated, one or both children might be put to death. In Buganda, admiration was ascendant. Twins were therefore allowed to live and the parents were held in honour (the king was addressed as 'Father of Twins' whether he had earned the distinction or not), but they had to go through an elaborate rite called *okumenya olukanda* (seemingly 'the breaking of the fence'), which simultaneously celebrated the achievement and purged the offence against nature.[3]

For Kateregga, the rite took place in the presence of his family head, King Kimbugwe. The mother was not fit to make the journey, and so he took another wife to perform the rituals in her stead. Kimbugwe discovered the substitution, a bitter quarrel ensued, and Kateregga went home in anger, throwing the ritual impedimenta into the Nonve stream on the way. War then broke out, and Kateregga prepared a fetish in the form of a magic bird, which fell onto Kimbugwe's head and killed him. And so he became king in his cousin's stead.[4]

There is nothing about this episode that says 'myth' – certainly not the sorcery, which would have been automatically alleged in the case of such a convenient death. It would be idle to speculate whether Kimbugwe really died of natural causes or was assassinated or defeated in battle. The point is that there was conflict and Kateregga came out on top.

Yet the stated cause of the quarrel is distinctly odd. Kateregga's behaviour may have been a grave ritual offence, but it is not easy to see why it should have so enraged the king. The key, it is suggested, is not the presence of a 'wrong' woman, but her identity. She was Nalugwa of the Sheep clan, bearer of the same title as Kimbugwe's mother. So prince Kateregga was flaunting a marriage alliance that Kimbugwe would have considered to be in his own gift and had probably intended for his son. (There was a son, Kamyuka, who is remembered with scorn because he failed to fight for his father's cause.) And we have seen that alliance with the maritime Sheep clan was very much worth having. But the question then poses itself: with precisely what power were the Sheep folk making an alliance?

Ssekamaanya and his son Kateregga are identified, as explicitly as any of the kings, with the old ritual nucleus in north Busiro. Their shrine-capitals at Kongojje and Buteregga were both in the immediate vicinity of Bakka hill. Ssekamaanya's mother was said to have been Nakku daughter of Walusimbi, and Kateregga, like his 'grandfather' Mulondo, was a nephew of the Mushroom clan. The shrines of Ssuuna and Kimbugwe, on the other hand, were located in central Busiro, several miles south of Bakka though still well away from the Lake shore. It seems likely that in reality the Nonve stream separated two distinct micro-polities, and that each sought the alliance of the maritime Sheep, who in the end preferred the northern kingdom, which could give them deeper penetration. Kateregga was thus enabled to absorb the intervening country of Kimbugwe and much else besides.

It has been realised for a long time that the reigns of Kimbugwe and especially Kateregga mark the beginning of Buganda's territorial expansion, which would eventually transform an obscure little kingdom, one of dozens in the forest lands fringing the Lake, into the formidable state 'discovered' by Speke and Grant in 1862.[5] And we can now glimpse something of the dynamics of its political growth. C. P. Kottak perceptively remarked that Kateregga's reputed harem, with nine wives, a hundred 'reserve wives' or concubines and two hundred servant-girls, was far larger than any credited to previous kings;[6] and it is not to be supposed that this was just a personal predilection. Like the story of his failed or irregular initiation, the statement signifies the breakdown of the old ritual system. No longer will the king of Buganda live in incestuous seclusion. Instead he will engage in exogamous and plural unions, which will bring him affines and thus allies in the quest for power. So in place of ritual there will be politics; in place of recurrence, historic change; in place of stability, aggrandisement and strife. The new system was inherently dynamic; for as wife-takers members of the royal house had to be constantly seeking new resources with which to compensate the groups that lost their daughters to them.

Kimbugwe is said to have appointed a kinsman, Mpadwa, as 'Kayima', which was in later times the title of the governor of Mawokota, the deeply indented coastland to the west of Busiro. By defeating Kimbugwe, Kateregga thus won control of Mawokota, which, I have suggested, was the object of the whole exercise. North of Mawokota there is an irregular sliver of land called Butambala: not a complimentary term, for it means 'the country of people who do not wear clothes'. To the Ganda of historical times full covering of the body was perhaps the most important token of civilisation, the chief outward sign of their superior culture. Clearly Butambala was inhabited at that time by non-Ganda barbarians; and we find Kateregga appointing a man of the Sheep clan – that is to say, a kinsman of his wife Nalugwa – to govern it. The office of 'Ka-tambala' remained a prerogative of the Sheep clan until 1893, when it was given as a consolation prize to the defeated Muslim faction. In the same context, it is reported that Kateregga persecuted the Leopard clan, which had its headquarters in Butambala, killing four hundred of its members and causing others to conceal themselves in the Genet clan of Mawokota.[7] Given the pre-eminent role of the Leopard folk in the cult of Kintu, it must be expected that the event thus briefly related would have far-reaching consequences.

North and west of Butambala lies the district called Gomba (or Butunzi), which was assigned by Kateregga to 'his man' Balamaga Wasswa, a member of the otherwise obscure Duiker clan, who became Ki-tunzi. Wasswa is remembered as an outstanding warrior, who seems to have conquered the land himself but to have been prepared to hold it as a fief of the Buganda kingdom. There is no evidence, admittedly, that he was Kateregga's brother-in-law; but other marriages appear to have brought an even more important accession of territory and power. Besides the mother of his twins, Kateregga married two other women of the Monkey clan. (This is the grey or vervet monkey, *Cercopithecus aethiops*,[8] not to be confused with the black-and-white colobus.) The Monkey territory lay to the south-east of Bakka, north-west of Kampala; and it seems likely that his marriages gave Kateregga control over this strategically vital territory, which provided access to the open waters of Murchison Bay.

It will have been noted that, in sharp contrast to the procedure adopted hitherto, the traditional account of Kateregga's reign has been accepted here as being quite straightforwardly historical, with relatively minor inventions and suppressions. This may appear arbitrary, especially as the reign is placed in Generation Nine, well outside the normal range of reminiscence. However, we shall find reason to bring it down to a somewhat more recent date than the one that is genealogically suggested. More important, there is no reason *not* to grant it essentially historical status. The events narrated do not conform to any pattern of myth or ritual – in fact they explicitly reject such a pattern – and they add up to a coherent and convincing picture of political change, which will be further developed in the story of the next reign. There is, it is true, one possible counter-indication: a brief reference in an Nkore tradition to a divinity being accompanied by 'his Muganda servant Kataraiga'.[9] Since this is the Nkore pronunciation of Kateregga the identification is practically certain; and the allusion might be taken to mean that the king of Ganda tradition was himself really a divinity, an imaginary being. However, it more probably signifies that Kateregga was the first ruler of Buganda to impinge on the consciousness of the western peoples. If we are not wholly mistaken, by the end of his reign he controlled a not inconsiderable territory, extending from somewhere north of the Mayanja Wasswa to the Lake shore and from the vicinity of Kampala to the edge of the western grasslands, and covering the whole of the modern county of Busiro with small parts of Bulemeezi and Kyaddondo and large sections of Mawokota, Butambala and Gomba. His son and successor, Mutebi, would add largely to this domain, chiefly on the north-west, and would also accentuate the political processes that he had originated.

This continuity strongly suggests that Mutebi was indeed the immediate successor – but not necessarily the son – of Kateregga, even though the tradition is not unanimous on the point; one version puts him in the 'Mulondo' position, directly after Nakibinge. And the first thing we hear about him is that he killed seven hundred people in order to secure the throne.[10] 'Seven hundred' is the conventional term for a large number and is not to be taken literally, but it is clear that violence was now a normal feature of Ganda politics. This signifies that the kingship had become a valuable prize, no longer an onerous ritual burden but a source of pleasure, pride and posterity, worth killing for. It also means, of course, that ambitious politicians could raise armed followings. The shadow of the warboy, the political thug (to use modern West African terminology) had fallen across the land. And Mutebi had at once to find ways of distributing offices to 'the men he had come to the kingship with'.[11]

His first thought was to depose the Mugema, who besides being head of the Monkey clan held a very important ritual office, but from this act his counsellors dissuaded him; and so the head of the Monkey people retained his position within the Ganda state. Restraint was also shown to the Kaggo, holder of a similar office that belonged to a lineage of the Colobus Monkey clan. So Mutebi turned his eyes about and launched a series of moves against chieftains on his western borders. Officially he was suppressing rebels against his authority, but there is little doubt that in reality the people concerned were being subjugated for the first time. In western Mawokota there is a cluster of clan centres. Most of the clans are of rather minor importance: Yam, Genet, Jumping Rat, Cane-rat. At the centre of the group, however, is the Bushbuck clan; and the bushbuck, *ngabi*, is the royal animal *par excellence* of the Lakes region, no doubt because of its erect horns of power and its auspicious red-and-white colouring. It is probably related etymologically to *mu-gabe*, title of the king of Nkore, and to *mu-gabe-kazi*, the queen-mother or 'female king' of Rwanda; and it served as emblem for the widely ramifying ruling clan of Bunyoro, the Ba-Bito. The head of the Ganda Bushbucks, Nsamba (who later claimed to be a foster-brother of Kimera), had thus undoubtedly had royal status; and Mutebi, in defeating this 'rebel', was incorporating another little kingdom, in which the other west-Mawokota clans probably stood to Nsamba in much the same kind of ritual relationship as the Colobus and Mushroom folk had stood to the lords of Bakka. Nsamba preserved his status as a clan head within the Buganda system, but unlike Mugema he stayed aloof from government and court and did not present girls or page-boys to the king. It is not clear whether this was a privileged exemption or a precautionary exclusion, but it did have the result that before the colonial period the Bushbucks had never enjoyed the position of maternal uncles to a young ruler or brothers-in-law to a mature one.

Further north, Mutebi put an end to the pretensions of Chief Kajubi in the district known to the Ganda as Busujju, 'Pumpkin-land', and of Kaweewo in Ssingo – probably just the southern fringe of what would later be the great north-western marcher province. Like his predecessor, he employed 'new men' to execute these conquests. Kalali of the Pangolin clan was the slayer of Kajubi and was rewarded with the office of Kasujju (lord of Busujju), which was held by his heirs until colonial times. Another ambitious warrior, Lubulwa of the Oribi Antelope (*mpeewo*) clan took the title of Mukwenda from Kaweewo (which name, perhaps significantly, is the diminutive form of *mpeewo*). He did not succeed in making it hereditary, but a new office, that of Kibaale, was created for the head of the Oribi clan, whose base was in northern Kyaddondo.

Not surprisingly, of the five wives of Mutebi whose names are recalled, three were daughters of the Pangolin and one belonged to the Oribi clan. And the basis of his power is well illustrated in a 'short story' attributed to his reign.[12] For the most part it is a familiar kind of folk-tale – and was sometimes told without any historical context.[13] A man is brewing beer by the roadside. A woman, passing by with a child on her back, stops to talk and sets the baby down against a banana stem. A man on the way to a hut-building also stops, propping his pole against the same stem. Another man joins the party and tethers a sheep to the stem. Then a hunter with his dog comes by. The dog flies at the sheep, which pulls at the stem, which dislodges the pole, which falls on the child and kills it. Who is guilty – builder, shepherd, hunter, brewer, or the mother? The local chief cannot resolve the problem and refers it to the royal court; but Mutebi and his counsellors are also baffled. Then a little herdboy standing on the fringe of the crowd comes forward and offers a solution: the pole, the stem, the sheep and the dog are all guilty and should be burnt, but the human defendants should go free. There is general acclamation, but then the boy reveals the sting in the tail of his judgment: since the dead child was female, the king had been deprived of a future wife, and so all those concerned must pay a fine in women. Even so, they are glad to have escaped death, but it is naturally the king who is most pleased by the precocious judgment; and the young sycophant is richly rewarded.

He was in fact Kalali, the future Kasujju and one of the great men of the realm. Although, as the kingdom developed, Busujju became one of its smallest counties, the heirs of Kalali remained very powerful figures. They were custodians of the royal princes and so had at least a formal say in the selection of the next king, taking over this role from the Mugema. Thus the ancient motif of the Wise Child was used as the charter of the Kasujju office but also, more importantly, to establish the fundamental principle of the Ganda polity, the doctrine that all the women of the kingdom were in law the king's property. The point was succinctly expressed in a wry lament said to have been composed in the reign of Mawanda (G.6), a king even richer and more powerful than Mutebi:[14]

> I would buy me a woman, the pick of the bunch
> To dig in my garden and cook me my lunch
> But I'd have to make do with a skinny old thing
> For all the fair wenches are wives of the king.

This doggerel does not convey the sharp precision of the original; 'skinny old thing', for example, translates the one word *ekkadde*, a 'neuter' and thus contemptuous form of the regular term *mukadde*, 'old person'. But the cynical message of the royal eulogy (and Mawanda had it played by his musicians) is unmistakable.

The obvious reasons for the kings' appropriation of women were certainly present but not a sufficient explanation. Nineteenth-century rulers of Buganda had female households that far exceeded the dreams of sexual avarice, and they begot far more children than were needed to guarantee the survival of their genes. Of course the women tilled the royal gardens and served the royal feasts, but their principal function was to be given away in return for political services. An ugly reminiscence of Muteesa's grandfather Kamaanya (the Second) may suffice to make the point.[15] This king, when disposed to reward a loyal chief, would lift up his bark-cloth in order to estimate whether five or ten or twenty women would be the appropriate gift. Women, in short, became commodities – Mawanda's poet spoke unequivocally of 'buying' one – and counters in the game of power. The result was the extreme patriarchy that struck every observer of recent Buganda, where heads of households had absolute authority over both children and wives. The degradation of women led inexorably to instability of marriage, generally 'permissive' morals and, by the early twentieth century, a very high incidence of venereal infections.

The royal control over sexual exchange, which seems to have been initiated by Kateregga and Mutebi, can also be seen as the source of Buganda's bias towards expansion and aggression. An ordinary citizen could satisfy his needs for sex, children, horticultural and domestic service only by seeking women from a political superior, who in turn would have obtained them ultimately by royal gift. Conversely, power and status were granted only to those who gave their daughters to the king. The model is of course highly simplified and not to be taken literally; it is not implied that kings exercised their option on all the women of the land. But in theory there was an efficient cycle, which, however, operated in a way that produced wide inequalities even among men. As the poet complained, there were great differences in the satisfactions enjoyed by those in positions of power and the rest of the population, who must far more often have been faced with genetic death. That is the normal condition of African and other polygamous societies. But the extreme concentration of women that took place in Buganda had a further consequence: at any one time a considerable number of women were, so to speak, out of circulation, in that they were being held in stock in the excessive harems of the king and the great chiefs. Adulterers, who were numerous in spite of the ferocious penalties for detection, corrected the balance to some extent, but probably not completely. To fill the deficit and to make inequality more acceptable, it was necessary to add continually to the total supply of women; and the only way to do that was to steal them from communities outside the system. That became the principal object of the military machine that was built up in Buganda during the eighteenth and the early nineteenth centuries.

The second function of the army was to increase the supply of livestock, especially cattle, the only commodity, apart from political service, for which women might be exchanged. Now, whereas Kateregga's annexations were directed towards the Lake, Mutebi's shifted the centre of Buganda's gravity temporarily to the north-west, to the edge of the short-grass country where cattle throve. He established his own court in Busujju and swam in Lake Wamara, which forms its western boundary. More important, it is remembered that he levied dues on the cattle coming from

Mitiyana, still further to the north-west. That is to say, he added to his wealth by controlling the drover route along which cattle had already been brought from the pastoral districts to meat-scarce central Buganda.

To all appearance, then, by Generation Eight, presumably by the latter part of the seventeenth century, Buganda was already set on the courses of centralisation, expansion and militarisation that would bring it to its known mid-nineteenth-century structure and extent. The next chapters of the tradition, however, indicate that things were not in reality quite so simple.

The clay boat: an interlude

With Ssekamaanya, Kateregga and Mutebi we have a coherent sequence of events and an analysable political process. The history is not to be compared with that which is based on contemporary records or recent oral testimony, but it is recognisably history. After Mutebi, however, there is a curious retrogression. The stories of the next reigns, in Kaggwa's compilation,[16] are again fanciful, inconsequent and unbelievable, and it becomes hard to see what is really going on.

Mutebi, who apparently died a natural death, was succeeded by his full brother Jjuuko. Also by the same mother (a woman from Nankere's branch of the Lungfish clan but not a daughter of 'Lord Frog' himself) there was a third son of Kateregga called Kayemba, and this man disturbed the right order of things by marrying Nakku, the woman who in each generation was reserved for a ritual marriage to the reigning king. This was high treason, yet Jjuuko felt unable to proceed openly against him. Instead, he gave him command of an expedition to the Buvuma islands, and secretly ordered that he should be tricked into embarking in a boat made of clay. Kayemba was warned at the last moment, and took refuge in Busoga beyond the Nile. After a while Jjuuko lured him back by putting out a rumour of his own death and ordering the people of the eastern marches to stop cultivating so as to make it appear that the land was in mourning. When Kayemba got near the capital he found that life was going on normally but by then it was too late to turn back. The brothers then seemed to achieve an uneasy reconciliation, but Kayemba was planning a bizarre vengeance. Nakku had been delivered of a child more monstrous even than the serpent that she bore to Kimera; for he had no arms or legs and he was called Kawumpuli, which is to say, 'Plague'.

When the German adventurer 'Emin Pasha' reconnoitred Buganda in 1877 he passed through a village that showed all the signs of hurried evacuation. His escort hurried him past, muttering a word which he heard as 'Kampoddi', and he jumped to the conclusion that this was a cryptic reference to the tyrant Muteesa, who must have sacked the place.[17] But on this occasion, at least, Muteesa was innocent. Kawumpuli was a demon of lethal epidemics. It is not certain that his name necessarily referred to bubonic fever; and even if it did we could not infer that the disease was already present in the heart of Africa in the seventeenth century, to which generation-dating would assign Jjuuko and Kayemba. Even if Jjuuko had been a real, datable character, the stories about him could well have been elaborated in the generation or two before Kaggwa wrote.

In the story as it stands, Kayemba and Nakku installed their monstrous offspring in Bulemeezi, the district north of the Mayanja that was thought of as the country of death; and it was known that if ever Jjuuko looked towards him he would fall sick and die. For some time the plot was foiled by his devoted wife Nalunga who, when he walked abroad, held up a cloth to screen him from the fatal glance. But one day when she was indisposed Jjuuko went out alone, his eyes strayed northwards – and very soon Kayemba was sitting on the throne in his stead. We can be fairly sure that this was really a ritual reminiscence, not a historical incident – that at one time all kings had been prohibited from looking in that dangerous direction.

It has been suggested that Jjuuko must at some time have had a particularly imaginative Nnaalinnya, the woman who was installed at the king's tomb and charged with preserving his memory.[18] But that is not a sufficient explanation for the oddity of his biography, behind which there surely lies not just fantasy but myth. Even the one apparent piece of historical realism, the campaign against Buvuma, is certainly anachronistic. These islands lie just off the far end of the Kyaggwe coast, close to the exit of the Nile. They remained unsubjugated until the colonial era, even repulsing a full-scale assault in 1875 in which the explorer Stanley outrageously took part; and the tradition gives clear indications that the intervening coastlands were not brought under Ganda control until the middle of the eighteenth century, two generations after the apparent time of Jjuuko and Kayemba. In fact, the topography of the story is partly in the 'Monkey' area near Kampala and partly in the ancient nucleus around Bakka, from where it is possible to look across the Mayanja stream to Bulemeezi.

With Jjuuko, of course, we are back where we started. For it was in his time that the sun fell out of the sky at Bakka and was put back in its place by Wanga the divine Artificer. It must be suspected therefore that this king's real home was in the world of Genesis. Indeed it was proposed earlier that his name reveals him as God, in His Nilotic manifestation, *juok*. Here, however, there is an example of a recurrent puzzle of Ganda (and doubtless other African) philology: the presence of two quite different but equally plausible derivations of the same word. Such problems result from the people's delight in puns, which allow them to bring into association two concepts that would otherwise have been kept far apart. 'Jjuuko' may evoke the Lwo idea of God, but the name also has a simple meaning in the Ganda language; it is a 'passive' nominal form derived from the verb *ku-juuka*, 'to scold'. 'The thing that is scolded' is of course a child. And so the sixteenth king of Buganda can be seen to belong both to a myth of genesis, of the Creation, and to a myth of perpetual return, being yet another representation of the ever-recurrent Child King.

The juvenility of Jjuuko is evident from everything we hear about him. The woman Nalunga who so carefully protected him, not only from the eyes of Death, but also, as a sacred king should be protected, from public view and the sun's rays, was surely nurse or mother rather than wife; and we are told that he loved her, like a spoilt child, because she was good at cooking his favourite dish of cocoyam.[19] (This is no more a datum of agricultural history than the plague-child was a clue to the history of disease. Cocoyam, or taro, *Colocasia antiquorum*, is a plant of south-east Asian origin which may have been introduced to Buganda before the end of the seventeenth century but is just as likely to have been inserted in the story at a later date.) Nalunga, like Jjuuko, we have met before. She was the daughter of the Seed clan chief whose home in central Kyaddondo, the 'land of the [king's] finding', was the place where a king spent the first night of the *okukula* ritual, recapitulating his childhood before he essayed the adventure of initiation. Yet Na-lunga belongs also to the other, divine aspect of the 'Jjuuko' concept; for her name is based on the same stem as Ka-lunga and Mu-lungu, two of the commonest Bantu names of God.

The 'death' of the Child King is of course initiation, after which he will emerge with a new personality and name – in this particular version, as Kayemba. The name was not idly chosen; it is a diminutive form of Jjemba (originally I-yemba), which belongs to the brother and successor of Mulondo, and the story of his accession has unmistakeable ritual allusions. Having procured Jjuuko's death, the vengeful Kayemba tried to eliminate him totally by having the jawbone, vessel of his spirit, thrown into the Lake. But the local chief, Kinyolo, a 'son' of the Monkey chief Mugema, looked into the bag and covertly substituted some stones, then preserved the precious bone until it could be properly bestowed. Here, surely, is a faint but unmistakable echo of the ancient Nile valley rite whereby the spirit of kingship had to be recovered from the river so that the continuity broken by death could be restored. And the motif of the clay boat also finds a precedent in the literary heritage of Egypt, in the great mythical drama wherein Horus, divine counterpart of the young pharaoh, strives endlessly against the ill-will of his rival Seth, projection of the powers of darkness.[20]

The boat that Seth was at one point induced to enter was made of stone, not clay, but that is hardly a significant variation. At both ends of the great valley the episode certainly recalled one of the ritual tests that the royal initiate had long ago been caused to pass.

There was an oddity about Jjuuko's shrine: it contained two jawbones, one on top of the other. For this a seemingly absurd explanation was offered. Jjuuko, it is said, had forced his brother at one point to carry the *katikkiro*, Mulwana, on his back as a penance or humiliation; and so Kayemba got his own back by making Jjuuko 'carry' the man in death. And again there is an echo from the Egyptian drama. When Seth had been captured the (other) gods invited Osiris to sit on him and (it is explicitly stated) to sodomise him, this being the extreme humiliation inflicted upon a defeated enemy.[21] It is at any rate clear that Jjuuko's jawbone temple, which is described not by the normal term *ssiro*, but, like Nakibinge's, as a *ssabo*, a 'praying place', was a religious rather than a dynastic monument.

It must also be significant that the chief Kinyolo, rescuer of Jjuuko's jawbone, regularly had an important part to play in the inauguration of a new reign.[22] When the young king had completed his father's (or brother's) obsequies he sat on the Namulondo stool and Kinyolo presented his daughter to be his first wife, who was always called Kaddu-lubare, 'Servant of the gods' (or of God) – as was the senior wife of any substantial citizen. In this instance, however, we are told that she was not a real wife (the king was after all a child) but was 'for ritual purposes'. It was also Kinyolo's function to tell the king that it was time for him to marry, and as a result of his services to Jjuuko he and his successors were given a role in the performance of the royal 'growing up'.

Nothing in the traditions of Jjuuko and Kayemba suggests political history, and the story of Buganda went on as though they had not been. Besides Kawumpuli Kayemba had two other sons called Ssematimba, 'Chief Python', and Wakayima, 'Hare', neither of whom sounds like a human prince; and though Ndawula (K.19) is described as Jjuuko's son he is, as we shall see, even more obviously unreal. But the question then poses itself: what are these mythical figures doing here in Generation Eight, in the middle of the dynastic sequence, after Kateregga and Mutebi, who to all appearance were real-life politicians? It is possible, of course, that the sequence is distorted; indeed, the alternative 'Mugwanya' version places Kateregga considerably lower down the list. But it puts Mutebi even higher up, and we would still have to ask why the distortion occurred. The most likely answer is that those who later put the tradition together did not want the actual sequel to Mutebi's reign to be remembered, or could not agree on how it should be presented. At this point in the country's affairs a veil was drawn over events; mythical matter was inserted to conceal a real turbulence.

The kings in the forest

Kayemba (Kaggwa tells us) was succeeded by his nephew Tebandeke, son of the former king Mutebi by one of his Pangolin wives. The name Te-ba-n-deke means 'Let-them-not-leave-me' and might be taken as the cry of a reluctant 'saviour', pleading not to be left in the hands of the enemy; he would then represent, like Nakibinge, the recurrent figure of the Old King, who closed the cycle by a sacrificial death in the hands of the enemy, so that his successor might renew the realm. His extant biography, however, includes no story of that kind, and a different cyclical role is on the whole more probable. Moreover, Tebandeke's story introduces a new theme, the relation between kingship and the gods.

A striking feature of the Ganda tradition is that the 'early' kings do not belong to history, being imaginary characters or ritual stereotypes, but the gods do.[23] That is to say, they were believed to have become active in the affairs of the kingdom at a definite point in dynastic time, when the hero-king Nakibinge (K.8, G.12) sought their help against an invasion from Bunyoro. Kibuuka the Flyer was not the only one of the gods who came to the mainland from the Ssese islands at that time, when, as was noted earlier, they are said to have overrun the whole country. Mutebi (K.15, G.8 – but in one list Nakibinge's immediate successor) showed especial favour to them – that is, of course, to the men and women who interpreted their messages. ('He was a very bad king, that one,' wrote Kaggwa the Christian convert; 'he was devoted to the gods.')[24] But his son Tebandeke would go further. In the early years of his manhood he found that he was not begetting children and sought help from the mediums, who detected the malign influence of the 'twin' of his great ancestor King Kimera. When the missing cord was located and honoured the king's generative faculty was restored. There was, however, an unhappy sequel. Tebandeke was angered by the exorbitant fees that the gods publicly claimed for their services, so he slew a number of them and sacked their shrines. Anyone who disputes professional charges does so at his peril, even if he is a king, and the great god Mukasa retaliated by driving him mad, so that he went and hid in the forest. Now the regular remedy for mental illness was a homoeopathic one: the afflicting deity or spirit was induced by appropriate ritual to take over the sufferer in a regulated and socially productive way, making him, or more often her, a counsellor and therapist. That was done with Tebandeke, who became himself a medium of Mukasa.[25]

Generation

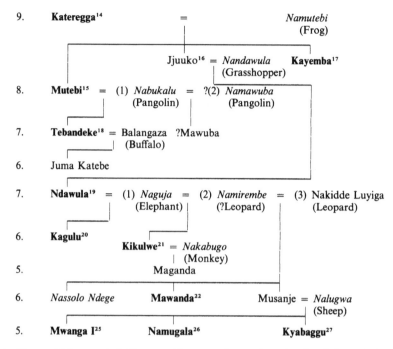

Note: Names of kings are in **bold** type, with superscript numbers showing their position in the list. Names of females are in *italics*, with their clan in brackets. Generations are counted back from the time of first record, with Muteesa I (1856–84) as Generation 1.

Fig. 8   The eighteenth-century crisis

This Pauline conversion was not well received in the country, as it was clearly wrong that a king should play such a dual role. And when Tebandeke died steps were taken to prevent a repetition. His successor should have been his young son Juma Katebe, but his cousin Ndawula, reputedly a son of King Jjuuko, roughly intervened, saying to Juma: 'You can inherit the gods, but I'll take the kingdom.'[26] Thereafter a youth representing Juma Katebe would be formally installed together with each new *kabaka* but would then retire into obscurity. The episode has been seen by historians as marking a decisive stage in the secularisation of the monarchy, but that seems a rather doubtful interpretation. For one thing the Juma figure seems to have played no greater part in religion than in politics, so that the significance must be sought elsewhere than in the separation of the sacred and the profane. In fact, it must be suspected that the whole story was invented in an attempt to explain a piece of ancient ritual that was no longer understood. In any case it does not describe the emancipation of kingship from religious controls but rather a new priestly aggression against the monarchy, which had been the centre of the people's religious life. There is evidence, in fact, that the practice of spirit-mediumship, the claim of certain individuals to act as spokesmen or more often spokeswomen for imaginary but supposedly potent beings, spread rapidly over the whole Lakeland during the seventeenth and eighteenth centuries, in response to the stresses of social and political change. Everywhere the behaviour of the mediums was called *ku-bandwa*, 'to be pressed down', a term which tries to describe the experience of possession; and there are many other similarities in the ritual apparatus and terminology, in the training of mediums and in the names of the possessing deities which, as Iris Berger has shown,[27] imply a loosely organised cult that transcended political boundaries. Buganda shared some of these features, including the gods Mukasa (Mugasa), Wamala (Wamara) and Ddungu (Irungu); but, Berger also makes clear, there was an important structural difference. Elsewhere, in Bunyoro, Nkore, the Haya states and Rwanda, large sections of the population went through a process of religious initiation; but in Buganda the cults were kept in the hands of professionals known as *mmandwa* (from *m-bandwa*) and *ba-lubaale*.

The offensive of the mediums that seems to be described in the stories of Tebandeke and Ndawula was evidently checked by the royal power, but their influence certainly did not disappear from the political scene. And any explanation of this part of the tradition has to confront the awkward fact that the apparently secularising ruler Ndawula was himself a god.

Perhaps it may be thought over-sceptical to suggest that the nineteenth king of Buganda was an imaginary person, that in the seventh generation before the written record we are still in the realm of religious myth. Ndawula is certainly the name of a fairly well-known *lubaale*,[28] but could not a prince have been named after a god, as many other Ganda children were and are? That simple explanation, however, will not do. In the first place Ndawula is the name of a *Nyoro* god, and his foreign origin was never forgotten; in mid-colonial times his medium still spoke in the Nyoro tongue.[29] The name is in fact the Ganda pronunciation of the great Ndahura, founder of the divine Cwezi dynasty which, according to some, had held sway in middle-earth before the second great disaster (see above, pp. 39–40); and it would surely be strange if this alien power had provided a personal name for a Ganda prince. But more decisive is the evidence that 'King' Ndawula was linked with myth and cult in ways that put his divinity beyond doubt.

The god Ndahura had his main centre of worship at Mubende, an isolated hill that rises from the plain of Buwekula to the north-west of

Buganda. On its summit is a grove of trees dominated by an ancient many-buttressed *pterygota*, which is itself called *ndahura*, and here the priestess Nyakahima carried on a cult which had every sign of great antiquity.[30] The root of the name, *bende*, crops up as a term of divinity from eastern Uganda to southern Zaire; and recent investigations have confirmed that the site was occupied in the fourteenth century; there is even evidence of an Early Iron Age settlement, perhaps a thousand years before that.[31] The area was Nyoro territory at least till about 1820, when it was overrun by Ganda. It had been indeed the heart of the Nyoro realm. Each new king had to ascend the hill with only four companions to receive the blessing of his divine ancestor. He was then taken to stand on the sacred anthill called *epyemi*, not far away, and only then was he truly king.[32] These rites are believed to have been carried on in secret even after the area had come under Ganda control. In addition, Mubende was a great centre of pilgrimage, which did not altogether cease when the British built a district headquarters at the foot of the hill. (The place is high enough to be almost malaria-free, and at one time there was talk of making it Uganda's 'Simla'.) Ndahura was also linked with the far west of the Nyoroan zone. He made the crater lakes and stocked them with hippos, and some say that he lives still among the snows of Gambalagala, Mt Ruwenzori, which is sometimes visible from Mubende. Since this was the most heavenward point within Nyoro or Ganda knowledge, it must be inferred that Ndahura was really the High God. His name, however, makes him 'the Oppressor', God in his destructive aspect; and in recent times he was especially thought of as the cause, and therefore the possible cure, of smallpox – as was Katabi or Kataai, the Creator god worshipped in western Tanzania. Whether or not plague and smallpox were endemic in these parts, they became far more rife in the latter half of the nineteenth century, as the region was opened up to commercial and other contacts with the outer world; and the recent worship of Ndahura/Ndawula, like that of Kawumpuli, has been very much a cult of affliction.[33]

However, such was the plasticity of religious thought that Ndahura had another, apparently different role as a hero of the kingship myth. He was begotten by a bold hunter on a princess whose father had forbidden her to conceive, cast at birth into the water, rescued by a potter and brought up incognito until it was time for him to assume the kingship (see above, p. 39). The story follows a very familiar pattern, but it has especially close affinities with the Ganda tale of Kimera. Indeed the Ganda seem to have recognised that their 'King' Ndawula was a virtual duplicate of Kimera. Each was reputedly a son of the Grasshopper folk on his mother's side, and Na-ndawula, like Na-kimera, is a favourite name for daughters of that clan. What is more, Kalemeera, who figures in the official tradition as

Kimera's father, appears in the alternative king-list immediately before Ndawula. The biography of Kimera ends in effect with his accession; for when the young king was ready for his initiation he ceased to be Kimera and became Ttembo instead. In Bunyoro, however, the story of Ndahura goes on to tell how he was suddenly swallowed up in the earth, or alternatively was captured by Bwire-butakya, the King of Eternal Night. Either way, he managed to escape on the third day with the help of his faithful servant Nyamutare, but did not resume his reign.[34] As I pointed out long ago, the god who returns after two nights in the land of darkness has to be the moon[35] – or, as I would now say, is the projection of kingship in its lunar aspect. The recurrent crisis of the moon provides a powerful analogy for the human crisis of initiation, which is a singular event for the individual but a recurrent one for society and kingdom. Like the moon, initiated boys, for whom in these countries the young king stood proxy, return (with luck) from the sojourn in the camp which is their first death.

A similar myth is central to the Ganda tradition of Ndawula, as usual in impoverished form but with unmistakably the same meaning.[36] It says that, suffering from eye disease, he went to hide in the forest, just as his predecessor had done. There he met a poor man with the strange name Siroganga, 'I never practise witchcraft' (or in another version Sseroganga, 'chief witch'),[37] and swore him to secrecy. But the man, having exchanged clothes with the king, went to court, where his finery gave rise to comment, and under questioning he gave way and led the queen-mother and the katikkiro to the king's hiding-place. Ndahura speared the traitor but was persuaded to return to his people. Now all solitary sojourns in the forest, like journeys to the underworld, are echoes of the initiatory experience; and it seems therefore that both Tebandeke and Ndahura play the role of Ttembo, the king as initiand. They do so, however, in the framework of a more complex society, in which some of the roles of the sacred king have been transferred to gods.

To suggest that both Siroganga and Nyamutare (a minor Cwezi deity) represent the evening star, who accompanies the moon on his return from the darkness, would be no more than a conjecture; but the lunar associations of the Ganda Ndawula receive support from the researches of Benjamin Ray into royal ritual and especially the regular new-moon ceremonies. 'During these liminal periods of darkness (enzikiza)', he writes, when 'time itself is temporarily abolished', princes and princesses and others attend court at the tombs of dead kings; and the hymn sung there 'speaks repeatedly of Ndawula'. 'All the ceremonies', in fact, 'repeat this legendary act' – his return from the forest. That forest, moreover, is identified in myth with the one into which Kintu disappeared and in ritual with the sacred area behind the screen of royal tombs.[38]

Ndawula, in short, has a place at the very centre of the Ganda sacral kingship, and it is hardly conceivable that the name merely belonged to an individual and not very ancient holder of the royal office. But then other questions present themselves. Why was such a role assigned to a character who was at home in Nyoro mythology? And why was he placed, not at or near the beginning of the dynasty, but in Generation Seven, only just before the threshold of genuine remembered history? Part of the answer seems clear: like his 'father' Jjuuko, he was used as a cover for events that the tradition-makers wished to expunge from the national consciousness.

The fall of the tyrant

Ndawula was followed in the chronicle by Kagulu, his son by a woman of the Elephant clan. Unlike his father, who had a reputation for mild government that was strangely at variance with his character as a deity, Kagulu, also called Tebucwereke, or 'More than the land can endure', is described as an insane tyrant. He devised curious ordeals for his courtiers and servants, making them prostrate themselves on iron spikes and decreeing that the labourers who built his palace should carry reeds upside down on their heads, presumably with the sharp ends piercing the skull.[39] Exaggerated and bizarre reports of royal cruelty are a commonplace of African tradition and are not of course to be taken literally. There was for example a king of Kasanje in Angola who, when he wished to rise from his seat, levered himself up by plunging knives into the backs of slaves kneeling at either side.[40] Such fantasies probably expressed the awe, almost horror, that was one of the emotions aroused by the notion of a king, a human being who had the right as well as the power to take human life.

Allegations of tyranny can also serve in retrospect to justify rebellion, as they did in this case. King Ndawula had also taken wives from the Leopard clan, and by them he had had several children: the princess Nassolo Ndege and the princes Kikulwe, Mawanda, Musanje and Segamwenge. Musanje unfortunately killed a half-brother called Luyenje in a wrestling match, and although the death was an accident he was executed on his father's orders. So Nassolo Ndege, fearing for the lives of her other brothers, took them, together with the four young sons of Musanje, and fled towards Bunyoro. The fugitives actually got no further than a place called Busunju on the Busiro–Ssingo border, which was then the border between Buganda and Bunyoro, and there they were befriended by a local chief, Mawuba, who entered into blood-brotherhood with Mawanda. In *The Kings of Buganda*, Kaggwa did not identify this mysterious personage, the reason being that his case was then *sub judice*. His descendants were claiming princely status, saying that he had been a son of King Mutebi and had himself briefly held the kingship after Kagulu. It was not until 1926 that the *kabaka*'s court finally ruled against them and assigned them to the Lungfish clan.

According to Professor Kiwanuka, Mawuba is remembered in Ssingo as a great magician;[41] and it was by supernatural or symbolic rather than by military means that he contrived the tyrant's overthrow. The story says that he took 'a little antelope' (*kaweewo*, diminutive form of the regular *mpeewo*) and a coucal bird (*tuttuma*), doctored them and sent them to the king's court. Kagulu's people drove the antelope away and it ran back to Mawuba, but the damage had apparently been done; the defenders were deprived of power or will to resist, and the rebel princes took possession of the capital. Kagulu fled into the coastlands of Kyaggwe, at that time the home of small independent communities, but Mawanda and his formidable sister tracked him down and captured him with the connivance of a local chief, and Ndege had him drowned – or according to another account burnt his body and threw the ashes in the Lake. The princes then offered the throne to Mawuba but he declined it, and Kikulwe, the oldest of them, was chosen king.

That was not the end of the turmoil, for Kikulwe soon became suspicious of his more valiant and popular brother Mawanda, and plotted to do away with him, using the stereotyped device of the staked pit, which as usual the intended victim managed to evade.[42] That, at any rate, was the story put about by Mawanda's partisans to justify or excuse the successful coup he organised against his brother, who was deposed and killed after a reign of probably no very long duration. His own reign was one of great achievements, which will need separate treatment. Here it is necessary to pause and to consider the implications of Kagulu's fall.

The tyrant was reputedly the son of an Elephant woman, and her brother Ntambi had been his *katikkiro* and the chief instrument of his oppressive rule. So after his death the victorious 'Leopard' princes threatened to execute Walusimbi, lord of Bakka, head of the Elephant clan, for being the parent of a double evil. He, however, managed to deflect the odium on to his brother (or by some accounts his blood-brother) Mukalo, who lived at Kambugu not far away. 'I', he said, 'am only the begetter [of kings] by day, he is the begetter by night.' Mukalo was duly put to death with many of his kin, and thereafter it was his heirs who bore the notorious Elephant badge, while the heirs of Walusimbi acknowledged the Civet instead.[43] It was also alleged that there had been doubt about Kagulu's selection, inasmuch as the ritual of accession required the new king to jump over an elephant's tusk, an act which in his case would be tantamount to incest. So his maternal grandfather Mukalo, head of the Elephant clan, had taken counsel with the *katikkiro* Walusimbi, head of the Civets, and they decided to join the two clans, so that Kagulu's mother could become an honorary Civet; they agreed to share the offices of the king's uncles.[44] Others, however, maintained that the Walusimbi of that time had lied to save his skin and that he really was the Elephant chief and the parent of the tyrant's mother.

Clearly the tradition was treading on very delicate ground at this point; and the matter was further confused by later developments. After the death of Kagulu and Mukalo it was decreed that the Elephants should have no further connection with the kingship; yet only a generation later a woman of the clan, Nanteza, not only married the reigning king, Kyabaggu (K.25), but saw her two sons, Jjunju and Ssemakookiro, succeed one another on the throne. (By one account the king married her under the impression that her father was a high-ranking Civet; by another she was captured in a razzia on the Ssese islands and so dazzled the king by her beauty that he took her to bed without enquiring into her parentage.) The come-back of the Elephants was completed by the accession of Muteesa I, whose mother also came from that clan. Ssemakookiro (K.27) had already 'joined together' the Elephants and the Civets, or perhaps re-joined them.

But this cannot be the whole of the story. Stanley, who retailed the earliest version of Kimera's founding of the kingdom, did not hear it at court but as a tale told at the camp-fire by one of his porters, a man of Ganda origin called Kaddu. And he had described Kimera's father Kalemeera as a man of the Elephant clan, 'one of the four royal clans of Buganda'.[45] To anyone familiar with Ganda ethnography this must be a disconcerting remark; no other testimony attributes royalty to the Elephants, and the ruling patriline was supposed to have no totem of its own. Yet Stanley could not have invented such a statement, nor could Kaddu have been so far mistaken about his country's basic institutions. The truth is almost certainly that the kings who ruled from Bakka had indeed recognised the Elephant as their emblem; and it begins to appear that the overthrow of 'Kagulu' disguises a truly revolutionary act, the ending of the royal line. There emerges also a motive for the invention of 'King' Ndawula, who provided an august, even divine parentage for usurpers with no legitimate claim to royalty.

If, however, the Elephants had been kings in Busiro, what were the Civets before the upheaval of Generation Six? The answer is probably that they were the group that regularly supplied the mothers of the kings. The mothers of princes, even in later times, were sometimes called *ba-ma-fumbe*, 'people of the Civet'. Moreover, during the ritual of his growing the young king spent a night with a Civet girl called Nabitalo, 'Mother of marvels', and this is a synonym of Na-bijjano, which in turn was an alternative title for the woman more commonly called Namasole, the queen-mother. It is also remarkable that nearly half the *katikkiros* listed by Kaggwa, up to and including the reign of Ndawula – ten out of a total of twenty-two – were members of the Civet clan. If we allow for fictitious claims inserted on behalf of other clans, it is possible to suggest that in appointing his mother's brother to that office Kagulu had been following ancient custom – that is to say, the *katikkiro* had regularly been the king's mother's brother and a member of the Civet clan.

An arrangement of this kind, in which the king's parents came always from the same two clans, was found in the kingdom of Rwanda and may be seen as historically intermediate between royal incest and indiscriminate royal polygamy. It was probably difficult to sustain for very long, and in Buganda the story of the fall of Kagulu seems to describe its collapse. Thereafter the *katikkiro* became an appointed official who could be drawn from any clan, as could the mother of the king. These changes were made possible by a drastic discontinuity, the ending of the ancient lineage of the kings. It is possible, as we shall see, that it was restored after an interval; but those who henceforward claimed to belong to the patriline of the *balangira*, 'the rulers', would acknowledge no totemic emblem. The kingship was detached from its origins and was free to manipulate the clans, including the Elephant and the Civet, and to arbitrate between them.

The sons of Ndawula are located in Generation Six, only just beyond grandfathers' recollections, and it cannot be doubted that the narrative outlined above deals with real events, indeed with the main formative events of Buganda's history. But it is certainly neither the whole truth nor wholly true. Doubts arise not only or mainly because of the fanciful elements such as the ominous antelope or the conventional episode of the pit trap, which could be mere arabesques on an essentially factual report. It is the personages, or some of them, that are suspect. There must have been a real man behind the political achievements credited to Mawanda, and the dynamic role of his sister would not have been assigned to a woman by later tradition if it had not first impressed contemporaries. Kagulu, however, is another matter. The name is related to the word for 'sky', *ggulu*, and was commonly applied to hills, including a prominent one overlooking the Lake in Kyaggwe, in the area where the king was said to have met his death. One tradition claims that Ggulu, 'Heaven', was the father of Mbaale, the rocky home of the god Kibuuka, and of Kagulu, whose fifteen 'children' were probably lesser hills in the vicinity.[46] The Ganda were fond of tales of political and amorous intrigue in which the actors were hills and streams; and it seems clear that one such fantasy has been superposed on the saga of dynastic strife. This almost certainly indicates that some aspect of reality has needed to be disguised.

One clue is surely the statement that Kagulu's rebel siblings fled towards Bunyoro. The narrative admittedly claims that they stopped at or near the border; but there must be a suspicion that in reality they owed their triumph not to magic but to Nyoro power. At any rate we can no longer delay discussion of the Nyoro factor in the history of the Buganda state.

9   Foreign affairs

The enemy kingdom

One of the popular topographical legends in Buganda features a character called Kkungu, who decided that he would like to be king and so set off for Bunyoro to get himself appointed.[1] But when he got as far as the home of Kibaale, chief of the Oribi Antelope clan, about a dozen miles north of Kampala, he began to feel tired and was tempted to take a couple of days' rest. The delay was fatal, for the (unnamed) reigning *kabaka* got wind of the plot and took steps to foil it. There was then nothing for Kkungu to do but turn into the rocky hill (a standard difficult climb, according to a colonial enthusiast)[2] that now bears his name. K-kungu (from *i-kungu*) is a depersonalised form of the word *mu-kungu*, 'chief'; and by a neat inversion Ki-baale, the name of the chief who resides at the foot of the hill, is a personifying form of *i-baale* or *m-baale*, an old word for 'rock'.

The story was of course a joke about procrastination: '"I might as well stop here for the week-end", he said, and there he is still!' Sometimes it was told simply as such, without any political content.[3] Its interest for us, however, is the plain assumption that the way to become the *kabaka* of Buganda was to seek authority from Bunyoro. In fact the name Kkungu probably contains a punning allusion to prince Kakungulu, brother of Kamaanya (G.3), who did seek and win Nyoro support in his bid for the Ganda throne, though it proved unavailing. That would have been some time in the first decades of the nineteenth century; but even three generations later the idea surfaced again in the full light of recorded history, during the factional fighting that accompanied the European intrusion. Having been driven from the capital by the Christians, the Muslim Ganda sought refuge and assistance in Bunyoro. It seems unlikely that they would have behaved in this treasonable way if there had not been a lingering belief that the king of Bunyoro had the right to decide who should hold power in Buganda. Certainly the Nyoro thought that he had. The *mukama* Kamurasi told Samuel Baker in 1866 that Buganda had been a dependent province until the previous generation, when Muteesa's father had rebelled.[4] That was clearly nonsense. Nyoro historians in fact accept that three generations before Kamurasi the Ganda had wrested control of the key province of Buddu from Bunyoro and had inflicted a great defeat on the *mukama* Duhaga which resulted in his suicide.[5] Further territorial gains had followed, and through most of the nineteenth century they were regularly raiding into Bunyoro and meddling in its politics; for a time the Ganda managed to maintain a client on the throne of the breakaway province of Toro, which had been part of the Nyoro heartland. Yet Kamurasi's assertion cannot be dismissed as pure fantasy. Like the ritual claim of Tudor monarchs to the throne of France, it must have had some kind of reference to an earlier historical reality. And there are ample indications in Ganda tradition that Bunyoro had at one time enjoyed influence, probably suzerainty, perhaps outright dominion, in the lands that came to be Buganda.

First there is the rather dim figure of the second *kabaka*, Cwa, who fills a gap between his 'father', the genesis hero Kintu, and his 'grandson' Kimera, reputedly the effective founder of the dynasty. Cwa is not otherwise a Ganda name, but it was of great renown in Bunyoro. It labelled one of the dominant 'Bushbuck' clans, second only in status to the ruling Bito; and it was also the regnal name of several Nyoro kings, including the last independent ruler Kabarega, the unfortunate Duhaga and an earlier warrior leader who was remembered as a formidable enemy in the sagas of Rwanda and Nkore. Its appearance in the prologue to the Ganda king-list looks like a half-suppressed memory of Nyoro supremacy. The traditional associations of this *kabaka*, moreover, are with the north-west of the country, close to the old frontier with Bunyoro. He had particular links with the Dog clan, based at Gguluddene in the north-west corner of Busiro, and his reputed capital was at Bbigo, near the intersection of Busiro, Busujju and Ssingo counties; he was supposed to have disappeared while wandering on the nearby plain of Ddavula. These places are well to the west of Walusimbi's ancient domain, and yet Cwa has the surname Na-bakka, Lord of Bakka, which seems to place him at the very centre of Ganda ritual tradition.

Then there is the brief statement that Kiggala (K.5) slew 'a Nyoro man called Toko'[6] who had established himself at Mugganvula, just north of Kampala. One might almost suppose that Kaggwa or his informant was gifted with prophetic vision, for a Colonel Toko was one of the most prominent leaders of the northern army of occupation that was driven from Kampala in 1985. The coincidence is intriguing, but perhaps not all that remarkable. Toko is presumably a Lwo name, and there was always a Lwo-speaking element in the population of Bunyoro. It is not a name that the Ganda would have chosen for a character of myth or fantasy; and so we must assume that a fragment of historical saga has been preserved concerning a Nyoro incursion into the heart of the country. The incident was attached to the reign of Kiggala, who was a god, probably because Mugganvula was the scene of the incest that made him 'the Father of the Rivers'. This mythical context would have helped to make the unwelcome memory less damaging.

The main evidence, however, for a Nyoro contribution to the history of Buganda remains the highly charged story called 'The Coming of Kimera', to the analysis of which it is necessary to return. Back in 1959 I implicitly dismissed this episode from history, explaining it as a dramatic presentation of the routine transition from one reign to the next.[7] Now I feel less confident that one can ignore the plain statement that Kimera came from Bunyoro – not from the symbolic east like Kintu and Mulondo, but from the north-west. In the meantime Matthias Kiwanuka has produced an interesting alternative theory, accepting the basic historicity of Kimera but arguing that the 'Bunyoro' from which he came was not the recent historical kingdom of that name but the older 'Cwezi' realm supposedly called Kitara, with its base in the great earthworks at Biggo on the Katonga.[8] It is not unfair to point out that Kiwanuka is a Ganda patriot and was writing at a time when relations between the two kingdoms were severely strained. (In fact, he was continuing the quarrel that had allowed the northern politician Milton Obote to destroy them both.) Bunyoro's claims to a great imperial past were anathema to him,[9] and especially hard to take was the idea that his own country had begun life as a mere colonial dependency. By transferring Kimera to 'Kitara' he could make Buganda, no less than Bunyoro, a direct successor to the glorious, but safely defunct, empire of the Cwezi. But political bias does not necessarily make a historical proposition false, and this one does not lack supporting evidence. Speke was told that Kimera came to Buganda from the west (not the north-west), hunting his way down the Katonga valley – that is, from the direction of Biggo. In addition there is Kimera's link with the Grasshopper clan, who claim that his mother Wannyana was their daughter. Na-kimera ('Kimera's mother') is also a favourite name for girls of that clan, and one so named was regularly presented to the young *kabaka* as the first of his ritual wives. Now the Grasshopper folk, otherwise known as Ba-Songa, were widely distributed over the Lakeland, especially in the more pastoral districts. The Ganda section derived from settlements in the western borderlands, not far from Biggo, and their leaders operated what had clearly once been independent chiefdoms. It is clear, however, that their incorporation dates from the reigns of Kateregga and Mutebi, far removed in dynastic time from Kimera.[10] Also, the oldest versions of the Kimera story, those of Stanley and Le Veux's *Manuel*, make no mention of

Grasshopper kinsfolk. It seems likely therefore that the connection was a relatively recent invention designed to improve the clan's status within the Ganda state. The claim was known to King Muteesa I, for when he appointed a member of the clan to the sacred office of Mugema (the preserve of the Monkey clan), he tried to justify the innovation by asserting that the Grasshoppers were his true 'mothers'.[11] But the original context was probably the reign of his grandfather Kamaanya, when the dynastic tradition took on something like its definitive shape. For that king was indeed the son of a Grasshopper mother, and his maternal kinsmen (including Kaggwa's great-grandfather) had spells of high favour both in his father's reign and in his own, though on each occasion the end was disastrous. It is likely that in that brief political heyday the clan, though unable to conceal its foreign origin, inserted itself into the deepest roots of the royal genealogy. The silence of Stanley's informants shows, however, that the clan was not universally accepted, and it was doubtless the literate authority of its son, Apolo Kaggwa, that gave it canonical status.

In any case the weight of the traditional evidence is that Kimera came from Bunyoro – not from the hypothetical realm of the Cwezi to the south-west but from the heartland of the recent northern kingdom, starting from Kibulala in Ssingo, the known capital of a former Bito king. He is said to have been accompanied to Buganda not only by his Grasshopper uncles but also by founders of the Buffalo and Squirrel clans, both of which have their main domains in the formerly Nyoro province of Ssingo, and the Buffalo folk came to play a major role in Ganda politics and ritual. His escort also included the ancestors of the ba-m-bowa, the Binders, the kabaka's bodyguards and executioners; and it is in the Nyoro, not the Ganda language that ku-bowa (or rather ku-boha) means 'to bind'. The young king's closest associate, however, was his foster-brother Katumba, founder of the Grey Monkey clan, on whom he conferred the ritual title of Mugema (probably 'Protector'), otherwise known only at the court of Bunyoro.[12] Second only to Mugema in ritual importance was his 'son' Kinyolo, a title which actually means 'the man of Bunyoro'. And there is much else in the apparatus of Ganda kingship, from the name of the great battery of royal drums, mujaguzo, 'that which is made to cause jubilation', to terms of chiefship such as mukungu and mutongole, that has specific Nyoro origin.

The geography of the Kimera tradition is rather contradictory. On the one hand, he has a shrine at Bumera, 'Kimera's place', which is close to Bakka, and a grave at Kanzize in Bulemeezi, the ancient country of death. On the other, the drama of his advent is located to the south, on the borders of Busiro and Kyaddondo, nearer the nineteenth-century centre of the kingdom. Here are Temangalo, 'Chop-finger', probably the place where the wildling's nails were clipped to prepare him for entry into civilised society, and Gganda, where he ousted the regent Ssebwana. It is difficult to decide whether the locale was shifted to correspond to new political realities, or whether the whole story was developed after those realities had taken shape. The place-name Gganda is formed from the same stem as Bu-ganda, and it is possible that the kingdom only acquired its modern name when its centre of gravity moved towards the Kampala area. Gganda and Temangalo are in the territory of the Monkey clan, and it is likely that this clan, rather than the Grasshoppers, originally inserted him into the dynastic history.

In so doing, they duplicated the personality of the Child King, a role already played by Mulondo. There is a difference, however. It is likely that the actual practice of installing a small boy as king was abandoned long ago, so that the picture of Mulondo on his mushroom throne was a kind of snapshot from the distant past, a literary *donnée* without real meaning for recent Ganda. The 'Kimera' ritual, by contrast, was still operated in the nineteenth century, each new king being saluted as his incarnation, and the linked myth thus remained lively and productive; the assertion of a 'grant from Kimera' was the best possible title to inherited land or office, superior even to a grant from 'Nakibinge'.

The conclusion is that, whereas the original pattern of the complex tale of Kimera comes from neolithic myth and ritual, its proximate source is to be found in local political relations of recent centuries, and that it contains a particular allusion to an act of homage paid by new kings of Buganda to their Nyoro overlord. It is well established that until the early nineteenth century the rulers of Kiziba, the little kingdom on Buganda's southern border, had to journey to Bunyoro to be confirmed in office, and there is nothing to prevent us from supposing that at some stage the kings of Buganda had done the same. The story of Kalemeera would then reflect, at one level, the outward journey (the 'trade-goods' that he took with him may be a disguise for tribute) and 'Kimera' is the prince who returns in ceremonious triumph with the blessing of the over-king. A local and transient political drama was thus grafted onto one far older and of universal relevance, and the assimilation of the two themes in the myth of Kimera was the easier because both referred to recurrent acts, not singular events. Not once but very many times had the millet grown and the boy become a hunter and the young king come to take his father's place. The visits of client princes to the Nyoro court were less numerous, but still they happened often enough to take on the form of a ritual and to be remembered in the language of a myth.

It is not suggested here that Nyoro activity had anything to do with the *origins* of Buganda. The beginnings of both systems lie far back in the Early

Iron Age, beyond the reach of tradition. But it is hard to doubt that the political development of the area was decisively shaped by a period of Nyoro hegemony. This conclusion will doubtless be unpalatable to Ganda patriots, and it may not be welcomed by neutral historians either. For it makes Buganda appear as a 'secondary state', the product of foreign intervention, and thus may seem to deprive its history of theoretical interest. The crucial question of how and why complex political systems arise in the first place is simply pushed back into the history of Bunyoro. Many analysts today would like to see every polity as the result of internally generated change, from which it may be possible to construct developmental laws or models, not dependent on accidents of history. Some are tempted to forget that conquest, acculturation and institutional transfer are facets of reality, not just figments of colonial prejudice. In any case, to acknowledge that Buganda owed much to an external stimulus is not to deprive it of originality. For in the end it evolved on lines peculiar to itself, and the ways in which it differed from Bunyoro and from all other Lakeland polities are at least as interesting as the ways in which it resembled them.

The 'empire' of Kitara

The cumulative evidence from tradition, ritual and political institutions makes the reality of Nyoro supremacy inescapable. What it does not tell us is when the supremacy began or how long it lasted. Since all the early names in the Ganda tradition are those of imaginary or symbolic personages there is no point in counting the generations backwards in order to provide Kimera with a date. To have any hope of arriving at a chronology it would be necessary to use Nyoro traditions as well, but unfortunately these are uncertain, ambiguous and confused. Bunyoro's historians, it was shown earlier (p. 38), divided the past into three ages, each dominated by a distinct line of kings, though tenuous genealogical links preserved a continuity that went back to the beginning of the world. The first two, divine, 'dynasties' need not here concern us, and we can concentrate on the dominion of men, represented by the human Bito rulers. In the first three decades of this century no fewer than nine lists of these found their way into print.[13] All were in accord on the four generations preceding the last independent ruler, Kabarega, but beyond that there was no agreement on the names, let alone the sequence, of the Bito rulers, and the number of generations assigned to the dynasty varied from nine to fourteen. It seemed clear that beyond the reach of secondary reminiscence in Generation Five or possibly Generation Six those who reported on Nyoro history had only vague ideas about the names of kings and the sequence they occurred in. In 1935–7 an attempt was made to clear up the confusion by no less a person than the reigning king, Tito Winyi IV, writing in the *Uganda Journal* over the initials K. W.[14] His version expanded the Bito dynasty to seventeen generations, thus nearly closing the embarrassing gap that had opened up between Bunyoro and Buganda. (Kimera, G.18, was supposed to be the junior twin of the first Nyoro king.) After the war the senior chief John Nyakatura, the king's principal consultant if not the real author of his articles, published an expanded version in book form.[15]

Scholars generally welcomed this apparently authoritative revision and most of what has written in the 1950s and 1960s, and even more recently, about the history of Bunyoro and of the Lakeland as a whole took the K. W./Nyakatura genealogy as a datum. It has, however, been seriously undermined by David Henige's searching critique, which showed that it was the product of research rather than of tradition, and of a research plainly motivated by the need to compete historically with Buganda.[16] The authors lengthened the first dynasty from six to nineteen names by such devices as the conversion of a religious invocation *Nkya ka Nkya*, 'Dawn of dawns', into two kings called Nkya I and Nkya II – a procedure which hardly inspires confidence. And with regard to the Bito a profusion of royal praise-names enabled them to multiply the bearers of the recurrent names Winyi, Olimi, Cwa and Kyebambe. One of Henige's most telling points concerned the title of the author himself. At the time when he wrote his articles King Tito Gafabusa allowed himself to be called in English fashion Winyi IV. This accorded with his history of the dynasty, which included three previous bearers of the royal Winyi name. Yet in 1924, when he became king, he had been content to be Winyi II. At that time, therefore, he cannot have believed that more than one of his predecessors had been so styled. That does not make the new genealogy wrong, but does rob it of the claim to privileged knowledge. Thus the sequence and dating of reigns and events in Bunyoro has to be regarded as largely indeterminate. It is much the same in the kingdom of Nkore to the south, which made up a kind of triangle of interlocking data with Bunyoro and Buganda. Here too there were several early colonial dynastic lists, followed in 1955 by an official history[17] which was clearly a riposte to Nyakatura and had at least as much to do with the status of Nkore in the emergent state of Uganda as with the authentic past.

The first rule of source-criticism is that, other things being equal, the earliest testimonies are the best. Tentatively, therefore, we may take Ruth Fisher's narrative, which appeared in 1912, as the most likely to represent authentic Nyoro tradition. It must be said, however, that though her story of the Bito dynasty purports to describe the rule of mortal kings in contrast to the earlier reigns of divinity, it is itself not free from myth. The founder,

Winyi, also known as Isingoma, Mpuga and Rukidi, who came from beyond the Nile to claim the kingship left vacant by the departing Cwezi, is an archetype, both of kingship and of a new generation; and the 'sons' who followed him belong to the domain of theology. Ocaki is the Lwo Ocaak, the First Man or the Creator, and his brother Oyo Ka-bamba-iguru, 'He who pegs out the sky' (like a drying hide), can only be God. More doubtful is the next character in her story, the great warrior king Cwa. The name may be of (Nilotic) Lwo origin, but *ku-cwa* is a (Bantu) Nyoro verb of violent action, meaning 'break', 'chop', and the like. So this character was dubbed *Cwa-mali*, 'Cwa indeed', ('Smasher by name and smasher by nature'), and *Cwa eya-cwire ente z'Nkore*, 'Cutter who cut off the cattle of Nkore'. (He is also remembered as Cwa ya Runege or Runego, a name which caused people to credit him with a mother called Runego, or Dunego. But men in this part of the world are not usually called after their mothers, and the real meaning is likely to have been that he was well equipped with balls, *binege*!) Like his Ganda namesake, Cwa disappeared, in his case while campaigning in the south. According to Fisher, he was lured into the forest by Cwezi spirits, who imitated the lowing of cattle, and was never seen again. He left an infant or posthumous son, who played out the classic role of the lost heir.

In spite of these mythical overtones, it is unlikely that there were no real events behind the story of Cwa. The traditions of Nkore, Karagwe and Ihangiro all recall a devastating invasion which they say was repelled by kings who took the title of Nyoro-slayer, and usually the enemy leader is named as Cwa.[18] The chronology, however, is very uncertain. Cwa is placed by Fisher in Generation Nine, and by others still further back, but the Nyoro-slayers belong at most to Generation Seven. Help may perhaps be sought from Rwanda, whose traditions also speak of a major assault by Nyoro forces, the enemy commander being named in one source as Cwa.[19] This testimony has to be taken seriously, since it is definite and elaborate and Rwandan historical literature was exceptionally rich. The invaders were described as formidable warriors armed with iron spears that were all of one piece. (Bunyoro was rich in iron ore and the processing was highly developed.) They also made a great impression by their voracity, and the Rwanda were especially shocked by the way they slaughtered and ate the captured cattle. This clearly indicates that they were something other than Lakeland pastoralists of the normal kind, to whom cattle were capital, not to be recklessly consumed. Their historicity is confirmed by the presence in the Rwanda pantheon of a deity called Munyoro ('the Nyoro man'); for the regular way of coping with unpleasant phenomena, especially new and alien ones, was to turn them into gods, who could be manipulated and appeased.

The Rwanda kings usually associated with the invasion were the first Kigeri and the first Mibambwe, who are assigned to Generations Fifteen and Fourteen. However, it was argued earlier (p. 137) that the first cycle in Rwanda provided a model of kingship, not a record of events. So we must suppose that the Nyoro onslaught was projected back into a mythical past, much as the invaders themselves were turned into a personifying deity. There is some reason to believe that the invasion cannot be placed much later than Generation Eleven, for allusions to it, as to a well-remembered event, appear in highly stylised dynastic poems that are alleged to have been composed as early as Generation Seven and recited ever afterwards without alteration. Doubt has recently been cast on that claim, however,[20] and the dating has to remain tentative.

All the same, the faint outlines of a political history for the northern Lakeland do begin to emerge from these fragments of saga. They suggest a period of far-reaching Nyoro aggression and expansion datable at least as far back as Generation Nine (the position assigned to Cwa by Ruth Fisher), that is, to some time in the seventeenth century. This is more or less consistent with the picture that archaeologists are starting to present, and also with the claims made by Nyoro spokesmen in the nineteenth century. Their ancestors, they told Speke and other early reporters, had controlled a great kingdom called Kitara, or Bunyoro–Kitara, which extended from the Victoria Nile in the east to Lakes Albert and Edward in the west and southward to the Kagera river.[21] Again, it would be unwise to reject such early and explicit testimony. Nor should it be assumed that, insofar as the claim has any substance, it referred to the Cwezi empire of glorious memory, of which Bunyoro and other nineteenth-century kingdoms were the somewhat degenerate successors. The Cwezi in turn have been customarily linked with the visible signs of ancient organised settlement at Ntusi and Biggo (above, p. 77). However, it has come to be widely recognised that the Cwezi tales are myths of paradise lost which, if they carry any reference at all to a fourteenth-century political structure, give a very exaggerated impression of its size and splendour. It also appears from recent investigations that Ntusi and Biggo were something less than imperial capitals.[22]

Edward Steinhart, indeed, has gone so far as to argue that the process of state-formation hardly started in the Lakeland before the seventeenth century. The construction of the Biggo earthworks, he believes, need imply no more than 'ritual control or kin-based labour recruitment'.[23] This is not entirely convincing, but he is surely right to insist that 'Kitara' did not denote the Biggo system but the later construction based further north in Bunyoro, which claims it as its alternative name, and that it was created, not destroyed, by the Bito dynasts. This system is unlikely to have been a tightly organised state like the later Buganda or Rwanda, or even the Bunyoro of Kamurasi and Kabarega, but rather a loose network of tribute-paying clients round a central core. Even so, it must have been a considerable political achievement, which can be seen as the result of pressures that had been building up in the central Lakeland for several centuries, ever since cattle-keeping had become a major component of the economy, apparently about the beginning of the present millennium. Cattle are a form of wealth that does not have to be transported, since (like human beings) they can be driven. They thus lend themselves to armed robbery; and indeed the quickest as well as the most exciting way of acquiring a large herd is to steal it from other people. So when cattle (or slaves) have become the principal currency of power and status it can be expected that organised violence will be the norm. There is, however, no necessary connection between pastoralism and state-formation. The Maasai of Kenya and northern Tanzania, among others, bore witness that the forcible acquisition of cattle could be managed very successfully without any kind of hierarchical government; and their relations with the agricultural Kikuyu showed that the juxtaposition of herding and cultivating groups did not necessarily lead to government either. The reason why military government did emerge in the Lakeland is, I believe, that monarchical communities existed there before the coming of cattle. Outside and on the fringes of the main Lakeland power-structures there were, even in the late nineteenth century, simple herdfolk for whom cattle were a means of livelihood and a way of life, not a source of wealth and status, and these were not noted for their martial qualities. For their part, kings of the sort whose ritual biographies have been explored in this book were not originally rulers or organisers of war, but they could become such when the need and the opportunity arose. Cattle-raiding bands would be more effective when centrally controlled, and by exploiting such bands a formerly symbolic figure could become a wielder of wealth and power. There was thus a coalescence of Early Iron Age kingship, with its apparatus of ritual and myth and its high emotional potency, and the crude vigour of the warrior-herdsmen who came to dominate the Later Iron Age scene. Whether the old kings acquired military forces or the new military leaders took over the old ritual systems, the result would have been much the same. And the contrast between the large, undefended mixed settlement at Ntusi, which flourished between about the middle of the eleventh century and the beginning of the fourteenth, and the protective earthworks at Biggo, which clearly succeeded it, is mute evidence of the growth of violence.

The chronology of Biggo is rather uncertain; for though carbon dates exist they are few and were taken a long time ago, when the technology was not highly refined. So far as they go, they suggest that the earthworks were in use from the fourteenth century and perhaps as late as the seventeenth.[24] By the end of that century, however, they had certainly been abandoned, and by the nineteenth century the whole area that includes Biggo and Ntusi was almost empty of people. This is the driest part of the Lakeland, and it may be that the accumulation of cattle had been too much for the vulnerable pastures to bear. Population, wealth and power had clearly moved elsewhere. To the north, in the southern parts of the historic kingdom of Bunyoro, there are many signs of fortified settlements.[25] One set of earthworks, at Munsa, though now dilapidated, could once have been as large as Biggo, and scattered over the area are trenches which commonly ring a defensible hill or outcrop of rock. Nor were the means of protection always physical. There were also the shrines of powerful divinities, which were sanctuaries as well as places of pilgrimage. Ndahura's shrine on Mubende hill was one such refuge. Another was the great temple of Wamara at Masaka on the north bank of the Katonga.[26] And at the south end of Lake Albert was the home of the Ba-yaga, or 'Wind-folk', who made their first fortune by controlling the weather in that dangerous storm-funnel, but who also owned the potent Cwezi deity Murindwa.[27] It was said that their hill-shrine could not ever be approached either by agents of the Nyoro state or by the marauding Ganda armies of the nineteenth century. This combination of 'burgs' and 'abbeys' strongly suggests a time of troubles, otherwise known as a heroic age, when there was no large-scale government, and cattle-rieving bands strove for ascendancy on the grasslands. In time, competition led to new aggregations of power. South of the Kagera, the dominant force that had emerged by the seventeenth century was the group of war-bands that called themselves the Ba-Hinda, which could mean either the 'Stormers' or the 'Protectors'. There is no evidence that they operated a unified state, but they established or remodelled the kingdoms of Karagwe, Kyamutwara, Ihangiro and Buxinza and also the nuclear kingdom of Nkore just to the north of the river. Away to the south-west the highly specialised Ba-Tutsi warriors achieved spectacular successes, making themselves masters of the whole of the fertile hill country; sub-groups called the Ba-Nyiginya, the 'Handsome ones', and the Ba-Ganwa, the 'Renowned', founded or more probably took over the kingdoms that became Rwanda and Burundi. But perhaps even greater was the achievement of the bands known as the Ba-Bito, the 'Favourite sons', creators of the northern state of Kitara.

Their environment gave the Bito certain advantages. It included high-quality agricultural as well as pastoral land; and it contained superior supplies of iron, the raw material of war among other things, and precious deposits of salt at Kibiro on Lake Albert and at Katwe near Lake Edward. It is possible too, though ethnic stereotypes must be used with caution, that the tough Nilotic farmer-fishers who formed part of the population of 'Bunyoro' were more apt for war than either the depressed Ba-iru peasants or the simple herdfolk.

The northern earthworks are as yet undated, but the archaeologist Peter Robertshaw, who has carried out a preliminary survey of the area, infers from pottery styles that large settlements on ridges and hilltops, some of them entrenched, were older than the smaller homesteads on lower ground that constitute the modern pattern of settlement.[28] He suggests that the abandonment of the hill villages indicates a population decline caused by warfare between 'chiefdoms', and perhaps by famines and epidemics, and that the Bito dynasty moved into a vacuum, uniting the region into 'basically a single state administered by a bureaucracy capable of resolving conflicts over access to scarce resources'. This interpretation reflects the common view of the Bito as an intrusive Nilotic force. By my reckoning, however, the Nilotes had been present since the beginning of the millennium, and the Bito were a group that rose to power in the late sixteenth or early seventeenth century within the ethnically mixed population of the northern Lakeland.[29] Originally among the disturbers of the peace, they used both military and ritual resources to recreate a system of order, as Robertshaw describes. It was, I suggest, the security they provided that made hill villages unnecessary and allowed the people to disperse over the land.

The vast kingdom of Bunyoro–Kitara created by the Bito did not last long, for without either writing or a monopoly of weaponry a system of that size could not be sustained. The temptation for distant governors and client princes to withhold tribute and ignore the distant government would soon have become too strong, notwithstanding the mystical potency that it deployed. So it is not surprising that by the time we reach Generation Seven, probably the early years of the eighteenth century, 'Kitara' had been reduced to not much more than the historic kingdom of Bunyoro. By then the remnants of the invaders of Rwanda had been absorbed into that rapidly growing political system and no more was heard there of Nyoro attacks. Around the peripheries of the old Kitara there were now small independent or at least semi-independent kingdoms, such as Nkore, Mpororo, Igara, Buhweju[30] – and, almost certainly, Buganda.

Central Buganda, with its over-lush vegetation, would not have been a prime target for invaders whose main interest was in cattle. Nevertheless it is very probable that the power of the Bito kingdom in its heyday was felt there, as throughout the northern Lakeland, its advent being represented, as elsewhere, by the figure of King Cwa. According to the Ganda genealogy, the king who bore that Nyoro name lived far back in

Generation Twenty. But that genealogy is a construction that cannot be used for dating purposes; and there is no impediment to the assignment of the Nyoro impact on Buganda, as on Rwanda, to Generation Twelve or a little later, probably the late sixteenth or early seventeenth century. Cwa became Na-bakka, Lord of Bakka, and Walusimbi, heir of the ancient ritual kingdom focused on that hill, became his local viceroy; tradition indeed remembers him as Cwa's *katikkiro*. The subsequent period of dependence was then both preserved and disguised by the related symbolic figures of Kimera and Ndawula.

The postulated Nyoro incursion would accord well with the Ganda traditions relating to the wars of Nakibinge (G.12). Now the Ganda did not know the name of the king who led the invasion, but 'K. W.' supplied it. He was not Cwa, but Olimi I, called Rwita-mahanga, 'Slayer of nations', fourth of the Bito line, who, having settled matters with Buganda, made a highly improbable long march through Kenya and Tanzania and then turned up in Nkore, where he defeated a ruler called Nyabigwara. But the sun fell into a small lake nearby, and so he thought it better to return home.[31]

At one time there were high hopes that eclipse stories could provide the beginnings of an absolute chronology for African kingdoms, and in particular that the report of an eclipse in Nkore could be used to date Olimi I, and thus Nakibinge. Much of that confidence has now evaporated, for the complications are many. If partial eclipses are included, the solar events are too numerous for dating; but if only total eclipses are counted they are often, as in this case, difficult to fit with the traditional data.[32] The stories themselves, moreover, need critical inspection; and here it seems to have escaped notice that in the Nkore text it was the moon that fell into the lake, resuming its place in the sky after sacrifices of white cows and sheep.[33] It is true that there was also said to have been darkness in daytime; but the tradition is altogether too uncertain to bear the weight of chronology that some have imposed on it.

But K. W. did not pluck the name of Olimi out of thin air. A quarter of a century earlier Ruth Fisher's sources had given her much information about a king of that name. She did not give him a number – and of course the numbering of kings is a European practice quite out of place in an authentic African tradition. She described him as an extremely dynamic ruler and a monster of cruelty, known to his people as the 'Vulture' (a soubriquet not attached to any Nyoro king in any other text). On his accession, she wrote,

he immediately set out plundering and ravaging all the countries that were in open rebellion against Bunyoro and had followed the example of Buganda in declaring themselves independent. He first journeyed into Buganda and laid waste the whole country, raiding cattle, women and children. The ruling chief, Maganda, fled to an island on the Victoria Lake; but Olimi sent messengers after him, calling for an armistice, that they might arrange terms of peace. So Maganda came back, and they decided that the boundary between Buganda and Bunyoro should lie at the Miyanji River; all the territory and tribes to the north should be ruled over by Olimi, while the district to the south should be independent of Bunyoro and under the control of Maganda.[34]

Olimi then 'forced Nkore into submission', sought to increase his security by carrying out an exchange of population between Toro in the south of his domain and Chope in the north, and raided Bukidi, the country to the east of the Nile.

For Fisher this Olimi was the grandson of Cwa-mali and the grandfather of the next Cwa king, called Duhaga, and therefore belonged to Generation Seven – or more precisely, since the Nyoro and Ganda royal generations overlap, to Generation Six-and-a-half. In fact, he may be even more recent. She reports that he was deposed by his son Isansa, but in all other sources there is a single king called Olimi Isansa, Olimi being one of the recurrent regnal names while Isansa was a personal nickname. If, as is likely, she was confused on this point, the invasion would have taken place between the Ganda Generations Six and Five. At all events it was clearly the traditions of this comparatively recent ruler that were picked up by K. W., and transferred to a more distant past in order that they might correspond with the Ganda story of the defeat of Nakibinge. In fact he appears to have conflated two different and widely separated episodes in the relations between his country and Buganda. One, associated with the name of Cwa, inaugurated a period of Nyoro hegemony during which the *kabaka* was a tribute-paying dependent. The other, linked with Olimi, was much more recent. It was an attempt on the part of a revitalised Nyoro kingdom to restore a supremacy that had been effectively lost. And it is clear even from the Nyoro account that, though Olimi scored some initial successes, the attempt ended in failure, Buganda's independence being confirmed and its territory only slightly reduced.

That admission makes the tradition reported by Fisher worthy of credence. Moreover, if her genealogy can be trusted, it deals with events close to the edge of reminiscence and well within the range of authentic saga. Yet Ganda tradition seems to know nothing about them. The only Nyoro invasion that it does admit is assigned to the reign of Nakibinge some six generations earlier, and it recognises no *kabaka* by the name of Maganda. That name, however, does appear in the royal genealogy. It belongs to a prince of whom nothing is remembered except that he was a son of Kikulwe (K.21),[35] the king dispossessed and killed by his brother

Mawanda, and should thus be placed in Generation Five. This would make him a very possible target for the aggression of Olimi Isansa; and the suspicion grows that a major disturbance has been edited out of the collective memory of the fairly recent past. But to have any hope of reading this riddle we must pick up the Buganda story where we left it, at the point where the twenty-second king, Mawanda, had forced his way to the throne.

10   The making of the state

Memories of crisis

Commentators have long recognised the reign of Mawanda (K.22) as the main formative period in the history of the Ganda state. He found a still fairly small kingdom near the north-west corner of the Lake and left it a major power, which stretched from the Katonga to the Nile and far into the interior, having created a hierarchy of appointed officers to govern it.[1] The orientation of the kingdom was also significantly altered. The earlier expansion in the time of Kateregga and Mutebi had been to the west, with the incorporation of Butambala, Gomba, Busujju and part of Ssingo; and it was clearly in this part of the kingdom that Mawanda's power-base lay. His first capital was at Katakala in southern Ssingo and he claimed to be a nephew of the Leopard clan, keepers of the shrine of Kintu at Magonga in Busujju. We saw, too (above pp. 117–18), how he attempted to enlist the great Ancestor as the patron of his rule. But from this western base Mawanda pushed Ganda power far to the east. According to the story, it was the pursuit of the tyrant Kagulu that first brought him and his sister Ndege into the coastlands east of Murchison Bay, where he developed contacts with local groups which were incorporated into Buganda as the Sprat and Jackal clans, and with others that recognised the Sheep and Bean emblems. Once on the throne, he organised this area together with its hinterland as the rich marcher province of Kyaggwe,[2] and used it as a base for profitable raids on the people of south-west Busoga beyond the Nile.

The governorship of this province was conferred on Nkalubo of the Cane-rat clan, who assumed the title of Ssekiboobo, Lord of the Fly-whisk, which had presumably belonged to some indigenous kinglet. Now the Cane-rats were a somewhat parvenu group. Natives, they said, of the Ssese islands, they had settled on the mainland in Mawokota, and Nkalubo had become a palace servant in the time of King Ndawula. The ruler remembered by that name had a wife called Nakidde Luyiga of the Leopard clan, who had the misfortune to cough while serving the king's food. This was a capital offence, and she was handed over to Nkalubo for execution. But when the man realised that she was carrying a potential future *kabaka* he killed his own pregnant wife instead and in due course presented the king with a fine baby son, to be fully rewarded for his loyal disobedience.[3] That his conduct was in any way reprehensible does not seem to be suggested.

The story is a cliché, told also of a Nyoro king of about the same period,[4] and is in fact a variation on the familiar theme of the royal infant providentially rescued from his father's malevolence. But its particular meaning in this context is not easy to read. It could have been put about by the Cane-rats to explain and consolidate their position in the state. It could have been a libel spread by Mawanda's enemies and supplanters, casting doubt on his legitimacy. But the most likely interpretation is that it was an attempt by his partisans to deny what everyone knew, that he was in truth the son of a menial and a complete interloper.

Being in that precarious position, he would naturally rely on the support of his real kinsmen; and so it is not surprising that Nkalubo became in the first instance Ssebugwawo, keeper of the king's privy. This was a much more important office than it might appear, for it included the vital task of preventing sorcerers from getting access to the royal excreta. It became the permanent prerogative of the Cane-rat clan, who developed it into Buganda's secret service. They did not, however, retain the governorship of Kyaggwe. Nkalubo did have one successor from his own clan, but by the nineteenth century the eastern march was ruled by whichever of the reigning king's officers and courtiers was currently in favour. It was this that differentiated Mawanda's annexations from the earlier, western fiefdoms. These too had originally been granted to 'new men', who managed, however, to establish local sub-dynasties. In much the same way, Kyaddondo, 'the land of the finding' to the east of Busiro, was constituted by Mawanda as a province under an officer called the Kaggo, 'He of the staff'. Hitherto this office had been combined with that of Ssebatta, 'Chief executioner', and had been the property of a Colobus Monkey lineage, but it was now conferred on a man of the Pangolin clan and was thereafter at the king's disposal.

Mawanda also strengthened Buganda's control over the land to the north of the Mayanja Wasswa, creating the province of Bulemeezi.[5] This had been the name of a small area containing the royal burial grounds, but it was now greatly extended, taking in what had been the Nyoro district of Rugonjo, and the title of the displaced Nyoro governor, Kangaho (Kangawo in Ganda pronunciation), was conferred on Matumpaggwa ('Big-ears'), another of Mawanda's trusties. He is said to have ousted the hereditary official called Nabugwamu, of the Lungfish (Frog) clan; and historians have inferred a general substitution of royal nominees for autonomous clan chiefs. This is a slightly misleading formulation, however. Nabugwamu, like Kaggo, was a ritual officiant (see above, p. 152) and had in no sense been a territorial chief, though he had, and retained, a small domain to the north of the river. In fact, a new kind of chief was emerging to cope with the needs of a new kind of state, too large and complex to be governed directly from the centre. If this construction was to endure, provincial governors had to be prevented from acquiring hereditary rights. But the clans did not, then or later, lose their role as basic components of the state, though their character evolved over time.

Officers such as the Ssekiboobo, the Kangawo and the new-style Kaggo, together with their subordinates, were classed as *bakungu*, an already familiar term for a non-sovereign office-holder. But Mawanda is credited also with the institution of the first *batongole* chiefs, young men with careers still to make who could be relied on to do the king's bidding. Some of these, if we can go by later practice, were captains of troops stationed around the capital to ensure his safety; and it was one such that was his undoing. Mawanda had three young nephews, sons of his brother Musanje, who had been put to death by Kagulu, and the time came when they conspired against him. It is said that they procured his assassination at the hands of a certain Dibongo, commander of the Batamannyangamba, 'Those who do not know the speech', presumably a company of foreigners. (Dibongo is a name of Nyoro form.) Others claim that the princes did the deed themselves, and afterwards framed Dibongo. Certainly their first action on taking over the kingdom was to liquidate the Batamannyangamba, in accordance with the most cynical principles of statecraft.

The three leading conspirators were all sons of the same mother, a daughter of the Sheep clan who was called Nalugwa, like the woman who had been the occasion of war between Kateregga and Kimbugwe. She was also styled Nabulya, 'She who ate the kingship', indicating that she became a queen-mother. In fact, she ate it three times over, since her sons would follow one another on the throne. The first, called Mwanga, lasted only nine days, and was therefore ignored by the compilers of some king-lists. His first action was to order the killing of his mother's brother's son, having been advised that this would assure him a long reign.[6] He could hardly have been more mistaken, for the boy's outraged father lost no time in taking his revenge. There is a clear echo here of the nine-day ritual of the king's growing. For the centrepiece of that ancient drama was the murder of a son of Nankere, who for the purposes of the rite was the king's mother's brother. Mwanga, it seems, was trying to be a Frog's Nephew, carrying out a prescribed killing. But it is a sign of the revolutionary times that he had heard only a garbled version of the ritual and understood nothing of the context that gave it meaning and the sanction of tradition.

Namugala, who succeeded his brother, drew the conclusion that the new regime needed a completely new process of sanctification; and his advisers thought up an elaborate ceremony of installation, which would be performed for all his successors – even, with suitable modifications, those of the colonial epoch (and later). It took place at Naggalabi, 'where evil is shut out', part of the hill called Buddo in the south of Busiro, not far from the Lake, thus well away from the old ritual centres of the kingdom.

The alleged assassins of Mawanda were now executed, but Namugala could not bring himself to kill their leader, to whom he was bound by the formidable tie of blood-brotherhood. His brother, who had no such scruples, deprived him of the kingship and Dibongo of his life. Namugala was allowed to live in retirement, but not long afterwards died as the result of a fall. Kyabaggu had a long and in some ways successful reign, but in the end fell victim to one of his own sons.

The period covered by Generation Six and Five was manifestly a very disturbed one in Buganda. According to the tradition, six men held the office of *kabaka* in that time, and at least five of them came to a violent end. By contrast, in the nineteenth century four successive kings, spanning four generations, would die from natural causes after reigns of some duration. On the face of the narrative the turmoil had purely internal causes, consisting in fact of strife within the royal house. There are faint hints of Nyoro influence: the infiltration of the king-list by a Nyoro deity, and the flight of the 'Leopard' children to the Bunyoro border, the incident that triggered the disorder. But there is no sign of a war between the *mukama* Olimi (Isansa) and a Ganda ruler called Maganda. Must we then discard Ruth Fisher's testimony, despite its realistic character, the early date of its recording and its consequent freedom from contamination by colonial politics? Probably not. There is reason to think that the events she describes are in fact present in the Ganda tradition, but have been relegated there to a more distant past. The story of Nakibinge, besides alluding to the ancient cyclical myth of kingship, seems to have been used for veiled references to eighteenth-century events which some parties in the state did not wish to be clearly remembered.

At first sight there is no great likeness between the story of Nakibinge and the events referrable to Generations Six and Five. Yet there are certain suggestive repetitions. In both there is a character called Juma who competes unsuccessfully for the throne: in one, he is Nakibinge's cousin who called in a Nyoro army; in the other, he is set aside by his father's cousin Ndawula. In both stories a prince called Luyenje (like Juma, a name that occurs nowhere else) is killed in the margin of the action – by Juma's treacherous servant Namunkululu or by his brother Musanje. In both cases

the slayer is killed in his turn – by unnamed Nyoro or by King Kagulu. Nor
are these the only echoes. Both Nakibinge and Mawanda – and these kings
only – are said to have sought an audience with Kintu at Magonga. There is
also a curious story in which Mawanda's soldiers burned down the shrine
of Nakibinge at Bbumbu in Kyaddondo and a spark from the fire scorched
the queen-mother's breast, which could not be healed until the shrine had
been rebuilt. But perhaps the most significant resonances link the
Nakibinge saga with the new accession ritual devised for Namugala.[7] On
the face of it the Buddo rites, which by common consent were first
performed in Generation Five, cannot throw light on events that took place
some two centuries earlier. Yet the echoes are hard to ignore. To begin
with, the clans chiefly concerned in the ancient story and in the recent ritual
were the same. Nakibinge belonged to the maritime Lungfish group on his
mother's side. The guardian of Buddo, Ssemanobe, was of that clan, and
most of the hill was Lungfish property. Namugala's maternal kinsmen, for
their part, were Sheep, as were the guardians of Kibuuka's shrine at
Mbaale. The new king's first call at Buddo was actually to the shrine of
Sserutega, Kibuuka's 'twin' – that is to say, his umbilical cord. (That he was
supposed to have a cord at Mbaale as well is no more to the point than the
impossible multiplicity of sacred relics in medieval Europe.) Also, the
climax of the ceremonies came when the young *kabaka*, accompanied by
his sister the *lubuga*, climbed on to a mound of beaten earth from a termite
hill. This mound became the heart of the realm, the most sacred spot in all
Buganda; and it was called Na-kibuuka. The name could mean 'mother of
Kibuuka', but it is also an apt title for an anthill – 'mother of that which
flies'. It begins to appear that the great war-god may have had his origin in a
kind of pun, and that the myth of his and Nakibinge's heroic deeds may
have been adapted (like the fable of Snake and Tortoise) to serve as the
charter of the Buddo ritual, which itself validated a drastic eighteenth-
century reconstruction of the kingdom.

Another group prominent in Generations Twelve and Five, and barely
mentioned in between, was the Seed clan (the conventional English label of
the people who avoided the fruit of a wild pod-bearing shrub, *Rhynchosia
sp.*, known to the Ganda as *nvuma* or *kati-nvuma*.) This clan, which
specialised in priestly activities, kept the shrine of Nakibinge at Bbumbu,
and their son Kigali was reputed to have served him as *katikkiro*. Another
clansman with a very similar name, Kagali, performed the same office for
King Namugala. But more significant was the role of the Leopard clan,
organisers of the Kintu cult and maternal kinsmen, or so it was claimed, of
Kings Kikulwe and Mawanda, of their sister Ndege and of the prince
Musanje whose sons would inherit the kingdom. In the Nakibinge
narrative they are represented by his faithful wife Nannono ('Lady of

Nnono', the centre of the cult) who acted as regent after the hero's death and would have become the queen-mother if her child had been male. It seems that in this version too the Leopards originally had a major role in the dynastic succession but that it was later played down. In the new dispensation they would have little connection with kingship or government, though they retained the ceremonial priesthood at Magonga.

There is still the problem of Maganda, the Ganda ruler who, according to the Nyoro, fought and negotiated with the *mukama* Olimi in Generation Six. If this testimony is accepted, it would appear that Ganda tradition, though preserving the name, has entirely suppressed the memory of his eventful reign. There is another possibility, however: he may have been the same person as Mawanda. The two names are not phonetically interchangeable, but 'Mawanda', which means spittle or urine, could have been an offensively punning nickname conferred by the enemies who overthrew him. It is possible that Mawanda is also alluded to in the story of Namunkululu, 'the Devourer', an obviously hostile nickname, the double traitor of the Nakibinge narrative, who first brought in the Nyoro to back his political ambitions and then tried to play them false. The uncertainties are many, but by putting together the various partial and tendentious narratives produced by rival interests and assigned by the tradition-editors to very different periods of dynastic time, it is possible to discern a dim outline of actual events.

The story probably begins in the early seventeenth century with the arrival of Nyoro warriors, who were then carrying all before them. it is unlikely that their great leader Cwa-mali was present in person, but his was the name that remained in the consciousness of the Ganda people, who, however, also disguised the occupying forces under the mythical names of Kimera and Ndahura. Faint echoes of this invasion, overlaid both by myth and by memories of later events, can be detected in the story of Nakibinge; and it was probably at that time that elements of the old regime of Bakka first made contact with the coastal and island communities. Whether a Nyoro governor took over at Bakka or whether the ancient lineage of the *balangira* was allowed to continue, Buganda (as we may call it) remained for some time, perhaps for more than a century, a tributary kingdom, whose leaders had to visit the Nyoro court to be confirmed in office. But the Bito power could not be long preserved in its original extent. Overambitious campaigning in the south and subsequent succession struggles made it unable to control the outlying provinces; and the *kabaka*s re-emerged as effectively independent rulers. Their character, however, had profoundly changed. They were now more like Bito warlords than sacral kinglets. We have seen how Sse-kamaanya violently subverted the rite of the King's Growing, how Kateregga distorted the twin ritual and how he and Mutebi broke away from royal monogamy to build up marital alliances and so extend the frontiers of the kingdom. Symbolic of the new order is the virtual dismissal of poor little Juma Katebe; for the surname 'Little chair' evokes the image of Mulondo on his mushroom stool, and 'Juma' has a variant form, Jjumwa, which would be a near-synonym of Jjuuko, the Child King. His suppression would then mark the final disappearance of the archaic cycle of ritual kingship. But the new aggressive monarchy incurred many enmities. The heirs of the slaughtered Frog-chief Nankere in western Busiro seem to have turned themselves into Lungfish in order to win the support of the powerful coastal groups that were united by that emblem. The Leopard priests of Magonga, persecuted and dispersed by King Kateregga, also fled south, into Mawokota, where they concealed themselves for a time in the Genet clan. Meanwhile Mutebi's incursions into Busujju and Ssingo, which brought him close to the Bito heartland, must have caused resentment and alarm at the Nyoro court, where the ruthless *mukama* Olimi (Isansa) was bringing about a military renaissance.

So there were internal and external threats to the growing Ganda power, but it seems to have been tensions within the ruling house that actually set off the upheavals of Generation Six, around the middle of the eighteenth century. These are presented negatively in the Nakibinge story, which tells us of Juma's treacherous alliance with Bunyoro against the legitimate rule of his kinsman (a reversal of the historical reality), and positively in the saga of the revolt led by the princess Ndege and her brothers against the infamous tyrant they called Kagulu. The ensuing turmoil opens the way to the adventurer who was later presented by some as the legitimate state-builder Mawanda and by others as the treacherous usurper Namunkululu. After this there are two possible scenarios. In one, Mawanda is attacked at the beginning of his reign by the Nyoro but (notwithstanding the tradition of Namunkululu's quick come-uppance) he rallies support from the coastlands and islands and negotiates a Nyoro withdrawal which leaves him in possession of the bulk of his domain. The terms of the settlement need inspection. The 'Miyanji river', specified in Fisher's text as the new frontier, might be taken to mean the Mayanja Wasswa, with the implication that Buganda was deprived of the Bulemeezi march. However, while some early British writers on Uganda would have been capable of such a garbling of an African place-name, Mrs Fisher was usually accurate, and she was working from written Nyoro texts. It is more likely therefore that the reference was to a place called Myanji on the Ssingo border to the west. For his part K. W., besides imagining a campaign by a much earlier Olimi, reported that King Olimi Isansa (of G.6) recovered Buwekula (the area round Mubende) and Ssingo from the Ganda. It is significant that, though Ssingo was supposed to have been conquered in the reign of Mutebi

(K.15), no holder of the office of Mukwenda, governor of the Ssingo province, is mentioned in the lists of chiefs between his reign and that of Namugala (K.24). It seems then that the outcome of Olimi's campaign was a temporary rolling back of Buganda's north-western frontier, but not much more.

Mawanda then compensates for losses in the west by making large territorial gains in the east, building up a large state by the use of Nyoro administrative and military techniques. In this story, the Company of Foreigners who eventually bring his reign to an end are simply mercenary troops suborned by the sons of Musanje, who take over Buganda as a more or less going concern.

The other, and perhaps preferable, scenario allows Mawanda to prosper for a considerable time as a Nyoro client, who eventually incurs their displeasure and is removed by his Nyoro minder Dibongo. On this view the renewal of Nyoro occupation comes at the end of his reign, and it is the sons of Prince Musanje and their Sheep kinsfolk who take the credit for the easing out of the Nyoro and the construction of what was in some respects a new state.

The politics of this period (roughly the middle quarters of the eighteenth century) were clearly very complex, with shifting alliances between a number of competing groups, including the Leopard priesthood of Magonga, the maritime Sheep and Lungfish clans (probably at first rivals but eventually collaborators), the Nyoro would-be overlords and the ancient patriline of the *balangira*, which probably was continued by the sons of Musanje, perhaps after an interval. In fact the marriage of Musanje to the Sheep woman Nalugwa is likely to have prepared the way for a grand alliance which would be the framework of the new Buganda. Namugala and his advisers must indeed be credited with a statesmanlike policy of conciliation and comprehension that found a place for all the recently contending parties in the state and began the construction of a national identity. He took wives not only from the Lungfish, Seed and Leopard clans, but also from the Mushrooms and the Elephants, components of the Bakka complex, as well as from the important western Grasshopper group.[8] It was because of the delicate balance between these groups, recent rivals and mostly recent collaborators with the Nyoro power, that historical memory had to be so carefully managed, some events being suppressed and others reported in duplicate from varying perspectives.

The new installation at Buddo clearly played a major part in Namugala's statecraft, but perhaps even more important was the related cult of Kibuuka at Mbaale, which was managed by the Sheep clan. Kibuuka was the divine enemy of Bunyoro, and there was a saying: 'If you don't want to stay among Nyoro, go to Mbaale where the true Ganda dwell' (literally, 'where the Ganda filter themselves').[9] It is remembered that the Mbaale area in Mawokota was once a borderland where communities of Ganda and Nyoro speech were intermingled;[10] and it is usually in such areas, where language difference is a matter of common experience, that ethnic consciousness becomes most intense. It can also be surmised that Olimi's incursion served as the catalyst for the combination of many competing groups against an enemy whom all could recognise as foreign.

The upshot was clearly a decisive shift in the centre of gravity of the kingdom, away from the inland areas vulnerable to Nyoro attacks and towards the more defensible coastlands and islands. (Buddo is within easy reach of the Lake shore and a finger of the Lake reaches to Mbaale.) Yet the sons of Musanje seem to have been able to take over the whole of the realm created by Mawanda and to lay the foundations for the triumphs of the following century.

The wars of the princes

Neither the overthrow of Mawanda nor the disappearance of the Nyoro nor the subtleties of the Buddo ritual brought peace to the land. On the contrary, the next two generations were a period of recurrent internal strife of an intensity hitherto unknown. They were also a time of decisive territorial growth, as Mawanda's conquests were consolidated and extended. There is no contradiction here: it is a commonplace of statecraft that the best way of coping with stresses within a society is to export them. The military forces needed for the enlargement of the state can also plunge it into disorder, and conversely the armies recruited by political rivals can be deployed against foreigners in the intervals of civil war.

After the bloodless deposition of King Namugala and the elimination of Dibongo, last of Mawanda's assassins, the new regime headed by Kyabaggu (K.25) might have been expected to enjoy a period of stability, but it was not to be.[11] In the first place, the sanction of blood-brotherhood proved its power, for some physical ailment persuaded Kyabaggu that he was being literally gnawed by Dibongo's ghost. His response was to leave the country, taking an army across the Nile to resume Mawanda's raiding of Busoga on a larger scale. It would be natural to rationalise his behaviour and to assume that his malaise was a sign of continuing political tensions which he tried to divert into external aggression. However, it seems clear that his departure really was a kind of flight, for after initial successes in Busoga he announced that he would make his permanent base there, beyond the reach of the vengeful spirit, leaving other members of the royal house to rule Buganda. The crossing of the Nile was seen as a momentous break with the past, quite unlike the earlier encroachments into Bulemeezi

Generation

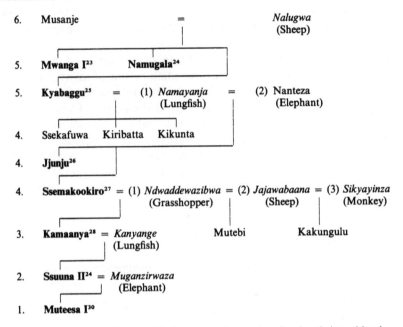

Names of kings are in **bold** type, with the superscript number showing their position in the official list. Names of females are in *italics*, with their father's clan in brackets.

Fig. 9   The new state

and Kyaggwe. Kyabaggu had soil brought from Buganda to be mixed symbolically with the alien earth; but Busoga, though repeatedly harried during the next century, was never integrated into the Ganda state.

This effective abdication encouraged new conflict within the kingdom. Mawanda had left several sons, and two of them, Bengo and Mulere, managed to raise enough support to challenge for their father's throne. Kyabaggu's sons defeated the rebels and, in an attempt to destroy the spirit with the body, had them burned to death – they were the first of many dissidents to meet that fate in the course of the next century or so: Bengo's pyre was lit at Namugongo, which would be the scene of Muslim martyrdoms in 1876 and Christian martyrdoms ten years later. Kyabaggu now returned to Buganda, perhaps because he felt more secure, but more probably because he had no option; it is fairly clear that the Soga had rallied and compelled the Ganda to withdraw. Like the British, the Ganda were good at presenting military reverses in a heroic light, and the retreat was remembered chiefly for the deeds of a warrior called Wakiwuugulu, who was still famous at the end of the nineteenth century.[12] The dominant mode of the narrative, in other words, is now saga, and while valour may be exaggerated and motives distorted there is no doubt that the tradition from now on deals with real events and is true in its main outlines. There is no longer any question of disentangling history from myth. Instead, the historian faces the normal problems of sifting rumour, propaganda and the self-serving statements of interested parties. But the testimonies are still far fewer than he would like, and none of them are contemporary. Above all, of course, he has to do without the letters, diaries and other documents not meant for public record which are the most reliable witness to the realities of a literate society. There are extant two different, though not absolutely contradictory, accounts of the events about to be described, and it is hard to tell which is closer to the truth. However, it does not really matter much, for the general tenor and outcome are not in doubt.

For some time after Kyabaggu's return from Busoga, it seems, peace did prevail, but it was broken by a storm within the royal house. According to Kaggwa it was set off by a trivial incident, a quarrel between the royal herdsman and one of the king's adult sons, Ssekafuwa, who complained that the cattle were trespassing in his gardens. Getting no satisfaction, he killed one of them and sent a joint of its meat to his mother. Next morning he went with other princes to attend the court and found her dead body lying naked in the road. In response to this brutal outrage he took counsel with her brother and her two other sons and organised his father's assassination. It is evident that the royal court was a far smaller and simpler affair than it would become in the later nineteenth century, when a family coup of this kind would have been hard to imagine. In fact, later generations heard with some surprise tht the only resistance came from one of the king's wives, who speared two of the assailants before she and her husband were overcome.

Kyabaggu's other sons, led by prince Jjunju, sought to avenge his death, and after two hard battles near the modern Kampala the assassins were defeated and slain. The victors then fought among themselves for possession of the late king's body which, as in Bunyoro, conferred legitimacy on the successor. Jjunju, with the help of his full brother Ssemakookiro, emerged victorious; it is interesting to note that his surviving rivals fled to Bunyoro.

The other story makes no mention of Prince Ssekafuwa and incriminates Jjunju as the leader of the conspiracy against Kyabaggu.[13] According to this account he and Ssemakookiro grew up believing that they were sons of the same mother, Nanteza of the Elephant clan – as the official tradition continued to affirm. They were puzzled, however, because, though not twins, they were almost the same age; and at last Nanteza revealed to them that Jjunju was really the son of her sister, who had been done to death by the king. That provided him with the motive for revolt.

The upshot was in any case that Jjunju became the twenty-sixth king, and one of Buganda's greatest heroes. His reign was marked above all by the annexation of Buddu, the rich province in the south-west which was the last major addition to the territory of the pre-colonial state. Separated from the rest of the kingdom by the Katonga, the broad, swampy river that wends its slow way to the Lake at its north-western corner, Buddu is ecologically an extension of inner Buganda, having a very similar soil, climate and agriculture. Up to this time it had been ruled by local chieftains nominally subject to the king of Bunyoro. Of slightly more consequence was the kingdom of Kkooki to the south-west, where a cadet branch of the Nyoro royal house held sway; and there is some evidence that it encouraged and assisted the Ganda intervention, hoping to win full independence as well as a share of the spoils. Kaggwa says merely that Jjunju was tempted by Buddu's wealth in cattle; but that would have prompted raiding rather than conquest, and in any case Buddu is no better cattle country than Buganda proper. The Nyoro form of the name, Bw-iru, proclaims it as the land of mere cultivators, ba-iru, distinct from the grasslands to the west where the ba-hima herdfolk lived. It did, however, make a valuable base for Ganda raids into the pastoral country.[14] Another tradition recalls Kyabaggu's official sister, the lubuga, who was established in a domain in the west of the country, then quarrelled with her brother and crossed the Katonga to take refuge with one of the local chiefs. It is said that at first the people of Buddu were glad to have a Ganda royal personage in their midst as a counter to their Nyoro overlords, but that she overplayed her hand and was killed. By this account Jjunju's object was at least in part to avenge her death.[15]

Whatever may have been the occasion of Buganda's expansion onto the west shore of the Lake, the consequences were far-reaching. Not only did the state acquire a large tract of fertile and populous country and a launching pad for plundering excursions to the west and south, but it also gained access, by way of friendly Kkooki, to the great market in Karagwe, south of the Kagera river, and so to the network of world trade of which it was then the furthest outpost. It would be a couple of generations, however, before that commercial link became really significant.

The people of Buddu appear to have offered only sporadic and feeble resistance to Ganda rule, and they were not treated as colonial dependants. This most recent acquisition, indeed, throws much light on the processes by which the Ganda state and society were expanded. The population history of the area, it is true, is confused by the great upheavals at the turn of the present century, when a new distribution of lands and offices caused major two-way displacements of people. Even in the twentieth century, however,

while many of the mainstream clans were present, a substantial part of the
Buddu population still owed allegiance to the original clans of Nyoro type,
such as the Tailless Cow. There were also many Bushbuck folk, probably
descended from indigenous royalties and not related to the Ganda clan of
that sign. Gradually, however, the native sections were assimilated to the
Ganda pattern. Thus in 1902 the three different groups that abstained from
eating the hearts of animals came together to form the Heart clan, whose
enterprising leader would before long insert his ancestor into the central
Ganda myth of Kintu.[16] So there is reason to think that the indigenous
people were not killed or driven out in any numbers but that they were very
thoroughly absorbed. After four generations at the most, there was no
trace of the original Nyoro language, and the people spoke the king's
Ganda without even an inflexion. From the beginning Buddu took its
place, along with Ssingo, Bulemeezi and Kyaggwe, as one of the four great
outer provinces, and its governor, the Ppookino (a title which is not Ganda
and must have been taken over from a native chieftain), ranked as one of
the magnates of the realm. There was the usual hierarchy of subordinate
administrators, with perhaps more than an average number of enclaves
allotted to *batongole* who reported directly to the king. And yet there was a
certain feeling that the Katonga remained a frontier and Buddu a land
apart. In post-colonial politics it has often been at odds with the rest of
Buganda. That is mainly because it was the largest district to be assigned to
the Catholic party in the early colonial settlement; and was thus in some
degree alienated from the continuing Protestant ascendancy; but there was
probably also a legacy from its distinct pre-colonial past.

Jjunju's bold aggression had another consequence of even greater
import for the future. The king of Bunyoro, Cwa Duhaga, felt bound to
react to this insolent trespass on his domain, however distant and
ineffectively ruled it may have been. He had reached the phase of his reign
that should have precluded him from going to war (did Jjunju know this
and believe it therefore safe to act?), but he nevertheless collected an army
and marched on Buganda, only to suffer a disastrous defeat, which Nyoro
historians fully acknowledge. The battle took place within the borders of
Ssingo, and the result was to undo the work of the previous king, Olimi,
and return this debatable land to Ganda rule, at least in part. The Nyoro
should really have won, but a Ganda commando gained access to the
poorly guarded royal camp, and in the ensuing affray Duhaga was slightly
wounded, whereupon his army fled and he felt bound to kill himself.[17] A
damaged king, it was believed, would damage the land if he allowed
himself to go on living. It is possible to suspect that his suicide owed more
to a ruined ego than to immemorial custom. Yet it does seem that Nyoro
behaviour was still partly constrained by the laws of the sacred kingship,

whereas in Buganda the laws of the spear were by now almost totally ascendant.

Those laws continued to hold sway within the kingdom as well as in its dealings with the outer world, and Jjunju's victories did not bring him lasting peace or allow him to perpetuate his line. By now there were only two sons of Kyabaggu left – or only two with the ability and ambition to compete for power – but that proved to be one too many. There was normally a powerful bond between sons of the same mother, as Jjunju and Ssemakookiro were by upbringing at least, but the systemic stresses made it difficult for them to coexist. The tradition (which of course derives from the victor) lays the blame for the rift on Jjunju's brutality; by one barely credible account he sent for his brother's wife when she was pregnant, started an argument with his courtiers about the sex of the child, and settled it by having her opened up. It is even suggested that he made a habit of this atrocity.[18] Ssemakookiro bided his time, building up a power-base in the far east of the country, to which he had been effectively exiled, and then, urged on by his mother, made his bid for vengeance and for power. The crunch came when a royal emissary (the chief Kinyolo, whom we have met as a ritual functionary) came demanding a present in token of allegiance. Ssemakookiro made the derisory offering of a goat – a black goat, moreover, thus ill-omened and offensive. The ensuing struggle was desperate, and at one point the rebel prince was saved only by the valour of his young sons Kamaanya (the future king) and Kakungulu. But the tide turned, Jjunju's power was broken in battles at the hub of the kingdom in the Kampala area, and he himself was hunted down, killed and mutilated. The tradition can by now recite the places where they fought, the names of the captains on either side and the songs that were sung to taunt the vanquished.[19]

And so the kingdom was established in the hands of Ssemakookiro. His accession no doubt seemed at the time just one more turn in an unending spiral of violence, but it would prove to be a decisive moment in the consolidation of the state. For the new king, ruthless even beyond the measure of his predecessors, brought the forces of contention under a control that would hold firm for nearly a century.

The peace of the kings

The slayer of King Jjunju reported back to base with great complacency, expecting congratulation and reward. But Ssemakookiro's brow was dark, as he professed that he had not wished his brother dead. A commoner who took it upon himself to shed the blood of a king, and to dishonour him as well, deserved only death; and sentence of execution was passed not only on the actual killer but on the whole company to which he belonged, the Ba-Kunta.[20] In fact many members of this group, which was evidently a large one, managed to escape. Some fled west, eventually settling among the Konjo of the western mountains where, as Roland Oliver discovered,[21] their saga was imposed as the tradition of origin of the whole people. Others took to the Lake and found their way to the islands of Rusinga and Mfangano near its eastern shore. Here too, Michael Kenny has shown,[22] their leaders were integrated in ingenious and often bizarre ways into local genesis myths. Even in flight, Ganda warriors were clearly people of formidable authority.

But who exactly were these Bakunta? Kenny argues that they were predominantly members of the Lungfish clan, whose wide network of lacustrine operations, originally independent of the Ganda state, has already been noted (see above, pp. 167–8), and it is true that Ssemakookiro took strong measures against that clan, launching a razzia on its strongholds in Ssese. (Among the captives brought back to the court was a girl called Kannyange who caught the king's fancy. After his death she was taken over by his successor Kamaanya and became the mother of King Ssuuna.[23] Life in Buganda was full of such peripeties.) Yet the equivalence of Lungfish and Bakunta was certainly not complete. Other sources suggest that they were drawn in the main from the Reedbuck clan,[24] natives of the far east of Buganda where Ssemakookiro was living in semi-exile, and Roland Oliver found several different clans represented among the descendants of Bakunta refugees in western Uganda. Even if Lungfish men were indeed numerous it was not because clan allegiance was politically significant but because their traditional mode of life made those hardy, lightly rooted rovers of the Lake good material for a warrior band – and that is what the Bakunta ('the Stormers') were, a *kitongole*, a company of fighting men. Here indeed is a sign of a profound change in the character of Ganda politics. In the conflicts of the previous two or three generations the players were clearly clans: Elephant, Leopard, Sheep, Lungfish, with lesser roles for others such as the Seed, the Pangolin, the Civet and the Grasshopper. At first sight the strife of the sons of Kyabaggu conforms to the same pattern, since Ssekafuwa and his allies were Lungfish and the victors, Jjunju and Ssemakookiro, were sons of the Elephant. But the bond that held the princely factions together was not really that of clanship but a much closer tie: they were sons of the same mother. So little were clans now relevant that Jjunju could appoint a Lungfish man as his *katikkiro*. Clan affiliation remained of great sentimental and practical importance to the Ganda. Indeed, to be a citizen of Buganda was to be a member of a recognised totemic group, and in the nineteenth century whole clans were held responsible for the political misdeeds of their individual sons. But the idea that a clan that succeeded in making one of its daughters the queen-mother was guaranteed collective power and fortune does not survive close inspection. Of the seven kings from Namugala through Muteesa I, three were sons of Elephant women, two of Sheep and one each of the Lungfish and the Grasshopper. During the same period, of the high, non-hereditary offices held by commoners the largest number (fourteen) went to the Lungfish clan, but it was closely followed by the Pangolins (thirteen) and the Buffaloes (twelve) who contributed no queen-mothers. The Grasshoppers secured nine offices, but so did the Seed and Cane-rat clans. The Sheep achieved six posts and the Elephants only four. Vast numbers of offices were indeed reserved for particular clans, but most of them were ceremonial and traditional, and real power increasingly belonged to individual politicians, whose ambitions were often fulfilled through the leadership of a *kitongole*, a war-band.

The phenomenon of the band, or more bluntly the armed gang, has attracted less attention from students of Africa than it deserves[25] – probably because it was hardly visible under the colonial peace. It is not of course a peculiarly African phenomenon. The fact that many young men love to go about in intimidating groups has been painfully evident to peace-loving citizens in many lands in recent decades, from the streets of Beirut to the vicinity of English football grounds. But the conditions of eastern and southern Africa, which in many respects were those of a frontier society in late pre-colonial times, gave unusual scope for the indulgence of violent energies. Indeed, the very rapid spread of Bantu speech and Early Iron Age technology does not look like the work of farming communities, but conjures rather the picture of highly mobile groups of adventurous hunters and artisans who only incidentally brought with them the means to establish themselves on the land when their wandering years were over. And Bantu-speaking people seem to have retained the ability to form similar bands whenever the opportunity arose. The simple truth is that for many young men life in such a group, which might engage in various combinations of hunting, trading and plundering, was much more enjoyable, even though it might well be briefer, than the staid and arduous existence of those who stayed at home to ply the cutlass and the hoe.

Some may think this is putting the matter in too positive a form. In European and West Asian history there are many examples of groups that alternated banditry with mercenary service, from the *'apiru* of the Late Bronze Age Levant, in whom many see the origin of the 'Hebrew' tribes, through the *bagaudae* of the late Roman Empire and the Vikings to the *Landsknechten* of sixteenth-century Germany, and all are commonly seen as people who were not so much attracted to a violent way of life as forced into it by their landlessness. But this explanation does not carry much weight in Africa where, so far as can be discovered, there was rarely a lack of land to till. It is rather that other ways of life were so much more rewarding than tillage. However, the two modes, the productive and the rapacious, the sedentary and the mobile, were not mutually exclusive. Hunting, trading and warfare were usually dry-season activities; and even the semi-professional fighter would hope to settle down when he had the means to acquire the women who would feed him and bear his children.

Band organisation took many forms at different times and places in Bantu history. Nineteenth-century Tanzania was infested by freebooting gangs known as *ruga-ruga*, as well as by professional elephant-hunters who often used their guns to terrorise the local populations. This was a rather special situation, when the slave and ivory trades were spreading rapidly into the far interior and newly imported firearms were upsetting the balance of military power. Also partly a by-product of external influences were the Chikunda warriors of the Zambezi valley, clients and sometimes rivals of the Portuguese settlers who in the eighteenth century combined the roles of plantation-owner and feudal lord.[26] More debatable were the allegedly cannibal hordes encountered by the Portuguese soon after their arrival on both the coasts of peninsular Africa and known as Jaga ('Stormers') and Imbangala ('Rangers') in Angola and as Zimba (probably 'Water-demons') in East Africa. These seem to have resulted from the snowballing of originally small warrior bands, which recruited new members from the young men of the villages they ravaged on their way. The Portuguese certainly made use of these people as allies and mercenaries and as suppliers of ivory and slaves, but whether they actually brought them into being must remain an open question, for until there were Portuguese there was no recorded information.

The crucial relationship is that between war-band and state, which was one of complex interaction. There is some reason to think that Zimba and Jaga began as the military forces of small states but broke away to operate far beyond the authority of their original employers. Conversely the kingdoms of Kasanje and Matamba, which flourished in the interior of Angola from the seventeenth to the nineteenth centuries, were founded by the leaders of Imbangala bands, who realised that raiding had become less profitable than the organisation of trade between central Africa and the west coast. Either way, the trick for political leaders was clearly to persuade young thugs that they had more to gain by acting as enforcers for a central power than as freelance brigands. Among the most successful in this were the kings of Lunda in southern Zaire; and we have a vivid description of one of their tribute-gathering bands descending on a village that had supposed itself independent. The headman flees into the bush but is caught and haled before the gang-leader, who contemptuously tells him that he is confirmed in his position but must henceforward have a Lunda minder at his side.[27] The distinction between state exploitation and banditry turns simply on whether the 'tribute' stays with the collectors or is brought back, at least in part, to the royal capital.

It is often and rightly stated that it was difficult to create and maintain states or any other structures of class power in sub-Saharan Africa, because the usual means of domination were lacking. Since land was not scarce, the feudal mode of exploitation could not function. Capitalist enterprise being undeveloped, no one could be made permanently subject to the power of money. The proposition sometimes heard, that the men of power therefore 'had to' resort to slavery instead, is lacking in logic. In the first place, there was no necessity about it; political structures could have been left unbuilt, and often were. In the second place, it remains to ask where power came from in the first place, how it was possible for people to be deprived of liberty. For the physical instruments of coercion were not usually such as could be monopolised. All men carried spears, and no man had any more lethal weapon. Exceptions prove the rule. The great states of the western Sudan were created by Saharan commerce, certainly, but also by the horse, a military asset that only rulers could afford and only specially trained warriors could use. In southern West Africa, where military states also flourished from the seventeenth century on, there were firearms, which could easily be controlled by political authorities and then used to consolidate and extend their power.[28] But horses could not be easily maintained in equatorial Africa, and firearms did not reach most parts of East Africa until the last pre-colonial decades. Yet states did exist there, most notably in the Lakeland, and some were highly organised and more than ephemeral. The Lunda episode shows how they could be made to work, even in the absence of high technology. Villagers had spears and were unlikely to be cowards, but they could not cope with the sudden descent of a large group of organised fighters. The ability to control and direct such groups was the key resource of royal power and the means by which an original nucleus of sacrality could be transformed into large-scale secular authority.

It was suggested earlier that the rise of cattle-herding, and therefore of cattle-stealing, as a way of life on the western grasslands, gave a special stimulus to the formation of armed gangs, some of which went on to become the rulers of extensive states, most notably the one known as Bunyoro–Kitara. But cattle were not the only cause of militarisation. Equally important, so far as Buganda is concerned, was the growth of trade along the shores of Nalubaale and the building of large canoes whose crews could easily become contingents of a fighting force. Certainly by Generation Four Buganda was full of underemployed youths for whom violence was a principal means of livelihood. Just before Ssemakookiro's rebellion his mother sent him seventy fighting men (the word is *bazira*, 'braves'), with the message that since he was evidently a woman he should let them use him as one.[29] (It would be pleasant to suppose that women were always an influence for peace in Africa, but the truth is otherwise; a great deal of its violence has always had machismic motives.) It may be assumed that by now everyone of wealth and standing had some spearmen at his or her command, and the supreme power would go to whoever could rally the largest number to his side.

To win power, you must have spears behind you; to keep it, you must ensure that they are not plunged into your back. Thus the ruthless destruction first of the Batamannyangamba and then of the Bakunta was clearly crucial to the consolidation of the Ganda state. After that (and similar though smaller purges were repeated at intervals) armed companies were unlikely to step out of line. But to carry out these liquidations the kings must obviously have had other armed men who saw their interest in obedience. There had to be, in other words, a carrot as well as a stick. It consisted partly in the power the fighters were given over the rest of society, especially the women, and partly in the spoils of foreign war. Consolidation of the state was not merely consistent with but demanded the expansion of its power.

Even though he was the sole survivor of his princely generation and had put the fear of death into the war-bands, Ssemakookiro was still nervous. He had sons who were already grown at the time of his accession. Might they not do to him what his brothers had done to his father? Rumours – or, for all we know, hard information – that some were in fact plotting against him drove him to an extreme act: he decided to eliminate all but three of his numerous male offspring. Prince Kakungulu had to be spared because he had begotten twins and was thus sacrosanct, perhaps also because he had fought for his father while still a lad, but he was banished to Bunyoro. From that kingdom, which doubtless saw a chance to recover its lost hegemony, he obtained armed assistance. The invasion was beaten back with some difficulty, but Kakungulu escaped and remained a threat until well into the next reign. Of the others, Prince Mutebi was the preferred successor, but Kamaanya was also spared, perhaps out of a sense of obligation (he too had rendered valiant service at a crucial moment of the war against Jjunju) or in order to provide a reserve successor. Even when Kamaanya was implicated in another alleged conspiracy he was allowed to live, though his mother was executed along with the leading members of his clan, the Grasshoppers (among them Kaggwa's great-grandfather). And it was he who was the victor in the succession war that followed Ssemakookiro's death. The forces behind the two rival princes were evenly matched, and the battle raged long over the Kampala hills before Kamaanya's men prevailed and he could eat the kingdom.

According to later testimony,[30] it was the god Mukasa who had counselled Ssemakookiro to his extreme measures, and the medium had asked for the court to be cleared so that he could make his point to the king alone. For in truth the enormity of Ssemakookiro's deed can hardly be overstated. Africans, even more decidedly than other peoples, look on descendance as the chief aim of life, and the final object of political endeavour. What, many would ask, is the point of amassing power, and therefore wives, if you then destroy nearly all the sons they give you? Certainly the deed was not repeated, and at the end of the next three reigns there were numerous princes to choose from. Kamaanya did kill one of his sons, but that was a special case and a horrifying one even in the context of its violent age. When the defeated Mutebi was put to death Prince Nakibinge, who was still a child, protested; and Kamaanya, a man of ungovernable rages, forced him to put his head between the thighs of his already murdered mother and then told the guards to set fire to him.

What the slaughter of the princes did achieve was the ending of fraternal succession which, as we have seen, had hitherto been frequent, though not necessarily a rule of the constitution. From now on it was established that, in the words of King Ssuuna's personal motto, *batanda b'ezaala*, 'sovereigns beget themselves'[31] – that is to say, only a son of the last reigning king was eligible. The events of the previous two generations had shown beyond doubt that fraternal succession did not work, since the king in possession could not trust his brothers to wait for him to die. It is often asserted that Buganda in the nineteenth century had found a solution to the perennial problem of royal succession in a polygamous society where primogeniture was not recognised, inasmuch as the brothers of the chosen king were killed as a matter of systematic policy.[32] The reality, however, was not so clear cut. Kamaanya, thanks to his father's ruthlessness, had only two brothers to contend with; one he defeated in battle, the other, Kakungulu, continued to intrigue against him from beyond the borders but finally died in Busoga. On his own deathbed Kamaanya adjured his magnates not to fight over the succession, and his son Ssuuna did become king without overt contention. The unsuccessful princes, some sixty in number, were not immediately put to death, but they were kept under strict surveillance and their lives were precarious. Ssuuna II, by all accounts an even grimmer despot than his father, did eventually massacre all but two of them. His motive, however, was to protect the interest of his grown-up sons; and since he was only a lad when he came to the throne, the slaughter must have been deferred until late in his reign.

On the next succession there is fuller information. The heir indicated by Ssuuna himself was Prince Walugembe, also called Mukaabya, but a strong party among the chiefs preferred another son, who bore the legendary name Kimera. The *katikkiro*, Kayira, himself leant in that direction, but at the last moment he was persuaded by the argument that Kimera's mother's kinsmen were over-powerful people and that Mukaabya would be a safer choice.[33] So next morning, when Ssuuna's sons were paraded, it was Mukaabya who was ordered to stand forth. Kayira had made his military dispositions and the nomination was not immediately contested. Soon afterwards, however, the opposing faction managed to spirit Kimera and some other princes out of the stockade where they were confined. But the rebellion, though backed by several of the leading provincial chiefs, was quickly put down and the escaped princes were executed along with their backers. And so Mukaabya, who adopted the name Muteesa, 'He who keeps things in good order', became king and reigned for nearly twenty-eight years without open opposition.

There was no general massacre of Muteesa's brothers at this time, for Grant actually saw them in his company, 'a mob of little ragamuffins'.[34] Some were in handcuffs, but they were alive four years after his accession. Speke was told that they would be 'guarded until the prince-elect should reach maturity and be crowned', when all but two would be burned to death; one of the survivors would be banished to Bunyoro and the other pensioned off.[35] Their actual fate has been a matter of some dispute.[36] However, there seems no good reason to doubt the usual story, which allows them to have remained alive until the arrival of Stanley and de Bellefonds in 1875. Then the queen-mother, it is reported, feared that the foreigners might intrigue with the princes, as they had done in Bunyoro, and so to defend her son she had them put in a closely guarded stockade and left to starve to death. Only Prince Mbogo, later the leader of the Muslim faction, and one other survived this horror. It seems therefore that the elimination of royal brothers was a contingent measure, not a prescriptive custom, and only Ssemakookiro slaughtered his own sons. It was not really systematic murder that brought the wars of the princes to an end, but rather the development of an efficient intelligence service, which nipped conspiracies in the bud and, more importantly, the collective realisation by the palace officials, provincial governors and military leaders that there was more to be gained by the operation of a stable and effective state than by factional violence.

On the death of Muteesa in 1884 the accession of his son Mwanga was contrived without trouble, but only four years later the system broke down under the stress of religious factionalism and foreign intrigue. In the upheavals of the next two years all Mwanga's brothers perished and so did his young sons – and his daughters too, for his enemies argued that the

British interlopers, who themselves had a female ruler, might be so perverse as to set a princess on the throne. The upshot was that at the end of the century, apart from princes claiming descent from pre-nineteenth-century rulers, the royal house was represented only by Mbogo and his sons, by the *kabaka* Daudi Cwa, who had succeeded his deposed father in 1897 at the age of two, and by his still younger brother. Thus the patriline of the *balangira* had made singularly poor use of the biological advantage conferred by unlimited access to the most beautiful and fertile women both of Buganda and of neighbouring countries. Or perhaps it could be said that it had sacrificed its genetic interests to the good of the kingdom, securing three generations of nearly unbroken internal peace.

It needs to be stressed that throughout the bloody conflicts of Generations Six to Four the survival and integrity of the kingdom itself were never in doubt; the only question was who was going to rule it. Buganda was already displaying its special character, which has been well described as the capacity for 'fissures without fracture'.[37] The final conflict of Generation Four, for example, had a marked geographical aspect, Jjunju's main support coming from the western part of the country while Ssemakookiro raised his forces in the east, but neither seems to have considered the possibility of partition. The prize fought for was always the whole state. Likewise when factional fighting broke out again and Catholics were forced to flee from the capital or even from the country, their one thought was to return in greater strength, not to create a state of their own. Eventually they allowed the British to impose a power-sharing settlement, but within a kingdom that was as unitary as it had ever been. This continuity was more remarkable than it might seem to those accustomed to the solidity of modern states. In the Lakeland, at about the same time as the wars of the Ganda princes, the substantial kingdom of Mpororo had completely disintegrated, much of it being swallowed up by Nkore; the kingdom of 'Greater Kyamutwara' had split into three fragments after being taken over by adventurers called Nkango; the six nineteenth-century kingdoms of Buha, a very homogeneous culture, had in all probability been one at no very distant date. In the mid-century, when Buganda's cohesion was at its greatest, Bunyoro was plagued by secessions and lingering rebellions. In this context the preservation of the Ganda state through a period of great turbulence has to be seen as a political *tour de force*, however high the cost.

We have now reached the point at which history can be made respectable by the attachment of approximate dates to political successions. Sir John Gray made a careful study of the evidence, and with some reservations his chronology can be accepted.[38] Arab witnesses testified that King Ssuuna II, father of Muteesa, died in the same month as Sultan Said of Zanzibar, that is to say, in October or November 1856. He had come to the throne at the age of twelve according to Kaggwa, or sixteen according to Stanley's informant. This does not mean that anyone had been counting the years but that his sister and other aged witnesses reported that he was then what Englishmen called a twelve-year-old (or sixteen-year-old) boy. Since he had already been on campaign the latter estimate is more likely to have been accurate. By the same kind of reckoning he was about forty when he died, succumbing to smallpox while conducting a military expedition, so his accession can be dated to about 1830. It is remembered that he was born when his father was living at his second capital; and since the kings moved their headquarters every two or three years for sanitary reasons it is likely that Kamaanya's accession took place around 1812. Beyond this it is impossible to go with any real confidence. But when Ssemakookiro ousted his brother he had sons who were old enough to fight and he can hardly have been less than thirty-five. There is no suggestion that he lived to an advanced age. (For what it is worth, the story of his death suggests that, like many people in the pre-scientific age, he was the victim of his doctors.) Long life was not in fact to be expected in that time and place, least of all perhaps by kings, who had every opportunity for every kind of physical excess. None of the *kabaka*s whose dates are historically known lived beyond what would now be called early middle age: Muteesa I died at about forty-five, Mwanga II at thirty-seven, Daudi Cwa at forty-four and Muteesa II at forty-eight. There is thus no reason to doubt the testimony that Ssemakookiro's reign lasted no more than ten years. Moreover it is said that when he seized the kingship his son Kamaanya already had a daughter, Tajuba;[39] and if this is correct his reign cannot possibly have begun before 1800, for Tajuba was alive and in possession of her faculties in the 1890s, when she became one of Kaggwa's principal informants. It is likely that Jjunju's reign, though eventful, was also quite short and that Kyabaggu's ended some time after 1790. The date of Namugala's accession, the beginning of the modern kingdom, can then be guessed at between 1760 and 1770.

11 Reflections

Political economy

By the later eighteenth century the kingship of Buganda was evidently a prize for which ambitious men were willing to compete with desperate ferocity, staking their own lives and killing without mercy, while other men, not eligible for the supreme position, strove no less avidly for a share in the spoils of power. There was in other words a large surplus to be seized, and obvious questions follow. How did the surplus arise? How was it extracted, and from whom? And these are part of the larger questions about state formation which have been the main themes of African historical studies since their academic beginnings some forty years ago.

Structures of political authority of the kind that Europeans could recognise as states were by no means universal in sub-Saharan Africa, and where they existed they were generally smaller, weaker and less durable than those of Asia and Europe. This undeniable fact has troubled African intellectuals and foreign sympathisers, because states are commonly regarded as the proper mode of political existence and have now become the compulsory mode. Africans thus appeared to have fallen behind in the normal journey of political development, with the natural implication that they were deficient in some crucial capacity, either genetic or environmental. Colonial apologists had welcomed this inference, since government was held to be chief among the blessings conferred on Africa by European rule. Hardliners among them had seen the deficiency as incurable and the foreign rule therefore necessarily eternal. Liberals had thought it possible to implant new political organs and withdraw when they were capable of autonomous functioning. But even this more hopeful version of colonial theory was naturally rejected as patronising and offensive by those Africans whose education had made them aware of it.

For colonialists, indisputable states such as Buganda had to be exceptions that proved the rule; and the universal explanation of them was that they were the result of conquest by people of Hamitic stock who, though native to the African continent, were distinct, biologically or

230

culturally or both, from the mass of the sub-Saharan population. Needless to say, the opposition denied this claim, but beyond that its stance was ambiguous. Once Hamites had been eliminated from the argument, Buganda was welcome proof that genuine black Africans could construct states, but did not by itself refute the proposition that they usually did not. The tendency of anti-colonial and post-colonial thought was therefore to deny that the exceptions were truly exceptional, to present them as merely outstanding products of an evolutionary process that was everywhere in motion. That denial, however, was not easy to maintain, so great were the differences between African polities in both size and structure. At the least, there was still a need to explain why some had advanced so much further towards statehood than others.

One popular answer lies in exposure to long-distance, especially extra-African, commerce, in gold or ivory or slaves, which permitted new concentrations of wealth and power. There are problems about this explanation, however. For instance, the Igbo-speaking people of south-east Nigeria were stateless in a double sense: they lived in autonomous village-groups which recognised no superior authority, and within each village power was widely diffused among lineage elders and priests, with no clear structure of government. Yet the Igbos had been involved in long-distance trade for as long as we have knowledge of them. Their society was not primitive or anarchic, but its complexity took a non-state form, communities being linked by subtle and wide-ranging networks of kinship, age-fellowship, functional association and religious cult. It was in most ways more 'developed' than most of the Bantu societies of eastern Africa, which were generally apical in form, vesting authority in an individual or small group, but which did not usually create or sustain articulated structures above the village or at most the district level. The axis of centralisation, in other words, is not the only one on which African societies should be measured. Trade would undoubtedly lead to greater social complexity, but not necessarily to the special kind of complexity that is called a state.

On the other hand, there is plausibility in the converse proposition, that it would be difficult to form states in Africa without the help of trade. For the great problem facing would-be dominators, where everyone possessed the means of subsistence and little more than subsistence was to be had by anyone, was how to persuade men to serve them rather than to serve themselves; and it was here that the exotic goods brought in by long-distance commerce made their impact. Either by levying tolls on merchants or by asserting the sole right of purchase, an East African chief could become rich in imported cloth, beads, brass and iron wire, and then at last he had the means to reward servants and enforcers and so to intensify and expand his power. It was not that the new commodities made life vastly better. Cotton cloth was preferable to skins or bark but it was not essential; beads and wire had no function other than the ornamental. But such goods were the mark of success and pride in societies where the quest for status was the great game of life,[1] and those who could control them were assured of followers. The model does not of course explain the origins of political differentiation, for it assumes that 'chiefs' existed before they were empowered by commerce. That, however, ceases to be a problem when it is accepted that sacred authority-figures were of immense antiquity in Africa.

The difficulty with regard to Buganda and the rest of the Lakeland is not with the theory but with the historical evidence. There is in fact very little to show that trade with the east coast and the world beyond it was here of any importance until well into the nineteenth century. Further south it is obvious – if only from the presence of Chinese porcelain – that foreign commerce supplied at least part of the wealth that enabled the lords of Zimbabwe to create their famous monuments.[2] But Great Zimbabwe stood guard over the road to a rich goldfield, and the Lakeland had no gold to speak of nor any other comparable asset. There was an abundance of ivory, but only when demand was exceptionally strong could it bear the huge cost of transport to the coast in the pre-railway age. So it is not surprising that archaeological sites have yielded no porcelain and that only a few glass beads and cowrie shells of not very certain date attest contact with the coast before about 1800. Some of these may belong to the thirteenth or fourteenth century, a period of active trade in the Indian Ocean region and high prosperity in the East African coastal towns. There are signs, however, that this was on the wane even before the sixteenth century, when the Portuguese seized control of the trade and sucked it dry. The next and much greater commercial boom had to wait for the Industrial Revolution in Britain and America and the rise of a bourgeoisie which, thanks to the British involvement with India, made ivory one of its principal status symbols. The price of this commodity rose almost continuously from about 1800 to 1890 and, as elephants were killed off near the coast, the supply network stretched rapidly into the far interior.[3]

By the early nineteenth century, however, there is no doubt at all that the historic Lake kingdoms, including Buganda, were almost fully formed, so it is hard to see the coastal trade as a contributor to any but the final stages of their growth. The first mention of it in Ganda tradition comes from the reign of Kyabaggu (K.25), who received a gift of cups and plates[4] – a great novelty for people who ate off banana leaves and drank mostly from gourds with the aid of straws. The episode seems to belong to the latter part of his reign, thus probably to the 1780s. It is reported as a curiosity and there is no reason to think the acquisitions were more than an incidental by-product of

Kyabaggu's wars. Nor was there any sequel. Crockery was not a regular item in the nineteenth-century Lakeland or anywhere in the East African interior. In the next generation we hear that Ssemakookiro sold ivory in Karagwe in return for cowrie shells and the dark blue Indian cloth called *kaniki*. Again the exchange seems incidental and not especially important. As Kaggwa tells the story[5] the energetic king organised a general drive against elephants as a measure of crop protection, found himself with a large stock of ivory (everywhere in East Africa rulers had by ancient custom the right to at least one tusk from every carcase) and disposed of it on the market to which the conquest of Buddu had opened the road. And again there appears to have been no early follow-up. It was two generations later, in the 1840s, that coastal merchants appeared in person at the court of King Ssuuna II, and only then did regular commerce make a start. After a while Ssuuna broke off contact with the traders, evidently finding their offerings dispensable; and at the time of Speke's visit in 1862, while cotton cloth was in use at the Karagwe court, the dignitaries of Buganda were still dressed in bark-cloth and antelope skins. After that time the trade grew rapidly and visitors in the mid-1870s found Muteesa arrayed in Arab splendour, while cotton cloth had become the normal wear at court, though not to any extent beyond it.

Extra-African commerce has thus to be ruled out as a cause of the Buganda state, but the 'trade and politics' model need not be discarded altogether. All over the Lakeland, copper artefacts served as emblems of sacred dignity, being used as bracelets and anklets, in the royal drums and in the magical spears that were a key item of the regalia. There is some copper in the western mountains, but even in the colonial era it was exploited only in boom periods and there is nothing to show that it was even known about in earlier times. The source of the Lakeland treasures was undoubtedly the Copperbelt, the great metalliferous plateau that separates the Zaire and Zambezi basins, where copper was mined at least from the seventh century, and by the fourteenth had given rise to a regional network covering much of south central Africa. However, there is no sign of copper at Ntusi or indeed in any archaeological site except for a fragment of uncertain date at Biggo;[6] so it was probably at least the middle of the millennium before the Lakeland was added to the commercial complex. It is then possible that the arrival of the southern merchants and their attractive and semi-magical substance had something to do with the rise of the kingdoms. As a primary factor, however, the copper trade does not really carry conviction. More to the point was the internal trade of the Lakeland, and especially that which was focused on the inland sea of Nalubaale. There was in the first place the commerce generated by the Lake itself. Members of the royal family and some other dignitaries had privileged access to the Ssese island fisheries; and this was certainly a major source of income, for the dried fish from the Lake was in great demand on the protein-hungry mainland. In addition, the cost advantage normally enjoyed by water-borne transport was especially great in a region lacking beasts of burden, where everything not carried in a canoe had to be balanced on a human head. The Lake thus fostered longer-distance exchanges than were possible elsewhere, and its coastlands and islands witnessed a busy trade in skins, bark-cloth, pottery and iron manufactures. Buganda had its own distinctive export products; its soft and supple bark-cloths were widely demanded, and so was the fruit of the robusta coffee tree, which grew wild and partly tended in the warm, moist northern and western coastlands of the Lake.[7]

So there is much to be said for C. P. Kottak's view that the trade of the Lake was a very important factor in the rise of Buganda.[8] We have seen that a crucial step towards the formation of the state was the breakthrough to the Lake achieved by hinterland kinglets, first Kimbugwe and then Kateregga. And since cattle, the usual motive for Nyoro aggression, were not abundant in Buganda it is likely that the Nyoro rulers who intervened there also had the Lake commerce in their sights. However, this argument comes up against problems of both time and space. The material conditions for the vigorous lacustrine trade were present long before the seventeenth century, the apparent beginning of the turbulence out of which the Ganda state arose – and indeed before the thirteenth century, to which Kintu is assigned by those who believe in his historicity. It is indeed possible that the traffic received a new stimulus in the later seventeenth century, not from the east or the south but from the west. The Atlantic commerce initiated by the Portuguese had by then penetrated into eastern Zaire and probably into Rwanda and Burundi, and perhaps its furthest ripples, following the channels of the copper trade, may have flowed into Nalubaale. But there is scant positive evidence for this, either material or traditional, and there is the anomaly that trade was more active in the northern than in the southern sector of the Lake. The famous sewn-plank canoes, for example, belonged to the north, especially Buganda and Ssese, and elsewhere there were only dugouts. What is more, extreme political development took place only in one segment of the northern Nalubaale coast; east of the Nile and south of the Katonga, units remained small and power modest. Clearly this specificity requires a specific explanation.

A more obvious line of enquiry focuses on the virtues of the land of Buganda, its fertile soil and the easy living it offers to its fortunate inhabitants. It would be strange if exceptional state development were not somehow related to an exceptional environment. The nature of the link, however, needs inspection. When I first wrote about this matter I took the kindness of nature to be permissive, freeing the men of Buganda from most of the drudgeries of subsistence and so leaving energies free for politics.[9] Behind this argument was the assumption that states are normal, so that, where they do not take shape, something must be wrong. Since I rejected the idea that there was anything wrong with Africans as people, the reason for the absence or weakness of states in most of the continent had to be its environmentally determined poverty. Where, as in Buganda, that constraint was relaxed, states would naturally arise. I was aware of a possible objection: some East Africans had even more favourable habitats, notably the rich volcanic slopes of the rain-attracting mountains of Elgon, Kenya and Kilimanjaro, yet they lived in small chiefdoms or in communities without formal government. However, it could be argued that mountain ridges made communication difficult and kept political units small, and so the general explanation could be saved.

In the newer perspective state-formation no longer appears automatic (or automatically admirable)[10] and a simpler view of the environmental basis now presents itself. Specially productive land is eagerly coveted. It is therefore competed for and if necessary fought over, and so gives rise to the military organisation that we call a state. For it cannot be too strongly insisted that, whatever other roles may have been found for them, the historical function of states, the real reason for their existence, is to wage war – defensive war in the first instance, but turning easily to aggression.[11]

Those who contested for the rich land of Buganda were not struggling for the means of existence, which were found easily enough in most other parts of the Lakeland. The prize at stake was not an ample diet but power. In fact a kind of political spiral was in operation. Anyone who already had enough power to assert control over more land than he needed for his family's subsistence could use it to attract followers, both by the grant of smallholdings and by the hospitality made possible by the surplus output of his womenfolk, and so augment his power in the land. But again there is a problem of timing. The natural advantages of Buganda did not come into being in the seventeenth century or in the thirteenth. So why did the state not emerge much earlier? One possible answer may lie in the history of crop plants. What made Buganda supremely desirable was fertile soil and reliable rainfall plus bananas. There is no direct evidence for the date of the arrival of this exotic plant in Buganda; but I have argued elsewhere[12] that the full development of the banana economy there may have been as recent as the sixteenth or seventeenth century. If this is so – and the hypothesis is far from being proven[13] – there would be a causal innovation at the right period and of the right potency.

A form of agricultural production that needs very little male labour might seem to place a premium on women and so enhance their social power. But things do not usually work out like that, and certainly did not here. Instead, male power-holders set out to make female labour abundant by importing it, and by the early nineteenth century there was a massive influx of captured women from most of the surrounding lands. Here, then, is one principal link between the banana economy and the state. The military organisation that was the Buganda kingdom was built up in the first instance to defend the land, to reserve it for the clan groups and war-bands that constituted the state and to exclude foreigners. (Some of those who did the excluding were probably themselves of recent alien origin.) But defensive organisations, when successful, regularly pass over to the offensive.[14] The result was that outsiders were not denied access to the land that the bananas had made one of the most desirable in east Africa, but they were forced to enter it on disadvantageous terms, most of them women who can only be described as slaves. For a slave is by definition a person without rights; in Africa rights are asserted by kin; and people separated from their kin are therefore rightless.

The result was that women in general were devalued by their abundance and by the servile origins of some of them. It may be recalled that the poet at Mawanda's court in the mid-eighteenth century spoke unequivocally of 'buying' a woman to tend his garden, even though he knew that only inferior grades were available on the open market (above, p. 176). The further consequences of this commoditisation are easy to imagine: there was a general loosening of sexual mores. The large harems of sometimes elderly chiefs were a standing temptation to adultery, no matter how harsh the penalties of detection. In the colonial period, though most Ganda accepted the ideal of the Christian family and quite a number came close to realising it, the people as a whole were well known for the lack of marital fidelity on the part of both sexes; and it is likely that before the churches made their effort marriage had been even less of a bar to self-indulgence. By the later nineteenth century, at any rate, venereal diseases were rife, at least in the vicinity of the court; and in the early twentieth century the authorities were so alarmed by the disappearance of taxpayers and producers that they set up a VD clinic – the first and for some time the only public provision of medical treatment for the African population.

Pre-colonial medical and demographic history in Africa is a desert in which facts are as scarce as trees in the Sahara, yet a historian cannot avoid conjecture about matters so crucial to the unfolding of his story. In the present century we have a little more to go on and some inferences about earlier trends may be possible. Between about 1880 and 1920 Buganda unquestionably suffered a severe loss of population, due to the bloodshed and turmoil of the civil wars that accompanied the transition to colonial rule and to the epidemics that came in the wake of commerce and conquest, above all the calamitous onslaught of sleeping sickness. Similar demographic reverses were suffered all over East Africa in that period, but in the 1920s and 1930s the regional population began to grow, and by the 1950s its expansion was becoming explosive. In Buganda, however, revival was distinctly sluggish. The land began to fill up, but much less from natural increase than from further immigration, powered this time by economic, not military, compulsions and taking the form of an influx of workers and settlers from outer areas of Uganda and from Rwanda and Burundi. By this time the slow growth, perhaps even stasis, of the native population was clearly not due to specially high mortality but to low fertility, of which venereal infections were almost certainly the most important cause.[15] Since the social relations that made them endemic were well established by the nineteenth century, it is reasonable to suppose that the cause was already operative then. Indeed, for what it may be worth, another piece of doggerel attributed to the court of King Mawanda suggests that syphilis was rife by the middle of the eighteenth century:

> The pox! It makes our fingers swell.
> The pox! It makes them hurt like hell![16]

If fertility was already impaired well before the colonial era, a new twist would be given to the spiral of conflict. For when the Ganda male elite found that their wives were not bearing live children, the obvious response would be to add to the stock by rounding up yet more foreign women – not just for economic purposes but in order to ensure descendance. So there was a new motive for individuals to acquire power within the state, and thus a larger share of its child-bearers, and for the state to exert power over neighbouring peoples, so as to augment the total supply. Internal and external politics thus became ever fiercer. It would be difficult in this context not to advert to AIDS, which looks like being the worst of all the disasters that have afflicted the Ganda people. To suggest, however, that it is a consequence of specifically Ganda sexual behaviour would be obviously unfair as well as heartless, for the disease is a regional one, affecting a vast tract of central Africa and societies of many different kinds. Besides, the sexual 'grazing' (as the people describe it) that has helped to spread the infection is a modern rather than a traditional phenomenon, the obligatory promiscuity of the urban migrant and the lorry-driver. But it is possible that AIDS is relevant to our story in another way.

There is no question but that the dramatic increase in immunity-deficiency illness in central Africa during the 1980s was a real one, and not simply a product of new medical knowledge (or medical theory). The people coined the term 'slim disease' to describe an affliction that they had not known before. At the same time, there is growing reluctance to believe that the current epidemic has no history. It seems likely that the virus has been present in a muted form for generations, perhaps even for millennia, and for some reason still unknown acquired a new potency a decade or two ago. If so, without wreaking havoc on the present scale, it could have been a cause of early mortality for a long time past. Until very recently such deaths, even if they came to the notice of Western medicine, would have been attributed to one of the opportunistic infections that deliver the *coup de grace* to AIDS sufferers. This condition could then share with conventional venereal diseases the explanation of perhaps the most puzzling feature of Buganda's history: despite its advantages for food production, the land remained so far from over-populated that labour was the scarce factor, causing its rulers to organise the abduction of women, who would both work themselves and produce the next generation of workers.

With or without the AIDS hypothesis, which the reader will easily recognise as speculative, a dynamic model of Buganda's development can now be summarised. Rich soil and reliable rainfall, married to the banana plant, made the land a highly desirable asset. To regulate the ensuing competition and to ensure that the asset did not have to be divided between too many groups, a military state was developed out of long-pre-existing ritual institutions. The special character of the banana economy put a premium on female labour, and the military organisation of the state was used to procure additional supplies. The very success of this operation aggravated the problem, inasmuch as the status of women declined and promiscuity became the norm; the resultant infections brought about a fall in fertility, so that women were in even greater demand than before. Clearly such a system was not in equilibrium, since its maintenance required a continuous input of foreign goods and labour; and even before the tidal wave of Western ideology and power broke over East Africa there were signs of growing crisis in Buganda, as the military supremacy on which all else depended began to weaken.[17]

This model, however, cannot be a self-sufficient explanation of the course of Ganda history. It would be sufficiently time-specific only on the assumption that the banana economy did not develop fully until the seventeenth century; and it also lacks the necessary specificity of place. Banana cultivation of the Ganda kind extends all the way from the Mpologoma swamp (on the eastern border of Busoga) to the Kagera river, but the political explosion was confined in the first place to a much more limited area between the Katonga river and the Murchison bay. Perhaps the presence of the ancient Magonga cult system had something to do with this. But it is probably necessary to reintroduce trade into the equation, so that the material basis of the kingdoms is seen to consist both of agricultural excellence and of commercial opportunities. More especially, central Buganda was the area that lay between Bunyoro, rich in iron and salt, and the fisheries and traffic of the great Lake. What is certain is that during the seventeenth and eighteenth centuries the land of Buganda was the scene of complex competition between indigenous kinglets, Nyoro empire-builders, canoe-borne adventurers, freebooting war-bands and the organisers of shrine cults; and that a series of able and ruthless leaders, probably continuing an ancient royal lineage and certainly making use of its millennial rituals and emotions, created unprecedented order out of exceptional turmoil.

The society that emerged from this tumultuous history is not easy to fit into a conventional category. In the first place, it was not a class society. The concept of class in fact assorts ill with the realities of pre-colonial Africa, and neo-Marxists have been obliged to devise an 'African' or 'tributary' mode of production in order to describe them. In this general scheme, small, non-productive groups extracted surplus directly from the masses, partly by force and partly as more or less voluntary payments for judicial, peace-keeping and mystical services. The extractors did not usually form a closed class, and least of all was that so in Buganda, where large numbers of individuals were constantly climbing or falling off the ladder of power and status. The way onto the ladder lay through youthful service to a man of power who, if satisfied of the boy's loyalty and diligence, would help him up the first rungs. (The psychological consequences of this early removal from the natal home, similar to the experience of upper-class English boys, are a matter of speculation but were probably serious.) Best of all, of course, was to become a 'page' in the king's service. In theory, this was a privilege for the sons of senior office-holders; but, since the royal court was a place of peril as well as opportunity, caring parents are believed to have quite often sent other men's sons instead. In any case, opportunity did not guarantee success, and no one, however advantaged by birth and family connection, could climb far without personal gifts of energy, courage and political acumen. So, while there was a tendency for status to persist over the generations, lineage membership was less significant than in most African societies and the system was genuinely open to the talents.

The ladder, moreover, had many rungs, and there was no point at which the climber moved into a clearly defined class. A distinction was drawn, it is true, between *ba-kopi*, the 'common people', those undistinguished by any kind of office, and *ba-ami*, the generic term for 'chiefs', whether in the clan hierarchy (the *bataka*) or the administrative one (*ba-kungu* and *ba-tongole*). But the category of *mw-ami* (which in Rwanda and elsewhere was the title of the king) was here a very inclusive one, which covered everyone from the lord of a great province or the head of a great clan down to (as a British officer sourly remarked) the 'headman of a dozen tottering huts'. Properly speaking, however, everyone was a *mu-kopi* unless he was a *mu-langira*, a prince of the royal house; and although the *ba-langira* did form a class apart in terms of status, they were, as we have seen, systematically excluded from real power. Buganda, in short, was a ranked society, in which meaning was attached not to categories but to precise positions.

To what extent it was a slave society is a matter of difficult debate. There was certainly a class of people who, having been captured or purchased, were not part of Ganda society and were therefore rightless.[18] They could be bought and sold, were not entitled to burial and were more likely than others to be killed or tortured. They were sometimes described as *nvuma*, an offensive term meaning 'reviled ones' and belonging to a grammatical class normally used for the names of animals. However, this was not the commonest designation. Unfree persons of female gender were more often described as *bazaana*, a term which is probably best rendered as 'servant-girls'. In spite of their dependent status it does not appear that their lot was an intolerable one; and the children they bore to a free Ganda man would themselves be free: as it was said, 'your mother may have been a Nyoro but she bore you into the clan',[19] and so into citizenship. It is true that one way of destroying a political rival was to put it about, with or without truth, that he was the son of a foreign woman; but this tactic worked only if the victim's career was already on the slide, and in general the distinction between 'true' Ganda and others was quietly ignored.

There were, however, some males who were called *ba-ddu*, a term commonly rendered as 'slaves'. Some were foreign captives, but these were far fewer than the women; most of the men in the villages attacked by Ganda raiders were either killed or driven off. Others were unfortunates, who had been sold or pawned by parents in desperate straits. The total number is unknown, but they were certainly not a majority of the non-office-holding population. Nor is 'slave' an entirely accurate description of their status. The term *ba-ddu* is the Ganda version of the Nyoroan *ba-iru*, which denoted the mass of the population, cultivators as opposed to stock-owners and commoners as opposed to rulers. The first contrast was irrelevant to Buganda, and in the second the semantic equivalent of *ba-iru* was, as we have seen, not *ba-ddu* but *ba-kopi*; and the people classed as *bakopi*, though their services and even their lives were at the disposal of political superiors, were independent householders and full members of Ganda society. To suggest that they were slaves is to misunderstand the nature of their subordination. Buganda is probably best seen as an army. Its population lived under military discipline, which had always included an obligation to work at call for the state and its officers. (In one sense everyone was a 'slave' of the *kabaka*.) This customary subordination was very useful to the colonial regime in its early years, when money economy and wage labour were in their infancy. British officials, theoretically opposed to slavery, were glad to have manpower placed at their disposal by the chiefs. Indeed, Michael Twaddle is certainly right to say that, for men at least, the burden of unwilling labour was much heavier in the early colonial period than in the old Buganda.[20]

Moral economy

When the American adventurer Colonel Chaillé-Long visited the Buganda court in 1874 as an emissary from General Gordon in the Sudan, Muteesa greeted him with the carefully staged execution of thirty men, who were seized by the Binders and killed in his presence.[21] Later, in Mwanga's time, before the mass purge of Christian converts, three lads living in the British missionaries' household were seized and put to death, among them a small boy to whom Robert Ashe was greatly attached, and he learnt that the child was dismembered before being thrown into the flames.[22] It is not surprising that he went home in 1886 crying '*Delenda est Buganda*' (Buganda must be destroyed) – and helped to move public opinion in Britain towards annexation.

The missionaries, it must be stressed, had not arrived with consciously imperialist intentions. They had believed Stanley's claim that king and people were ready to receive the gospel, which would of itself bring enlightenment and prosperity. Ten years of alternating hope and despair led them to invoke the secular power, but even then they were not acting as British imperialists; the greatest of them, Alexander Mackay, would have been happy to see Buganda taken over by Germany, a civilised and Protestant power. So there is no question of the horrors being invented or exaggerated. Buganda in the later nineteenth century, or at any rate its capital, really was a place of cruelty and slaughter.

The killings were not all of the same kind. There were, in the first place, the executions of those held to be guilty of serious crime or sedition. These were numerous and often extremely brutal – but perhaps not much more barbaric than the hangings, drawings and quarterings or the breakings on the wheel that had been routine in European countries only a century or two earlier. And when Muslim and Christian visitors protested, they got always the same answer from the king and others: the choice was between despotism and anarchy. Without the prospect of an agonising death, it was argued, the behaviour of the people would soon be completely out of hand. This Hobbesian thesis was widely accepted, even outside the ruling elite, and not only in Buganda but also in Bunyoro and other Lakeland kingdoms. And behind this consensus, it seems clear, was the apparent lesson of history: the time of troubles that preceded the consolidation of the historic kingdoms had left deep scars on the public memory, conditioning people to accept any authority, however harsh, so long as it supplied order and peace.

The rule of the *kakaba* provided positive benefits even to the humblest of his subjects. It gave them undisturbed occupancy of a rich land and a share in the spoils of consistently victorious war. But the loyalty of the people went beyond such calculations of material gain. The king's government was not just tolerated in spite of its severities; it was applauded because of them. The dark view of human nature that informed Ganda political thought is not in any way unusual. Within a state such as Britain, where internal order has been established for centuries, humane and liberal values may be allowed to prevail, but on the international stage – we are constantly assured – they cannot be indulged. For the hearts of the nations are perpetually inclined to war, and so only the threat of nuclear annihilation is deemed sufficient to preserve the peace.

Thus the self-righteousness of Europeans is wholly out of place, for nothing in the known history of Africa (until 1994) compares in horror with the mass slaughter of women during the so-called witch craze that ravaged western Europe in the seventeenth century, not to mention the Jewish Holocaust and the saturation bombing of cities in our own century. But there is one feature of the killings that we may reasonably complain about: the punishments were not only cruel but also arbitrary, resulting often from nothing more than the ruler's caprice. There is, for instance, the much-quoted incident reported by Speke, who presented Muteesa with a hunting-rifle, whereupon the king handed it to one of his pages and told him to go and shoot a man in the outer court. The boy returned in a few moments with a broad grin on his face, mission clearly accomplished.[23] Speke was also distressed to witness sentences of instant execution being passed on several of the king's women for trivial misdemeanours. He managed to beg a reprieve for one of them, but Muteesa clearly considered his concern eccentric.[24]

Personal character is certainly relevant. Muteesa's father Ssuuna was by all accounts a real brute, a grim autocrat wholly devoid of human feeling – though he decreed national mourning for his dog – but Muteesa himself was a more complex personality. Travellers and missionaries treated him with respect and even a reluctant liking, for to them he was generally affable and he had undoubted presence and authority. At the time of Speke's visit he was barely out of his adolescence, and much of his behaviour could be excused as that of a self-willed youth, exuberant in his new-found power and determined to use it to the full. Thirteen years later Stanley persuaded himself (and his readers) that, thanks to greater maturity and civilising

Arab influences, he had become a very different man, worthy of the patronage of Christian philanthropists. Stanley was not aware of the liquidation of the king's brothers that probably took place during his visit, admittedly on the initiative of the queen-mother, or of another murder of which the king was the sole author. Muteesa took advantage of Stanley's presence to launch a large-scale expedition against the stubbornly independent people of the Buvuma islands, and failed to subdue them. When he returned home, one of his wives teased him about his ill-success. She thought she was safe, because she was his favourite, probably the only person apart from his mother that he actually loved. But she had presumed too far, and was hurried off to be drowned.[25]

Some apparently capricious killings, however, were coolly calculated. Muteesa was a highly intelligent man and a very skilled political operator. When Speke arrived he had already escaped from the leading-strings of the very powerful official Kayiira, who as *katikkiro* had given him the throne but was soon forced into a humiliating resignation.[26] And he was no less adroit in his dealings with foreigners. Even in Stanley's time he knew so little of the outer world that he thought Queen Victoria would be gratified by his offer to take one of her daughters to wife; yet he had a shrewd idea of the forces converging on his country and played them off with consummate craft.[27] He knew, for instance, that Colonel Chaillé-Long served a power that had designs on his kingdom, and staged the killing of thirty men to demonstrate that he was a hard man, firmly in control of the country. In fact these murders had a double purpose. The victims were *lubaale* priests, whose sudden deaths were meant to warn their colleagues not to challenge the Islamising king's authority.

Yet political expediency, personal brutality and a passion for law and order do not, even in combination, explain all the bloodshed in Buganda, some of which seems to derive from a less rational kind of thinking. For a long time the term 'human sacrifice' was effectively banned from academic discourse on Africa; for example, the reader who looks for it in the index to Ivor Wilks's great work on the Asante kingdom is instructed to 'see "capital punishment"'.[28] As disillusion about Africa's current performance has set in there has been less reluctance to mention that its past was not an unblemished model of enlightenment. Even so, it took courage for Robin Law to point out not long ago that the ceremonial beheadings that took place with great frequency in Asante and other West African states cannot be subsumed under the criminal justice system.[29] Some of the victims were prisoners of war, but many were innocent citizens who were required to lose their heads in order that king and kingdom might prosper. And there is no reason to doubt that these eighteenth- and nineteenth-century killings had very ancient precedents.

In Buganda we know that the 'Frog' boy and several others had to die so that the young king might grow up (above, pp. 150–4); and in Burundi there was a still stranger expression of the same sacrificial theme. We learn of it from reports of an incident that took place during the interregnum between German and Belgian rule. The king-elect, Mwambutsa, a child of three, was to be carried across the sacred stream so that he might begin his reign, but before that crucial transition could be achieved there was a price to be paid. Cows were tethered a short distance away and prevented from drinking for a day and a night. Between them and the stream a shallow trench was dug and a man was made to lie down in it. The other members of his clan, whose doom was to provide this victim, had scattered to the ends of the kingdom on the news of the old king's death, but he had been too slow. So he was in no sense a volunteer but now, well primed with hydromel and encouraged by the crowd, he accepted his fate quietly. At a given signal the cows were released. They stampeded for the water and he died under their hooves. And then, to enormous jubilation, the king could cross the river.[30]

To the modern mind such proceedings cannot but seem senseless as well as brutal, yet they are also strangely moving, as is the ritual suicide of the king's horseman that followed the death of the king of Oyo – at any rate when portrayed with the art of Wole Soyinka.[31] Such sacrifices certainly do not imply that human life is held cheap. On the contrary, they signify it as a gift so precious that someone must surrender it in order that others may possess it. And after all the same proposition is at the base of Christian civilisation: 'It is expedient that one man should die for the sake of the people.' One man, perhaps. Several men, just possibly. But in nineteenth-century Buganda this concept had given birth to the monstrous institution called *kiwendo*, whereby from time to time several scores, probably hundreds, of people were seized on the roads and clubbed, strangled, burned, drowned or hacked to pieces for the health of the kingdom.[32] There was no suggestion of all or most of the victims having committed an offence, other than that of being in the wrong place at the wrong time. Typically they were peasants bringing supplies into the capital; and *kiwendo* means simply 'making the number up'.

The link with ancient ritual was explicit. For instance, when a captive claimed to belong to Nankere's branch of the Lungfish clan (and thus, like all those with traditional functions, sacrosanct) he was released with the scornful jibe: 'You're going to die from the pummelling anyway!'[33] But *kiwendo* was not itself a ritual, for it was not performed at set intervals or on specific occasions, but whenever the king and his advisers saw fit, probably on average once every five or ten years. His own ill-health was certainly one cause, and otherwise it was decreed, according to Kaggwa, when there had been trouble in the court, when there were too many idle youths around, when the roads had been fouled or princesses seduced, or when the diviners needed the bodies of people with physical peculiarities for their medicines. This last can be taken as incidental, a bonus for a special-interest group. The general cause was a feeling that the state was out of joint and that blood-letting was needed to put it right.

The reference to there being 'too many young men' has both a general and a particular significance. There is no question but that life in nineteenth-century Buganda *was* held cheap, both by those who took it and by those who had it taken from them, whether on the execution pyres or on the battlefield. The victories of the Ganda army were not free of cost, and all observers commented on its reckless bravery. A missionary eyewitness reported that a Ganda force lost half its men in one (successful) engagement.[34] In 1898 those Ganda who had thrown in their lot with the British helped them to contain a nearly disastrous mutiny of their Sudanese mercenary troops. They repeatedly charged against a stockade defended by well-armed professionals, suffering very heavy casualties.[35] Certainly warriors hoped for honour, promotion and reward, but survival was in itself clearly of little account; and it is possible to discern behind this behaviour a sense that men were more than usually redundant in a country where the basic work was done by women, that their deaths did not really matter.

The alleged excess of young men at the capital also alludes more especially to the constant dilemma of the nineteenth-century *kabakas*, who surrounded themselves with armed youths in order to protect and enhance their power but lived in fear that their weapons – which by the mid-1870s were firearms – might be turned against them. The conversion of many of the palace guards to Islam and Christianity was a particular worry, since it gave them an allegiance to foreigners and filled their heads with subversive ideas. Thus the martyrdoms of Muslims in 1876 and of Christians in 1886 were clearly precautionary measures. The charge against the young Muslims was they had rejected their meat rations, products of non-Islamic butchery. The specific offence of the Christians was not made public but was rumoured to be that they would not submit to King Mwanga's sexual demands.

These 'religious' purges have been shown to have many of the features of a *kiwendo*, even though the victims were more clearly targeted than usual. It is also established that they believed themselves to be dying, not only for Islam or for Christ, but also for their king,[36] and it was this thought, as well as the prospect of paradise, that made them go cheerfully to the flames. Likewise, observers noted with astonishment that those despatched in an 'ordinary' *kiwendo* offered no resistance or even protest, nor was the general loyalty to the *kabaka* at all diminished by what seemed to

Europeans to be his unspeakable tyranny. Yet should we really be surprised? In the entirely pointless holocaust that was the First World War millions of young Europeans went uncomplainingly to their muddy deaths, believing it right that they should give their lives for the fatherland, for king and country. The power of the moloch state to command sacrifice is indeed mysterious, but it is not a peculiarly African mystery.

At least part of the problem seems to lie in an improper transference from small scale to large. Local communities had always required their young men to risk their lives in order to protect them from wild beasts and human raiders. That was mainly what young males were for, and from a biological point of view most of them were readily expendable. But the emotions and expectations that belong to the defence of the homestead and the village have been translated to the service of a purely metaphorical hearth and home, the territory and economic interests of the nation-state, with disastrous consequences. And in much the same way the mystique of sacred kingship, created by and for primitive face-to-face communities whose survival was constantly in question, was carried over into the era of large military states, the leaders of which were clothed in spurious awe. Muteesa I of Buganda was not a god, nor was he in any meaningful sense sacred, nor were the four or five predecessors of whom we have some genuine knowledge. They were tough-minded secular politicians placed at the head of an elaborate structure of police power. But, as Benjamin Ray rightly insists, the quality of the allegiance given to them cannot be adequately explained in pragmatic terms, as a simple return for the material and psychic satisfactions that chiefs and people derived from the operation of the military state. The kingship, Ray explains, was a cultural, not just a political, creation.[37] He, however, assumes that the ideology of the Ganda kingship was developed *pari passu* with the structures of the state. My thesis, by contrast, is that kingship is far older than the Ganda state, and that the historically known *kabaka*s were illegitimate heirs of kings who had not been despots or even rulers, but the suffering servants of their people.

Luc de Heusch has well said that 'kingship, when founded on a transcendental basis, always introduces a threat of tyranny . . . The African societies that adjusted to sacred kingship in the Utopian hope of increasing their control over nature remained dimly conscious that they were playing with fire.'[38] There are two reservations to be made, however. The rulers of Buganda did not pretend to control the forces of nature, and that Frazerian function had always, I believe, been secondary to the real task of kings, which was to control time. Also, de Heusch suggests that in the acceptance of sacred kingship 'lies the upsetting of archaic society'. But it is here contended that the institution was itself archaic, and it was in the course of later economic and military transformations that it became corrupted. It is true, none the less, that the possibility of corruption was present from the neolithic beginnings. Kingship, as I have said (above, p. 128), is the most imaginative of the devices by which humanity has tried to cope with the flux of time; but like all such devices it is fundamentally flawed. It was, and is, wrong to compel selected individuals to perform the drama of life and death on our behalf; and we pay the price when our puppets take the opportunity to become our masters. Then we are likely to suffer the *kiwendo*, which is made more dreadful by our consent.

So it is necessary to pose again the question asked at the beginning: what went wrong in Buganda? Some of the economic and political reasons for the extreme concentration of power have been discussed, but there is still an outstanding issue of constitutional morality. Why did this society fail to develop checks and balances? Since the king had broken the bonds of kingship and had ceased to be sacred, since the solidarities of kin and neighbourhood had been eroded by the dominance of the political order, it might have been expected that the gods would act as countervailing powers. (What else are gods for?) Now gods did emerge, and did on occasion contest the royal will, but evidently with no lasting effect. There are even suggestions that they actually incited the kings to their worst excesses. We saw that it was the spokesman of Mukasa who counselled King Ssemakookiro to slaughter his own sons. In Muteesa's time one of the last and worst of the sacrificial massacres was attributed to the demands of the river-god Mayanja.[39] Likewise the Christian and other victims were told by their executioners not to be angry with them, nor with the king, since it was Kibuuka and Mukasa who were the cause of their deaths.[40] That, however, was a transparent attempt to deflect their ghosts from taking vengeance, and the gods can probably be absolved from the instigation of slaughter. It does not appear, however, that they did much, or indeed anything, to prevent it.

Mukasa was regarded by the Ganda as a beneficent deity who, it was pointedly remarked, did not kill people; and his influence was a moral one inasmuch as theft was said to be unknown throughout the coastlands and islands of north-western Nalubaale that made up his domain.[41] Yet, while he was sometimes at odds with the *kabaka*, the occasions for quarrel seem curiously trivial or self-interested. In the not easily decipherable story of his feud with King Tebandeke (above, pp. 182–4), the original cause of dispute was the fee charged by his medium for medical advice. There was a similar encounter with Kyabaggu, when the mediums (this time identified as people from Ssese) cured the king's illness but again made the mistake of demanding too large a share of his meat-feasts. Kyabaggu not only put them to death but sent an expedition to Ssese and slew Gugu, the chief medium of Mukasa. Again the god struck back, causing the capital to be infested by rats, whose bites caused the people to sicken and die. Kyabaggu organised rat hunts (did he really, as Kiwanuka suggests, understand the aetiology of bubonic plague?), but the sickness continued. So he sued for peace, building a new shrine for Mukasa and richly endowing it.[42]

Mukasa was active again in the reign of Kamaanya, whose most successful general, Ssewankambo, campaigning on the eastern borders, carried out a surprise attack by having canoes hauled over dry land. Canoes belonged to Mukasa, and to take them out of his domain was to commit sacrilege. So Ssewankambo was summoned to the capital and stripped of his office and property.[43] In this case, however, it must be suspected that the alleged anger of the god was a pretext for pulling down an overmighty subject. If the god was involved at all, it was as an ally and instrument of the king.

Then there is the dramatic story of the prophet Kigemuzi, spokesman of Kiwanuka the lightning-god, who articulated popular resentment of sanitary measures ordered by King Ssunna II. Commanded to cease his complaints, he threatened the king with the wrath of his patron. Ssuuna replied with scornful arrogance: 'Kiwanuka may be god in the sky but I am god on earth', and told his guards to stitch the man's lips together. Kigemuzi defied him, saying: 'Yours will be stitched too.' And sure enough, in the night lightning struck the palace, and the king was temporarily deprived of speech.[44] Stories of this sort are of course priestly propaganda, but the very fact that they circulated shows that, while the profession of the spirit-mediums was a high-risk one, they were in a position to challenge the king's power. But they also show that the aims they pursued had nothing to do with morality or the real good of the people. (Ssuuna's sanitary regulations, after all, may have been unpopular but were presumably necessary.) The tyranny of nineteenth-century Buganda can thus be seen as a failure of its intellectuals.

Michael Nsimbi retails a story which, whether true or not, accurately portrays the contempt in which the Ganda deities were held by Muteesa, and by most members of his court.[45] It probably dates from the time when his naturally sceptical temper had been reinforced by exposure to comparative religion. Having summoned all the balubaale mediums to court, he put a fruit-stone in his mouth and invited them to diagnose his swollen cheek. Most were too stupid to detect the deception or too timid to expose it, but a minor deity called Namalere did conjuring tricks which caused the king to open his mouth in laughter, whereupon he pointed to the obstruction. Muteesa admired the man for his chutzpah (as he did that of some European visitors) and rewarded him for it, but he was confirmed in the belief that the gods were frauds.

However, unbelief is not always proof against real illness, and from 1876 onwards Muteesa was a sick man, stricken by a venereal infection. The missionaries could not help him and so, to their great dismay, he turned to the old gods. At the beginning of 1879, for the first time since his involvement with Islam, Mukasa and other deities were invited in all earnest to his presence. Evidently briefed by discontented factions at the court, they ascribed his sufferings to his breaches of ancient custom, especially the appointment of a court favourite to the ritual office of Mugema, even though he did not belong to the Monkey clan, which had owned it from ancient times.[46] Muteesa gave way on this and some other matters, but it did him little good. His illness worsened and he died in 1884, when in his mid-forties.

This episode has been given rather exaggerated importance by scholars of Buganda, for instance inspiring Michael Kenny to an article called 'Muteesa's crime: hubris and the nemesis of African kings'.[47] His argument is eloquent but perhaps a little overstated. Muteesa's nemesis was gonorrhoea. His crimes were many, but those that offended clan heads and spirit mediums were by no means the worst. His kingdom was indeed doomed as an independent power, but that was due to forces far beyond his power to control. And his temporary submission to the gods is in no way surprising. To this day many urban Africans turn to ancient forms of treatment when Western medicine has failed them, just as in the West the mortally ill may resort to 'alternative' therapies. The political revival of the *balubaale* in 1879 was a brief interruption of their terminal decline, and under Muteesa's successor Mwanga, as the structural crisis deepened, government slid further into arbitrariness and iconoclasm. It was this king's pleasure to travel round the country with his retinue of armed youths, looting his own people with no regard for custom or privilege. When he arrived at the great shrine of Nende at Bukeerere the priest warned him that so holy a place could not be plundered, but he replied: 'There is no place that I can't plunder.' The story says that the priest then predicted an early end to his reign, which indeed came to pass, but that has all the marks of a prophecy after the event. Certainly his young men were unabashed. They made up a song about their exploit, telling how they had been warned that Nende was sacrosanct but had bravely cooked and eaten one of his goats. Nine of them took part, and not one even got indigestion![48]

These irreverent youths, or others of the same kind, would soon drive King Mwanga from his throne and so inaugurate a new phase in Buganda's history. In one sense they were a new generation of Bakunta, but they were Bakunta with a difference; for by then they had given their allegiance to the Islamic or the Christian faith. For the missions, Buganda was unique in

East Africa and exceptional in the whole continent of Africa, inasmuch as a significant number of people were recruited there before the colonial conquest gave the new religion the prestige of overriding power. Conversion, moreover, did not start at the top, but among the young men who would in any case have formed the next generation of the governing elite. The phenomenon has been analysed mainly in terms of sociology and politics, but it also has a properly religious aspect. The foreign faiths triumphed because the decay of the indigenous ones had left 'a partial belief vacuum',[49] because the young especially felt that they had nothing to live by or for. What Islam and Christianity offer above all (though it may be unfashionable to say this) is life after death; and the Ganda responded to this inducement because the usual modes of African survival, as members of a lineage and of a perpetual kingdom, had been cast in doubt. Lineage bonds were weak and the status of an ancestor not especially attractive, and the nineteenth-century *kabaka*s were not plausible symbols of eternal life. There was something strained and artificial about the pseudo-religious veneration they received from their subjects. Neither the despotic military state nor the corrupt cluster of charlatans who ran the national 'religion' could satisfy the hunger of many Ganda either for transcendental faith or for a political ethic more in tune with common humanity.

The gods had failed but there was still one potent figure who could be enlisted in the cause of reform; that was Kintu, Stanley's 'mild, humane and blameless patriarch' who had left the world in disgust at the behaviour of his descendants. Missionaries appealed to this tradition, and the Ganda agreed that Kintu did stand for values similar to those of Christianity.[50] Yet there was an apparent contradiction, for in Kaggwa's stories it was Kintu himself who had brought death and violence into the world. And John C. Yoder has used this difference to draw a picture of ideological conflict in the reign of Muteesa.[51] The traditions repeated by Kaggwa, he argues, represented the official propaganda, which legitimised royal violence by ascribing it to the reputed founder of the kingdom. Stanley, however, whose informant was a young officer called Sabaddu, had picked up a subversive doctrine current among young men of the kind who would soon go over to foreign faiths. (Sabaddu would become commander of the palace troops and leader of the Muslim faction in the coup of 1888.) In the stories he heard, Kintu serves as an implied critique of the contemporary methods of government. This, however, is to misunderstand the language of myth, which regularly describes an ideal time of peace and virtue, but does not effectively challenge the purveyors of war and oppression, because it locates Eden in an irrecoverable past. In the real world, as the men of power confidently remind us, things have to be done differently. All the same, Yoder (and Stanley) were right, in that 'Kintu' of Magonga did belong to an older and gentler (and not unreal) world; but the independent power of his shrine had been broken long ago.

A different approach to Buganda is that of Eli Sagan, who takes it, together with Hawaii, as the type of a tyrannical society.[52] His perspective is not that of a historian but of a social psychologist with a strongly evolutionary bias, who believes that 'the energy that drives the whole history of the world is the force of the psyche struggling to fulfil its developmental destiny'.[53] The progress of individuals from infancy to maturity, he argues, is the 'paradigm for the development of society and culture'.[54] The psyche, moreover, is the prime mover. It is because people strive to grow up, to liberate themselves from their parents, to achieve individuation and emotional autonomy, that societies strive to escape from the primitive constraints of kinship. Societies are therefore classified and ranked according to their progress along this historical path. The first kind of complex society, in which behaviour is not wholly determined by the kinship system, is a chiefdom. Buganda was one step up from this, being an advanced complex society, which however is one step short of an archaic civilisation such as Egypt or Babylonia.[55]

The insights of psychoanalysis are often useful to historians, and Sagan has much to say about Buganda, especially on the links between family and political relationships, that is truly enlightening. It would be widely agreed, however, that his analysis is fundamentally flawed. There is no analogy, and certainly no causal connection, between human adolescence and the elaboration of social and political institutions. People who live in primitive communities are poorer and have narrower horizons than the citizens of capitalist democracies, but they are not less human, less individual or less adult. And a state such as Buganda is not an exemplar of an evolutionary stage but the product of a particular historical conjuncture. It was what its people, its environment and its inheritance of ideas and institutions had made it, and there is no reason to suppose that it was on the way to becoming something else.

Further, evolutionist theories of society often lead to overindulgent judgements. It is implicit in Sagan's work that the mutilations and burnings inflicted by Ganda rulers on their own subjects, the depredations and enslavements they inflicted on other people were a reasonable price to pay for the emancipation that followed liberation from earlier kin-dominated forms of society. I must confess that this is an opinion that I was myself helping to propagate thirty years ago, but it is one that I now disown. Cruelty is evil and cruel government is tyranny. No long-term benefit, material or psychic, could compensate for the sufferings it causes – even if long-term benefits had accrued.

This brings me to a final question: what did the Buganda state have to show? When this question is put to the much-admired kingdom of Asante, a broadly similar though larger and more complex African system of which I have only a second-hand acquaintance, the answer seems to be: not very much. Its florescence coincided with the explosive transformation of Western economy in Europe that is called the Industrial Revolution, but the military state that was Asante did not significantly raise the level of culture and technology beyond that already achieved by the Akan peoples, nor did any useful capital formation occur. There was a hugely elaborate exchange of goods and power and status, but the only visible end-product was the royal treasury – a house full of European junk.[56]

On Buganda a Polish sociologist passed a similar judgement.[57] Ganda time, he wrote, was 'statistical and cumulative' in the political domain, but 'mechanical and stationary' in all others; there was progress towards bureaucracy but no new production methods or technical innovation, and the systems of kinship and worship were unchanged. Consequently Buganda has to be classed as an example of 'pre-cumulative, post-stationary time'. With reservations about its evolutionary assumptions, and some qualification with regard to kinship and worship, this statement seems to me broadly correct. The state was able to demand and reward high standards in leather-working, pottery, bark-cloth-making and especially in canoe-building and weaponry, but with the single exception of gun-repairing in the final years there was no new kind of industrial production. The *kabaka*'s palace and tomb were as large and imposing as thatched huts could possibly be, but they were still thatched huts. The outstanding neatness and productivity of Ganda banana groves owed much to the social discipline imposed from above, and there were some minor new crops in the nineteenth century, but agricultural methods were basically unchanged. There had always been some local and regional trade, and it increased considerably in the nineteenth century, but as John Tosh noted, no professional traders emerged and 'the resultant commercial structure was very elementary'.[58] And even in the political domain there must be doubts. Within its fairly extensive borders the state maintained peace and order, but it also caused war and rapine beyond them, and the balance-sheet is hard to draw up.

And yet, it is difficult to forgo altogether my early conviction that there was something special about Buganda. To ask what would have happened if it had continued to be exposed to foreign commerce and ideas but had been allowed an autonomous adaptation is to pose a counterfactual question of an extreme kind. Perhaps the society might have been creatively transformed from within. Who can tell?

Notes

1 PREAMBLE

1 The standard work, which the present study does not attempt to replace, is M. S. M. Kiwanuka, *A History of Buganda from the Earliest Times to 1900* (London, 1971). Other important studies, wholly or partly historical, include L. P. Mair, *An African People in the Twentieth Century* (London, 1934); T. Irstam, *The King of Ganda* (Uppsala, 1944); D. A. Apter, *The Political Kingdom in Uganda* (Princeton, 1961); M. Southwold, *Bureaucracy and Chiefship in Buganda*, East African Studies no. 14 (Kampala, 1961); and 'The history of a history: royal succession in Buganda', in I. M. Lewis (ed.), *History and Social Anthropology*, (London, 1968); L. A. Fallers (ed.), *The King's Men* (London, 1964); C. P. Kottak, 'Ecological variables in the origin and evolution of African states: the Buganda example', *CSSH* 14 (1972), 351–80; M. Twaddle, 'On Ganda historiography', *HA* 1 (1974), 85–99; Walter Rusch, *Klassen und Staat in Buganda vor der Kolonialzeit* (Berlin, 1975); Benjamin C. Ray, *Myth, Ritual and Kingship in Buganda* (Oxford, 1991).

2 J. H. Speke, *Journal of the Discovery of the Source of the Nile* (Edinburgh and London, 1863); J. A. Grant, *A Walk across Africa* (London, 1864).

3 H. M. Stanley, *Through the Dark Continent* (New York, 1878), vol. I.

4 For the early missionary story see R. Oliver, *The Missionary Factor in East Africa* (London, 1952); J. V. Taylor, *The Growth of the Church in Buganda* (London, 1958); A. Philippe, *Au coeur de l'Afrique, Ouganda: un demi-siècle d'apostolat au centre africain* (Paris, 1929).

5 J. M. Gray, 'Mutesa of Buganda', *UJ* 1 (1934), 22–33

6 J. F. Faupel, *African Holocaust* (London and New York, 1962); John A. Rowe, 'The purge of Christians at Mwanga's court', *JAH* 5 (1964), 55–72; D. A. Low, 'Converts and martyrs in Buganda', in his *Buganda in Modern History* (Berkeley and Los Angeles, 1971), 13–74.

7 Ahmed Katumba and F. B. Welbourn, 'Muslim martyrs of Buganda', *UJ* 28 (1964), 151–63; Arye Oded, *Islam in Uganda* (Jerusalem, 1974), 152–61.

8 For the events thus briefly summarised see Kiwanuka, *History*, 192–263; Michael Wright, *Buganda in the Heroic Age* (London and Nairobi, 1971); Michael Twaddle, *Kakungulu and the Making of Uganda* (London and Kampala, 1993), 33–134.

9 See Apter, *Political Kingdom*; but also L. A. Fallers, 'Despotism, status culture and social mobility in an African kingdom', *CSSH* 2 (1959), 11–32.

10 E. Sagan, *At the Dawn of Tyranny: The Origins of Individualism, Political*

Oppression and the State (New York, 1985). See p. 251.

11 C. C. Wrigley, 'Buganda: an outline economic history', *Economic History Review* n.s. 10 (1957), 69–80; and his 'The Christian revolution in Buganda', *CSSH* 2 (1959), 33–48; also his 'The changing economic structure', in Fallers, (ed.) *The King's Men*, 16–63.

12 For these and subsequent events see P. M. Mutibwa, *Uganda since Independence* (London, 1962).

13 J. Vansina, *Oral Tradition as History* (London and Nairobi, 1985), 201.

14 Apolo Kagwa, *The Kings of Buganda*, trans. and ed. M. S. M. Kiwanuka (Nairobi and Kampala, 1971).

15 M. B. Nsimbi, *Waggumbulizi* (Kampala, 1952); and *Amannya Amaganda n'Ennono Zaago* [Ganda Names and Their Meanings] (Kampala, 1956).

16 See *Munno* 4 (1914), 61–3, 72–5; 5 (1915), 6–8, 62–4, 92–5, 156–9, 173–6, 188–91; 7 (1917), 22–6; 8 (1918), 164–5; 10 (1920), 121–2, 131–2, 150–1. Of Gomotoka's unpublished six-volume work, *Makula* [Treasury] only one volume survives at Makerere, and I have had access only to one short extract. For a thorough review of the sources see John A. Rowe, 'Myth, memoir and moral admonition: Luganda historical writing, 1893–1969', *UJ* 33 (1969), 17–40.

17 James Miti, 'History of Buganda' (1939; ms held at the School of Oriental and African Studies, London).

18 M. I. Finley, 'Myth, memory and history', *History and Theory* 4 (1965), 281–302.

19 J. C. Miller (ed.), *The African Past Speaks* (Folkestone, 1980), 10.

20 Kaggwa's sources are listed in his *Mpisa za Baganda* [The Customs of the Ganda] (London, 1905), v–vi.

21 T. L. Thompson, *The History of the Patriarchal Narratives* (Berlin, 1974); J. van Seters, *Abraham in History and Tradition* (New Haven, 1975).

22 *The World of Odysseus* (2nd edn, Harmondsworth, 1979), 177. For the previously orthodox view see C. W. Blegen, *Troy and the Trojans* (London, 1963), 20.

23 David P. Henige, *The Chronology of Oral Tradition: Quest for a Chimera* (Oxford, 1974), 71–94.

24 See H. F. Morris, *The Heroic Recitations of the Bahima of Ankole* (Nairobi, 1964).

25 E.g. A. de Rop, *Lianja, l'épopée des Mongo* (Brussels, 1964); J. Jacobs, 'Het epos van Kudukese', *Afrika-Tervuren* 9 (1963), 33–6; D. Biebuyck and K. Mateene, *The Mwindo Epic of the Banyanga* (Berkeley, 1969). See also I. Okpewho, *The Epic in Africa* (New York, 1979).

26 J. Roscoe, *The Baganda, Their Customs and Beliefs* (London, 1911; repr. 1965), 35.

27 H. M. and N. K. Chadwick, *The Growth of Literature*, vol. III (Cambridge, 1940), 587.

28 E.g. Iris Berger, 'Deities, dynasties and oral tradition: the history and legend of the Abacwezi', in Miller (ed.), *The African Past Speaks*, 61.

29 C. C. Wrigley, 'Some thoughts on the Bacwezi', *UJ* 22 (1958), 11–17; and 'Kimera', *UJ* 23 (1959), 38–43.

30 For a partial rehabilitation of diffusionism see the important work of I. Kopytoff, *The African Frontier: The Reproduction of African Traditional*

Societies (Bloomington, 1987). See also p. 51.
31 Grant, *A Walk across Africa*, 232.
32 The essay by Michael W. Young, 'The divine kingship of the Jukun: a re-evaluation of some theories', *Africa* 36 (1966), 135–53, was ahead of its time and was generally ignored. More recently, see J. H. Vaughan, 'A reconsideration of divine kingship', in I. Karp and C. S. Bird (eds.), *Explorations in African Systems of Thought*; G. Feeley-Harnik, 'Issues in divine kingship', *Annual Review of Anthropology* 14 (1985), 273–313; A. Adler, *La mort est le masque du roi* (Paris, 1982).
33 Ray, *Myth, Ritual and Kingship*, 8.
34 Michael G. Kenny, 'Mutesa's crime: hubris and the control of African kings', *CSSH* 30 (1988), 606.
35 Ray, *Myth*, 203–4.
36 *Ibid.*, 3.
37 *Ibid.*, 183–99.
38 C. Renfrew and J. F. Cherry (eds.), *Peer Polity Interaction and Socio-political Change* (Cambridge, 1986).
39 Ray, *Myth, Ritual and Kingship*, 5–9.
40 'Royal shrines and ceremonies of Buganda', *UJ* 36 (1972), 35–48; 'Sacred space and royal shrines in Buganda', *History of Religions* 16 (1977) 363–73; 'Death and kingship in Buganda', in Earle H. Waugh and Frank E. Reynolds (eds.), *Religious Encounters with Death* (Pennsylvania, 1977), 56–69; 'The story of Kintu: myth, death and ontology in Buganda', in Karp and Bird (eds.), *Explorations*, 60–79.

2 THE STORY AND ITS MAKING

1 J. W. Nyakatura *Ky'Abakama ba Bunyoro–Kitara* [The Kings of Bunyoro–Kitara], trans. T. Muganwa (St Justin, Quebec, 1947), and ed. G. N. Uzoigwe as *The Anatomy of an African Kingdom* (New York, 1973), 209.
2 Speke, *Journal*, 205.
3 H. H. Johnston, *The Uganda Protectorate*, vol. II (London, 1902), 680.
4 Stanley, *Through the Dark Continent*, vol. I, 221.
5 Cf. A. H. Cox, 'The growth and expansion of Buganda', *UJ* 14 (1950), 153–9.
6 This valuable notation was devised by D. W. Cohen, 'A survey of interlacustrine chronology', *JAH* 11 (1970), 177–99.
7 J. Gorju, *Entre le Victoria, l'Albert et l'Edouard* (Rennes, 1920).
8 J. M. Gray, 'The early history of Buganda', *UJ* 2 (1935), 259–71.
9 Southwold, 'The history of a history'. Cf. his 'Succession to the throne of Buganda', in J. Goody (ed.), *Succession to High Office* (Cambridge, 1966), 82–126.
10 Kagwa, *The Kings of Buganda*, supplemented by his *Mpisa za Baganda* (Kampala, 1905; 3rd edn London, 1918), partially trans. by E. B. Kalibala and ed. May Mandelbaum as *The Customs of the Baganda* (New York, 1934).
11 R. Oliver, 'The royal tombs of Buganda', *UJ* 23 (1959), 124–33.
12 Ray, 'Royal shrines'; 'Sacred space'; and *Myth, Ritual and Kingship*, 108–59.
13 Kagwa, *The Kings of Buganda*, 57.
14 David P. Henige, '"The disease of writing": Ganda and Nyoro kinglists in a

newly literate world', in Miller (ed.), *The African Past Speaks*, 240–61.

15 Ray, *Myth, Ritual and Kingship*, 207–10.

16 J. F. Treharne, *The Glastonbury Legends* (London, 1967).

17 Kagwa, *The Kings of Buganda*, 65.

18 *Munno* 6 (1916), 117–19.

19 D. H. Johnson, 'Fixed shrines and spiritual centres in the Upper Nile valley', *Azania* 25 (1990), 41–50.

20 Johnston, *Uganda Protectorate*, vol. II, 681.

21 C. E. S. Kabuga, 'The genealogy of Kabaka Kintu and the early Bakabaka of Buganda, *UJ* 27 (1963), 205–16; cf. Nsimbi, *Amannya Amaganda*, 153; and Nsimbi, *Waggumbulizi*, 3–8. See also Twaddle, 'Ganda historiography'.

22 See Kabuga, 'Genealogy'.

23 Kagwa, *Mpisa*, 5–8; J. T. K. Gomotoka in *Munno* 4 (1914), 156–9, 173–6, 188–91; A. I. Richards, *The Changing Structure of a Ganda Village* (Nairobi, 1966), 34–49. Cf. Ray, *Myth, Ritual and Kingship*, 84–6.

24 R. Baskerville, *The Flame Tree* (London, 1925), 107–13.

25 Stanley, *Through the Dark Continent*, vol. I, 271–3; F. Stuhlmann (ed.), *Die Tägebücher von Dr Emin Pasha*, vol. I (Berlin, 1916), 381 (trans. J. M. Gray, 'The diaries of Emin Pasha – extracts', *UJ* 26 (1962), 95); C. T. Wilson and R. W. Felkin, *Uganda and the Egyptian Sudan*, vol. I (London, 1882), 197 (also R. W. Felkin, 'Notes on the Waganda tribe', *Proceedings of the Royal Society of Edinburgh* 13 (1885/6), 740). See table 2.

26 See table 2, and for fuller discussion C. Wrigley, 'The king-lists of Buganda', *HA* 1 (1974), 129–39.

27 F. Stuhlmann, *Mit Emin Pasha ins Herz von Afrika* (Berlin, 1894), 192–3.

28 J. Kasirye, *Obulamu bwa Stanislas Mugwanya* [The Life of Stanislas Mugwanya] (Dublin, 1962), 1.

29 Johnston, *Uganda Protectorate*, vol. II, 681.

30 I am grateful to the archivist of the White Fathers in Rome for a copy of this document, which was the source of the king-list presented by the Polish anthropologist Jan Czekanowski in his *Forschungen im Nil–Kongo Zwischengebiet* (Leipzig, 1917), vol. I, 60.

31 A. Kagwa, *Ngero za Baganda* [Ganda Tales] (London, 1902; repr., 1949).

32 L. Livinhac and C. Denoit, *Manuel de langue luganda* (2nd edn, Einsiedeln, 1894). A much expanded edition, but with the same texts, appeared under the name of R. P. Le Veux (Algiers, 1914).

33 Henige, '"Disease of writing"', 253. The Wilson–Felkin king-list began without reservation 'Kintu, or Ham'!

34 Henige, '"Disease of writing"', 248–54.

35 'Ganda historiography', 96.

36 The influence of Frazer on Roscoe is discussed much more fully by Ray, *Myth, Ritual and Kingship*, 23–53. See also J. A. Rowe, 'Roscoe's and Kagwa's Buganda', *JAH* 8 (1967), 163–6. For the intellectual background see R. Ackerman, *J. G. Frazer and the Cambridge Ritualists* (New York, 1991).

37 'Notes on the manners and customs of the Baganda', *JAI* 31 (1901), 117–30; and 'Further notes on the manners and customs of the Baganda', *JAI* 32 (1902), 25–80.

38 Kagwa, *Mpisa*, 319.

39 For an overview see E. Mworoha, *Peuples et rois de l'Afrique des lacs: le Burundi et les royaumes voisines au xixe siècle* (Dakar, 1977).

40 J. Vansina, *L'évolution du royaume rwanda dès origines á 1900* (Brussels, 1962).

41 A. Kagame, 'Le code ésotérique de la dynastie du Rwanda', *Zaire* 1 (1947), 363–86; and M. d'Hertefelt and A. Coupez, *La royauté sacrée de l'ancient Rwanda* (Tervuren, 1964).

42 A. Coupez and T. Kamanzi, *Récits historiques rwanda* (Tervuren, 1962); A. Kagame, *La poésie dynastique du Rwanda* (Brussels, 1951); A. Coupez and T. Kamanzi, *Littérature du cour au Rwanda* (Oxford, 1971), 159–97.

43 A. Pagès, *Un royaume hamite au coeur de l'Afrique* (Brussels, 1933); L. de Lacger, *Ruanda*, 2 vols. (Namur, 1939), vol. I, *Le Ruanda ancien*; A. Kagame, *La notion de génération appliquée à la généalogie et à l'histoire du Rwanda* (Brussels, 1959).

44 'Rwandan chronology in regional perspective', *Cahiers africains* 4/5 (1993), 163–208.

45 J. Vansina, *La légende du passé: traditions orales du Burundi* (Brussels, 1972), 219.

46 'Tels qu'en eux-mêmes l'éternité les change': J.-P. Chrétien and E. Mworoha, 'Les tombeaux des *bami* du Burundi', *Cahiers d'études africaines* 10 (1970), 40–70.

47 *Ibid.*, 76.

48 R. Fisher, *Twilight Tales of the Black Baganda* (1911, reissued with an introduction by M. Posnansky, 1965). The wholly inappropriate title was chosen by her publishers, who knew that the Ba-ganda had much greater market appeal than the Ba-nyoro. See also P. Bikunya, *Ky'Abakama ba Bunyoro* [The Kings of Bunyoro] (London, 1927).

49 Wrigley, 'Some thoughts on the Bacwezi'.

50 For the Cwezi (or Chwezi) see Iris Berger, *Religion and Resistance: East African Kingdoms in the Precolonial Period* (Tervuren, 1981) and J.-P. Chrétien, 'L'empire des Bacwezi: la construction d'un imaginaire géopolitique', *Annales ESC* 40 (1985), 1335–77.

51 See J. Beattie, *The Nyoro State* (Oxford, 1971).

52 See below, pp. 197–206, where the historical significance of the tradition is discussed.

3 INTRODUCTION TO MYTH

1 The controversy did not reach the English language until after the Second World War. For a summary see I. Henderson, *Myth in the New Testament* (London, 1951).

2 See Adam Kuper, *Anthropology and Anthropologists: The British School, 1922–72* (2nd edn, London, 1983).

3 Talal Asad (ed.), *Anthropology and the Colonial Encounter* (London, 1973); also Richard Brown, 'Passages in the life of a white anthropologist', *JAH* 20 (1979), 525–41.

4 A. I. Richards 'Social mechanisms for the transfer of political rights in some African tribes', *JRAI* 90 (1960), 177.

5 See especially J. M. Onyango-ku-Odongo and J. B. Webster (eds.), *The Central*

Lwo during the Aconya (Nairobi, 1976); and J. B. Webster (ed.), *Chronology, Migration and Drought in Interlacustrine Africa* (London and Dalhousie, 1979).

6　J. B. Webster, 'Dating, totems and ancestor spirits: methods and sources in African History', *Journal of Social Research* [Malawi] 5 (1978); and his 'The reign of the gods', in Webster (ed.), *Chronology, Migration and Drought*, 126–41.

7　Review in *IJAHS* 11 (1978), 157. See also I. Okpehwo, *Myth in Africa: a Study of its Aesthetic and Cultural Relevance* (Cambridge, 1983).

8　Miller, *The African Past Speaks*, 30.

9　E. R. Leach, *Genesis as Myth and Other Essays* (London, 1969). For one of many criticisms see B. Nathhorst, *Formal or Structural Analysis of Traditional Tales* (Stockholm, 1969), 60–70.

10　E. R. Leach and D. A. Aycock, *Structuralist Interpretation of Biblical Myth* (Cambridge, 1983).

11　C. Lévi-Strauss, *From Honey to Ashes*, trans. J. and D. Weightman (London, 1973), 475.

12　C. Lévi-Strauss and D. Erébon, *De près et de loin* (Paris, 1988), 195.

13　J. S. Mbiti, *African Religions and Philosophy* (London, 1969), 22–6.

14　H. Baumann, *Schöpfung und Urzeit im Mythus der Afrikanischen Völker* (Berlin, 1936), 268–78; H. Abrahamsson, *The Origins of Death: Studies in African Mythology* (Uppsala, 1951), 1–39 (an expanded version of the previous item).

15　C. Lévi-Strauss, *The Naked Man*, trans. J. and D. Weightman (London, 1981), 693–5.

16　R. R. Atkinson, 'The traditions of the early kings of Buganda: myth, history and structural analysis', *HA* 2 (1975), 17–57.

17　J. Jensen, 'Mythen und historische Legenden von Ostafrika', *Paideuma* 22 (1976), 170–88.

18　The literature on the beginnings of food production in sub-Saharan Africa is now voluminous. For some of the more recent discussions see J. D. Clark and S. A. Brandt (eds.), *From Hunters to Farmers* (Berkeley, 1984); L. Krzyzaniak and M. Kobusiewicz (eds.), *Late Prehistory of the Nile Basin and Sahara* (Poznań, 1989); R. Haaland, *Socio-economic Differentiation in the Neolithic Sudan*, BAR international series 350 (Oxford, 1987); and R. Haaland, 'Fish, pots and grain: early and mid-holocene adaptations in the central Sudan', *AAR* 10 (1992) 43–64.

19　Kopytoff, *The African Frontier*, 9–10.

20　D. P. Henige, 'Truths yet unborn? Oral traditions as a casualty of culture contact', *JAH* 23 (1982), 395–412.

21　C. Lévi-Strauss, *The Raw and the Cooked*, trans. J. and D. Weightman (London, 1970), 8.

22　*Ibid.*, Lévi-Strauss and Erébon, *De près et de loin*, 180–2.

23　L. de Heusch, *Le roi ivre ou l'origine de l'état* (Paris, 1972), trans. Roy Willis as *The Drunken King* (Bloomington, 1982); C. C. Wrigley, 'Myths of the savanna, *JAH* 15 (1974), 121–39.

24　J. P. Crazzolara, *The Lwoo*, part I (Verona, 1950), 179–83; A. Southall, 'Cross-cultural meanings and multilingualism', in W. H. Whiteley (ed.), *Language Use and Social Change* (London, 1971) 388–9.

25　E.g. J. Fontenrose, *The Ritual Theory of Myth* (Berkeley, 1960), 15–20, who

nevertheless did 'not believe in the historicity of Arthur or Agamemnon'.
26 C.-H. Perrot, 'Anyo Asema: mythe et histoire', *JAH* 15 (1974), 199–223.
27 (*O*)*musota* is the ordinary word for a snake. The meaning of Bemba can be inferred from the verbs -*bemba*, 'to form a scab' and -*bembula*, 'to remove skin'.
28 Gray, 'Early history', 260.
29 B. A. Ogot, 'The Great Lakes region', in *General History of Africa*, vol. IV: D. T. Niane (ed.), *Africa from the Twelfth to the Sixteenth Century* (Paris, 1984), 521.
30 M. Twaddle, 'Ganda historiography', 96.
31 G. Dumézil, *Horace et les Curiaces* (Paris, 1942), 64–8. Cf. his *Les dieux des Indo-européens* (Paris, 1951), 127–8.

4 INTRODUCTION TO BUGANDA

There is no space or need for anything more than an indication of the main features of land and society that are relevant to the themes of this book. A good ethnographic outline is in Margaret C. Fallers, *The Eastern Lacustrine Bantu* (London, 1960), and Rusch, *Klassen und Staat*, provides a comprehensive analysis of the late nineteenth-century data from a Marxist perspective, with a full bibliography of contemporary sources. The earlier anthropological studies by Roscoe and Mair remain indispensable. Other important secondary contributions, besides those listed in note 1 to chapter 1, are M. Twaddle, 'Ganda receptivity to change', *JAH* 15 (1974), 303–15; John A. Rowe, 'The pattern of political administration in precolonial Buganda', in Ibrahim Abu-Lughoud (ed.), *African Themes* (Evanston, 1975); P. C. W. Gutkind, *The Royal Capital of Buganda* (The Hague, 1963); and a valuable but elusive essay, of which I became aware only in the final stages of preparation: R. D. Waller, 'The traditional economy of Buganda', unpublished MA dissertation, London, 1971.

1 Speke, *Journal*; Grant, *A Walk Across Africa*.
2 For further information and references see C. C. Wrigley, 'Bananas in Buganda', *Azania* 24 (1989), 64–70.
3 For discussions of the Lakeland clans see Carole A. Buchanan, 'Perceptions of interaction in the East African interior; the Kitara complex', *IJAHS* 11 (1978), 410–28; M. d'Hertefelt, *Les clans de l'ancien Rwanda* (Tervuren, 1971); and D. S. Newbury, 'The clans of Rwanda: an historical hypothesis', *Africa* 50 (1980), 389–403. For lists of the Ganda clans see Apolo Kagwa, *Bika bya Baganda* (London, 1912); Roscoe, *The Baganda*, 128–72; Nsimbi, *Amannya Amaganda*, 182–319; and his 'The clan system in Buganda', *UJ* 28 (1964); and A. J. Lush, 'Kiganda drums', *UJ* 4 (1937), 1–25.
4 Kagwa, *Mpisa*, 144–46.
5 Beattie, *The Nyoro State*, 254.
6 'I. K'. in *Munno* 2 (1912), no. 24.
7 Lawrence D. Schiller, 'The royal women of Buganda', *IJAHS* 23 (1990), 455–74.

5 THE REMOTER PAST

1 John Sutton, 'The aquatic civilisation of Middle Africa', *JAH* 15 (1974), 527–46; Haaland, 'Fish, pots and grain'; Clark and Brandt, *From Hunters to*

Farmers.

2 S. H. Ambrose, 'The introduction of pastoral adaptations to the Highlands of East Africa', in Clark and Brandt, *From Hunters to Farmers*; P. Robertshaw and D. P. Collett, 'A new framework for the study of pastoral communities in East Africa, *JAH* 24 (1983), 289–303.

3 R. C. Soper, 'Early Iron Age pottery types from East Africa', *Azania* 6 (1971), 39–52; M. C. Van Grundebeek, E. Roche and H. Doutrelepont, *Le premier âge du fer au Rwanda et Burundi: archéologie et environnement* (Brussels, 1983); F. van Noten, 'The Early Iron Age in the interlacustrine region: the diffusion of iron technology', *Azania* 14 (1979), 61–80.

4 B. Clist, 'A critical appraisal of the chronological framework of the Early Urewe Iron Age industry', *Muntu* 6 (1987), 35–62; F. J. Kense, 'The initial diffusion of iron to Africa', in R. Haaland and P. Shinnie (eds.), *African Iron Working: Ancient and Traditional* (Oslo and London, 1985), 11–35; P. R. Schmidt and S. T. Childs, 'Innovation and industry during the Early Iron Age in East Africa', *AAR* 3 (1985), 53–94.

5 P. R. Schmidt, 'A new look at interpretations of the Early Iron Age in East Africa', *HA* 2 (1975), 127–36; F. van Noten, *Les tombes du roi Cyirima Rujugira et de la reine-mère Nyirayuhi Kanjogera* (Tervuren, 1972).

6 The standard work for Africa as a whole is still J. H. Greenberg, *The Languages of Africa* (2nd edn, Bloomington, 1966). For the Lakeland there is the comprehensive study by David L. Schoenbrun, 'Early history in eastern Africa's Great Lakes region: linguistic, ecological and archaeological approaches', unpublished Ph.D. thesis, Los Angeles, 1990, partly summarised in '"We are what we eat": ancient agriculture between the Great Lakes', *JAH* 34 (1993), 1–31. See also C. Ehret and M. Posnansky (eds.), *The Archaeological and Linguistic Reconstruction of History in East Africa* (Berkeley and Los Angeles, 1982).

7 Jan Vansina, *Paths in the Rainforests* (Madison, 1990).

8 D. Nurse, 'Bantu expansion into East Africa', in Ehret and Posnansky (eds.), *Archaeological and Linguistic Reconstruction*, 199–222.

9 M. McMaster, 'Patterns of interaction in the Uele region of Zaire, c.500 BC to AD 1900', unpublished Ph.D. thesis, Los Angeles, 1988, 110–15.

10 Schoenbrun, '"We are what we eat"', 13–15, 30.

11 C. Ehret, *Ethiopians and East Africans: The Problem of Contacts* (Nairobi, 1974), table 10; Schoenbrun, '"We are what we eat"', 15–17, 31.

12 John Sutton, 'The antecedents of the interlacustrine kingdoms', *JAH* 34 (1993), 33–64; P. Robertshaw, 'Archaeological survey, ceramic analysis and state formation in western Uganda', *AAR* 12 (1994), 105–32.

13 Sutton, 'Antecedents', 48–52.

14 R. Soper, 'Roulette decoration in African pottery: technical considerations, dating and distribution', *AAR* 3 (1985), 29–51; and, with a different approach, Christine Desmedt, 'Poteries anciennes décorées à la roulette dans la région des Grands Lacs', *AAR* 9 (1991), 161–96.

15 J. P. Crazzolara, 'The Lwoo people', *UJ* 5 (1937), 1–21; R. Oliver, 'The Nilotic contribution to Bantu Africa', *JAH* 23 (1982), 433–42; and his 'The East African Interior', in R. Oliver (ed.), *Cambridge History of Africa*, vol. III (Cambridge, 1977), 621–69. See below, pp. 287–8.

16 In what follows I rely heavily on Schoenbrun, 'Early history'.

17 *Ibid.*, 136; C. Ehret, 'The East African Interior', in *General History of Africa*, vol. III, M. Elfasi and I. Hrbek (eds.), *Africa from the Seventh to the Eleventh Century* (Paris, 1988), 616–42. These authors actually place the split a little earlier, but there is reason to think that African linguistic dates are generally too old.

18 M. Posnansky, 'Bigo bya Mugenyi', *UJ* 33 (1969), 125–50.

19 Vansina, *Paths in the Rainforests.*

6 GENESIS

1 Kagwa, *The Kings of Buganda*, 47–8.

2 Romans 9:38.

3 J. S. Mbiti, *Concepts of God in Africa* (London, 1970), 45.

4 Cf. E. Dammann, 'A tentative philological typology of some African high deities', *Journal of Religion in Africa* 2 (1969), 87–8. For the ancestral vocabulary of Bantu languages see M. Guthrie, *Comparative Bantu*, 4 vols. (Farnborough, 1967–71).

5 For the *ba-lubaale* see Roscoe, *The Baganda*, 273–7, 290–323; Kagwa, *Mpisa*, 209–37; Nsimbi, *Amannya Amaganda*, 119–48; F. B. Welbourn, 'Some aspects of Kiganda religion', *UJ* 26 (1962), 171–82.

6 Nyakatura, *Ky'Abakama ba Bunyoro-Kitara*, p. 14.

7 Nsimbi, *Amannya Amaganda*, 194.

8 *Ibid.*, 124. Bakka was also called Namwezi, 'the place of the moon'.

9 J.-C. Muller, 'Le royauté divine chez les Rukuba', *L'Homme* 15 (1975), 5–27.

10 L. de Heusch, *Why Marry Her?* (Cambridge, 1981), 23. Cf. P. S. Garlake, *The Kingdoms of Africa* (Oxford, 1978), 22.

11 Pagés, *Royaume hamite*, 312; de Lacger, *Le Ruanda ancien*, 78–80.

12 L. Viaene, 'L'organisation politique des Bahunde', *Kongo-Overzee*, 18 (1952), 8–34; R. Sigwalt, 'Early Rwanda history: the contribution of comparative ethnography', *HA* 2 (1975), 137–46.

13 J. Osogo, *A History of the Baluyia* (Nairobi, 1966).

14 Van Noten, *Les tombes du roi Cyirima Rujugira*, 7; P. R. Schmidt, *Historical Archaeology* (Westport, Conn. and London, 1978), 292.

15 See below, pp. 150–2. This pattern, in which a ruling lineage is surrounded by a small group of clans, each having a specific ritual function, seems to be very widespread in Africa. It occurs, for example, among the Alur of north-west Uganda (A. Southall, *Alur Society* (London, 1956), 88) and far away among the Mundang of Chad (Adler, *La mort est le masque du roi*, 83–5).

16 J. Maquet, *Les civilisations noires* (Paris, 1962), 109.

17 T. N. Huffman, 'The rise and fall of Great Zimbabwe', *JAH* 13 (1972), 353–66.

18 A. Reid, 'Ntusi and its hinterland', *Nyame Akuma* 33 (1990), 26–28.

19 L. Krzyzaniak, 'New light on early food production in the central Sudan', *JAH* 19 (1978), 169; and his 'Early farming in the Middle Nile basin: recent discoveries at Kadero', *Antiquity* 65 (1991), 515–32.

20 The name of the First Man of Rwanda, Kigwa, means 'the Fallen', and so does Apodho, the First Man of the Lwo-speaking peoples.

21 Stanley, *Through the Dark Continent*, vol. I, 218–20; cf. Felkin, 'Notes on the

Waganda tribe', 764.
22 Kagwa, *Ngero*, 56–7.
23 R. Baskerville, *King of the Snakes, and Other Stories* (London, 1922), 17–19; F. Rowling, *The Tales of Sir Apolo* (London, n.d.), 27–9.
24 Ray, 'The story of Kintu', 60–79; and his *Myth, Ritual and Kingship*, 54–73.
25 Wilson and Felkin, *Uganda and the Egyptian Sudan*, vol. I, 220.
26 Johnston, *Uganda Protectorate*, vol. II, 700–5.
27 Roscoe, 'Notes on the manners and customs', 124–5; 'Further notes', 26; and *The Baganda*, 460–4.
28 See Baskerville, *King of the Snakes*; and (the best version in English) Alice Werner, 'African Mythology', in J. A. MacCulloch (ed.), *The Mythology of all Races*, vol. VII (Boston, 1925), 152–4, 172–4.
29 Le Veux, *Manuel*, 449–58.
30 The former view was taken by B. Kirwan, who first drew attention to the significance of millet in this tale: 'Place names, proverbs, idioms and songs', in M. Posnansky (ed.), *Prelude to East African History* (London, 1966), 161.
31 Gorju, *Entre le Victoria*, 183; F. L. Williams, 'Myth, legend and lore in Uganda', *UJ* 10 (1946), 69.
32 Kagwa, *Ngero*, 28–30.
33 Roscoe, *The Baganda*, 136.
34 Abrahamsson, *Origins of Death*, 40–65. H. Tegnaeus, *Le héros civilisateur* (Stockholm, 1950), assembles much information on African founders, including Kintu, and in particular cites (101) a Nigerian myth about the ancestress who came from the sky and whose brother was the god of death.
35 Romans 5:12–14; I Corinthians 15:21–2.
36 J. R. L. Macdonald, *Soldiering and Surveying in British East Africa* (London, 1897), 134–5, citing the missionary Robert Ashe. Cf. Johnston, *Uganda Protectorate*, vol. II, 606.
37 V. W. Turner, *The Forest of Symbols* (London, 1970), 59–72.
38 C. Lévi-Strauss, *The Origin of Table Manners* (London, 1978), 505.
39 E. S. Hartland, review of Roscoe's *The Baganda*, *Folklore* 23 (1912), 134.
40 Dumézil, *Les dieux des Indo-européens*, 98.
41 The *Mabinogion*, trans. and ed. G. and T. Jones (2nd edn, London, 1974), 95–136.
42 G. Pagès, 'Au Ruanda, sur les bords du lac Kivou', *Anthropos* 15 (1920), 962–6; Pierre Smith, *Le récit populaire au Rwanda* (Paris, 1975), 128–33.
43 De Heusch, *Roi ivre*, 47–96; C. C. Wrigley, 'The river-god and the historians: myth and history in the Shire valley', *JAH* 29 (1988), 367–83.
44 Adler, *La mort est le masque du roi*, 99.
45 J. Roscoe, *The Northern Bantu* (Cambridge, 1915), 247. For an interesting variation see E. K. Akimbisibwe, 'Death and the hereafter among Banyankole', *Journal of African Religions and Philosophy*, 1 (1990), 7–25.
46 A. D. Roberts, *History of the Bemba* (London, 1973), 39.
47 L. Décle, *Three Years in Savage Africa* (London, 1898), 439.
48 Wilson and Felkin, *Uganda and the Egyptian Sudan*, vol. I, 220–1.
49 Le Veux, *Manuel*, 27–30.
50 Pagès, 'Au Ruanda', 940–6.
51 E. Césard, 'Comment les Bahaya interprètent leurs origines', *Anthropos* 22

(1927), 447–53.

52 Thomas Malory, *Le Morte d'Arthur* (London: Everyman edition, 1906), book I, 76, 172.

53 F. X. Lwamgira, History of Kiziba, trans. E. R. Kamuhangire (Makerere, 1965), 6–7. For a darker version from Zaire see L. Frobenius, *Atlantis*, vol. XII (Jena, 1928), 26–7.

54 Kagwa, *Ngero*, 9–13; Roscoe, *The Baganda*, 465–7; Le Veux, *Manuel*, 443–6; and, without the Faustian theme, Baskerville, *King of the Snakes*, 12–15.

55 Kagwa, *The Kings of Buganda*, 6–7, and his *Bika*, 8–9. See also Roscoe, 'Further notes'; and Nsimbi, *Amannya Amaganda*, 222–3. The more accessible versions are too brief to be informative.

56 Chadwick and Chadwick, *Growth of Literature*, vol. III, 589.

57 E. W. Smith and A. M. Dale, *The Ila-speaking People of Northern Rhodesia* (London, 1920), vol. II, 182.

58 Smith, *Récit populaire*, 232–40.

59 Bikunya, *Ky'Abakama ba Bunyoro*, 6.

60 W. Fagg, *Nigerian Images* (London, 1963), plate 61.

61 A. Droogers, *The Dangerous Journey: Symbolic Aspects of Boys' Initiation Rites among the Wagenia of Kisangani*: (London, 1980), 94.

62 Fisher, *Twilight Tales*, 102–4.

63 Grant, *A Walk across Africa*, 170.

64 Décle, *Three Years in Savage Africa*, 440.

65 I. Schapera, *The Khoisan People* (London, 1930), 376–7.

66 *Mabinogion*, 37.

67 Chrétien de Troyes, *Perceval, The Story of the Grail*, trans. N. Bryant (Cambridge: D. S. Brewer, 1982), 32–40.

68 *Volsunga Saga*, trans. W. Morris (New York, 1962), 129–31.

69 E. Césard, 'Le Muhaya', *Anthropos* 32 (1937) 32–7; Lwamgira, History of Kiziba, 51–62.

70 Apolo Kagwa, *Basekabaka b'e Buganda* (London, 1912), 6.

71 *Ibid.*, 297.

72 J. S. Boston, 'The hunter in Igala legends of origin', *Africa* 34 (1964), 116–26.

73 The story was told in Kagwa, *The Kings of Buganda*, 5–7, and in his *Bika*, 41. The fullest account, however, is in J. F. Cunningham, *Uganda and its Peoples* (London, 1905), 170–8.

74 Nsimbi, *Amannya Amaganda*, 184.

75 Tobi Kizito in *Munno* 5 (1915), 92–5.

76 J. G. Frazer, *Folklore in the Old Testament*, 2 vols. (London, 1918), vol. I chap 2; Leach, *Genesis as Myth*. Cf. B. Otzen, 'The concept of myth', in B. Otzen, H. Gottlieb and K. Jepperson (eds.), *Myths in the Old Testament* London, 1980), 1–21.

77 See E. A. Speiser, 'Akkadian myths and legends', in J. B. Pritchard (ed.), *Ancient Near Eastern Texts Relating to the Old Testament* (Princeton, 1950), 60–119.

78 These and other versions are reviewed in Elizabeth Brewer, *From Cuchulainn to Gawain* (Cambridge: D. S. Brewer, 1973).

79 Atkinson, 'Myth, history and structural analysis'.

80 E. Hurel, *La poésie chez les primitifs* (Brussels, 1922), 15, 41.

81 Wrigley, 'Some thoughts on the Bacwezi', 13.

82 Ray, *Myth, Ritual and Kingship*, 83.
83 Stanley, *Through the Dark Continent*, vol. I, 218–26.
84 *Ibid.*, 239.
85 Wilson and Felkin, *Uganda and the Egyptian Sudan*, vol. I, 197. See Henige, '"Disease of writing"' for comment.
86 See Edith R. Sanders, 'The Hamitic hypothesis, its origins and functions in historical perspective', *JAH* 10 (1969), 521–32.
87 W. C. Willoughby, *The Soul of the Bantu* (London, 1928), 43. Cf. H. P. Gale, 'Mutesa I – was he a god?', *UJ* 20 (1954), 72–87; and for a more nuanced view see Gorju, *Entre le Victoria*, 95–102.
88 Johnston, *Uganda Protectorate*, vol. II, 680.
89 Roscoe, *The Baganda*, 137.
90 Twaddle, 'Ganda historiography'.
91 Kagwa, *Basekabaka*, 13.
92 J. T. K. Gomotoka, quoted by Twaddle in 'Ganda historiography', 95.
93 Kizito in *Munno* 5 (1915), 92–5.
94 D. W. Cohen, *The Historical Tradition of Busoga: Mukama and Kintu* (Oxford, 1972), 84–123.
95 Twaddle, 'Ganda historiography'.
96 Daudi B. Musoke in *Munno* 5 (1915), 112–15; P. S. Kakulu in *Munno* 8 (1918), 116–17.
97 W. MacGaffey, 'Oral tradition in central Africa', *IJAHS* 7 (1974), 421.
98 Lawi Sekiti in *Munno* 6 (1916), 6–10.
99 Kabuga, 'Genealogy'; Nsimbi, *Amannya Amaganda*, 151–4.
100 J. T. K. Gomotoka in *Munno* 8 (1918), 164–5.
101 Kagwa, *Mpisa*, 1–4.
102 Stanley, *Through the Dark Continent*, vol. I, 220–6. Also Kagwa, *The Kings of Buganda*, 71–3; Roscoe, *The Baganda*, 222–3.
103 M. Schoffeleers, 'Symbolic and social aspects of spirit worship among the Mang'anja', unpublished D.Phil. thesis, Oxford, 1968; and his 'The history and political role of the M'bona cult among the Mang'anja,' in Ranger and Kimambo (eds.), *The Historical Study of African Religion*, 73–94. For further references and comments see Wrigley, 'The river-god'.
104 Schoffeleers, 'Symbolic and social aspects', 412–15; and his 'The religious significance of bush fires in Malawi', *Cahiers des religions africaines* 10 (1971), 272–82.
105 H. Rehse, *Kiziba, Land und Leute* (Stuttgart, 1910), 89.
106 See Vansina, *Paths in the Rainforests*, chap. 4.
107 R. Dennett, *The Folklore of the Fjort* (London, 1898), 9.
108 M. Douglas, 'Animals in Lele religious thought', *Africa* 27 (1957), 46–58, repr. in J. Middleton (ed.), *Myth and Cosmos* (New York, 1964).
109 W. de Mahieu, *Qui a obstrué la cascade?* (Cambridge, 1985), 200.

7 THE CYCLE OF THE KINGS

1 Kagwa, *The Kings of Buganda*, 26–9.
2 *Ibid.*, 29–32. Supplementary details about reigns, capitals, wives and maternal kin are given in Kagwa, *Mpisa* (= Mandelbaum, *Customs*, 18–62).

3 Southwold, 'Succession to the throne of Buganda', 105.
4 Nsimbi, *Amannya Amaganda*, 232. J. S. Kasirye, *Abateregga ku Namulondo ya Buganda* [Sovereigns of the Throne of Buganda] (London, 1971), 11.
5 Roscoe, *The Baganda*, 213.
6 H. Frankfort, *Kingship and the Gods* (Chicago, 1948), 43; J. Cerny, *Ancient Egyptian Religion* (London, 1952), 35.
7 J. G. Frazer, *The Golden Bough* (3rd edn, London, 1911), vol. II, 18.
8 J. Gorju, *Face au royaume hamite de Ruanda: le royaume frère de l'Urundi* (Brussels, 1938), 25–6; Vansina, *Légende du passé*, 70–2.
9 Schmidt, *Historical Archaeology*, 308, 316.
10 C. C. Wrigley 'The story of Rukidi', *Africa* 43 (1973), 220.
11 J. P. Chrétien, 'Le Buha à la fin du xix° siècle', *Etudes historiques africaines* 7 (1975), 14. Cf. J.-P. Chrétien, 'Du hirsute au hamite: la variation du cycle de Ntare Rushatsi', *HA* 8 (1981), 3–41.
12 H. Jeanmaire, *Dionysos* (Paris, 1951/1971), 46.
13 de Lacger, *Ruanda*, vol. I, 80.
14 E. Simons, 'Coutumes et institutions des Barundi', *Bulletin des jurisdictions indigènes* 12 (1944), 144, 194.
15 H. Meyer, *Die Barundi* (Leipzig, 1916), 91.
16 Stuhlmann, *Mit Emin Pasha*, 189.
17 Speke, *Journal*, 207.
18 Felkin, 'Notes on the Waganda tribe', 739, 741.
19 Especially influential was E. E. Evans-Pritchard, *The Divine Kingship of the Shilluk of the Nilotic Sudan* (the Frazer Lecture for 1948, repr. in E. E. Evans-Pritchard (ed.), *Essays in Social Anthropology* (London, 1962)).
20 G. P. Murdock, *Africa: Its Peoples and their Culture History* (New York, 1959), 36–9; R. Oliver and J. D. Fage, *A Short History of Africa* (London, 1962), 44–65. However, I believe that Murdock's idea of a common template for African kingdoms was correct.
21 Vaughan, 'A reconsideration of divine kingship'.
22 See E. H. Kantorowicz, *The King's Two Bodies* (Princeton, 1957), 8. See also W. MacGaffey, 'Kingship', in M. Eliade (ed.), *Encyclopaedia of Religion* (New York, 1987), vol. VIII, 325–7; and Ilse Hayden, *Symbol and Privilege: The Ritual Context of British Royalty* (Tucson, 1987), 16–17.
23 Kagwa, *The Kings of Buganda*, 31; Nsimbi, *Amannya Amaganda*, 234.
24 Nsimbi, *Amannya Amaganda*, 234.
25 E. Steere, *Swahili Tales* (London, 1869), 478–9.
26 J. E. Harrison, *Themis: A Study of the Social Origins of Greek Religion* (London, 1911), 1–29.
27 C. Laye, *L'enfant noir* (Paris, 1953), 117–41.
28 W. F. Otto, *Dionysus, Myth and Cult* (Bloomington, 1965), 167.
29 Jeanmaire, *Dionysos*, 48–50.
30 Biebuyck and Mateene, *The Mwindo Epic*.
31 See also D. Biebuyck and K. Mateene, *Anthologie de la littérature orale nyanga* (Brussels, 1970).
32 So J. Kingdon, *East African Mammals*, vol. I (London, 1971), 387.
33 Biebuyck and Mateene, *Anthologie*, 54.
34 D. Biebuyck, *Hero and Chief: Epic Literature from the Banyanga* (Berkeley,

1978).

35 O. Rank, *The Myth of the Birth of the Hero* (New York, 1959); D. B. Redford, 'The literary motif of the exposed child', *Numen* 14 (1967), 209–28.

36 Rehse, *Kiziba*, 133; H. Cory and M. Hartnoll, *Customary Law of the Haya Tribe* (London, 1945), 272.

37 See H. L. Ginsberg, 'Ugaritic myths and legends', in Pritchard (ed.), *Ancient Near Eastern Texts* 129–55; G. R. Driver, *Canaanite Myths and Legends* (Edinburgh, 1956); and, most illuminating, B. Margalit, *A Matter of Life and Death: A Study of the Baal–Mot Epic* (Neukirchen-Vluyn, 1980).

38 J. van der Burgt, *Un grand peuple de l'Afrique orientale* (Bois-le-duc, 1903), 35–6; Meyer, *Die Barundi*, 91–2; Gorju, *Face au royaume hamite*, 105; Simons, 'Coutumes et institutions', 194; Vansina, *Légende du passé*, 75–95; G. Sandrart, *Cours de droit coutumier* (Astrida, 1939), 11; Pagès, *Royaume hamite*, 126; Coupez and Kamanzi, *Récits historiques*, 173–87 and 216–17. Most sources make it clear that they are dealing with popular fantasy or stories about the distant past, and that the succession, at any rate in recent times, had been governed in reality by the normal play of power politics.

39 Simons, 'Coutumes et institutions', 152; de Lacger, *Ruanda*, vol. I, 194; Coupez and Kamanzi, *Récits historiques*, 184–7, 218–21; Vansina, *Légende du passé*, 55–73; Chrétien and Mworoha, 'Les tombeaux', 71.

40 E. Césard, 'Histoire des rois de Kyamtwara', *Anthropos* 26 (1931), 539; Schmidt, *Historical Archaeology*, 291, 313.

41 So L. de Heusch, *Rois nés d'un coeur de vache* (Paris, 1982), 156.

42 Pagès, *Royaume hamite*, 126. Coupez and Kamanzi, *Récits historiques*, 173–87.

43 D'Hertefelt and Coupez, *La royauté sacrée*, 94–153.

44 See below, pp. 199–200.

45 Kagwa, *The Kings of Buganda*, 10–14; and more revealingly Le Veux, *Manuel*, 53–7; and Nsimbi, *Amannya Amaganda*, 38–42.

46 H. M. Stanley, 'How Kimyera became king of Uganda', in his *My Dark Companions and their Strange Stories* (London, 1893), 126–60 (republished in W. H. Whiteley, (ed.), *A Selection of African Prose*, 2 vols. (Oxford, 1964), vol. I, *Oral*, 113–28).

47 Wrigley, 'Kimera'.

48 Biebuyck and Mateene, *The Mwindo Epic*, 68.

49 For this, see J. E. Harrison, *Prolegomena to the Study of Greek Religion* (Cambridge, 1903), 32–76; Jeanmaire, *Dionysos*, 48–53. For the relationship with the *Choephoroe* see R. Fagles, *Aeschylus: The Oresteia* (London, 1976), 42.

50 Stanley, *My Dark Companions*, 133–4.

51 Nsimbi, *Amannya Amaganda*, 52.

52 H. Trevor-Roper, *The Rise of Christian Europe* (London, 1965), 9.

53 Cf. Roberts, *History of the Bemba*, 48. Even more illuminating is Michael G. Kenny, 'The stranger from the lake: a theme in the history of the Lake Victoria shorelands', *Azania* 17 (1982), 2–26.

54 Richard D. Sigwalt, 'The early history of Bushi', unpublished Ph.D. thesis, Wisconsin, 1975, 5, 275–97; Y. Tambwe ya Kasimba, 'Essai d'interprétation du cliché de Kangere', *JAH* 31 (1990), 353–72. An unusual variant is found among the Fipa of western Tanzania: see R. G. Willis, *A State in the Making* (Bloomington, 1981), 15.

55 G. A. Akinola, 'The origin of the Eweka dynasty of Benin: a study in the use and abuse of oral traditions', *Journal of the Historical Society of Nigeria* 8 (1976), 21–35.

56 Kagwa, *The Kings of Buganda*, 16–17.

57 Kagwa, *Mpisa*, 22–36 (= Mandelbaum, *Customs*, 16–18); Roscoe, *The Baganda*, 210–13; S. K. Kakoma, A. M. Kayonga and M. S. Kasolo, *Abakyanjove ab'e Mmamba mu Siiga lya Nankere e Bukerere* (Kampala, 1959), 15–17.

58 Kiwanuka, *History*, 106, admittedly on the authority of Kagwa, *Mpisa*, 7.

59 Roscoe, *The Baganda*, 210. 'When the king had reigned for two or three years, two men were brought before him. One of these he speared, the other was spared ... The next important event in the life of the king was his visit to Nankere.' Still earlier witnesses (Speke, *Journal*, 205; Wilson and Felkin, *Uganda and the Egyptian Sudan*, vol. I, 200) make it clear that there was an interval between the king's accession and his 'coming of age'.

60 Ray, *Myth, Ritual and Kingship*, 46.

61 Simons, 'Coutumes et institutions', 175–6.

62 Willis, *A State in the Making*, 15.

63 E.g. J. Vansina, 'Initiation rituals of the Bushong', *Africa* 25 (1955), 138–53; Turner, *Forest of Symbols*, 151–279; Droogers, *Dangerous Journey*. For a review of the whole subject from a social-anthropological perspective see J. S. La Fontaine, *Initiation*, 2nd edn (Manchester, 1986); also the pregnant essay by James L. Brain, 'Sex, incest and death: initiation rites reconsidered', *CA* 18 (1977), 191–8.

64 J. H. Grisward, 'Ider et le tricéphale', *Annales ESC* 33 (1978) 279–93.

65 Lévi-Strauss, *Origin of Table Manners*, 1–220. See also Geza Róheim, *Animism, Magic and the Divine King* (New York, 1930), 234–6.

66 Kagwa, *The Kings of Buganda*, 18, 20–3.

67 Viaene, 'L'organisation politique des Bahunde', 9. For the general subject see L. de Heusch, *Essais sur le symbolisme de l'inceste royale en Afrique* (Brussels, 1958).

68 Biebuyck and Mateene, *Anthologie*, 28–47.

69 Kagwa, *The Kings of Buganda*, 24.

70 *Ibid.* and Kagwa, *Bika*, 67–72.

71 Le Veux, *Manuel*, 328–42.

72 For Nalubaale as an 'image of natural power' and water as a 'liminal and mediatory element' see Michael G. Kenny, 'The powers of Lake Victoria', *Anthropos* 72 (1977), 713–33.

73 R. P. Ashe, *Chronicles of Uganda* (London, 1894), 96. J. M. Gray, 'Kibuka', *UJ* 20 (1956), 52–71 is a thorough survey of the sources for this popular story. See also J. Roscoe, 'Kibuka, the war-god of the Baganda', *Man* 7 (1907), 161–6.

74 Kagwa, *The Kings of Buganda*, 28.

75 Roscoe, *The Baganda*, 308n. See also F. B. Welbourn, 'Kibuka comes home', *Transition* 2 (1960), 15–17, 19.

76 A. T. Matson, 'The Samson and Delilah story', *UJ* 25 (1961), 217–23.

77 Le Veux, *Manuel*, 330. Cf. Kagwa, *Ngero*, 105–8.

78 Frazer, *Golden Bough*, vol. III, 36.

79 Stuhlmann, *Mit Emin Pasha*, 189.

80 See above, fig. 2.

81 Coupez and Kamanzi, *Récits historiques*, 187.

82 Kagwa, *Mpisa*, 5.

83 Johnson, 'Fixed shrines and spiritual centres'.

84 The material has been reviewed by W. Arens, 'The demise of kings and the meaning of kingship', *Anthropos* 79 (1984), 355–67; and by B. Schnepel, 'Continuity despite and through death: regicide and royal shrines among the Shilluk of southern Sudan', *Africa* 61 (1991), 40–70.

85 D. S. Oyler, 'Nikaung's place in the Shilluk religion', *Sudan Notes and Records* 1 (1918), 286–92; Kagwa, *Mpisa*, 2.

86 Schnepel, 'Continuity', 52. Cf. W. Hofmayr, *Die Schilluk* (Mödling bei Wien, 1912), 14.

87 E. A. Wallis Budge, *Osiris and the Egyptian Resurrection*, 2 vols. (London, 1911), vol. I, vii, 222–30, 234–46, 361–83 and throughout.

88 C. G. Seligman, *The Races of Africa* (London, 1930); and his *Egypt and Negro Africa* (London, 1934).

89 Frankfort, *Kingship and the Gods*, 16; and H. Frankfort, 'Ancient Egyptians and the Hamites', *Man* 49 (1949), 95–6.

90 E.g. Cheikh Anta Diop, *The African Origin of Civilisation: Myth or Reality?* trans. Mercer Cook (New York, 1966).

91 Ray, *Myth, Ritual and Kingship*, 184–99.

92 F.J. Simoons, 'The antiquity of dairying in Asia and Africa', *Geographical Review* 61 (1971), 431–9.

93 Le Veux, *Manuel*, 331.

94 Kagwa, *Bika*, 35–9, 66–7; Roscoe, *The Baganda*, 148–50; Nsimbi, *Amannya Amaganda*, 253–5, 293–4.

95 Stanley, *Through the Dark Continent*, vol. I, 259.

96 Kagwa, *Bika*, 38.

97 J. Jensen, 'Die Erweiterung des Lungenfish-Clans in Buganda', *Sociologus* 19 (1969), 153–66; and his 'Die nsuma-fisch-totem Gruppen auf Buvuma', *Paideuma* 22 (1976), 97–107.

98 Michael G. Kenny, 'The relation of oral history to social structure in South Nyanza, Kenya', *Africa* 47 (1977), 276–85.

99 The importance of the 'maritime' factor in Buganda's development has been noted by many, especially Kiwanuka, *History*, 26; and Kottak, 'Ecological variables'.

100 Kagwa, *Bika*, 35; Nsimbi, *Amannya Amaganda*, 253.

101 Atkinson, 'Myth, history and structural analysis', 43.

8 FRAGMENTS OF HISTORY

1 Kaggwa, *The Kings of Buganda*, 36–7.

2 For this legendary Sudanese monarch see Frazer, *Golden Bough*, vol. III, 15.

3 Roscoe, *The Baganda*, 64–73.

4 Kagwa, *The Kings of Buganda*, 38.

5 Cox, 'Growth and expansion', 153–9.

6 Kottak, 'Ecological variables', 374; Kagwa, *Mpisa*, 39. Bishop Gorju (*Entre le Victoria*, 120) noted as a redeeming feature that the early kings were 'almost monogamous'.

7 Kagwa, *Bika*, 64; Gorju, *Entre le Victoria*, 89.
8 The genus *Cercopithecus* includes many closely related species, several of which are or were present in Buganda. It does not appear that Ganda terminology consistently distinguished them.
9 A. G. Katate and L. Kamugungunu, *Abagabe b'Ankole* [The Kings of Ankole] (Nairobi, 1955), 22.
10 Gorju, *Entre le Victoria*, 80n.
11 Kagwa, *The Kings of Buganda*, 44.
12 Nsimbi, *Amannya Amaganda*, 46–9.
13 Kagwa, *Ngero*, 19.
14 Kagwa, *Mpisa*, 264.
15 Kagwa, *The Kings of Buganda*, 108.
16 *Ibid.*, 47–55.
17 Stuhlmann, *Die Tägebücher von Dr Emin Pasha*, 44–7.
18 Kirwan, 'Place names, proverbs, idioms and songs', 160.
19 *Ibid.*; Nsimbi, *Amannya Amaganda*, 232.
20 Miriam Lichtheim, *Ancient Egyptian Literature*, vol. II (Berkeley and Los Angeles, 1976), 220–1.
21 Budge, *Osiris*, vol. I, 27.
22 Kagwa, *Mpisa*, 19–22.
23 For references on the gods see above chap. 6, n. 5, p. 261.
24 Kagwa, *The Kings of Buganda*, 45.
25 *Ibid.*, 56–7.
26 *Ibid.*, 59; Roscoe, *The Baganda*, 220.
27 I. Berger, 'The Kubandwa religious complex of interlacustrine East Africa: an historical study', Ph.D. thesis, Wisconsin, 1973. An abridged version, with a stronger sociological orientation, was published as *Religion and Resistance; East African Kingdoms in the Precolonial Period* (Tervuren, 1981).
28 Wilson and Felkin, *Uganda and the Egyptian Sudan*, vol. I, 207.
29 Mair, *An African People*, 271.
30 E. C. Lanning, 'Some vessels and beakers from Mubende hill, Uganda', *Man* 53 (1953), 181–2; also his 'Excavations at Mubende hill', *UJ* 30 (1966), 153–63; and his 'The surviving regalia of the Nakaima, Mubende', *UJ* 31 (1967), 210–11; K. Babiiha, 'The Bayaga clan of western Uganda', *UJ* 22 (1958), 125; H. Ingrams, *Uganda* (London, 1960), 183; Berger, 'The Kubandwa religious complex', 87, 100.
31 P. Robertshaw, 'The interlacustrine region: a progress report', *Nyame Akuma* 30 (1988), 37–8.
32 H. B. Lewin, 'Mount Mubende, Buwekula', *Uganda Notes* 9 (1908), 91–2; repr. in *UJ* 13 (1949), 98–100.
33 For this term see V. W. Turner, *Drums of Affliction: A Study of Religious Processes among the Ndembu of Zambia* (Oxford, 1968).
34 Fisher, *Twilight Tales*, 84–98.
35 Wrigley, 'Kimera'.
36 Kagwa, *The Kings of Buganda*, 60–1.
37 Le Veux, *Manuel*, 24–7.
38 Ray, 'Royal shrines', 38; see also his 'Sacred space'. Professor Ray is not responsible for the gloss I have placed on his report.

39 Kagwa, *The Kings of Buganda*, 62–3.
40 O. Schütt, *Reisen im Südwestlichen Becken der Congo* (Berlin, 1881), 79. See J. Vansina, 'The foundation of the kingdom of Kasanje', *JAH* 4 (1963), 359, 363.
41 Kiwanuka, *Kings of Buganda*, 65.
42 Kagwa, *The Kings of Buganda*, 67–8.
43 Kagwa, *Bika*, 29; Nsimbi, *Amannya Amaganda*, 251.
44 P. M. Gulu in *Munno* 6 (1916), 117–9.
45 Stanley, *My Dark Companions*, 133–4.
46 Lawi Sekiti in *Munno* 6 (1916), pp. 6–10.

9 FOREIGN AFFAIRS

1 Nsimbi, *Amannya Amaganda*, 299.
2 R. M. Bere, 'Kungu – the sacred rock', *UJ* 7 (1940), 185–9. There is a photograph in Roscoe, *The Baganda*, 272.
3 F. Lukyn Williams, 'Myth, legend and lore in Uganda', *UJ* 10 (1946), 66.
4 S. W. Baker, *The Albert N'yanza* (London, 1866), vol. II, 428.
5 Nyakatura, *Ky'Abakama ba Bunyoro–Kitara*, 87.
6 Kagwa, *The Kings of Buganda*, 21.
7 Wrigley, 'Kimera'. See above, pp. 139–45.
8 Kiwanuka, *History*, 40–1, 53–63.
9 M. S. M. Kiwanuka, 'The empire of Bunyoro–Kitara: myth or reality?', *Canadian Journal of African Studies* 2 (1968), 27–48; repr. as Makerere Historical Paper No. 1 (Kampala, 1968).
10 Kagwa, *Bika*, 14.
11 *Ibid.*, 17.
12 Nsimbi, *Amannya Amaganda*, 38–44.
13 These comprise two narrative histories, Fisher, *Twilight Tales*, 114–72; and Bikunya, *Ky'Abakama ba Bunyoro*, 34–69; a shorter account by Kagwa, appended to the second and subsequent editions of *The Kings of Buganda* (*Basekabaka b'e Buganda*), 297; and lists reported by George Wilson in Johnston, *Uganda Protectorate*, vol. II, 600; Czekanowski, *Forschungen*, vol. I, 56; Roscoe, *The Northern Bantu*, 16–17; Gorju, *Entre le Victoria*, 61–2 and 64 (report of Fr Torelli); and J. Roscoe, *The Bakitara or Banyoro* (Cambridge, 1923), 88.
14 K. W., 'The kings of Bunyoro–Kitara', *UJ* 3 (1935), 155–60; *UJ* 4 (1936), 75–83; and *UJ* 5 (1937), 53–69.
15 J. W. Nyakatura, *Abakama ba Bunyoro–Kitara* (St Justin, Quebec, 1947), trans. T. Muganwa and ed. G. N. Uzoigwe as *The Anatomy of an African Kingdom: The History of Bunyoro–Kitara* (Garden City, N.Y., 1973).
16 Henige, *The Chronology of Oral Tradition*, 105–14; also his 'K. W.'s Nyoro king-list: oral tradition or applied research?' (paper presented at the 15th annual meeting of the African Studies Association, Philadelphia, 1972); and 'Royal tombs and preternatural ancestors: a devil's advocacy', *Paideuma* 23 (1977), 205–19.
17 Katate and Kamugungunu, *Abagabe b'Ankole*. The standard academic history is S. R. Karugire, *A History of the Kingdom of Nkore in Western Uganda to 1896* (Oxford, 1971).

18 Karugire, *History*, 156–60; O. Mors, *Geschichte der Bahaya* (*Ostafrika*) (Freiburg, 1957), 24, 75; I. K. Katoke, *The Karagwe Kingdom* (Nairobi, 1975), 44–7; Césard, 'Comment les Bahaya interprètent leurs origines', 458–9. In the lake-shore countries 'Cwa ya Runege' tended to become a Ganda raider, no doubt under the influence of nineteenth-century events.

19 Pagès, *Royaume hamite*, 121–3, 554–74; Coupez and Kamanzi, *Récits historiques*, 136–41; and their *Littérature du cour*, 59–61, 176–7.

20 Newbury, 'Rwandan chronology', 163–208.

21 Speke, *Journal*, 203; Baker, *The Albert N'yanza*, vol. II, 427–8.

22 The whole question is reviewed by John Sutton, 'Antecedents', 33–64. See also Robertshaw, 'Archaeological survey'; Reid, 'Ntusi and its hinterland'; and his 'The role of cattle in the Later Iron Age of southern Uganda', unpublished Ph.D. thesis, Cambridge, 1991.

23 E. I. Steinhart, 'From "empire" to state: the emergence of the kingdom of Bunyoro–Kitara, c.1350–1890', in Claessen and Skalnik (eds.), *The Study of the State*, 353–70.

24 Posnansky, 'Bigo'. See Sutton, 'Antecedents', 48–52.

25 E. C. Lanning, 'Ancient earthworks in western Uganda', *UJ* 17 (1953), 51–62; see also his 'The Munsa earthworks', *UJ* 19 (1955), 51–62; and his 'The earthworks at Kibengo', *UJ* 24 (1960), 183–96.

26 E. C. Lanning, 'Masaka hill, an ancient centre of worship', *UJ* 18 (1954), 24–30; I. Berger and C. A. Buchanan, 'The Cwezi cults and the history of western Uganda', in J. T. Gallagher (ed.), *East African Cultural History* (Syracuse, NY, 1976), 43–78; E. R. Kamuhangire, J. Meredith and P. Robertshaw, 'Masaka hill revisited', *Nyame Akuma* 39 (1993), 57–60.

27 Babiiha, 'The Bayaga clan'; Berger and Buchanan 'Cwezi cults', 56–7.

28 P. Robertshaw, 'Recent archaeological surveys in western Uganda', *Nyame Akuma* 36 (1991).

29 C. C. Wrigley, 'The problem of the Lwo', *HA* 8 (1981), 219–46.

30 Steinhart, 'From "empire" to state'; E. I. Steinhart, 'The kingdoms of the march', in Webster (ed.), *Chronology, Migration and Drought*, 189–213.

31 K. W., 'Kings', *UJ* 4 (1936), 78; cf. Nyakatura, *Ky'Abakama ba Bunyoro–Kitara*, 67–8.

32 See the discussions by J. Sykes, 'The eclipse at Biharwe', *UJ* 23 (1959), 44–50; and J. M. Gray, 'The solar eclipse in Ankole in 1492', *UJ* 27 (1963), 217–21.

33 Katate and Kamugungunu, *Abagabe b'Ankole* vol. I, 60.

34 Fisher, *Twilight Tales*, 137–8.

35 Roscoe, *The Baganda*, 177.

10 THE MAKING OF THE STATE

1 Kagwa, *The Kings of Buganda*, 69–76; Gorju, *Entre le Victoria*, 140.

2 Kagwa, *The Kings of Buganda*, 64–5; Viktoro Katula in *Munno* 2 (1912), 110–12.

3 Kagwa, *The Kings of Buganda*, 69–70; Nsimbi, *Amannya Amaganda*, 302–5.

4 Nyakatura, *ky'Abakama ba Bunyoro–Kitara*, 79.

5 Kagwa, *The Kings of Buganda*, 71; Tobi Kizito in *Munno* 6 (1916), 31–3.

6 Kaggwa, *The Kings of Buganda*, 77; Kasirye, *Abateregga*, 28.

7 For references to these see above, p. 256n. 23.
8 Kagwa, *Mpisa*, 35.
9 Nsimbi, *Amannya Amaganda*, 298.
10 Tobi Kizito in *Munno* 7 (1917), 22–6.
11 Kagwa, *The Kings of Buganda*, 82–9.
12 *Ibid.*, 86–7; Nsimbi, *Amannya Amaganda*, 197–9; Stanley, *Through the Dark Continent*, vol. I, 282; S. K. B. Mukasa, 'A legendary hero of Buganda', *UJ* 7 (1939), 49.
13 A. Aliwali in *Munno* 4 (1914), 38–40.
14 Kagwa, *The Kings of Buganda*, 90–1; E. C. Lanning. 'Notes on the history of Koki', *UJ* 23 (1959), 162–70.
15 A. Aliwali, in *Munno* 2 (1912) 40–2.
16 Kabuga, 'Genealogy'.
17 Nyakatura, *Ky'Abakama ba Bunyoro–Kitara*, 86–7. Strangely enough, Kagwa does not mention this battle.
18 A. Aliwali in *Munno* 4 (1914), 38–40, 57–8. Cf. Kasirye, *Abateregga*, 39.
19 Kagwa, *The Kings of Buganda*, 91–4.
20 *Ibid.*, 94–6.
21 R. Oliver, 'The Baganda and the Bakonjo', *UJ* 18 (1954), 31–3. Cf. J. Roscoe, *The Bagesu and Other Tribes of the Uganda Protectorate* (Cambridge, 1924), 159.
22 Kenny, 'Relation of oral history to social structure'. See also an unpublished paper by Henry Ayot, 'The eastern expansion of the Abakunta', Department of History, University of Nairobi, 1971/2.
23 Miti, 'History of Buganda', 39.
24 Nsimbi, *Amannya Amaganda*, 205.
25 But see Elizabeth Colson, 'African society at the time of the Scramble', in L. H. Gann and P. Duignan (eds.), *Colonialism in Africa*, vol. I (Cambridge, 1969), 27–65.
26 A. Isaacman, 'The origin, formation and early history of the Chikunda of south central Africa', *JAH* 13 (1972), 443–61.
27 Robert E. Schechter, 'A propos the drunken king: cosmology and history', in Miller (ed.), *The African Past Speaks*, 114–15.
28 Jack Goody, *Technology, Tradition and the State in Africa* (London, 1971); Robin Law, *The Horse in West African History* (Oxford, 1980).
29 Kagwa, *The Kings of Buganda*, 96–9.
30 Kagwa, *Mpisa*, 217. Cf. Wright, *Buganda in the Heroic Age*, 2.
31 Kagwa, *Mpisa*, 72.
32 Southwold, 'Succession to the throne of Buganda'; A. I. Richards, 'African kings and their royal relatives', *JRAI* 91 (1961), 135–149.
33 Kagwa, *The Kings of Buganda*, 141–6; B. M. Zimbe, *Buganda ne Kabaka* (Kampala, 1939), 21.
34 Grant, *A Walk Across Africa*, 224.
35 Speke, *Journal*, 205.
36 See the discussion by M. L. Nsibirwa and J. M. Gray, *UJ* 2 (1935), 84–5.
37 Apter, *Political Kingdom*, 108.
38 J. M. Gray, notes appended to A. M. K. Mayanja, 'Chronology of Buganda, 1800–1907, from Kagwa's Ebika', *UJ* 16 (1952), 148–58.
39 A. Aliwali in *Munno* 4 (1914), 57–8.

11 REFLECTIONS

1 L. A. Fallers, 'Social stratification and economic processes', in M. J. Herskovits and M. Harwitz (eds.), *Economic Transition in Africa* (London, 1964), 113–32.
2 P. S. Garlake, *Great Zimbabwe* (London, 1973).
3 R. W. Beachey, 'The East African ivory trade in the nineteenth century', *JAH* 8 (1967), 269–90; Abdul Sheriff, *Slaves, Spices and Ivory in Zanzibar* (London and Dar es Salaam, 1987), 185–200.
4 Kagwa, *The Kings of Buganda*, 99.
5 *Ibid.*
6 Eugenia W. Herbert, *Red Gold of Africa: Copper in Precolonial History and Culture* (Madison, 1984), 112.
7 John Tosh, 'The northern interlacustrine region', in R. Gray and D. Birmingham (eds.), *Pre-colonial African Trade*, (London, 1970), 102–18; G. W. Hartwig, 'The Victoria Nyanza as a trade route in the nineteenth century', *JAH* 11 (1970), 535–52; Kenny, 'The powers of Lake Victoria'; and Michael G. Kenny, 'Pre-colonial trade in eastern Lake Victoria', *Azania* 14 (1979), 97–107; Waller, 'Traditional economy'.
8 Kottak, 'Ecological variables', 357.
9 Wrigley, 'Buganda: an outline economic history'; and 'The changing economic structure'.
10 Cf. Basil Davidson, *The Black Man's Burden: Africa and the Curse of the Nation-State* (London, 1992).
11 Robert L. Carneiro, 'A theory of the origin of the state', *Science* 169 (1970), 733–8; also his 'Political expansion as an expression of the principle of competitive exclusion', in R. Cohen and E. R. Service (eds.), *The Origin of the State* (Philadelphia, 1978), 205–23; H. S. Lewis, 'Warfare and the origin of the state: another formulation', in Claessen and Skalnik (eds.), *The Study of the State*, 112–22.
12 Wrigley, 'Bananas in Buganda'.
13 It is rendered less plausible by the linguistic arguments of David L. Schoenbrun, 'Cattle herds and banana gardens: the historical geography of the western Great Lakes region', *AAR* 11 (1993), 39–72.
14 A similar point was made by Kottak, 'Ecological variables', 378. Every time I turn back to that impressive essay I am more dismayed to see how little I have added to his analysis.
15 This is the cautiously offered conclusion of A. I. Richards and P. Reining, 'Report on fertility surveys in Buganda and Buhaya, 1952', in F. Lorimer (ed.), *Culture and Human Fertility* (Paris: UNESCO, 1954), 403. Sir Harry Johnston noted as early as 1901 that 'from some cause or other the women of (Buganda) have become very poor breeders' (*Uganda Protectorate*, vol. II, 641.)
16 Kagwa, *Mpisa*, 264.
17 Waller, 'Traditional economy'. In 1886 the Ganda army suffered a heavy defeat at the hands of Bunyoro.
18 Rusch, *Klassen und Staat*, 108–14; M. Twaddle, 'The ending of slavery in Buganda', in S. Miers and R. Roberts (eds.), *The End of Slavery in Africa* (Madison, 1988), 119–49.
19 Nsimbi, *Amannya Amaganda*, 30.
20 Twaddle, 'Ending of slavery', 141.

21 C. Chaillé-Long, *Central Africa* (London, 1876), 106.
22 R.P. Ashe, *Two Kings of Uganda* (London, 1889), 136–47.
23 Speke, *Journal*, 242.
24 *Ibid.*, 289, 316.
25 H. Mukasa, 'Some notes on the reign of Mutesa', *UJ* 2 (1934), 65–70.
26 Kagwa, *The Kings of Buganda*, 149–52.
27 J. M. Gray, 'Mutesa of Buganda', *UJ* 1 (1934), 22–49.
28 I. Wilks, *Asante in the Nineteenth Century: The Structure and Evolution of a Political Order* (Cambridge, 1975), 594–5, 777.
29 Robin Law, '"My head belongs to the king": on the political and religious significance of decapitation in pre-colonial Dahomey', *JAH* 30 (1989), 399–415.
30 Simons, 'Coutumes et institutions', 195–6.
31 W. Soyinka, *Death and the King's Horseman* (London, 1975).
32 Kagwa, *Mpisa*, 141–52 (= Mandelbaum, *Customs*, 79–82).
33 Nsimbi, *Amannya Amaganda*, 260.
34 Wilson and Felkin, *Uganda and the Egyptian Sudan*, vol. I, 150.
35 Kagwa, *Basekabaka*, 211–32; H. H. Austin, *With Macdonald in Uganda* (London, 1903), 53, 90–105.
36 Gale, 'Mutesa I – was he a god?', 75–6.
37 Ray, *Myth, Ritual and Kingship*, 206.
38 de Heusch, *Why Marry Her?*, 25.
39 J. W. Harrison, *A. M. Mackay, Pioneer Missionary of the Church Missionary Society to Uganda* (London, 1890), 185.
40 Mandelbaum, *Customs*, 81.
41 Nsimbi, *Amannya Amaganda*, 126.
42 Kagwa, *The Kings of Buganda*, 82–4.
43 *Ibid.*, 110–11.
44 *Ibid.*, 118–19.
45 Nsimbi, *Amannya Amaganda*, 141–2.
46 Harrison, *A. M. Mackay*, 166–7; Zimbe, *Buganda ne Kabaka*, 54.
47 *CSSH* 30 (1988), 595–612.
48 Nsimbi, *Amannya Amaganda*, 104, 134.
49 A. B. K. Kasozi, 'Why did the Baganda adopt foreign religions in the nineteenth century?', *Mawazo* 4 (1975), 129–52.
50 See for instance Philippe, *Au coeur de l'Afrique*, 27.
51 John C. Yoder, 'The quest for Kintu and the search for peace: mythology and morality in nineteenth-century Buganda', *HA* 15 (1988), 363–76.
52 Sagan, *At the Dawn of Tyranny*.
53 *Ibid.*, 383.
54 *Ibid.*, 364.
55 *Ibid.*, xix–xxi.
56 T. C. McCaskie, 'Accumulation, wealth and belief in Asante history', *Africa* 53 (1983), 24–40.
57 Andrzej Zakaczowski, 'Change and development: problems of sociology of religion in Africa', *Africana Bulletin* 25 (1976), 115–25.
58 Tosh, 'The northern interlacustrine region', 118.

Bibliography

Abrahamsson, H. *The Origins of Death: Studies in African Mythology*, Uppsala, 1951.

Achte, A. 'Histoire des rois baganda', Kampala, 1896 (MS in archives of the Pères Blancs, Rome).

Ackerman, R. *J. G. Frazer and the Cambridge Ritualists*, New York, 1991.

Adler, A. *La mort est le masque du roi*, Paris, 1982.

Akinola, G. A. 'The origin of the Eweka dynasty of Benin: a study in the use and abuse of oral traditions', *Journal of the Historical Society of Nigeria* 8 (1976), 21–35.

Apter, D. A. *The Political Kingdom in Uganda*, Princeton, 1961.

Arens, W. 'The demise of kings and the meaning of kingship', *Anthropos* 79 (1984), 355–67.

Asad, Talal (ed.) *Anthropology and the Colonial Encounter*, London, 1973.

Ashe, R. P. *Two Kings of Uganda*, London, 1889.

Chronicles of Uganda, London, 1894.

Atkinson, R. R. 'The traditions of the early kings of Buganda: myth, history and structural analysis', *HA* 2 (1975), 17–57.

Babiiha, K. 'The Bayaga clan of western Uganda', *UJ* 22 (1958), 123–30.

Baker, S. W. *The Albert N'yanza*, 2 vols., London, 1866.

Ismailia, 2 vols., London, 1879.

Baskerville, R. *The King of the Snakes, and Other Stories*, London, 1922.

The Flame Tree, London, 1925.

Baumann, H. *Schöpfung und Urzeit im Mythus der Afrikanischen Völker*, Berlin, 1936.

Beachey, R. W. 'The East African ivory trade in the nineteenth century', *JAH* 8 (1967), 269–90.

Beattie, John *The Nyoro State*, Oxford, 1971.

Berger, Iris 'The Kubandwa religious complex of interlacustrine East Africa: an historical study', Ph.D. thesis, University of Wisconsin, 1973.

'Deities, dynasties and oral tradition: the history and legend of the Abacwezi', in Miller (ed.), *The African Past Speaks*, 61–81.

Religion and Resistance: East African Kingdoms in the Precolonial Period, Tervuren, 1981.

Berger, Iris and Buchanan, Carole A. 'The Cwezi cults and the history of western Uganda', in *East African Cultural History*, ed. J. T. Gallagher, Syracuse, N.Y., 1976.

Biebuyck, D. *Hero and Chief: Epic Literature from the Banyanga*, Berkeley, 1978.
and K. Mateene *The Mwindo Epic of the Banyanga*, Berkeley, 1969.
Anthologie de la littérature orale nyanga, Brussels, 1970.
Bikunya, P. *Ky'Abakama ba Bunyoro* [The Kings of Bunyoro], London, 1927.
Boston, J. S. 'The hunter in Igala legends of origin', *Africa* 34 (1964), 116–26.
Brain, James L. 'Sex, incest and death: initiation rites reconsidered', *CA* 18 (1977), 191–8.
Brown, Richard 'Passages in the life of a white anthropologist', *JAH* 20 (1979), 525–41.
Buchanan, Carole A. 'Perceptions of interaction in the East African interior: the Kitara complex', *IJAHS* 11 (1978), 410–28.
Budge, E. A. Wallis *Osiris and the Egyptian Resurrection*, 2 vols. [London, 1911], New York, 1973.
Burgt, J. van der *Un grand peuple de l'Afrique orientale*, Bois-le-duc, 1903.
Campbell, Joseph *The Hero with a Thousand Faces*, Princeton, 1949.
The Masks of God, vol. I, *Primitive Mythology*, New York, 1959.
Carneiro, Robert L. 'A theory of the origin of the state', *Science* 169 (1970), 733–38.
'Political expansion as an expression of the principle of competitive exclusion', in *The Origin of the State*, ed. R. Cohen and E. R. Service, Philadelphia, 1978.
Cerny, J. *Ancient Egyptian Religion*, London, 1952.
Césard, E. 'Comment les Bahaya interprètent leurs origines', *Anthropos* 22 (1927), 447–53.
'Histoire des rois de Kyamtwara', *Anthropos* 26 (1931), 533–43.
'Le Muhaya', *Anthropos* 32 (1937), 32–7.
Chadwick, H. M. and Chadwick, N. K. *The Growth of Literature*, vol. III, Cambridge, 1940.
Chaillé-Long, C. *Central Africa*, London, 1876.
Chrétien, J.-P. 'Le Buha à la fin du xix° siècle', *Etudes historiques africaines* 7 (1975), 9–30.
'Du hirsute au hamite: la variation du cycle de Ntare Rushatsi', *HA* 8 (1981), 3–41.
'L'empire des Bacwezi: la construction d'un imaginaire géopolitique', *Annales ESC* 40 (1985), 1335–77.
Chrétien, J.-P. and Mworoha, E. 'Les tombeaux des bami du Burundi', *Cahiers d'études africaines* 10 (1970), 40–70.
Chrétien de Troyes, *Perceval, the Story of the Grail*, trans. N. Bryant, Cambridge: D. S. Brewer, 1982.
Claessen, H. J. M. and Skalnik, P. (eds.) *The Study of the State*, The Hague, 1981.
Clark, J. D. and Brandt, S. A. (eds.) *From Hunters to Farmers*, Los Angeles/Berkeley, 1984.
Clist, B. 'A critical appraisal of the chronological framework of the Early Urewe Iron Age industry', *Muntu* 6 (1987), 35–62.
Cohen, D. W. 'A survey of interlacustrine chronology', *JAH* 11 (1970), 177–99.
The Historical Tradition of Busoga: Mukama and Kintu, Oxford, 1972.
Colson, Elizabeth 'African society at the time of the Scramble', in *Colonialism in Africa*, ed. L. H. Gann and P. Duignan, 4 vols., vol. I, Cambridge, 1969.
Cory, H. and Hartnoll, M. *Customary Law of the Haya Tribe*, London, 1945.
Coupez, A. and Kamanzi, T. *Récits historiques rwanda*, Tervuren, 1962.

Littérature du cour au Rwanda, Oxford, 1971.
Cox, A. H. 'The growth and expansion of Buganda', *UJ* 14 (1950), 153–9.
Crazzolara, J. P. 'The Lwoo people', *UJ* 5 (1937), 1–21.
The Lwoo, part I, Verona, 1950.
Cunningham, J. F. *Uganda and its Peoples*, London, 1905.
Czekanowski, Jan *Forschungen im Nil-Kongo Zwischengebiet*, 6 vols., Leipzig, 1917.
Davidson, Basil *The Black Man's Burden: Africa and the Curse of the Nation-State*, London, 1992.
Dècle, L. *Three Years in Savage Africa*, London, 1898.
Desmedt, Christine 'Poteries anciennes décorées à la roulette dans la région des Grands Lacs', *AAR* 9 (1991), 161–96.
Diop, Cheikh Anta *The African Origin of Civilisation: Myth or Reality?*, trans. Mercer Cook, New York, 1966.
Douglas, Mary 'Animals in Lele religious thought', *Africa* 27 (1957), 46–58.
Driver, G. R. *Canaanite Myths and Legends*, Edinburgh, 1956.
Droogers, A. *The Dangerous Journey: Symbolic Aspects of Boys' Initiation Rites among the Wagenia of Kisangani*, Zaire and London, 1980.
Dumézil, G. *Horace et les Curiaces*, Paris, 1942.
Les dieux des Indo-européens, Paris, 1951.
Ehret, C. *Ethiopians and East Africans: The Problem of Contacts*, Nairobi, 1974.
'The East African interior', in *General History of Africa*, vol. III, *Africa from the Seventh to the Eleventh Century*, ed. M. Elfasi and I. Hrbek, Paris: UNESCO, 1988.
Ehret, C. and Posnansky, M. *The Archaeological and Linguistic Reconstruction of East African History*, Los Angeles, 1982.
Eliade, M. *The Myth of the Eternal Return*, New York, 1954.
Birth and Rebirth, New York, 1958.
Evans-Pritchard, E. E. *The Divine Kingship of the Shilluk of the Nilotic Sudan*, the Frazer Lecture for 1948, repr. in *Essays in Social Anthropology*, ed. E. E. Evans-Pritchard, London, 1962.
Fallers, L. A. 'Despotism, status culture and social mobility in an African kingdom' *CSSH* 2 (1959), 4–32.
'Social stratification and economic processes', in *Economic Transition in Africa*, ed. M. J. Herskovits and M. Harwitz, London, 1964.
Fallers, L. A. (ed.) *The King's Men*, London, 1964.
Fallers, M. C. *The Eastern Lacustrine Bantu*, London, 1960.
Faupel, J. F. *African Holocaust*, London and New York, 1962.
Feeley-Harnik, G. 'Issues in divine kingship', *Annual Review of Anthropology* 14 (1985), 273–313.
Felkin, R. W. 'Notes on the Waganda tribe', *Proceedings of the Royal Society of Edinburgh* 13 (1885/6), 699–770.
Finley, M. I. 'Myth, memoir and history', *History and Theory* 4 (1965), 281–302.
The World of Odysseus, 2nd edn, Harmondsworth, 1979.
Fisher, Ruth *Twilight Tales of the Black Baganda*, London, n.d. [1911]; reissued with an introduction by M. Posnansky, London, 1965.
Fontenrose, J. *The Ritual Theory of Myth*, Berkeley, 1960.
Frankfort, H. *Kingship and the Gods*, Chicago, 1948.

'Ancient Egyptians and the Hamites', *Man* 49 (1949), 95–6.
Frazer, J. G. *The Golden Bough*, 3rd edn, 12 vols., London, 1911.
 Folklore in the Old Testament, vol. I, London, 1918.
Frobenius, L. *Atlantis*, vol. XII, Jena, 1928.
Gale, H. P. 'Mutesa I – was he a god?', *UJ* 20 (1954), 72–87.
Garlake, P. S. *Great Zimbabwe*, London, 1973.
 The Kingdoms of Africa, Oxford, 1978.
Ginsberg, H. L. 'Ugaritic myths and legends', in Pritchard (ed.), *Ancient Near Eastern Texts*.
Goody, Jack *Technology, Tradition and the State in Africa*, London, 1971.
Gorju, J. *Entre le Victoria, l'Albert et l'Edouard*, Rennes, 1920.
 Face au royaume hamite de Ruanda: le royaume frère de l'Urundi, Brussels, 1938.
Grant, J. A. *A Walk across Africa*, London, 1864.
Gray, J. M. 'Mutesa of Buganda', *UJ* 1 (1934), 22–49.
 'The early history of Buganda', *UJ* 2 (1935), 259–71.
 'Kibuka', *UJ* 20 (1956), 52–71.
 'The diaries of Emin Pasha – extracts', *UJ* 25 (1961), 1–10, 149–70; *UJ* 26 (1962), 72–95.
 'The solar eclipse in Ankole in 1492', *UJ* 27 (1963), 217–21.
Greenberg, J. H. *The Languages of Africa*, 2nd edn, Bloomington, 1966.
Grisward, J. H. 'Ider et le tricéphale', *Annales ESC* 33 (1978), 279–93.
Guthrie, M. *Comparative Bantu*, 4 vols., Farnborough, 1967–71.
Gutkind, P. C. W. *The Royal Capital of Buganda*, The Hague, 1973.
Haaland, R. *Socio-economic Differentiation in the Neolithic Sudan*, BAR international series 350, Oxford, 1987.
 'Fish, pots and grain: early and mid-holocene adaptations in the central Sudan', *AAR* 10 (1992), 43–64.
Haaland, R. and Shinnie, P. (eds.) *African Iron Working: Ancient and Traditional*, Oslo and London, 1985.
Harrison, J. E. *Prolegomena to the Study of Greek Religion*, Cambridge, 1903.
 Themis: A Study of the Social Origins of Greek Religion, London, 1911.
Harrison, J. W. *A. M. Mackay, Pioneer Missionary of the Church Missionary Society to Uganda*, London, 1890.
Hartwig, G. W. 'The Victoria Nyanza as a trade route in the nineteenth century', *JAH* 11 (1970), 535–52.
Hayden, Ilse, *Symbol and Privilege: The Ritual Context of British Royalty*, Tucson, 1987.
Henderson, I. *Myth in the New Testament*, London, 1951.
Henige, David P. 'KW's Nyoro king-list: oral tradition or applied research?', paper presented to the fifteenth annual meeting of the African Studies Association, Philadelphia, 1972.
 The Chronology of Oral Tradition: Quest for a Chimera, Oxford, 1974.
 'Royal tombs and preternatural ancestors: a devil's advocacy', *Paideuma* 23 (1977), 205–19.
 '"The disease of writing": Ganda and Nyoro kinglists in a newly literate world', in Miller (ed.), *The African Past Speaks*, 240–61.
 'Truths yet unborn? Oral traditions as a casualty of culture contact', *JAH* 23 (1982), 395–412.

Herbert, Eugenia W. *Red Gold of Africa: Copper in Precolonial History and Culture*, Madison, 1984.

Hertefelt, M. d' *Les clans de l'ancien Rwanda*, Tervuren, 1971.

Hertefelt, M. and Coupez, A. *La royauté sacrée de l'ancien Rwanda*, Tervuren, 1964.

Heusch, Luc de *Essais sur le symbolisme de l'inceste royale en Afrique*, Brussels, 1958.

Le roi ivre, ou l'origine de l'état, Paris, 1972; trans. Roy Willis as *The Drunken King*, Bloomington, 1982.

Rois nés d'un coeur de vache, Paris, 1982.

Why Marry Her?, Cambridge, 1981.

Hocart, A. M. *Kingship*, London, 1927.

Kings and Councillors, Cairo, 1936; new edn Chicago, 1970.

The Life-giving Myth and other essays, London, 1952.

Hooke, S. H. (ed.) *Myth, Ritual and Kingship*, Oxford, 1958.

Huffman, T. N. 'The rise and fall of Great Zimbabwe', *JAH* 13 (1972), 353–66.

Hurel, E. *La poésie chez les primitifs*, Brussels, 1922.

Irstam, Tor *The King of Ganda*, Uppsala, 1944.

Isaacman, A. 'The origin, formation and early history of the Chikunda of south central Africa', *JAH* 13 (1972), 443–61.

Jacobs, J. 'Het epos van Kudukese', *Afrika-Tervuren* 9 (1963), 33–6.

Jeanmaire, H. *Dionysos*, Paris, 1951/1971.

Jensen, A. E. *Myth and Cult among Primitive Peoples*, New York, 1963.

Jensen, J. 'Die Erweiterung des Lungenfisch-Clans in Buganda', *Sociologus* 19 (1969), 153–66.

'Die Nsuma-Fisch-Totem Gruppen auf Buvuma', *Paideuma* 22 (1976), 97–107.

'Mythen und historische Legenden von Ostafrika', *Paideuma* 22 (1976), 170–88.

Johnson, D. H. 'Fixed shrines and spiritual centres in the Upper Nile valley', *Azania* 25 (1990), 41–50.

Johnston, H. H. *The Uganda Protectorate*, 2 vols., London, 1902.

Jones, G. and Jones, T. (eds.) *The Mabinogion*, 2nd edn., London, 1974.

Kabuga, C. E. S. 'The genealogy of Kabaka Kintu and the early Bakabaka of Buganda', *UJ* 27 (1963), 205–16.

Kagame, A. 'Le code ésotérique de la dynastie du Rwanda', *Zaire* 1 (1947), 363–86.

La poésie dynastique du Rwanda, Brussels, 1951.

La notion de génération appliquée à la généalogie et à l'histoire du Rwanda, Brussels, 1959.

Kagwa, A. *Bakabaka b'e Buganda* [The Kings of Buganda], London, 1901; 2nd edn. published as *Basekabaka b'e Buganda* [The Former Kings of Buganda], London, 1912; ed. and partial trans.

M. S. M. Kiwanuka as *The Kings of Buganda*, Nairobi and Kampala, 1971.

Ngero za Baganda [Ganda Tales], London, 1902.

Mpisa za Baganda, Kampala, 1905; 3rd edn, London 1918; partial trans. E. B. Kalibala as *The Customs of the Baganda*, ed. M. Mandelbaum, New York, 1934.

Bika bya Baganda [The Clans of Buganda], London, 1912.

Kantorowicz, E. H. *The King's Two Bodies*, Princeton, 1957.

Karp, I. and Bird, C. S. (eds.), *Explorations in African Systems of Thought*. Bloomington, 1980.

Karugire, S. R. *A History of the Kingdom of Nkore in Western Uganda to 1896*, Oxford, 1971.

Kasirye, J. S. *Obulamu bwa Stanislas Mugwanya* [The Life of Stanislas Mugwanya], Dublin, 1962.

Abateregga ku Namulondo ya Buganda [Sovereigns of the Throne of Buganda], London, 1971.

Kasozi, A. B. K. 'Why did the Baganda adopt foreign religions in the nineteenth century?', *Mawazo* 4 (1975), 129–52.

Katate, A. G. and Kamugungunu, L. *Abagabe b'Ankole* [The Kings of Ankole], vol. I, Nairobi, 1955.

Katoke, I. K. *The Karagwe Kingdom*, Nairobi, 1975.

Katumba, Ahmed and Welbourn, F. B. 'Muslim martyrs of Buganda', *UJ* 28 (1964), 151–63.

Kenny, Michael G. 'The powers of Lake Victoria', *Anthropos* 72 (1977), 713–33.

'The relation of oral history to social structure in South Nyanza, Kenya', *Africa* 47 (1977), 276–85.

'Precolonial trade in eastern Lake Victoria', *Azania* 14 (1979), 97–107.

'The stranger from the lake: a theme in the history of the Lake Victoria shorelands', *Azania* 17 (1982), 2–26.

'Mutesa's crime: hubris and the control of African kings', *CSSH* 30 (1988), 595–612.

Kerenyi, C. *Dionysos, Archetypal Image of Indestructible Life*, Princeton, 1976.

Kingdon, J. *East African Mammals*, vol. I, London, 1971.

Kirwan, B. 'Place names, proverbs, idioms and songs', in *Prelude to East African History*, ed. M. Posnansky, London, 1966, 159–66.

Kiwanuka, M. S. M. 'The empire of Bunyoro–Kitara: myth or reality?', *Canadian Journal of African Studies* 2 (1968), 27–48 (also Makerere Historical Paper No. 1, Kampala, 1968).

A History of Buganda, from the Earliest Times to 1900, London, 1971.

(see also Kagwa, A.)

Kopytoff, I. *The African Frontier: The Reproduction of Traditional African Societies*, Bloomington, 1987.

Kottak, C. P. 'Ecological variables in the origin and evolution of African states: the Buganda example', *CSSH* 14 (1972), 351–80.

Krzyzaniak, L. 'New light on early food production in the central Sudan', *JAH* 19 (1978), 159–72.

'Early farming in the Middle Nile basin: recent discoveries at Kadero', *Antiquity* 65 (1991), 515–32.

Krzyzaniak, L. and Kobusiewicz, M. (eds.) *Late Prehistory of the Nile Basin and Sahara*, Poznań, 1989.

Kuper, Adam, *Anthropology and Anthropologists: The British School, 1922–72*, 2nd edn, London, 1983.

Kuper, Hilda, *An African Aristocracy*, London, 1947.

K. W. [Tito Winyi IV], 'The kings of Bunyoro–Kitara', *UJ* 3 (1935), 155–60; *UJ* 4 (1936), 75–83; and *UJ* 5 (1937), 53–69.

Lacger, L. de *Ruanda*, 2 vols., Namur, 1939: vol. I, *Le Ruanda ancien*.

La Fontaine, J. S. *Initiation*, 2nd edn, Manchester, 1986.

Lagercrantz, S. *Contributions to the Ethnography of Africa*, Lund, 1950.

Lanning, E. C. 'Some vessels and beakers from Mubende hill, Uganda', *Man* 53 (1953), 181–2.

'Ancient earthworks in western Uganda', *UJ* 17 (1953), 51–62.

'Masaka hill, an ancient centre of worship', *UJ* 18 (1954), 24–30.

'Excavations at Mubende hill', *UJ* 30 (1966), 153–63.

'The surviving regalia of the Nakaima, Mubende', *UJ* 31 (1967), 210–11.

Law, Robin *The Horse in West African History*, Oxford, 1980.

'"My head belongs to the king": on the political and religious significance of decapitation in pre-colonial Dahomey', *JAH* 30 (1989), 399–415.

Laye, C. *L'enfant noir*, Paris, 1953.

Leach, E. R. *Genesis as Myth, and Other Essays*, London, 1969.

Leach, E. R. and Aycock, D. A. *Structuralist Interpretation of Biblical Myth*, Cambridge, 1983.

Le Veux, R. P. *Manuel de langue luganda*, Algiers, 1914 (rev. edn of Livinhac and Denoit).

Lévi-Strauss, C. *Mythologiques*. 4 vols., Paris, 1964–71.

  The Raw and the Cooked, trans. J. and D. Weightman, London, 1970.

  From Honey to Ashes, trans. J. and D. Weightman, London, 1973.

  The Origin of Table Manners, London, 1978.

  The Naked Man, trans. J. and D. Weightman, London, 1981.

Lévi-Strauss, C. and Erébon, D. *De près et de loin*, Paris, 1988.

Lewin, H. B. 'Mount Mubende, Buwekula', *Uganda Notes* 9 (1908), 91–2; repr. in *UJ* 13 (1949), 98–100.

Lewis, H. S. 'Warfare and the origin of the state' in Claessen and Skalnik, *The Study of the State*, 201–22.

Lichtheim, Miriam *Ancient Egyptian Literature*, 2 vols., Berkeley/Los Angeles, 1976.

Livinhac, L. and Denoit, C. *Manuel de langue luganda*, 2nd edn, Einsiedln, 1894 (see also Le Veux).

Low, D. A. 'Converts and martyrs in Buganda', in D. A. Low, *Buganda in Modern History*, Berkeley/Los Angeles, 1971.

Lush, A. J. 'Kiganda drums', *UJ* 4 (1937), 1–25.

Lwamgira, F. X. 'History of Kiziba' (typescript translation by E. R. Kamuhangire, Makerere University, 1965.)

Mabinogion, see Jones

McCaskie, T. C. 'Accumulation, wealth and belief in Asante history', *Africa* 53 (1983), 24–40.

Macdonald, J. R. L. *Soldiering and Surveying in British East Africa*, London, 1897.

MacGaffey, W. 'Oral tradition in central Africa', *IJAHS* 7 (1974), 417–26.

  'Kingship', in *Encyclopaedia of Religion*, ed. M. Eliade, vol. VIII, New York, 1987, 325–7.

Mair, L. P. *An African People in the Twentieth Century*, London, 1934.

Malory, Thomas *Le Morte d'Arthur*, London: Everyman, 1906.

Mandelbaum, M. (ed.) *The Customs of the Baganda*, partial trans. by E. B. Kalibala of A. Kagwa, *Mpisa za Baganda*, New York, 1934.

Maquet, J. *Les civilisations noires*, Paris, 1962.

Margalit, B. *A Matter of Life and Death: A Study of the Baal–Mot Epic*, Neukirchen-Vluyn, 1980.

Matson, A. T. 'The Samson and Delilah story', *UJ* 25 (1961), 217–23.

Mayanja, A. M. K. 'Chronology of Buganda, 1800–1907, from Kagwa's Ebika', *UJ* 16 (1952), 148–58, with notes by J. M. Gray.

Mbiti, J. S. *African Religions and Philosophy*, London, 1969.

Concepts of God in Africa, London, 1970.

Meyer, H. *Die Barundi*, Leipzig, 1916.

Miller, J. C. (ed.) *The African Past Speaks*, Folkestone, 1980.

Miti, James 'A History of Buganda' (typescript translation in School of Oriental and African Studies, London, 1939).

Mors, O. *Geschichte der Bahaya (Ostafrika)*, Freiburg: Micro-bibliotheka Anthropos, No. 25, 1957.

Mukasa, H. 'Some notes on the reign of Mutesa', *UJ* 1 (1934), 116–33; and *UJ* 2 (1935), 65–70.

Simuda Nyuma [Progress], London, 1938.

Muller, J.-C. 'Le royauté divine chez les Rukuba', *L'Homme* 15 (1975), 5–27.

Munno [Your Friend], monthly journal published by the Roman Catholic mission, Kampala from 1911.

Murdock, G. P. *Africa: Its Peoples and their Culture History*, New York, 1959.

Mutibwa, P. M. *Uganda since Independence*, London, 1992.

Mworoha, E. *Peuples et rois de l'Afrique des lacs: le Burundi et les royaumes voisines au xixe siècle*, Dakar, 1977.

Nathhorst, B. *Formal or Structural Analysis of Traditional Tales* Stockholm, 1969.

Newbury, D. S. 'The clans of Rwanda: an historical hypothesis', *Africa* 50 (1980), 389–403.

'Rwandan chronology in regional perspective', *Cahiers africains* 4/5 (1993), 163–208.

Noten, F. van *Les tombes du roi Cyirima Rujugira et de la reine-mère Nyirayuhi Kanjogera*, Tervuren, 1972.

Nsimbi, M. B. *Waggumbulizi*, Kampala, 1952.

Amannya Amaganda n'Ennono Zaago [Ganda Names and their Meanings], Kampala, 1956.

Nyakatura, J. W. *Ky'Abakama ba Bunyoro–Kitara* [The Kings of Bunyoro–Kitara], St Justin, Quebec, 1947 (see also Uzoigwe).

Oded, Arye *Islam in Uganda*, Jerusalem, 1974.

Ogot, B. A. 'The Great Lakes region', in *General History of Africa*, ed. J. D. Fage and R. Oliver: vol. IV, *Africa from the Twelfth to the Sixteenth Century*, ed. D. T. Niane, Paris: UNESCO, 1984, 498–524.

Okpewho, I. *The Epic in Africa*, New York, 1979.

Myth in Africa: A Study of its Aesthetic and Cultural Relevance, Cambridge, 1983.

Oliver, R. *The Missionary Factor in East Africa*, London, 1952.

'The Baganda and the Bakonjo', *UJ* 18 (1954), 31–3.

'The royal tombs of Buganda', *UJ* 23 (1959), 124–33.

'The East African interior', in *Cambridge History of Africa*, ed. R. Oliver, vol. III, Cambridge, 1977, 621–69.

'The Nilotic contribution to Bantu Africa', *JAH* 23 (1982), 433–42.

Oliver, R. and Fage, J. D. *A Short History of Africa*, London, 1962.

Onyango-ku-Odongo, J. M. and Webster, J. B. (eds.) *The Central Lwo during the Aconya*, Nairobi, 1976.

Osogo, J. *A History of the Baluyia*, Nairobi, 1966.

Otto, W. F. *Dionysus, Myth and Cult*, Bloomington, 1965 (first published 1933).

Otzen, B. 'The concept of myth' and 'The use of myth in Genesis', in *Myths in the Old Testament*, ed. B. Otzen, H. Gottlieb and K. Jepperson, London, 1980, 1–21, 22–61.

Pagès, A. 'Au Ruanda, sur les bords de lac Kivou', *Anthropos* 15 (1920), 962–6. *Un royaume hamite au coeur de l'Afrique*, Brussels, 1933.

Perrot, C.-H. 'Anyo Asema, mythe et histoire', *JAH* 15 (1974), 199–223.

Philippe, A. *Au coeur de l'Afrique, Ouganda: un demi-siècle d'apostolat au centre africain*, Paris, 1929.

Posnansky, M. 'Bigo bya Mugenyi', *UJ* 33 (1969), 125–50.

Pritchard, J. B. (ed.) *Ancient Near Eastern Texts Relating to the Old Testament*, 1st edn, Princeton, 1950.

Raglan, Lord *The Hero*, London, 1966.

Ranger, T. O. and Kimambo, I. M. (eds.) *The Historical Study of African Religion*, London, 1972.

Rank, O. *The Myth of the Birth of the Hero*, New York, 1959 (1st German edn, 1905).

Ray, Benjamin C. 'Royal shrines and ceremonies of Buganda', *UJ* 36 (1972), 35–48.
'Sacred space and royal shrines in Buganda', *History of Religions* 16 (1977), 363–73.
'Death and kingship in Buganda', in *Religious Encounters with Death*, ed. Earle H. Waugh and Frank E. Reynolds, Pennsylvania State University, 1977, 56–69.
'The story of Kintu: myth, death and ontology in Buganda', in Karp and Bird (eds.), *Explorations in Africa Systems of Thought*, 60–79.
Myth, Ritual and Kingship in Buganda, Oxford, 1991.

Redford, D. B. 'The literary motif of the exposed child', *Numen* 14 (1967), 209–28.

Rehse, H. *Kiziba, Land und Leute*, Stuttgart, 1910.

Reid, A. 'Ntusi and its hinterland', *Nyame Akuma* 33 (1990), 26–8.
'The role of cattle in the Later Iron Age of southern Uganda', unpublished Ph.D. thesis, University of Cambridge, 1991.

Renfrew, C. and Cherry, J. F. (eds.) *Peer Polity Interaction and Socio-political Change*, Cambridge, 1986.

Richards, A. I. (ed.) *East African Chiefs*, London, 1959.
'Social mechanisms for the transfer of political rights in some African tribes', *JRAI* 90 (1960), 175–90.
'African kings and their royal relatives', *JRAI* 91 (1961), 135–49.
'Authority patterns in traditional Buganda', in Fallers (ed.), *The King's Men*, 256–93.
The Changing Structure of a Ganda Village, Nairobi, 1966.

Richards, A. I. and Reining, P. 'Report on fertility surveys in Buganda and Buhaya, 1952', in *Culture and Human Fertility*, ed. F. Lorimer, Paris: UNESCO, 1954.

Roberts, A. D. *History of the Bemba*, London, 1973.

Robertshaw, P. 'The interlacustrine region: a progress report' *Nyame Akuma* 30 (1988), 37–8.
'Recent archaeological surveys in western Uganda', *Nyame Akuma* 36 (1991).
'Archaeological survey, ceramic analysis and state formation in western Uganda', *AAR* 12 (1994), 105–32.

Robertshaw, P. and Collett, D. P. 'A new framework for the study of pastoral communities in East Africa', *JAH* 24 (1983), 289–303.

Róheim, Geza *Animism, Magic and the Divine King*, New York, 1930.

Rop, A. de *Lianja, l'épopée des Mongo*, Brussels, 1964.

Roscoe, J. 'Notes on the manners and customs of the Baganda', *JAI* 31 (1901), 117–30.

  'Further notes on the manners and customs of the Baganda' *JAI* 32 (1902), 25–80.

  'Kibuka, the war-god of the Baganda', *Man* 7 (1907), 161–6.

  The Baganda, Their Customs and Beliefs, London, 1911; repr. 1965.

  The Northern Bantu, Cambridge, 1915.

  Twenty-Five Years in East Africa, Cambridge, 1921.

  The Bakitara or Banyoro, Cambridge, 1923.

  The Bagesu and Other Tribes of the Uganda Protectorate, Cambridge, 1924.

Rowe, John A. 'The purge of Christians at Mwanga's court', *JAH* 5 (1964), 55–72.

  'Roscoe's and Kagwa's Buganda', *JAH* 8 (1967), 163–6.

  'Myth, memoir and moral admonition: Luganda historical writing, 1893–1969', *UJ* 33 (1969), 17–40.

  'The pattern of political administration in precolonial Buganda', in *African Themes*, ed. I. Abu-Lughoud, Evanston, 1975.

Rowling, F. *The Tales of Sir Apolo*, London, n.d.

Rusch, Walter *Klassen und Staat in Buganda vor der Kolonialzeit*, Berlin, 1975.

Sagan, E. *At the Dawn of Tyranny: The Origins of Individualism, Political Oppression and the State*, New York, 1985.

Sanders, Edith R. 'The Hamitic hypothesis, its origins and functions in historical perspective', *JAH* 10 (1969), 521–32.

Schapera, I. *The Khoisan People*, London, 1930.

Schechter, Robert E. 'A propos the drunken king: cosmology and history', in Miller (ed.), *The African Past Speaks*, 108–25.

Schiller, Lawrence D. 'The royal women of Buganda', *IJAHS* 23 (1990), 455–74.

Schmidt, Peter R. 'A new look at interpretations of the Early Iron Age in East Africa, *HA* 2 (1975), 127–36.

  Historical Archaeology, Westport, Conn. and London, 1978.

Schmidt, Peter R. and Childs, S. T. 'Innovation and industry during the Early Iron Age in East Africa', *AAR* 3 (1985), 53–94.

Schnepel, B. 'Continuity despite and through death: regicide and royal shrines among the Shilluk of southern Sudan', *Africa* 61 (1991), 40–70.

Schoenbrun, David L. 'Early history in eastern Africa's Great Lakes region: linguistic, ecological and archaeological approaches', unpublished Ph.D. thesis, Los Angeles, 1990.

  '"We are what we eat": ancient agriculture between the Great Lakes', *JAH* 34 (1993), 1–31.

  'Cattle herds and banana gardens: the historical geography of the western Great Lakes region', *AAR* 11 (1993), 39–72.

Schoffeleers, M. 'Symbolic and social aspects of spirit worship among the Mang'anja', unpublished D.Phil. thesis, Oxford, 1968.

  'The religious significance of bush fires in Malawi', *Cahiers des religions africaines* 10 (1971), 272–82.

Seligman, C. G. *The Races of Africa*, London, 1930.

Egypt and Negro Africa, London, 1934.

Seters, J. van *Abraham in History and Tradition*, New Haven, 1975.

Sheriff, Abdul, *Slaves, Spices and Ivory in Zanzibar*, London and Dar es Salaam, 1987.

Sigwalt, R. D. 'Early Rwanda history: the contribution of comparative ethnography', *HA* 2 (1975), 137–46.

'The early history of Bushi', unpublished Ph.D. thesis, University of Wisconsin, 1975.

Simons, E. 'Coutumes et institutions des Barundi', *Bulletin des jurisdictions indigènes* 12 (1944), 137–62 and 163–282.

Smith, E. W. and Dale, A. M. *The Ila-speaking People of Northern Rhodesia*, 2 vols., London, 1920.

Smith, Pierre *Le récit populaire au Rwanda*, Paris, 1975.

Soper, R. C. 'Early Iron Age pottery types from East Africa', *Azania* 6 (1971), 39–52.

'Roulette decoration in African pottery: technical considerations, dating and distribution', *AAR* 3 (1985), 29–51.

Southall, A. *Alur Society*, London, 1956.

'Cross-cultural meanings and multilingualism', in *Language Use and Social Change*, ed. W. H. Whiteley, London, 1971.

Southwold, M. *Bureaucracy and Chiefship in Buganda*, East African Studies No. 14, Kampala, 1961.

'Succession to the throne of Buganda', in *Succession to High Office*, ed. J. Goody, Cambridge, 1966, 82–126.

'The history of a history: royal succession in Buganda', in *History and Social Anthropology*, ed. I. M. Lewis, London, 1968.

Soyinka, Wole *Death and the King's Horseman*, London, 1975.

Speke, J. H. *Journal of the Discovery of the Source of the Nile*, Edinburgh and London, 1863.

Stanley, H. M. *Through the Dark Continent*, 2 vols., New York, 1878.

My Dark Companions and their Strange Stories, London, 1893.

Steere, E. *Swahili Tales*, London, 1869.

Steinhart, E. I. 'The kingdoms of the march', in Webster (ed.), *Chronology, Migration and Drought*, 189–213.

'From "empire" to state: the emergence of the kingdom of Bunyoro–Kitara, c. 1350–1890', in Claessen and Skalnik (eds.), *The Study of the State*, 353–70.

Stuhlmann, F. *Mit Emin Pasha ins Herz von Afrika*, Berlin, 1894.

Stuhlmann, F. (ed.) *Die Tägebücher von Dr Emin Pasha*, vol. I, Berlin, 1916.

Sutton, John 'The aquatic civilisation of Middle Africa', *JAH* 15 (1974), 527–46.

'The antecedents of the interlacustrine kingdoms', *JAH* 34 (1993), 33–64.

Sykes, J. 'The eclipse at Biharwe', *UJ* 23 (1959), 44–50.

Tambwe ya Kasimba, Y. 'Essai d'interprétation du cliché de Kangere', *JAH* 31 (1990), 353–72.

Taylor, J. V. *The Growth of the Church in Buganda*, London, 1958.

Tegnaeus, H. *Le héros civilisateur*, Stockholm, 1950.

Thompson, T. L. *The History of the Patriarchal Narratives*, Berlin, 1974.

Tosh, John 'The northern interlacustrine region', in *Pre-colonial African Trade*, ed.

R. Gray and D. Birmingham, London, 1970.

Treharne, J. F. *The Glastonbury Legends*, London, 1967.

Trevor-Roper, H. *The Rise of Christian Europe*, London, 1965.

Turner, V. W. *The Drums of Affliction: A Study of Religious Processes among the Ndembu of Zambia*, Oxford, 1968.

The Forest of Symbols, London, 1970.

Twaddle, Michael 'On Ganda historiography', *HA* 1 (1974), 85–99.

'Ganda receptivity to change', *JAH* 15 (1974), 303–15.

'The ending of slavery in Buganda', in *The End of Slavery in Africa*, ed. S. Miers and R. Roberts, Madison, 1988, 119–49.

Kakungulu and the Making of Uganda, London and Kampala, 1993.

Uzoigwe, G. N. *The Anatomy of an African Kingdom: A History of Bunyoro–Kitara*, Garden City. N.Y., 1973.

Vansina, Jan 'Initiation rituals of the Bushong', *Africa* 25 (1955), 138–53.

L'évolution du royaume rwanda dès origines à 1900, Brussels, 1962.

La légende du passé; traditions orales du Burundi, Brussels, 1972.

Oral Tradition as History, London and Nairobi, 1985.

Paths in the Rainforests, Madison, 1990.

Vaughan, J. H. 'A reconsideration of divine kingship', in Karp and Bird (eds.), *Explorations in African Systems of Thought*, Bloomington, 1980.

Viaene, L. 'L'organisation politique des Bahunde', *Kongo-Overzee* 18 (1952), 8–34.

Volsunga Saga, trans. W. Morris, New York, 1962.

Waller, R. D. 'The traditional economy of Buganda', unpublished MA dissertation, London, 1971.

Webster, J. B. (ed.) *Chronology, Migration and Drought in Interlacustrine Africa*, London and Dalhousie, 1979.

'The reign of the gods', in Webster (ed.), *Chronology, Migration and Drought*, 126–41.

Welbourn, F. B. 'Some aspects of Kiganda religion', *UJ* 26 (1962), 171–82.

Werner, A. 'African mythology', in *The Mythology of All Races*, ed. J. A. MacCullouch, Boston, 1925.

Whiteley, W. H. *A Selection of African Prose*, 2 vols., Oxford, 1964.

Wilks, I. *Asante in the Nineteenth Century: The Structure and Evolution of a Political Order*, Cambridge, 1975.

Williams, F. Lukyn 'Myth, legend and lore in Uganda', *UJ* 10 (1946), 64–75.

Willis, R. G. *A State in the Making*, Bloomington, 1981.

Wilson, C. T. and Felkin, R. W. *Uganda and the Egyptian Sudan*, 2 vols., London, 1882.

Wright, Michael *Buganda in the Heroic Age*, London and Nairobi, 1971.

Wrigley, C. C. 'Buganda: an outline economic history', *Economic History Review* n.s. 10 (1957), 69–80.

'Some thoughts on the Bacwezi', *UJ* 22 (1958), 11–17.

'Kimera', *UJ* 23 (1959), 38–43.

'The Christian revolution in Buganda', *CSSH* 2 (1959), 33–48.

'The changing economic structure', in Fallers (ed.), *The King's Men*, 16–63.

'The king-lists of Buganda', *HA* 1 (1974), 129–39.

'The problem of the Lwo', *HA* 8 (1981), 219–46.

'The river-god and the historians: myth and history in the Shire valley', *JAH* 29

(1988), 367–83.

'Bananas in Buganda', *Azania* 24 (1989), 64–70.

Yoder, John C. 'The quest for Kintu and the search for peace: mythology and morality in nineteenth-century Buganda', *HA* 15 (1988), 363–76.

Young, Michael W. 'The divine kingship of the Jukun: a re-evaluation of some theories', *Africa* 36 (1966), 135–53.

Zakaczowski, Andrzej 'Change and development: problems of sociology of religion in Africa', *Africana Bulletin* 25 (1976), 115–25.

Zimbe, B. M. *Buganda ne Kabaka*, Kampala, 1939.

Index

Achte, Père Auguste 31, 169–70
Adam 46, 93, 111, 114, 116, 121
agriculture
  African origins 50–1, 166
  in Buganda 60–1, 180, 235
  see also bananas
AIDS 237–8
Amin, Idi 6, 19
Anthesteria 143
archaeology 7, 50–1, 69–71, 73–6,
  200–3
Arthur, king 10, 27, 97, 136, 157, 162
Asante, kingdom 243, 252
Ashe, Robert P. 241
Atkinson, Ronald R. 49, 109, 168

Ba'al 135–6, 156
Bakka, ritual centre 79, 80, 83, 116, 122,
  148, 150, 151, 179, 188–9, 193, 212,
  214
bananas 60–1, 87, 235, 238
Bantu languages 71–2, 76–7
Bemba, snake-king 54–5, 105–10, 115
Berger, Iris 184, 254, 257, 269
Biebuyck, Daniel 131, 254, 265
Biggo, ancient site 74, 77, 194, 200–2,
  233
(Ba-) Bito, dynasty 40–1, 104, 124, 193,
  202–3
board-game, the 100–2
Buddo, ritual centre 23, 28–9, 58, 120,
  148, 211, 214
Buddu, county 58, 63, 159, 219
  annexation of 23, 193, 218
Budge, E. A. Wallis 163
Buffalo clan 195, 222
Buganda, eponymous 'king' 22, 28, 31
Bukerekere, ritual centre 80, 84, 150,
  154, 170
Bulemeezi, county 58, 63, 174, 208
  ritual role 162, 179
Bunyoro, kingdom 3, 20

British conquest of 4, 38
  myths of 39–40, 185–6
  in the nineteenth century 192–3, 228
  relations with Buganda 20, 66, 88, 122,
    140, 145, 147, 159–60, 192–7, 203–6,
    210–15, 218–19
  rise of 202–3
  traditions of 38–41, 197–200
Burundi, kingdom 36–7, 125, 149, 202,
  244
Bushbuck clan 175, 219
Busiro, county 22–3, 25–6, 58, 63–4,
  79–80
Busoga, country 23, 66, 114, 215–16
Busozo, kingdom 85, 125
Busujju, county 22, 58, 63, 117, 175, 176,
  207
Butambala, county 22, 58, 63, 173–4,
  207
Buvuma islands 58, 178–9, 243

Campbell, Joseph 14
Cane-rat clan 207–8, 222
cattle-keeping 72–3, 201–3, 224
Césard, Emile 97
Chadwick, Henry and Nora 13, 100
child kings 122–6, 136–45, 149, 180, 196,
  213
Chrétien, Jean-Pierre 124, 257, 265
Christians, in Buganda 113, 249–50
  see also martyrs, missionaries
Civet clan 83, 188–90
clans 25, 86
  in Buganda 64–5, 115–16, 189, 219,
    221–2
  see also Buffalo, Bushbuck, Cane-rat,
    Civet, Elephant, Grasshopper
    Leopard, Lungfish, Monkey, Otter,
    Pangolin, Seed, Sheep
class 239
Cohen, David W. 114, 116, 255
Cushitic languages 72–3, 78

Cwa, king
  I of Buganda 20, 21, 83, 122, 139–41, 193, 203
  I of Bunyoro 199, 203, 209, 212
  II of Buganda 123, 228, 229
  throne-name 193
(Ba-)Cwezi gods 39–40, 55, 97, 102, 199, 202
'empire' 75, 194, 200

David, king of Israel 125
demography 145–6, 236–8
diffusionism 15–16, 50–4, 165–6
Dionysus 125, 130–1, 134, 135, 143
Douglas, Mary 120
Duhaga, king of Bunyoro 193, 205, 219
Dumézil, Georges 14, 55, 95

Early Iron Age 70–1, 86, 88, 185, 196–7
eclipse stories 79, 204
Egypt
  and Buganda 124, 166, 180
  religion 18, 124, 165–6
Elephant clan 119, 187–90, 214, 222
Eliade, Mircea 14
Emin Pasha 29, 178
epics 13, 131, 135
Ergamenes of Kush 171
evolutionism 86, 111–13, 251–2

fables 47, 54, 106–7
Feierman, Steven W. 45
Felkin, Dr Robert W. 29, 90, 111, 113, 126
Finley, Moses I. 9
Fisher, Ruth 38, 198, 204–5, 213
Fisher King 103
folk-tales 47, 95–6, 175–6
form-criticism 32–4
Frankfort, Henri 165–6
Frazer, Sir James George 14, 17, 108, 126, 128, 162
  and Buganda 33–4
Freud, Sigmund 109
functionalism 18, 44–5

Gawain, Sir 108
Ggunju
  clan head 122, 128, 151
  dances 128, 132, 164
gods 12, 182–7, 247–50
  see also Baal, (Ba-) Cwezi gods, Dionysus, Horus, Isis, Osiris, (Ba-)Lubaale deities, theology
Golding, William 47, 105

Gomba, county 22, 58, 63, 173, 207
Gomotoka, J. T. K. 8, 256, 264
Gorju, Julien 24
Grant, James Augustus 3, 6, 227
Grasshopper clan 185, 194–5, 214, 222, 225
Gray, Sir John Milner 24, 54, 228, 253, 267, 272
Grisward, Joel H. 153

Ham, son of Noah 32, 52, 111
Hamitic hypothesis 72–3, 165, 230–1
Harrison, Jane Ellen 14, 129–30, 265, 266
Henige, David P. 11, 26–7, 32, 51, 198, 255, 256, 264, 270
Heusch, Luc de 14, 52, 246, 261, 266, 267, 274
Hocart, A. M. 14
Horus 124, 166, 180
human sacrifice 4, 243–6
  see also ritual murder

Igbo people 231
Ihangiro, kingdom 66, 97, 199
incest, royal 22, 155–7, 158–9
initiation, puberty 47–8, 108–10, 120, 148–54, 186
Irstam, Tor 17, 253
Isis 124, 166

Jacob
  and Esau 52–4, 106
  as First Man 93–5
Janjero, kingdom 124
Jensen, A. E. 14, 268
Jensen, Jürgen 49
Jjemba, king 21, 169, 170, 180
Jjunju, king 21, 23, 217–20, 221, 228
Jjuuko, king 30, 79, 81, 82–3, 170, 178–82, 187, 213
Johnston, Sir Harry H. 22, 30, 90, 112–13
Juma, rebel prince 156, 159, 210, 213
Juma Katebe, prince 183, 210, 213

Kabarega, king of Bunyoro 40, 193
Kagwa: see Kaggwa
Kaggwa, Sir Apolo
  ancestry 225
  as author 7, 9, 22, 23, 26, 30–4, 65, 90–2, 99–100, 104, 123, 148, 161, 182, 244
  career 9, 23–4, 123
Kagulu, king 27, 183, 187–91, 213
  hill 190

Kalemeera
  king of Kyamutwara   20–2, 30, 139–46,
    147, 185, 196
  prince   137
Kamaanya (II), king   33, 66, 176–7, 216,
  220, 225, 226
  see also Ssekamaanya
Karagwe, kingdom   2, 57, 66, 199, 202,
  218, 233
Kasujju, county chief   176
Kateregga, king   22, 26, 30, 170, 171–4,
  177, 207, 212
katikkiro
  individuals   7, 139, 160, 181, 186, 188,
    204, 211, 221, 227, 243
  office of   63, 190
  see also Kaggwa
Kawumpuli, plague-demon   178–9
Kayemba, king   30, 170, 178–81
Kayima, king   22, 159, 160
  county chief   159, 173
Kenny, Michael G.   221, 249, 255, 266,
  267, 268, 273
Kibaale, clan chief   175, 192
Kibuuka, war-god   28, 79, 161, 182, 211,
  214
  story of   160
Kiggala, king   22, 155–8
  and Bunyoro   193–4
  incest of   155
Kikulwe, king   187–8, 205, 211
Kimbugwe, king   171–2, 173, 234
  ritual office   63
Kimera
  and Bunyoro   143, 194–6, 204
  as dynastic founder   20, 22, 23
  prince   227
  story of   20, 22, 140–5, 147–8, 182
kingship
  myths of   15
  origin and functions   84–9, 126–8,
    246–7
  ritual cycle   133–9, 186, 213
  sacred, in Buganda   17–18
    in Britain   84, 127
    in Burundi   36–7
    in Rwanda   35–6
    of the Shilluk   163–5
  and the state   84, 86–8, 200–1, 246–7
  see also child kings, incest, matricide,
    regicide, state
Kintu
  cult of   117, 119, 211
  first king of Buganda   20, 21, 23, 24,
    112–20, 168, 234

First Man   20, 89–98, 108, 110, 114,
  115, 121, 164
  oracle of   117, 160, 211
  political role   115–16, 117–18, 207,
    250–1
Kinyolo   180, 181, 195
Kisolo   99–102
  see also otter
Kitara, 'empire'   77, 194, 197, 200–3
Kiwanuka, lightning-god   89, 248
Kiwanuka, M. S. M.   7, 24–5, 148, 149,
  169, 194–5, 248, 253, 267, 268, 270
kiwendo: see human sacrifice
Kiyimba, king   156, 157–8
Kiziba, kingdom   2, 66, 103–4
Kkooki, kingdom   2, 66, 218
Kopytoff, Igor   51, 254, 258
Kottak, Conrad P.   172, 234, 253, 268,
  273
K. W.: see Winyi
Kyabaggu, king   9, 23, 189, 210, 215–17,
  229
  and gods   247–8
  and trade   232
Kyaddondo, county   58, 63–4, 126,
  149–50, 174, 208
Kyaggwe, county   58, 63, 188, 208
  annexation of   207
Kyamutwara, kingdom   2, 66, 124, 202,
  228

Lacger, L. de   125
Lakeland   2, 19, 35
Lake Victoria: see Nalubaale
Laye, Camara   129
Leach, Sir Edmund   45, 46, 49, 108, 258
leopard
  clan   102, 117–18, 173, 187, 188, 207,
    211–12, 213, 214
  symbolic role   102, 119
Lévi-Strauss, Claude   14, 15, 46, 47, 48,
  50, 51–2, 53, 94, 97, 154
(Ba-)Lubaale
  deities   41, 82, 161, 167, 184–5
  mediums   182–4, 243, 247–50
  see also gods, Kibuuka, Kiwanuka,
    Mayanja, Mukasa, Muwanga, Nende,
    Wannema, spirit mediums
Lugard, Frederick J.   4, 29
Lumansi, prince   21, 22, 29, 147–8
Lungfish clan   150, 151, 159, 167–8, 178,
  211, 213, 214, 221, 222
Luyenje, princes   159, 187, 210
Lwo language   74–5, 83, 179
  see also Nilotic

MacGaffey, Wyatt 115, 265
Mackay, Alexander 241
Maganda, prince 205, 210, 212
Magonga, cult centre 58, 99, 117–18, 119, 207, 211, 238
marriage 172, 176–7, 189–96
  see also women
martyrs 4, 245
matricide, royal 142–3
Mawanda, king 23, 117, 119, 183, 187, 188, 190, 207–15, 216
  prince 67
Mawokota, county 22, 58, 64, 159, 173, 174, 175, 215
Mawuba, prince 187–8
Mayanja deity 247
  myth of 155
  Mayanja rivers 79, 84, 149, 155
Mbaale, cult centre 79, 80, 160, 161, 215
Mbogo, prince 227
migrations
  cause of 145–6
  symbolism of 146
Miller, Joseph C. 9, 45, 254
missionaries 3, 241
  and tradition 33–4. 111–13
Miti, James Kabazzi 8, 256
Monkey clan 171, 173, 174, 180, 195–6
  see also Mugema
Moses 134
Mubende, cult centre 184–5, 202
Mugema, office of 152, 174, 176, 180, 195, 249
Mugwanya, Stanislas 30, 31
Mukasa, deity 102–3, 135, 137, 160, 182, 184, 226, 247–9
Mulanga, son of Kintu 104
Mulondo, king 22, 30, 122–4, 139, 160, 168, 169, 170, 172
  in myth 122, 124, 126, 128–9, 144, 159
Murdock, George Peter 127
Musanje, prince 183, 187, 209–14
Mutabaazi, ritual saviour 139, 162
Mutebi, king 22, 30, 117, 170, 174–8, 181, 182, 187, 207, 212, 213
  prince 225
Muteesa I, king
  court of 59, 67
  and history 29, 32
  reign 3, 57, 67, 125, 179, 227, 229, 241–3, 244
  and religion 3, 26, 150, 248–9
Muteesa II, king 19, 21, 229
Muwanga, deity 82, 162
Mwanga I, king 209

Mwanga II, king 3, 5, 125, 229, 249
Mwindo, epic of 131–4
  hero 131–4, 136, 142, 148, 157
myth
  antiquity of 56–1
  categories of 48–9
  Celtic 95, 108, 153–4
    see also Arthur, Fisher King
  and Christianity 43–5
  and death 48, 52, 92–4, 98, 99, 100–1
  Egyptian 124, 166, 181
  Ganda 54–6, 79, 81, 83, 90–3, 95, 99–100, 105–7, 122, 171, 178–82, 186
  Greek 55, 101, 107–8, 129–31, 142–3
  Hebrew 52–4, 92–5, 108, 111, 115
  of the hunter 103–5
  Maravi 118
  Norse 163
  North American 154
  Nyanga 131–6
  Roman 55, 95
  Syrian 135–6
  in traditions 14–15, 45–46

Nabugwamu 152, 208
Nakibinge, king
  place in history 22–3, 159, 160, 174, 182, 204–5, 210–15
  as prince 226
  story 22–3, 30, 122, 159–66
Nakku, queen 141, 144, 147–8, 178–9
Nalubaale 2, 35, 59, 79, 80, 161, 167–8, 233–4
Nalugwa, royal wife 172, 173, 209, 214
Nalunga, royal wife 149, 179, 180
Nambi, wife of Kintu 20, 90–3, 96, 99, 116
Namugala, king
  accession rite 23, 120, 148, 210–14
  reign 9, 23, 210, 214, 229
Namulondo
  queen-mother 123, 159
  throne 59, 123–4
Namunkululu 159, 210, 212, 213
Nankere 148, 149, 150–1, 170–1, 213
Nannono, royal wife 122, 211–12
Nassolo Ndege, princess 187, 188, 190, 207, 213
Ndahura, Nyoro deity 39, 40, 184–6, 202
Ndawula
  Ganda deity 184
  Ganda king 30, 170, 182–4, 186–7
Nende, war-god 30, 249
neolithic
  culture 73, 166, 196

neolithic (*cont.*)
  economy 69
  era 50–1
Nilotic
  language group 74–5, 78
  people 203
  see also Lwo
Nkore, kingdom 2
  history 67, 202, 203
  traditions 174, 198, 199
Nsimbi, Michael B. 8, 83, 128, 248, 254, 263, 265, 269
Ntusi, ancient site 73, 75, 77, 87, 200, 201
Nyakatura, J. W. 198, 255, 261
Nyanga people 85, 131, 157
Nyikang 164, 166

Obote, Milton 6, 19, 194
okukula rite 126, 148–54, 170, 180, 209
Old Testament
  criticism 44, 45, 49
  myth 46, 92–5, 108, 111, 121
  traditions 10, 12, 40, 49, 51, 52–4
Olimi, king of Bunyoro 204–6, 210, 212, 213
Oliver, Roland 25–6, 127, 221
Oresteia 142–3
Orestes 142–3, 145, 157
Osiris 124, 166
otter
  clan 102, 117
  in myth 102–3, 119

pangolin
  clan 117, 120, 141, 175, 182, 221
  creature 106, 109, 120

queen-mother
  individuals 189, 209, 225, 227
  role 67, 150, 152, 154, 190
queen-sister 67, 157, 211, 218

Raglan, second baron 14
Ray, Benjamin C. 17–19, 25, 26 90, 92, 110, 149, 165, 186, 246, 255, 256, 262, 264, 269
regicide 17, 136, 138, 144, 162, 165, 219
ritual murder 149, 150, 152–3, 244–7
Robertshaw, Peter 203
Róheim, Geza 14
Roscoe, John 33–4, 90, 92, 113, 148–9
Rwanda, kingdom
  history and structure 1, 35–6, 85, 202
  royal cycle 36, 136–9

traditions 36, 109, 199–200
Ryangombe, deity 101, 163

saga 12–13, 200, 217
Sagan, Eli 251, 253, 274
Schoenbrun, David L. 72, 273
Schoffeleers, Matthew 118, 264
Seed clan 149, 167, 180, 211, 221–2
Seligman, C. G. 165
Seth, deity 133, 181
Sheep clan 119, 160, 167, 172, 207, 209, 214, 222
Shilluk, kingdom 163–5
slavery
  in Buganda 62, 236, 240–1
  general 224
  see also women
source-criticism 29–32
Southwold, Martin 20, 24, 123, 253, 255, 265, 272
Speke, John Hanning
  in Buganda 3, 6, 57, 59, 227, 242
  on traditions 22, 26, 110, 141, 194, 200
spirit mediums 59, 117, 182–4, 247
  see also (Ba-)Lubaale
Ssebwana, regent 141, 143–4
Ssese islands 22, 58, 155, 160, 167, 182, 247
Ssekamaanya, king 33, 169–71, 178
Ssemakookiro, king
  accession 220
  date 229
  reign 23, 189, 216, 220, 225
  and trade 233
Ssingo, county 22, 58, 63, 175, 187, 207, 213–14
Ssuuna I, king 26, 169, 170, 172
Ssuuna II, king 66, 125, 149, 226, 242
  date 229
  and gods 248
  and trade 233
Stanley, Henry Morton
  in Buganda 3, 179, 227, 242–3
  and traditions 22, 29, 31, 89, 111, 113, 117, 141, 144, 189, 250
state, the 1, 77, 230–1
  and ecology 234–5
  and kingship 84, 86–7, 201, 246–7
  origin and development 196–7, 200–3, 223–5
  and trade 231–4, 238–9
  and war 201–3, 235–6
Steinhart, Edward I. 200

structuralism 14, 45, 48–9, 51–2
see also Atkinson, Dumézil, Leach,
  Lévi-Strauss
Stuhlmann, Franz 29–30, 126

Tebandeke, king 26, 182–4
theology 81–2, 89
see also gods, myth
Tortoise 54–5, 106–7, 211
trade
  in copper 233
  with east coast 66–7, 87, 218, 232–3
  of Lake Victoria 233–4, 239
  and politics 87, 231–5
Ttembo, king
  murders Kimera 22, 147–8
  ritual role 148–54
  see also okukula rite
(Ba-)Tutsi 35–6, 73, 77, 202
Twaddle, Michael 33, 113, 114, 115, 253,
  259, 264

Uganda
  Republic 1, 6

Protectorate 4
Swahili for 'Buganda' 4–5
Ugarit, ancient site 135

Vansina, Jan 7, 78, 254, 266

Walumbe (Death) 92, 96–8, 100, 114, 116
Walusimbi, clan chief 83–4, 85, 89, 116,
  139, 141, 151–2, 188–9, 204
Wampamba, prince 22, 30, 156, 158–9
Wanfudu, *see* Tortoise
Wanga, deity 79–82, 88, 179
Wannema, deity 160–1
war 12–14, 199–201, 245–6, 252
  and state-formation 201–2, 224, 235
  war-bands 57, 63, 202, 221–5, 249
Wilks, Ivor 243
William of Malmesbury 153
Wilson, Charles T. 29, 90
Winyi IV ('K. W.') 198, 204, 205
women, role and status of 60, 62, 67,
  92–3, 96–7, 175–7, 225, 236–8, 240

Yoder, John C. 250, 274

Other books in the series

64 *Bankole-Bright and Politics in Colonial Sierra Leone: The Passing of the 'Krio Era', 1919–1958* Akintola Wyse
65 *Contemporary West African States* Donal Cruise O'Brien, John Dunn and Richard Rathbone
66 *The Oromo of Ethiopia: A History, 1570–1860* Mohammed Hassen
67 *Slavery and African Life: Occidental, Oriental and African Slave Trades* Patrick Manning
68 *Abraham Esau's War: A Black South African War in the Cape, 1899–1902* Bill Nasson
69 *The Politics of Harmony: Land Dispute Strategies in Swaziland* Laurel Rose
70 *Zimbabwe's Guerrilla War: Peasant Voices* Norma Kriger
71 *Ethiopia: Power and Protest: Peasant Revolts in the Twentieth Century* Gebru Tareke
72 *White Supremacy and Black Resistance in Pre-Industrial South Africa: The Making of the Colonial Order in the Eastern Cape, 1770–1865* Clifton C. Crais
73 *The Elusive Granary: Herder, Farmer, and State in Northern Kenya* Peter D. Little
74 *The Kanyok of Zaire: An Institutional and Ideological History to 1895* John C. Yoder
75 *Pragmatism in the Age of Jihad: The Precolonial State of Bundu* Michael A. Gomez
76 *Slow Death for Slavery: The Course of Abolition in Northern Nigeria, 1897–1936* Paul E. Lovejoy and Jan S. Hogendorn
77 *West African Slavery and Atlantic Commerce: The Senegal River Valley, 1700–1860* James Searing
78 *A South African Kingdom: The Pursuit of Security in Nineteenth-Century Lesotho* Elizabeth A. Eldredge
79 *State and Society in Pre-Colonial Asante* T. C. McCaskie
80 *Islamic Society and State Power in Senegal: Disciples and Citizens of Fatick* Leonardo A. Villalón
81 *Ethnic Pride and Racial Prejudice in Victorian Cape Town: Group Identity and Social Practice* Vivian Bickford-Smith
82 *The Eritrean Struggle for Independence: Domination, Resistance, Nationalism, 1941–1993* Ruth Iyob
83 *Corruption and State Politics in Sierra Leone* William Reno
84 *The Culture of Politics in Modern Kenya* Angelique Haugerud
85 *Africans: the History of a Continent* John Iliffe
86 *From Slave Trade to 'Legitimate' Commerce: the Commercial Transition in Nineteenth-Century West Africa* Edited by Robin Law
87 *Leisure and Society in Colonial Brazzaville* Phyllis M. Martin

Lightning Source UK Ltd.
Milton Keynes UK
UKHW03f1839220418
321463UK00001B/50/P